The Essential
Howard Gardner
on Education

The Essential Howard Gardner on Education

Howard Gardner

TEACHERS COLLEGE PRESS
TEACHERS COLLEGE | COLUMBIA UNIVERSITY
NEW YORK AND LONDON

Published by Teachers College Press,® 1234 Amsterdam Avenue, New York, NY 10027

Copyright © 2024 by Howard Gardner

Front cover art by Jay Gardner.

For permissions lines for individual essays, please see page 319.

All rights reserved. No part of this publication may be reproduced or transmitted in any form or by any means, electronic or mechanical, including photocopy, or any information storage and retrieval system, without permission from the publisher. For reprint permission and other subsidiary rights requests, please contact Teachers College Press, Rights Dept.: tcpressrights@tc.columbia.edu

Library of Congress Cataloging-in-Publication Data
Names: Gardner, Howard, 1943- author.
Title: The essential Howard Gardner on education / Howard Gardner.
Description: New York, NY : Teachers College Press, [2024] | Includes bibliographical references and index. | Summary: "A survey of Howard Gardner's contributions to our understanding of education across the age span and in many cultural settngs."—Provided by publisher.
Identifiers: LCCN 2023055112 (print) | LCCN 2023055113 (ebook) | ISBN 9780807769836 (hardcover) | ISBN 9780807769829 (paperback) | ISBN 9780807782453 (ebook)
Subjects: LCSH: Gardner, Howard, 1943- | Education—Philosophy. | Learning, Psychology of. | Multiple intelligences.
Classification: LCC LB885.G37 G37 2024 (print) | LCC LB885.G37 (ebook) | DDC 370.1—dc23/eng/20231206
LC record available at https://lccn.loc.gov/2023055112
LC ebook record available at https://lccn.loc.gov/2023055113

ISBN 978-0-8077-6982-9 (paper)
ISBN 978-0-8077-6983-6 (hardcover)
ISBN 978-0-8077-8245-3 (ebook)

Printed on acid-free paper
Manufactured in the United States of America

Contents

Acknowledgments	xiii
Introduction	xv

INFLUENCES

1.	Jerome S. Bruner as Educator	5
	References	10
2.	Harvard Project Zero: A Personal History	11
	Events Surrounding the Beginning of Project Zero	11
	Project Zero at Its Inception	14
	Leadership Transition	16
	Comments	18
	The Move to Educational Reform	18
	A Fateful Car Ride	19
	The 1990s: Going National and International	20
	Comment	21
	Beyond 2000—New Governance, New Opportunities, New Challenges	22
	Final Thoughts—The "Symptoms" of Project Zero	22
	References	23
3.	The Hundred Languages of Successful Educational Reform	24

CHINA: THE KEY IN THE KEY SLOT

4. **The Key in the Key Slot: Creativity in a Chinese Key**   31
   - I. A Recurring Incident   31
   - II. Childrearing in China: General Comments   32
   - III. Life as Performance   33
   - IV. The Arts as Beautiful and Good   35
   - V: The Importance of Hierarchy   37
   - VI. Shaping and Molding From Birth On   38
   - VII. Basic Skills Before Creativity   40
   - Toward a Productive Synthesis   41
   - Acknowledgments   43

EDUCATIONAL PHILOSOPHY

Progressivism—The True, the Beautiful, and the Good   45

5. **The Age of Innocence Reconsidered: Preserving the Best of the Progressive Traditions in Psychology and Education**   47
   Co-authored by Bruce Torff and Thomas Hatch
   - A Canonical View in Psychology and Education at Midcentury   47
   - New Insights   49
   - The Symbol Systems Approach   52
   - The View From Education   55
   - Closing the Loop: Innocence Recaptured   60
   - References   61

6. **Educating for the True, the Beautiful, and the Good**   62
   - Truth   63
   - Beauty   63
   - Goodness   64
   - Threats   66
   - Villains and Heroes   66

	Going Forward	67
	Reference	67
7.	**The Tensions Between Education and Development**	**68**
	I. Memories of Larry Kohlberg	68
	II. The Relation Between Development and Education	69
	III. Parameters of the Problem	71
	IV. Three Principal Ways of Representing Knowledge	72
	V. The Disjunctions Among Ways of Knowing	74
	VI. Possible Bridges Among Disparate Ways of Knowing	77
	VII. Closing Thoughts	78
	Acknowledgments	79
	References	79

INTRODUCING MULTIPLE INTELLIGENCES: CLAIMS, CRITIQUES, AND EDUCATIONAL IMPLICATIONS

	Overview of MI Theory	83
	References	84
8.	**Beyond IQ: Developing the Spectrum of Human Intelligences**	**85**
	References	92
9.	**Reflections on MI Myths and Messages**	**93**
	I. Breaking a Decade of Silence	94
	II. Myths of Multiple Intelligences	94
	III. Messages About MI in the Classroom	98
	Reference	102
10.	**"Multiple Intelligences" Are Not "Learning Styles"**	**103**
11.	**The Crystallizing Experience: Discovering an Intellectual Gift**	**106**
	Joseph Walters and Howard Gardner	
	The Biographies	110

The Interviews	116
Crystallizing Experiences	116
The Issue of Talent	118
In Conclusion	121
References	122

EDUCATIONAL EXPERIMENTS IN THE SPIRIT OF MULTIPLE INTELLIGENCES

12. MI Around the World — 125

The MI Meme	125
The Nature of the Soil	127
Why MI Takes Hold in Certain Soils	128
The Policy Level	129
Concluding Note: The Personal and the Political	130

IDENTIFICATION AND NURTURING OF INTELLIGENCES IN EARLY LIFE

Student Projects in the Pods at the Key School	131
The Artistic Intelligences: Can They Be Mastered and Measured in Adolescence?	132
References	133

13. The Spectrum Approach to Assessment: Nurturing Intelligences in Early Childhood — 135

Co-authored With Mara Krechevsky

The Spectrum Approach to Assessment	136
Implementation of the Spectrum Approach	137
Initial Results	139
Working Styles	140
A Comparison of Views: Parents, Teachers, and Spectrum	142
A Comparison of Spectrum Results With the Stanford-Binet Intelligence Scale	143

14. Projects During the Elementary Years — 149
    An MI School — 149
    Project Assessment — 151
    Project Scaffolding — 154
    References — 156

15. Arts PROPEL — 157
    Disciplined Inquiry in High School: An Introduction to Arts PROPEL — 157
    Building on the Theory of Multiple Intelligences — 157
    Alternative Accents in Arts Education — 158
    Disciplined Inquiry in High School: An Introduction to Arts PROPEL — 159
    The Project Zero Approach to Art Education — 159
    Arts PROPEL — 162
    Two Educational Vehicles — 163

CURRICULUM, PEDAGOGY, AND ASSESSMENT

    Acknowledgment — 175
    References — 175

16. The Unschooled Mind: Why Even the Best Students in the Best Schools May Not Understand — 177
    Reference — 191

17. Understanding Through the Disciplines — 192
    Three Puzzles — 192
    Vantage Points: From Puzzles to Concepts — 195
    The Patterns of the Scientist . . . and the Mathematician — 199
    The Beauty of the Artist — 201
    The Accounts of the Historian — 203
    In the Shopping Mall of the Disciplines — 205
    Reference — 209

18. **Teaching for Understanding Within and Across the Disciplines**   210
    Howard Gardner and Veronica Boix-Mansilla

    Understanding Within the Disciplines   211
    From Common Sense to Interdisciplinary Study   212
    Disciplinary Powers and Limitations   214
    Assessment Within and Across the Disciplines   215
    From Disciplinary to Personal Knowledge   215

19. **Assessment in Context: The Alternative to Standardized Testing**   217

    Binet, the Testing Society, and the "Uniform" View of Schooling   218
    Sources for an Alternative Approach to Assessment   220
    The Need for a Developmental Perspective   221
    The Emergence of a Symbol-System Perspective   221
    Emergence of a Multiple Intelligences Perspective   222
    A Search for Human Creative Capacities   223
    The Desirability of Assessing Learning in Context   224
    Locating Competence and Skill Outside the Head of the Individual   225
    General Features of a New Approach to Assessment   226
    Toward the Assessing Society   230
    References   234

HIGHER EDUCATION

20. **If We Were Designing a New College . . .**   237
    Wendy Fischman and Howard Gardner

    1. Why College?   238
    2. Less Is More   238
    3. More Alike Than Different   239
    Final Thoughts   239
    Reference   240

21. **Why We Should Require All Students to Take Two Philosophy Courses** — 241

CONTEMPORARY CHALLENGES AND OPPORTUNITIES

22. **Education in the Era of the Apps** — 247
    With Katie Davis
    Apps for a Better World — 254
    References — 256

23. **The Five Minds for the Future** — 257
    Cultivating New Ways of Thinking to Achieve Important Societal Goals — 257
    The Disciplined Mind — 257
    The Synthesizing Mind — 258
    The Creating Mind — 259
    The Respectful Mind — 260
    The Ethical Mind — 261
    Tension Exists — 262
    Wake-Up Calls — 262
    Role-Modeling — 263

24. **Synthesis 1.0: A Few Essential Tips** — 264

25. **Changing Minds** — 267
    80/20 and Seven R's — 267
    References — 274

26. **On Educating for the Three Virtues: A Hegelian Approach** — 275
    Toward a Synthesis — 279
    The Beauty of Truth-Seeking — 279
    The Conception of the Good — 280
    From Synthesis to Action — 281
    Lingering Questions — 282

Concluding Note 285
References 285

27. The Myths in "Neuromyths" 287
    References 289

28. Becoming a Good Person, a Good Worker, a Good Citizen
    in a Democratic Society 290
    The Challenge 290
    Framework 291
    The Lenses of Psychology 292
    A Recommended Course of Action 295
    Reference 298

29. To an Aspiring Researcher: Twelve Pieces of Advice 299
    A Thought Experiment 299
    Acknowledgments 306

Original Publication List 307
    Reference List 307

Index 311

Permissions 319

About the Author 320

Acknowledgments

In over a half century of research and writing, I've received wonderful help from hundreds of individuals—teachers, peers, students, editors, members of my research team, colleagues from institutions spread across the globe—and importantly, many generous funding agencies. When possible, I have acknowledged their help directly in these writings. But all too often, this has not proved possible. And so, with awareness of the inadequateness of the response, I voice my sincere gratitude to each and every one of you—invisible collaborators, so to speak.

In arranging for the publication of these volumes, I am tremendously indebted to Teachers College Press (TCP) at Columbia University. Brian Ellerbeck recognized the potential of this ambitious publishing venture and has been a true thought partner in the evolution from drafts of too many candidate pieces to the selection and presentation of the essays (in these two volumes). Thank you, Brian!

In addition, I am grateful to production editor, Mike Olivo; copy editor, Pam LaBarbiera; proofreader, Liz Welch; and their many responsible and responsive colleagues at TCP.

Only someone who has attempted to identify, track down, locate the appropriate personnel, and secure permissions from many outlets scattered around the world can appreciate the heroic work done by two unbelievably gifted and devoted colleagues, Shinri Furuzawa and Annie Stachura. In addition, Annie and Shinri have worked with me on countless details—not only taking care of them deftly, but calming me down when that was indicated.

Last, but also first, a profound thank you to my family. Above all to my wife, Ellen Winner, who has participated in every facet of this undertaking—problem-finding, problem-solving, and holding my hands, both literally and figuratively. And while they were largely spared any requests associated with these two volumes, my children, Kerith, Jay, Andrew, and Benjamin, have supported me over the decades—whether it was managing to fall asleep while I was typing late into the night, or giving me an idea for a study, or providing a critique—or simply a hug. I hope that if anyone asks them what their father accomplished in his research and writings, they will point to *The Essential Howard Gardner*.

Introduction

Since early childhood I've been in education. This has been true in the literal sense, ever since I attended Aunt Eunice and Uncle Gar's school for 3–4-year-olds in Scranton, Pennsylvania (nowadays, we'd call it Pre-K). In addition, while still a young child, I fantasized about one day teaching each of the grades from kindergarten through high school (college was not yet on my—or my family's—radar screen). And indeed, I coached Boy Scouts on some merit badges, and taught piano informally and intermittently in high school, college, and graduate school. I conducted a tutorial across the social sciences to undergraduates at Harvard College and did a stint as an apprentice teacher in a K–2 classroom in Newton, Massachusetts. Project Zero, my principal intellectual home since 1967, is located in Harvard's Graduate School of Education. My "CV" displays plenty of credentials in education.

My professional life is marked by sharp divide. In graduate school I became a dedicated empirical researcher, and for 15 years after receiving my doctorate I was a full-time researcher in developmental psychology and neuropsychology. Only when I accepted a teaching position at a school of education did my identity gradually shift: a researcher in developmental psychology and neuropsychology became a professor and researcher in education—where I have largely remained ever since.

My involvement in education has been broad. As a scholar who enjoys spending time in schools, I've worked in preschool education (Spectrum), K–12 (ATLAS and Harvard Project Zero) and college (The Real World of College); I have examined and written about education in areas ranging from the arts to technology; I've considered aspects of curriculum, pedagogy, and assessment. And I've had the privilege of visiting schools and interacting with scholars in education in many parts of the world. These diverse interests and experiences are drawn on and represented in this collection.

In terms of educational philosophy, I see myself in the tradition of John Dewey and Jerome Bruner, generally regarded in the United States as progressive educators. (While I myself attended traditional American public schools in Scranton, my four children attended schools considered progressive.) I've also been influenced significantly by my decades-long connection with early childhood education in the northern Italian city of Reggio Emilia—and via Reggio's leaders, I was exposed to the ideas of continental "educationalists" such as Friedrich Froebel, Nikolaj Grundtvig, Maria Montessori, Johann Pestalozzi, and Jean-Jacques Rousseau. It's not surprising that my mother had been studying to become a kindergarten teacher when her life was derailed by the rise of Hitler and the necessity of finding a safe haven outside of Nazi Germany. We might say that education was in my genes as well as in my environment—familial and cultural.

But while I might be considered a card-carrying supporter of progressive education, some of my ideas are more traditional, more conservative, more academic. I am a firm believer in the importance of disciplinary thinking—both on its own merits and as a necessary predecessor and indispensable ingredient of interdisciplinary thinking and intellectual synthesis. I cherish the idea of exposing young children to powerful ideas, but I don't believe that core disciplinary ideas and methods are easily understood or readily accepted; young children have strong preconceptions and stereotypes that interfere with more complex and less intuitive forms of thought. And while I hope that all children will find gainful employment and become caring citizens in their community, I believe that academic materials and goals need to be primary in formal education—otherwise, we would not need separate entities called schools, colleges, and universities. (How that agenda will be disrupted by increasingly powerful artificial intelligence instruments remains to be determined.) We can ask schools—from kindergartens to universities—to do many things, but we can't expect them to do everything. (And we benefit if family mores, community organizations, religious faiths, humanistic values, and various media are congenial with respect to consensual educational goals—rather than creating additional challenges and disruptions to their realization.)

In this volume, I lay out my principal ideas about education: its animating goals, as well as the specific curricula, pedagogies, and assessments that I have come to embrace. (A companion volume focuses on my research and views about the human mind, more broadly construed.) I make no claim to cover all of education—not even a graduate school of education can achieve that ambitious aspiration! But I do reflect on various areas of the curriculum—sometimes with special attention to the arts, spheres of personal passion. Moreover, I present the lessons that I've learned from decades spent working in American education (preschool through college) as well as insights gained from my experiences in China, northern Italy, Scandinavia, and elsewhere.

While education will continue to be a vital part of the human experience, the terrain changes quickly and unpredictably. I conclude with thoughts about education in a global era. At a time when technology (including artificial intelligence) looms ever larger, the quest for human values and practices that are powerful and positive is essential.

INFLUENCES

When I first started college, my roommates were surprised to discover that my parents had foreign accents—I seemed like the vast majority of my college peers, a typical American youth. But in fact my parents were Jewish refugees from Nazi Germany, having left just in time (they arrived in New York City on the notorious Kristallnacht, the so-called "Night of the Broken Glass.") I grew up with German as my first language (when I arrived in kindergarten I spoke English fluently but with a Bavarian accent!). My nuclear family, my extended family, and their circle of friends embraced longstanding European cultural values.

It is no surprise that I was attracted to subjects, hobbies, and professors who came from similar backgrounds: I studied history, music, the social sciences—areas that were populated by individuals of European and/or Jewish background (this would not have been true a generation earlier, when professors at major universities were largely Yankees of Protestant backgrounds), and it would have been less true in other areas of the curriculum, such as classics or engineering.

I benefited from studying with outstanding teachers and scholars. But I note with regret that very few of them were women or individuals of color or persons from parts of the world other than Europe and the United States. Fortunately, the situation has improved in recent decades, though not as quickly or completely as it should have. And the teaching that I encountered (while often excellent) was also quite conventional: hour-long lectures, rarely with time for questions and answers; sections headed by graduate students, some of whom were as much in the dark as their students; and standard midterm and end-of-the-semester written essay examinations. I happened to be a good test-taker and achieved high grades, but in retrospect I wish that I had experienced a more adventurous education.

At the beginning of graduate school, I was already married, and Judy and I had our first child in the middle of my graduate years. I was reading deeply in many areas and beginning to conduct empirical research—first in developmental psychology, then in neuropsychology (for samples of that work, see the companion volume—*The Essential Howard Gardner on Mind*). But only after a decade of studying and research was I stretched in other ways.

Specifically, courtesy of a generous grant from the Bernard Van Leer Foundation of the Netherlands, I was given the opportunity to travel widely. And indeed, I visited sites in Europe, Latin America, Africa, and several Asian countries. While these trips were typically short and tied to specific missions, I did have the opportunity to visit classes of various sorts and also to meet with scholars, particularly ones in education.

But what really opened my mind were visits to two societies that could not have been more distinct from one another in educational terms. On the one hand were the infant-toddler centers in Reggio Emilia, an affluent city in northern Italy. The Reggio schools were progressive in the optimal sense of the word: they took the thinking and feeling of young children very seriously; they created enticing learning opportunities for these youngsters; and they integrated education into the community so seamlessly that their schools would have delighted John Dewey. (I have continued to visit these schools and to gain sustenance from encounters over the decades.)

On the other hand, there were the schools in China in the early and middle 1980s—from preschool through secondary school—which were deemed excellent in quality, but the excellence was entirely different. The teachers and the curricula were completely scripted—minute-to-minute, it seemed—and followed essentially the same rigid script in classrooms in every city that I visited. Whether it was drawing or physical exercise, mathematics or political (moral) education, there were clear objectives, carefully described; routines scrupulously followed; and examinations that ascertained with precision what had been mastered and what had not.

It hardly needs to be said that I was more sympathetic to the Reggio approach—that's why I've returned there so many times and have recommended a visit to Reggio to numerous friends and colleagues (and skeptics!). And yet, it was important and salutary to witness an approach that was radically different—one that had stood the test of time and was allowing China once again to become a major player on the world scene.

(I should add that my one-time student Xin Xiang has now documented the full spectrum of educational approaches within contemporary China—ranging from what I saw 35 years ago to what one can see now in progressive schools in the United States and Western Europe.) Moreover, in my book *To Open Minds: Chinese Clues to the Dilemma of American Education,* I concluded that it was possible and perhaps desirable to realize the best features of both approaches—flexible approaches to the mastery of the disciplines, as well as an oscillation between exploration and discipline.

ESSAY 1

Jerome S. Bruner as Educator

In the late 1980s, in Paris, I attended an international conference on education. One evening I found myself having dinner with half a dozen people, none of whom I had known before, representing half a dozen different nations. As we spoke, a remarkable fact emerged. All of us had been drawn to a life in education because of our reading, years before, of psychologist Jerome Bruner's remarkable volume *The Process of Education* (1960).

At some point in their professional lives, many psychologists become involved in educational issues. Such engagement is especially likely in the United States, where educational theory and practice have been heavily influenced by contemporary work in psychology. It is possible that psychologists like B. F. Skinner or E. L. Thorndike have had more influence on specific educational policies, such as testing; but when it comes to enlarging our sense of how children learn and what educators could aspire to, Jerome Bruner has no peers.

Born in New York City in 1915, Jerome Bruner's professional life has been that of a prolific and versatile psychologist. Trained at Duke and Harvard, his first paper, published in 1939, was on "the effect of thymus extract on the sexual behavior of the female rat." During World War II, Bruner participated as a social psychologist, investigating public opinion, propaganda, and social attitudes. Thereafter, as one of the leaders of the postwar "cognitive revolution," his focus fell chiefly on human perception and cognition.

During the half-century since the war, Bruner investigated in turn a series of loosely related topic areas. In his work on the "new look" in perception, he emphasized the role of expectation and interpretation on our perceptual experiences. Maintaining this focus on the active role of the subject, he turned next to the role of strategies in the processes of human categorization. Becoming increasingly concerned with the development of human cognition, Bruner and colleagues at Harvard's newly formed Center of Cognitive Studies undertook a series of studies of the modes of representation used by children.

In the early 1970s Bruner moved from Harvard to Oxford University. There he continued his developmental studies of infant agency and began a series of investigations of children's language. Following his return to the United States a decade later, he showed a heightened concern with social and cultural phenomena. Rejecting the excessive computationalism of the cognitive perspective that he helped to found, he directed attention to human narrative and interpretive capacities, most recently in the law. And he helped to launch yet a third revolution in psychology, one centered around the lens and practice of cultural psychology.

It is important to sketch Bruner's contributions as a psychologist because they frame his involvement in educational issues. Reflecting his wide-ranging research interests and his own wide learning, Bruner has approached education as a broad thinker rather than as a technician. He has considered the full range of human capacities that are involved in teaching and learning—perception, thought, language, other symbol systems, creativity, intuition, personality, and motivation. He construes education as beginning in infancy and, especially in recent writings, has emphasized the role assumed in education by the gamut of cultural institutions. He has drawn on our knowledge of early hominids and has consistently viewed education from a cross-cultural perspective. (In the 1990s, he began to work regularly with the preschools of Reggio Emilia and other Italian communities; see Essay 3.) Indeed, in his most recent writings on cultural psychology, Bruner has proposed education as the proper "test frame" for constructing a full-fledged cultural psychology.

In the late 1950s, Jerome Bruner became explicitly involved in precollegiate education in the United States. At that time, following the Russian launching of the satellite Sputnik, many Americans felt that a greater portion of national resources must be devoted to education, particularly in science, mathematics, and technology. This interest occurred at the very time that the cognitive revolution, partly under the charismatic leadership of Bruner, had been launched. The influential National Academy of Sciences and the National Science Foundation convened a meeting of scientists, other scholars, psychologists, and educators at Woods Hole, Massachusetts, in September 1959. Bruner was the obvious chair for this meeting.

In his landmark book *The Process of Education* (1960), Bruner eloquently sketched the chief themes that had emerged at the conference. Against the widespread notion that youngsters should be learning facts and procedures, the conferees argued for the importance of the structure of scientific (and other) disciplines. If a student understood the principal concepts and procedures in a subject area, he or she could go on to think generatively about new issues. Against the view of the child as an assimilator of information, and as a little adult, the conferees put forth a still-unfamiliar view of the child: the child as an active problem-solver, who had his or her own ways of making sense of the world. Against the notion that certain subjects should be avoided until secondary school or later, the conferees argued for a spiral curriculum: in this formulation topics were introduced in appropriate ways early in school and then revisited, with added depth and complexity, at later points in schooling. This argument inspired the most quoted (and most controversial) line in the book: "We begin with the hypothesis that any subject can be taught effectively in some intellectually honest form to any child at any stage of development" (1960, p. 33).

The response to the book was swift and electrifying. The book was praised as "seminal," "revolutionary," and "a classic" by a range of scholars and policy leaders. It was translated into 19 languages and was for many years the bestselling paperback issued by Harvard University Press. Perhaps most important, *The Process of Education* catalyzed a range of important educational programs and experiments, both in the United States and abroad. As Bruner speculated some years later, "I think the book's 'success' grew from a worldwide need to reassess the functions of education in the light of the knowledge explosion and the new postindustrial technology."

Bruner became directly involved in educational efforts, first in the United States and later in Great Britain. He joined a number of committees and commissions. By far his deepest involvement was as chair and architect of a new curriculum for social studies to be used in the middle grades.

In 1964–1966, Bruner led the effort to design and implement "Man: A Course of Study." This ambitious effort to produce a full-fledged curriculum drew on the most current thinking in the newly emerging behavioral sciences.

In the late spring of 1965, as I was about to graduate from college, following a tip from a mutual acquaintance, I met Jerry Bruner, and shortly thereafter he offered me a summer job.

Little did I know that job would change both my personal and my professional life. The explicit job was to join something called IRG—the Instruction Research Group—to evaluate a new social science curriculum that was being developed for middle school called Man: A Course of Study, MACOS for short. And indeed, nearly every day for a month, a small group of us would evaluate sample lessons, how they worked, how they fell short, and how they might be revised and improved. Our efforts, along with that of dozens of other workers that summer and thereafter, eventually culminated in a brilliant curriculum that introduced kids from age 9 to 11 to gritty nutritious ideas and practices from the range of social science—from the principles of modern linguistics to the evolutionary similarities between human beings and higher apes. And on a personal level, Jerry himself introduced me to another researcher, "Judy Krieger, from UC Berkeley," whom I then married and who became the mother of three of my children.

In working on the curriculum, I was exposed not only to these important ideas but to many of the scholars who had developed them and were teaching them in universities. As one who had never taken a psychology course, I was introduced to cognitive and developmental psychology and soon made a career change to pursue that discipline.

If that was not enough, I also learned how to motivate and inspire a multidiscplinary team of students, scholars, teachers, and administrators. Jerry brought us together at times throughout the day. He asked questions, pointed us in new directions, improvised, joked, listened. In a brilliant move, he converted the basement of the Underwood School in Newton into a delicatessen, and each day, two assistants brought in delicious sandwich spreads. And then, in the evening, he and his wife, Blanche, opened up their spacious home near Harvard Square, and people of disparate ages, expertise, and status mixed freely. There I could actually talk to scholars who were at the forefront of their respective disciplines.

MACOS explored three guiding questions: What makes human beings human? How did they get to be that way? How can they be made more so? Only in recent years have I realized that much of my own research career has been devoted to answering these questions, and I hope that the way I approached them also bears the stamp of Jerry's way of thinking. And as I recently speculated, they seem attractive for a curriculum in an AI age (Gardner, 2023).

Reflecting Bruner's belief that even young children could tackle difficult issues, the curriculum presented themes that were "alive" in the behavioral sciences of the era. In light of linguistic analyses of Charles Hockett and Noam Chomsky, youngsters explored the nature of communication systems. Considering Sherwood Washburn's discoveries about the tool use of early man, students investigated ancient and modern tools and media. Inspired by discoveries about the social relations among primates (Irven DeVore) and the more complex relations among humans (Claude Lévi-Strauss), students explored kinship structures and social organizations of cultures. There was ample material on the art, myths, and childrearing practices of diverse groups. The ideas and themes were presented through rich ethnographic and filmic case studies, drawing in particular on the Netsilik Eskimos of Pelly Bay and the !Kung bushmen of the Kalahari Desert.

Years later Bruner wistfully recalled, "In the heady days of 1962, anything seemed possible" (1984, p. 190). As a young member of the research team in the summer of 1965, I can attest to the excitement that permeated this ambitious curriculum effort. Scholars, psychological researchers, curriculum planners, master teachers, and eager 5th-graders worked shoulder-to-shoulder each day to create and revise curricula that would engage and instruct the students. The resulting materials were made widely available and circulated through much of the United States and abroad in the late 1960s and early 1970s.

However, the euphoria surrounding such educational experimentation did not last. Within the United States, issues of poverty and racism erupted on the domestic front, and the increasingly frustrating and divisive war in Vietnam sapped the energies of reform. The Bruner curriculum was attacked by conservative political and social groups, which took objection to the intellectual aspirations (read: "elitist") and cross-cultural (read: "relativistic") sweep of the materials. Eventually, the National Science Foundation withdrew its support for the curriculum. Bruner conceded that the fault did not lie entirely with external critics. The curriculum worked best with well-prepared teachers working in schools with advantaged students. Bruner was fond of remarking, "We never quite solved the problem of getting the materials from Widener (the main library at Harvard University) to Wichita (largest city in Kansas, the heartland of America)." This issue remains alive in the 21st century.

Looking back on his educational work of the 1960s and early 1970s, Bruner came to recognize certain limitations. Part of the limitation represented the psychology of the era: an excessive focus on solo, intrapsychic processes of knowing. A complementary limitation came from a failure to recognize the depth and pervasiveness of societal problems, including poverty, racism, and widespread alienation. As Bruner commented, "It was taken for granted [at that time] that students lived in some sort of educational vacuum, untroubled by the ills and problems of the culture at large" (1996, xiii).

By the 1970s and 1980s, Jerome Bruner had emerged as a chief critic of the cognitive revolution that he had helped to launch. He saw it becoming an unwarranted reduction of human thought to a set of computational routines. With other colleagues, he called for the construction of a cultural psychology in which the historical background and current forces of a culture were given weight. In Bruner's view, such a rejuvenated psychology should discover what is meaningful to individuals and groups—and why it is meaningful.

In light of this framework, Bruner revisited educational issues in his 1996 book *The Culture of Education*. He proposed that education is not properly viewed simply as a function of the school, directed at the mind of individual students: "schools as now constituted are not so much the solution to the problem of education as they are part of the problem" (p. 198). One is more likely to achieve educational progress if one sees education as the function of the culture-at-large, and if one looks for learning amidst the interactions and joint constructions of students attempting to construct knowledge. No longer should educational theorists ponder the individual child (Piaget's "epistemic subject") puzzling about conservation of liquid or the subtlety of kinship relations. Rather, educationalists should direct their attention to groups of children attempting together—often with the aid of computer networks and remote experts—to understand the processes of biology, the nature of law, and even the ways in which they themselves learn. Successful students should tell one another what they have learned about the world and about the operations of their individual and collective minds.

Bruner's interest in educational experimentation continued throughout his life. In his later years, he made annual pilgrimages to Reggio Emilia. His own participation in the Italian educational efforts resulted in his being named an honorary citizen. When an observer pointed out that Bruner's ideas were more honored in Italy than in the United States, he quipped, "Well, then you've got quite a story."

I believe that Jerome Bruner was the most important American thinker and writer about education in my lifetime—equal in importance to John Dewey in an earlier epoch. Indeed, his influence may be greater than Dewey's, because Bruner wrote far more vividly and he entered directly into the classroom—politics and all!—in a way that Dewey was reluctant to do. In the first decades of the 21st century, neither Dewey nor Bruner is much discussed among political figures involved in education. But we will only have truly effective education in the United States, and the rest of the world, if we attend carefully to, and attempt to implement, the wisdom of these two scholarly giants.

REFERENCES

Bruner, J. *The process of education*. (1960). Harvard University Press.
Bruner, J. (1984). *In search of mind*. HarperCollins.
Bruner, J. (1986). *Actual minds, possible worlds*. Harvard University Press.
Bruner, J. (1990). *Acts of meaning*. Harvard University Press.
Bruner, J. (1996). *The culture of education*. Harvard University Press.
Gardner, H. (1989). *To open minds: Chinese clues to the dilemma of American education*. Basic Books.
Gardner, H. (2023). *Blog on AI and humanism*. https://www.howardgardner.com/howards-blog/a-hrefhttpsthegoodprojectsquarespacecomgood-blog202395chat-gpt-first-musingschat-gpt-first-musingsa

ESSAY 2

Harvard Project Zero
A Personal History

Until the middle 1950s, precollegiate education in America was primarily a local affair. But in 1957, the Soviets launched the satellite Sputnik. Democracies are slow to anticipate, but once attention-grabbing events happen, such nations are likely to react, and often overreact. Fearing that the Soviets were about to conquer Earth (if not outer space!), the U.S. federal government launched an expensive and aggressive campaign to upgrade precollegiate education. As in the early 21st century, the accent fell very much on science, engineering, and technology (what we now call STEM topics). Many people, including me, were beneficiaries of additional funds for education, particularly in the sciences.

In 1959, as part of the renewed focus on education, psychologist Jerome Bruner convened a distinguished group of scientists, psychologists, and educators at a conference center in Woods Hole, Massachusetts. Already a critic of Skinnerian behaviorism and traditional learning theory, Bruner and colleagues focused on a more constructivist, problem-finding (as well as problem-solving) approach. (See Essay 1.)

The "disciplinary turn" espoused by Bruner was not restricted to the sciences. In 1965, arts educator Manual Barkan convened a conference at Pennsylvania State University at which he built explicitly on Bruner's ideas. Barkan maintained that arts education (sometimes called aesthetic education) was also a discipline and should be taught and evaluated on that basis. This argument gave rise, decades later, to an explicit approach, funded by the California-based J. Paul Getty Trust, called "discipline-based arts education" (DBAE). By a strange twist of fate, work at Project Zero 2 decades later came to be framed or reframed, in part, as a critique of DBAE.

EVENTS SURROUNDING THE BEGINNING OF PROJECT ZERO

Shortly after the Woods Hole conference, with his colleague in psychology George Miller, Jerome Bruner launched the Harvard Center for Cognitive Studies. It soon became a unique venue. Outstanding scholars from a variety of disciplines, and from much of the Western world, came to Cambridge for a year or more of research and discussion as part of what we now call "the cognitive turn" in psychology. As it happens, in the early 1960s, three scholars did residencies at the Center: Paul Kolers, an ingenious experimental psychologist with interests both in visual perception and language; Nelson Goodman, a well-respected philosopher (with a focus on epistemology); and Noam Chomsky, already the leading iconoclastic theorist of linguistics and psychology, though not yet a well-known public intellectual (and, years earlier, a prize student of Goodman's at the University of Pennsylvania).

Moving away from a pure focus on psychological research, Bruner initiated a major curriculum effort for the middle grades. Called "Man: A Course of Study," it presented key ideas from psychology, linguistics, anthropology, and other social-scientific disciplines in ways that were intellectually respectable and yet could be grasped by 10-year-olds. I went to work for Bruner on this curriculum in the summer of 1965, literally weeks after I graduated from Harvard. (See Essay 1.)

Meanwhile, at the Harvard Graduate School of Education, Dean Theodore Sizer was reflecting on how the arts and arts education might become more central in a graduate school of education. And, coincidentally, meanwhile, Nelson Goodman, who had moved from Philadelphia to the Boston area, had already become disaffected with Brandeis University. He hoped to move back to his undergraduate and graduate alma mater, Harvard, and join the faculty of the distinguished Department of Philosophy. Assuming that such a position could be funded, Goodman moved temporarily to the Graduate School of Education in 1967.

As a graduate student in developmental psychology, I learned that a professor at Brandeis, Nelson Goodman, was looking for research assistants for a project in the arts. I had already been struck by the paucity, in developmental psychology, of *any* interest in artistic (as compared to scientific) development, and, accordingly, I had undertaken a study of creativity in the arts as well as the sciences. And so, in one of those episodes that can transform one's life, I drove out to the Brandeis campus in Waltham, Massachusetts, to meet Nelson Goodman.

While he was already one of the most esteemed philosophers in the English-speaking world, Nelson Goodman was scarcely a household name. Though considerably younger than Goodman, Noam Chomsky and Jerome Bruner were already much better known among the chattering classes. Nor, in that pre–search engine era, would it have been easy to get information about Professor Goodman.

Raised in the Boston area, Goodman had a blended love of philosophy and mathematics on the one hand, and the arts, particularly the visual arts, on the other. And indeed, in the 13 years between receipt of his undergraduate degree (1928) and receipt of his doctorate in philosophy (1941), Goodman ran his father's art gallery—said to be the first gallery in the Boston area to display the works of the once-controversial Pablo Picasso.

Goodman never relinquished his interest in the arts. He was married to Katherine Sturgis Goodman, a painter of some renown in New England. He collected works of art in a variety of styles and genres, and regularly attended art fairs. And in the 1960s, he directed his philosophical wits much more directly than before on the nature of artistic knowledge and practice. His John Locke lectures given at Oxford in 1962 transmogrified into a monograph, *Languages of Art* (1968), considered one of the chief contributions to aesthetics in the last half-century. (For some years, we at Project Zero referred to this book as "the Bible.") With little doubt, this rekindled professional commitment to the arts catalyzed Goodman's desire to launch a project focused on artistic knowledge and artistic education. Indeed, this immersion was foretold in the closing pages of *Languages of Art* (1968, p. 265):

> Once the arts and sciences are seen to involve working with—inventing, applying, reading, transforming, manipulating—symbol systems that agree and differ in certain specific ways, we can perhaps undertake pointed psychological investigation of how the pertinent skills inhibit or enhance one another; and the outcome might well call for changes in educational technology. Our preliminary study suggests, for example, that some processes requisite for a science are less akin to each other than to some requisite for an art. But let us forego foregone conclusions. Firm and usable results are as far off as badly needed; and the time has come in this field for the false truism and the plangent platitude to give way to the elementary experiment and the hesitant hypothesis.

Not a bad preamble for Project Zero (PZ), and a fair sample of Goodman's sharp and provocative literary style.

Goodman was a challenging personality. Nonetheless, he and I hit it off very well. He served as one of a small number of my "intellectual fathers." Goodman was a tireless worker, and while he taught me a lot about delegating, he did not neglect his students, nor his obligations as a head of a research project. And above all, his devotion to the arts was clear. At a time when the assassination of John F. Kennedy was still vivid in people's minds, Goodman regularly quipped, "Ask not what the arts can do for you; ask what you can do for the arts."

Speaking of quips, that may explain why we got the name Project Zero. As a former military man, Goodman thought easily in terms of finite projects. He also did not like to raise expectations! And so, rather than picking a descriptive name (like REsearch on Arts Education and Practice, which could be shortened to REAP), he picked a name that communicated nothing and promised nothing. Asked to explain the name, Goodman would say, "Well, there's lots of lore about arts education, but the general communicable knowledge about arts education is zero." Goodman would go on to explain that many practitioners of arts education knew what they were doing and seemed to do it effectively. But it was not easy to share such knowledge-in-practice with others, nor to know which practices could lead to general principles. So in effect, Goodman concluded, "we are starting from zero."

PROJECT ZERO AT ITS INCEPTION

In the fall of 1967, Project Zero was launched (without the slightest fanfare) at the Harvard Graduate School of Education (HGSE). The word "at" means notionally a part of the school budget, but we never had a permanent home and were moved regularly, sometimes as often as once a year and often without any advance notice. Indeed, as part-time inhabitants of a school in which arts education was hardly central ("invisible" would be closer to the truth), our housing received a Very Low Priority. Which allows me to cite an anecdote:

> Then as now, it was not easy to get furnishings from the school. At one time, we were in the possession of an extremely ratty rug; falling apart, malodorous, an eyesore. For months we tried to get it replaced. The bureaucrat to whom we plead for a replacement had a Dickensian name, Wormser. After the nth futile attempt to get a new rug, founding Project Zero member Paul Kolers asked, "Nelson, does this test your faith in human nature?" To which Nelson immediately retorted, "No, Paul, it *confirms* it."

Over the next 4 years (1967–1971), Project Zero functioned as a loosely knit think tank. At any one time, there were about a dozen persons associated with the project. (Writing in 2024, there are several dozen members and hundreds—if not thousands—of alums. This founding membership included David (Dave) Perkins in artificial intelligence, and I was in developmental psychology.)

What did we do? We met regularly, sometimes as often as once a week ("promptly," said Nelson, and he meant it!), to discuss issues that cut across the disciplines and across the arts, for example, the meaning and nature of style, metaphor, rhythm, expression, and other key concepts that spanned some or even all of the arts. Most of these were issues of interest to Goodman, ones that he had raised and probed, at least initially, in *Languages of Art*. We carried out small-scale experiments; for example, Dave Perkins probed which visual cues enable us to perceive cubic corners, and I examined the development in young children of sensitivity to artistic styles. Focusing more explicitly on education in the arts, we called in experts, those knowledgeable about education of young children, education at arts academies and museums, and education in high school, and made occasional site visits to highly regarded venues of education in the arts.

One encounter proved especially consequential for me. Early in 1969, both Goodman and I became interested in newly reported research on the division of labor between the two cerebral hemispheres (what we now call "right brain" and "left brain" thinking). Goodman's interest centered on the means by which different kinds of symbol systems are encoded and decoded; my interest was in how artists manage to orchestrate the many skills that go into the creation and perception of works of art.

We decided to invite as a speaker Norman Geschwind, a well-known neurologist with a special interest in higher cortical functions (thinking, not reflexes). Starting in the early afternoon, Geschwind gave a mesmerizing talk on the sequelae to different kinds of brain imaging. For example, he spoke about what had happened to composer Maurice Ravel and painter Lovis Corinth after each had suffered injuries to the brain. I had to go home for dinner, but the discussion continued until well into the night.

By the end of that day I had begun to rethink my future course of study. Instead of pursuing a faculty position in psychology, I would attempt to secure support for postdoctoral work with Geschwind at the local neurological unit that specialized in the study and rehabilitation of stroke victims. I'd rank the catalytic evening with Geschwind, and the 15 years of study and collaboration that followed, as equally important in my scholarly development to my involvements with my psychology mentor, Jerome Bruner, and my philosophy mentor, Nelson Goodman. Indeed, I ultimately had the privilege of dedicating books to each of these three remarkable scholar-mentors.

I was not heavily involved in the securing of funding for Project Zero during its early phases. The Harvard archives chronicle a set of correspondences between Ted Sizer at HGSE and Ernie Brooks at the Old Dominion Foundation. Sizer never received as much money as he asked for, but there was support sufficient to provide a modest base for PZ. I used to quip that Perkins and I were unpaid assistants, "a tradition that we have maintained until the present." Nonetheless, I was amused to discover that our unpaid ("volunteer" was the politically correct predecessor to "intern") status was enshrined in the Brooks-Sizer correspondence. Toward the end of Goodman's tenure as founding director, there were also modest funds from the U.S. Office of Education.

The other activity for which Project Zero was notable during the early years has been insufficiently acknowledged and heralded. Goodman believed passionately that artistic forms of knowledge were every bit as important, precious, and challenging as knowledge in the sciences and in other realms. In this respect, he was a faithful follower of epistemologically oriented philosophers Susanne Langer and Ernst Cassirer. He also believed, probably correctly, that most students at the Graduate School of Education (and, indeed, at the university more broadly) had little understanding of artistic practices and processes.

And so, with little fanfare, and a willingness to do most of the heavy lifting himself (neither Perkins nor I were much interested in being impresarios), Nelson launched a memorable series of 12 lecture performances at the Graduate School of Education. At each, a well-known artist invited the audience, which was often quite large, behind the scenes, so that attendees could understand the deep and complex thinking that went into quality artistic production and performance. And the series was deliberately broad: I. A. Richards (a university professor of literature) on poetry; Ladji Camara on drumming; Jacques Lecoq on mime; Ina Hahn and Martha Gray Armstrong on dance; George Hamlin and others on the directing of a play (with Christopher Reeve, then a high school student, as one of the actors); Alfred Guzzetti on photography; Leon Kirchner on composing. This kind of activity, had it been undertaken at the recently opened Lincoln Center, might have had a total budget of millions, but Goodman curated them on a shoestring, and those who attended (including me) were much affected. It was Nelson Goodman at his best!

I should mention some "products" (we came to use the even more deadly term "deliverables") of the first years of Project Zero.

Of singular importance was the final report of the first phase of Project Zero, co-authored by Goodman, Perkins, Vernon Howard, and myself (Goodman et al., 1972). It provided a synoptic view of the various activities undertaken during the 4 years of the Goodman era, and is an essential document for any future historian. The second is a book, published some years later, and edited by Perkins and Barbara Leondar, called *The Arts and Cognition* (1977). Contributors were other "principals" of Project Zero, and, like the "final report," this volume provides an excellent (and somewhat less technical) survey of the topics and conclusions reached during the first phase. Finally, there is a scholarly paper co-authored by David Perkins, Vernon Howard, and me called "Symbol Systems: A Philosophical, Psychological and Educational Investigation" (1972). Members of PZ also offered a course at the School of Education.

LEADERSHIP TRANSITION

By 1971, Goodman was well entrenched in the Harvard Department of Philosophy. I think that he felt that PZ had been successfully launched, and he was no longer that interested in the empirical and practical details of artistic education. And so, characteristically and epigrammatically, he said to Dave Perkins and me, "You can have the project." Which, as he then pointed out with glee, meant that from then on *we* had to raise the money.

For a year, while I was beginning postdoctoral studies with Norman Geschwind and others at the Boston Veterans Administration Medical Center, Dave was the sole director of Project Zero. In 1972, I joined him as co-director, and for the next 28 years (until 2000), we remained at the helm of the organization. Dave and I did not work closely together on projects. But we kept each other informed about our activities, applied together for funds for Project Zero, shared a secretary, and, when appropriate, worked together on writing and speaking projects. At various times we also hosted seminars and brown bag lunches at which visitors or members of Project Zero spoke. While we tried to ignite these discussions from time to time, they never worked as effectively, or for as long, as the Goodman-led weekly sessions of the late 1960s. I regret this—Goodman may have had a convening genius that we lacked.

The Psychology Decade

Any division of the 50-plus year period from 1972 to the present would be to some extent arbitrary. It seems fair to say that both Perkins and I remained interested in conceptual and analytic issues, but neither of us saw ourselves primarily as philosophers, and our contributions to the philosophical literature, if any, were incidental, not focal. During the decade after Goodman's resignation, Dave and I both operated primarily as psychologists, directing small research groups. At some point in that decade, we initiated an informal division of labor. Dave headed the "cognitive skills" group, which focused on cognitive processes involved in creativity and artistic perception and production, as well as other realms of thinking. I headed the "developmental" group. My group focused on the development, in normal and gifted children, of various forms of artistic and symbolic competences, and, to a lesser extent, on their breakdown under various forms of pathology.

With the support from the Old Dominion Foundation (which had morphed into the Mellon Foundation) at an end, Dave and I were expected to hone our own entrepreneurial skills. Sometimes we applied together to the government for research support. We had a fan at the National Science Foundation (a psychologist named Henry Odbert) and a friend at the National Institute of Education (named Martin Engel), and they provided sufficient support in the 1970s to keep us afloat. That a research project in the arts could be funded by NSF seems incredible—how times have changed!

The 1970s saw the first of several crises at Project Zero. In 1972, Sizer resigned the deanship at HGSE and became the head of Phillips Academy at Andover. His place was taken by Paul Ylvisaker, who had not previously been an academic (and, unknown to us, was already quite ill). Ylvisaker also inherited one of the periodic financial crises at HGSE. He did not see the point of having a research project in the arts, not least one headed by two young researchers without faculty appointments. And so he began to take steps to shut us down.

We were saved by two people. One was philosophy professor Israel Scheffler, who, while never an active member of Project Zero, was loyal to Goodman and saw us as a positive force at the School of Education. In effect, he said to Dean Ylvisaker, "These are bright guys who are bringing overhead to the school. Why thwart them . . . just leave them alone." The second was the dean's own sister, Barbara Y. Newsome, who worked in the arts for one of the Rockefeller philanthropies. Dean Ylvisaker sent Barbara some information about our project, and while she did not give us a ringing endorsement, she was enthusiastic enough that she contributed, if unwittingly, to our survival.

You might see this decade as a time when both Perkins and I were building up our résumés as researchers in psychology, broadly construed. If we taught at all, it was quite incidental. We neither duplicated Goodman's work in philosophy nor picked up his practical educational agenda, as in the lecture performances. And I began to work with a number of promising young researchers, including Dennie Wolf; Laurie Meringoff (who met her husband, noted children's book author Marc Brown, while conducting research on children's understanding of media); and Ellen Winner, who worked with me on metaphoric thinking and whom I married in 1982.

COMMENTS

It is worth noting that while Dave and I never collaborated on nonedited books, the subjects in which we became interested often paralleled one another—and this was probably not a coincidence. We both had longtime interests in the topic of creativity across the arts and sciences. We both devised original, iconoclastic theories in the area of intelligence. We both studied and wrote about leadership, with interests both in individual leaders and in the direction of organizations. We had a continuing interest in artistic perception, production, and education. And as we grew older, we became interested in ethical and moral issues, my research group looking at "good work," Dave and colleagues focusing on peace studies.

While a focus on education in the arts remained, Dave and I both branched out from that focus. Dave, for example, did work in standard visual perception, in everyday reasoning, and in creativity across the spectrum. I was looking at the development and breakdown (as a result of brain damage) of the full range of cognitive capacities, not just those in the arts. Nearly everyone who came to work at Project Zero had some background in the arts, and I think one can discern an "artistic touch" and an "artistic attitude" even in work that is not explicitly concerned with the arts.

THE MOVE TO EDUCATIONAL REFORM

Just as the launching of Sputnik in 1957 catalyzed a crisis in American educational policy, the publication in 1983 of the federal report *A Nation at Risk* by the National Commission on Excellence in Education galvanized reflections on the condition of K–12 education in the United States. It also generated more of a federal role in government and more funding from foundations, as well as more active attempts to affect curriculum, pedagogy, and assessment at the national level. It is not possible to say whether Project Zero would have moved increasingly into educational reform—particularly K–12 education—had it not been for the issuing of this influential report. But in any event, in the 1980s and thereafter, Project Zero became far more involved in educational theorizing and educational practice. Again, our two groups worked in tandem rather than closely together, but both were far more involved in schools, far more involved with teachers, and far more involved in curriculum and assessment than had been the case in earlier years.

This period ushered in the one sustained collaboration between our teams of researchers. At the urging of historian Lawrence Cremin, then the influential president of the Spencer Foundation, we began a lengthy examination of what we came to call "Teaching for Understanding." Partly conceptual, partly involving action research in schools, we sought to refashion what it means to understand concepts, topics, and disciplines, and to conceptualize "understanding as a performance." Not only did this undertaking provide a very rich vein for exploration; in recent decades, it has become perhaps the best-known educational product of Project Zero. (See Essays 17 and 18.)

I useed to quip that when Ronald Reagan became president in 1981, our funding from the government ended; and that is because Reagan thought that social science was socialism (he had said as much). Whether or not this remark is literally true, it *is* the case that nearly all of our more recent funding came from other sources, either foundations or wealthy individuals. Dave and I began to acquire a whole new set of skills.

I've long maintained that Project Zero carries out projects that fulfill two requirements: a) the projects are of interest to the researcher(s), and b) the researchers can secure money to execute it. If you look at the lengthy list of projects undertaken after 1980, you can certainly see a connection between the funder's interest and what work we carried out. But we never responded to contracts (and rarely to so-called RFPs), and we did not bend our work simply to please a funder. This independent trait places us in a very small category of research enterprises.

A FATEFUL CAR RIDE

In the late 1980s, I attended a conference on educational reform at a hotel in Cambridge. I don't remember the content of the conference and the conference itself was not very memorable.

Except for one thing.

After the end of the conference, an attendee who had been quiet during the conference asked if he could hitch a ride with me from the venue to his hotel in Harvard Square. I replied in the affirmative. On the way to the hotel, Ray Handlan told me that he was interested in our work and might be able to help with funding. Having tried to raise money for over half a century, I can assure you that this is a message all too seldom heard by petitioners!

It turned out that Ray represented a foundation that was unknown to the public, so secretive indeed that I did not learn its name for some time. Called the Atlantic Philanthropies, the organization funded work in many areas, including education, and did so generously, with the only proviso that its identity would be kept secret. And for close to a decade, its beneficiaries maintained the aura of secrecy, until the name Atlantic Philanthropies and that of its funder, Charles Feeney, was revealed in a front-page story in the *New York Times* (Miller, 1997).

Since I wanted to make sure that I was not accepting laundered funds, I checked with the powers that be at Harvard; I was assured that the Atlantic Philanthropies was a valid nonprofit and that it was appropriate to accept its support. My group was faithful to the directive of the foundation, so much so that we referred to Ray Handlan as "Rex Harrison," our program officer Angela Covert as "Agatha Christie," and the foundation itself as AF (for "anonymous funder"). Many other beneficiaries were much less compliant, though I don't know that any recipient was ever penalized by a withdrawal of funding.

While we continued to secure some funding from other sources, Project Zero was fundamentally—and in my view positively—transformed by the support from the Atlantic Philanthropies.

THE 1990S: GOING NATIONAL AND INTERNATIONAL

In the mid-1980s, having spent most of my adult life at Project Zero, and now beginning a career as a full-time faculty member at HGSE, I went to Tom James, the founding president of the Spencer Foundation (which supported PZ for 40 years!), and asked for his advice about Project Zero. He responded, in matter-of-fact fashion, "Either go international or give it a decent burial." On my own, I would not have followed either strand of advice. But the funding from the Atlantic Philanthropies, which lasted a solid decade, and often yielded one million dollars a year, fundamentally altered our organization. It both enhanced our organizational capacity and laid the groundwork for long-term stability.

For the first time, we were in a position to assemble a genuine secretariat. Before that time, Dave and I either shared a secretary or worked with one or more student assistants (now paid!). Thereafter, we were able to hire individuals who were in charge of finance, human resources, technology, publications, and other core needs of an organization, whose ranks swelled from roughly 15–20 individuals to more like 50–60. Without question, the extra support allowed us to focus much more on the research itself.

Of course, a large organization does not run itself, even when you are in a position to hire various kinds of experts. And so, during the 1990s, we experimented with different variations of governance. Dave and I retained our title roles, but we experimented with various kinds of managers and management teams. None of them was disastrous, but none of them worked seamlessly, either (nor should we have expected them to). And so Dave and I began to think about the issue of succession of leadership of the organization.

The second major change of Project Zero was the challenge of making our work, and particularly our work in education, better known, both nationally and internationally. For the most part, in its treatment of organizations that it funded, the Atlantic Philanthropies was admirably hands-off. Our valued program officers did not tell us what to study or how to study it. And yet our program officer made it clear to us that it did not suffice to "carry out research for research's sake."

This directive caused one of the few genuine crises in the history of Project Zero. As the major contact to the Foundation—one privy to its thinking—I recommended that we initiate a summer institute where we could present our ideas and practices to a large group of educators.

To my surprise, this suggestion led to almost unanimous opposition. To this day I don't quite understand the nature or the vehemence of the opposition, which suggests to me that it stemmed from many causes, ranging from resentment of the muscle that I was flexing in a famously flat organization to a feeling that each of us should be able to do whatever we wanted, no matter what the funder (or anyone else) requested.

At any rate, I became so frustrated that I finally announced, "If you all won't join me in mounting this institute, I'll simply do it myself." For some reason, this line in the sand calmed people down, and in the end almost everyone cooperated in carrying out a summer institute. It took us a few years to iron out various wrinkles, but quite soon our institutes were highly successful. We now carry out institutes each year in the United States; they are our major source of income for the core staff of the organization, and we have been carrying out conferences abroad for nearly a decade. (Alas, these off-site conferences had to be suspended during the pandemic of 2020–2022, but by the time you read these words, they will have been resumed—along with many offerings available online.)

COMMENT

It would be misleading to claim that the ideas and practices of Project Zero would win a plebiscite anywhere. We might like to think that that is because our ideas are too subtle, too progressive, and perhaps too sophisticated for many educators and parents, and that our ideas are destined to cede hegemony to more simplistic ways to think about learning and teaching.

But that's a self-serving analysis. I've come to believe that in almost any educational jurisdiction, there would be a portion of members who would find Project Zero ideas and practices appealing. And rather than trying to convert the resisters, we are better off trying to help those individuals and institutions, often early adapters, who already have some sympathy with our aims and our methods.

At various times we have created maps of where our ideas have taken root. In the United States, our ideas are best-known and most admired on the coasts. But if anything, our ideas have greater following outside the United

States, in particular, in parts of Latin America, Scandinavia, Australia, New Zealand, and, surprisingly, in pockets of China and India. Of course, the latter two countries are so populous that they cannot readily be compared to Colombia or to Denmark.

BEYOND 2000—NEW GOVERNANCE, NEW OPPORTUNITIES, NEW CHALLENGES

In 2000, Dave and I turned over the reins of Project Zero to Steve Seidel, a longtime researcher with Project Zero and soon to become head of the Arts in Education program at the school. We put together a small steering committee, composed of the three of us, with various managers in attendance on an ad hoc basis. Shari Tishman soon joined the steering committee, and in 2008, we had a smooth transition from Steve's to Shari's leadership. In 2015 we had another smooth transition to the leadership of Daniel Wilson (and his chief administrator, Faith Harvey), who built up the outreach of Project Zero and has also set up many more connections among the researchers and research projects currently under way.

With my urging, Project Zero recently set into motion a more formal mechanism for choosing leaders and lines of research. And in 2023, longtime researchers Liz Duraisingh and Carrie James became co-directors. And I voluntarily retired from the Executive Committee at the same time.

I quip that we have moved from a Politburo model to an Articles of the Confederacy model. And perhaps by the time you read these words, Project Zero will have established a well-entrenched mode for choosing leaders and paths of work.

FINAL THOUGHTS—THE "SYMPTOMS" OF PROJECT ZERO

According to Nelson Goodman, when trying to specify what makes a work or an experience "artistic," it does not make sense to set up a single, rigid definition. Rather, one should think of certain characteristics that, when all are present, suggest that we are in the realm of the arts; and when are all absent, signal that we are not involved in the arts.

Over the years, attempts to create a short and sharp mission statement for Project Zero have never succeeded. Project Zero is too loose a confederation of researchers and practitioners, and it is too much subject to the whims of national priorities and funding preferences to lend itself to a simple formulation as might be case for the Center for Cryogenics or the Center for Population Growth, or more recently the Center for Digital Thriving housed at PZ. In that sense, our "zero" is both a benefit and a curse.

That said, I'm willing to stick my neck out and delineate the symptoms, loosely grouped, that have characterized our endeavors over the decades:

- Focus on high-end cognition (e.g. problem-solving and problem-finding, not the identification of the alphabet or the ability to discriminate colors).
- Search for conceptual clarity; create frameworks that can be applied flexibly.
- Avoid linkages to specific age groups or specific disciplines; inherently multidisciplinary.
- Draw on artistic thinking and analyses, without being limited to the arts.
- Have resonance with educators, particularly those of a progressive frame of mind.
- Develop ideas and give them a push in the right direction (we don't run schools or museums, but give helpful input to many all around the world).
- Open up to collaboration to many individuals and organizations, but insist on quality partnerships.
- Avoid a party line—one is free to study what one wants, and no one legislates the findings or their interpretations.
- Carry out succinct projects (sometimes caricatured as project-itis) and make sure that they are well documented.
- Require a champion who is willing to take the lead in securing the funding and leading each project.
- Prefer support that is open-ended rather than tied to contracts and "deliverables."

As I write, Ellen Winner has launched a 3-year study of the impact of PZ ideas and practices around the world. Stay tuned!

REFERENCES

Gardner, H., Howard, V., & Perkins, D. (1972). Symbol systems: A philosophical, psychological and educational investigation. National Society for the Study of Education.

Goodman, N. (1968). *Languages of art.* Bobbs-Merrill.

Goodman, N., Perkins, D., & Gardner, H. (1972). *Basic abilities required for understanding and creation in the arts.* Final Report National Institute of Education.

Miller, J. (1997, Jan. 23). He gave away $600 million, and no one knew. *The New York Times.* www.nytimes.com/1997/01/23/nyregion/he-gave-away-600-million-and-no-one-knew.html

Perkins, D., & Leondar, B., Eds. (1977). *The arts and cognition.* Johns Hopkins University Press.

ESSAY 3

The Hundred Languages of Successful Educational Reform

> There are many ways of mediating among these human impulses and strains. To my mind, no place in the contemporary world has succeeded so splendidly as the schools of Reggio Emilia in northern Italy. When the American magazine Newsweek, in typically understated fashion(!), chose "The Ten Best Schools in the World" in December 1991, it was entirely fitting that Reggio Emilia was its nominee in the Early Childhood category. Reggio epitomizes for me an education that is effective and humane; its students undergo a sustained apprenticeship in humanity, one that may last a lifetime.

As is often quipped, success has a thousand parents, while failure is an orphan. By all accounts the infant-toddler centers and preschools of the municipality of Reggio Emilia are a singular success. Indeed, they are justifiably honored all over the world; thousands have admired them up close, and many dozens of schools have been created in their image. In so characterizing the schools, it is important to remember that most educational experiments fail without leaving a trace (hence embodying their orphan status). Moreover, even those experiments that have some success do not last long and/or fail to affect educational institutions elsewhere. Thus the collection of schools begun by Loris Malaguzzi and his close colleagues in the 1960s is important in addressing the questions of what makes for a successful educational experiment; how such experiments might be replicated; and, more troublingly, why the desire for such schools is found in a relatively small minority of the world's population.

Certainly the initial circumstances surrounding the Reggio endeavor were not favorable. In the latter 1940s Malaguzzi returned to a part of Italy that had been devastated by war, with few tangible assets and a significantly demoralized population. While comfortable Americans may have flocked to the Italian neorealist films of the late 1940s, the grim life that was captured in them hardly hinted at the potential for revolutionary new schools.

In any successful endeavor, a number of separate elements need to come together. As I read the evidence, there was the practical idealism (or idealistic practice) of Malaguzzi; the tradition of innovative schools in northern Italy and select parts of Central and Western Europe; a set of young educators, almost all women, who were attracted to the vision of a new kind of education; the willingness of the Reggio local and regional governments—largely Communist, or, less provocatively, communitarian—to invest generously and over a long time in these schools; a tradition of civil society, along with certain habits and attitudes of Catholicism, which have long marked this region of the world; the gradual prospering of northern Italy; and no doubt many other factors, some readily identifiable, others lost to history or mythology. (Writing in 2024, I would add the appeal—but also the limitations—of schools inspired by Italian educator Maria Montessori).

It would be instructive to know about the tipping points for the Reggio experiment—both positive and negative. Did these include the first signs of international interest in the 1970s; the launching of influential periodicals at the same time; the election of a particular mayor, *assessore* (councilor), or town council? And it would be equally important to specify what did go wrong, or could have gone wrong—the loss of a strategic ally, sustained public criticism of personalities or policies, the anger surrounding the sometimes violent Red Brigades, a push toward formal introduction of statewide curricula in the preschool years—just to name a few possible villains?

My colleague Dave Perkins has proposed a formula for successful educational innovation. He posits the need for three kinds of visionaries: a *theoretical* visionary, who develops the key ideas—for example, the basic contours of curricula, pedagogy, mission, and values; a *practical* visionary, who makes these ideas come alive on the ground; and a *political* visionary, who provides the resources and the protection so that the others can proceed with their work. From what I know and observed, I suspect that Loris Malaguzzi was primarily a theoretical visionary. However, the schools would not have succeeded had he not been a prime contributor to the practices that work and been able to attract and maintain co-workers who wanted to practice (as well as theorize) alongside him. Moreover, although he enjoyed resisting the political establishment—indeed, challenging *any* kind of establishment—I suspect that he was skilled at aligning the political forces needed to ensure that the educational experiments in Reggio would be successful.

Now for perhaps the most important reason for the success of the Reggio Schools—both the vision and the reality are singularly impressive. The schools are beautiful to behold, reflecting an exquisite sense of space and materials. The key instructors, called *pedagogistas* and *atelieristas*, are well trained, carry out their work excellently, and devote themselves unstintingly—indeed monastically—to their task. The parents and the surrounding community provide regular tangible support, as well as useful criticism. The techniques that have been developed—group learning, documentation, long-term projects, integration into the community, just to name a few—are innovations that actually work.

Most importantly, there is the capacious and inspiring conception of children as:

- active, engaged, exploring young spirits;
- capable of remaining with questions and themes for many weeks;
- able to work alongside peers and adults; and
- welcoming the opportunity to express themselves in many "languages"; to create new ones; and to apprehend and enter into those modes of expression that have been fashioned by their age mates.

I suspect that this conception may be the most important legacy of Loris Malaguzzi. Certainly it's what first brought me to Reggio in the early 1980s and catalyzed many memorable trips since, as it has moved many other visitors as well.

Not to imply that this vision was Loris Malaguzzi's alone. The same feeling of solidarity, collaboration, and mutual invention that characterizes the schools today—both teachers and students—is likely to have characterized Reggio from its early days. No doubt Malaguzzi could be difficult, stubborn, at times. And perhaps, as many of us do, he may have arrogated more credit to himself than was actually the case. The evidence that the schools have grown and thrived in the decades since his death speaks both to his capacity to create an institution that would survive him *and* to the enormous capabilities of his closest colleagues.

As an American educator, I'm struck by certain paradoxes. In the United States we pride ourselves on being focused on children, and yet we do not pay sufficient attention to what they are actually doing and expressing. We call for cooperative learning among children, and yet we rarely have sustained cooperation at the level of teacher and administrator. We call for artistic works, but we rarely fashion environments that can truly support and inspire them. We embrace parental involvement, but are loathe to share ownership, responsibility, and credit with supportive parents. We recognize the need for community, but we so often crystallize immediately into interest groups, if not into individual barracks or foxholes. We hail the discovery method, but we do not have the confidence to allow children to follow their own noses and hunches. We call for debate, but often spurn it; we call for listening, but we prefer to talk; we are affluent, but we do not safeguard those resources that can allow us to remain so and to foster the affluence of others.

Reggio is so instructive in these respects. Where we are often intent to invoke slogans, the educators in Reggio work tirelessly to solve many pedagogical and institutional challenges.

Why, I must ask again, when so many informed educators sing the praises of the Reggio schools, are there relatively few successful examples of such schools in other parts of the world? One reason, no doubt, is that such schools are difficult to launch, require much financial capital, and even more human capital, if they are to be sustained. But I contend that there is a deeper reason.

While the vision of children and human nature embodied in the Reggio schools is undoubtedly compelling, it can be threatening as well. It means that you trust children, you trust teachers, you trust the powers of the imagination. It means that you abandon an approach to life that is purely instrumental, purely financial, purely Darwinian if you will, in favor of one that recognizes the rights of children and the obligations of humanity.

Such a generous view of human nature has until now been a minority one all over the world—and while there are signs of it in Scandinavia, in Scotland, and perhaps elsewhere, it is certainly not the trend in the United States, England, or much of the rest of the "developed" and the "developing" world. For now, the Reggio schools remain more an existence proof rather than a harbinger of things sure to gel around the world. But they are far more than simply an existence proof; they stand as testimonials of what quality education can be like in early childhood.

CHINA: THE KEY IN THE KEY SLOT

In the 1980s, I had the invaluable opportunity to visit China several times. On the first trip, in 1980, China had just come out of the terrible experience of the Cultural Revolution and was seeking to establish ties to the West, particularly in areas like the arts and arts education. Because of my own (and Project Zero's) work in arts education, I was especially primed to make comparisons with Western practices. And through a combination of circumstances, I soon became the American leader of a cross-cultural exchange in the arts.

On one trip, taken with our young son Benjamin, I made a seemingly casual observation: how Chinese nationals reacted to Ben's playful exploration of a hotel key. As occasionally happens, this incident opened up my eyes to significant differences in attitudes toward the arts and education between China, on the one hand, and the United States (and other Western societies) on the other.

To some extent this essay is a period piece. China has changed enormously since 1980! But for that very reason, it seems valuable to try to capture that moment—and to note in which ways China has changed, and to ponder in which ways our respective societies are closer and in which ways they have drifted apart.

CHINA: THE KEY IN THE KEY SLOT

ESSAY 4

The Key in the Key Slot
Creativity in a Chinese Key

I. A RECURRING INCIDENT

At the Jinling, a comfortable hotel in Nanjing, the key to our hotel room was attached to a large plastic block with the room number embossed on it. When leaving the hotel, guests were encouraged to turn in the key, either by handing it to an attendant standing behind the desk or by dropping the key into a slot. Because the key slot was rectangular and narrow, the key with its plastic pendant had to be carefully aligned by hand so that it could fit into the snug slot.

Our 20-month-old son Benjamin (adopted from Taiwan a year earlier) loved to carry around the key and shake it with his hand. He also liked to attempt to place the key into the key slot. When my wife or I approached the hotel registration desk with Benjamin in our arms, he would bring the key to the vicinity of the slot and then try to shove it into the hole. Because of his tender age and limited understanding, he would usually fail to insert it into the slot. This lack of success did not bother Benjamin in the least. He loved to bang the key on the slot and to enjoy the sound it made, along with the kinesthetic sensation it produced.

My wife Ellen and I were both perfectly happy to allow Benjamin to bang the key in the vicinity of the key slot. But I soon observed an interesting phenomenon. Frequently, when there was a Chinese attendant nearby—and sometimes even when there was merely a Chinese passerby in the vicinity—that individual would come over to watch Benjamin. As soon as the observer saw what our son was doing and noted his lack of immediate success, she attempted to intervene. In general, she would hold onto his hand and, gently but firmly, guide it directly to the slot, reorient it as necessary, and then press the key-clutching hand into the slot. She would then smile somewhat expectantly at Ellen or me, as if awaiting a thank-you.

Alas, we were not particularly grateful for this intervention. After all, it was not as if Benjamin were running around wildly without supervision; clearly we—his parents—had been aware of what he was doing and had not ourselves intervened. However, it also became clear that we were dealing with a very different set of attitudes—assumptions concerning not only what children should be doing (or not doing), but also the proper role of other adults in their socialization. Perhaps, indeed, this recurring incident held part of the key to the mysteries of arts education that had brought us to China.

II. CHILDREARING IN CHINA: GENERAL COMMENTS

During the course of the months that we spent in China, it became clear to us that babies are "fair game" in China. Adults (and even adolescents) feel little compunction about intervening in the childrearing process. It was equally clear that the Chinese had a consensus on what was right or wrong in most situations; in their casual encounters with Benjamin, they were simply exhibiting their commonly held beliefs.

After I had gleaned what was going on, I began to incorporate this little key-slot anecdote into my talks to Chinese teachers, parents, and administrators. I would relate what had happened and seek audience reactions. With very few exceptions, my Chinese informants shared the opinions of the residents and attendants at the hotel. They put it this way: Since adults know how to place the key in the key slot; since that is the ultimate (if not the only) purpose of approaching the slot; and since the baby is not old (or clever) enough to consummate the action on his own, what possible gain is achieved by having the baby flail about? Why not show him what to do? He will be happy (those around will also be happy); he will learn how to do it sooner; and then he can proceed to more complex activities. We agreed that sometimes it is important to show the child what to do and that we certainly did not want to frustrate him. But we also pointed out that Benjamin was rarely frustrated by his attempts to insert the key in the slot—delight was a more common reaction. We then tried to communicate to our Chinese hosts that we had quite a different view about the significance of our son's behavior.

First of all, we did not care whether he succeeded in inserting the key into the slot; it was not important. He was having a good time and was exploring, which we liked. But here's the more important point: We were trying to teach Benjamin something in the process—that one can often solve a problem by oneself. This lesson reflects a principal value of childrearing in middle-class America: As long as the child is shown exactly how to do things—whether it be placing a key in a key slot or drawing a rooster—he is less likely to figure out himself how to do it. He is certainly less likely to arrive at an original way of doing it. And, in general, he is less likely to view life—as we do—as a series of situations in which one has to learn to think for oneself.

In reflecting on the recurrent scenario, I arrived at insights on some of the fundamental differences between Chinese and American society at the time. I describe these difference in terms of five points or assumptions. I see these five points as interconnected and perhaps inseparable, a series of interlocking concepts that fuse into a greater, one might almost say Confucian, whole.

One could discuss them in any order and reach the remainder of the set by several routes. Taken together, they help to explain not only differences that we continually observed in arts education, but also more pervasive differences that influence the range of activities in society.

To be sure, these are relative differences, and one finds examples of the opposite assumptions in each society. I state the five assumptions of Chinese society succinctly and then review each at somewhat greater and more nuanced length:

1. Life should unfold like a performance, with carefully delineated roles.
2. All art should be beautiful and should lead to good behavior.
3. Control is essential and must emanate from the top.
4. Education should take place by continual careful shaping.
5. Basic skills are fundamental and must precede any efforts to encourage creativity.

III. LIFE AS PERFORMANCE

The high value placed in China on performance dates back a long time. Twenty-five hundred years ago Confucius put forth a composite portrait—in words and in his own example—of how a gentleman should behave. Procedures for study, for the transmission of knowledge, and for the leading of a proper life were laid out carefully. The tradition of indicating the exact dimensions of a desirable performance has survived in China over the centuries. Indeed, by the time of the Ming dynasty (1368–1644), prescribed performances were expected of cultivated gentlemen or literati; one had to be able to perform music, paint, compose poems, and render calligraphy according to culturally agreed-upon standards, and one had to display proper responses to these performances as well.

But simply to talk about expected behaviors, or roles to be fulfilled, does not begin to convey the Chinese commitment to performance. Nearly everything that the visitor sees publicly in China appears to be a performance—and a very refined and finished one at that. From the young children sitting with hands folded at their desks or walking rhythmically into a room, to the headmaster describing her school with punctilious detail in a morning briefing, to the student answering questions with vivid expressiveness in a discussion with visitors, everything has been carefully scripted in advance. As children are performing, adults sit there mouthing the exact same words and gestures, as if to ensure that there's a model present for any confused child to consult. In addition, the arrangement and layout of these scenes look as if they could be the scenery for a play or if they could be put onto live television. Everyone knows just about what to expect and how it should look; any deviations are readily noticed and quite troubling to those who have "staged" the performances.

This commitment to an elegant and well-executed performance prompted the Chinese to correct Benjamin. His banging the key about is disorderly and disrupts the desire for smooth performance. The goal of the adults in correcting him is to ease his way to a well-executed key-slotting performance as soon as possible—a performance that all can admire.

We were impressed by the performances we constantly encountered, not only in arts classes but throughout our journey through the educational system. Yet we were also frustrated. To carry out our research mission, we wanted to see how polished performances *came to be achieved*—in other words, to peer behind the scenes; to see some rehearsals en route to the final version; to learn about curriculum selection, planning, and evaluation. We clearly saw instances of Chinese children learning new things, which were, in that sense, not performances. My guess is that it was not easy for Chinese to show us such incidents, since it permitted us to go "backstage."

Of course, an emphasis on performance is not necessarily an isolated or bad thing. In times past, our society had much more of a "public performance" dimension. During the age of nobility, the West featured public selves as stylized as those perceived today in China, but today there is much more of an emphasis on informality. Many Asian cultures continue to feature this penchant for performance, well described by anthropologist Clifford Geertz in his studies of Indonesia. Educated Chinese people often like to read European novels such as those of Jane Austen, or American novels like those of Edith Wharton, possibly because these works document societies that placed a great premium on performances.

I feel that it's good to foster performing and public speaking skills in children. But performing skills are not the same as a performing society. American students are often better at informal situations and at critical discussions; they are usually comfortable, where Chinese are not, with talking with strangers, with criticizing their own papers and those of other students. These are situations that cannot, by their nature, be rehearsed. But some American teachers, while agreeing with me, point out that Chinese students master the factual material much better and commit materials to memory with greater accuracy.

In many Western societies, one may contrast *performance* with *understanding*. We want, above all, for our students to dig beneath the surface and become able to grasp the meaning, including the underlying meaning, of writings, texts, scientific principles, and works of art. This emphasis dates back to Socrates (roughly a contemporary of Confucius), who valued knowledge and argument above all things, who was himself slovenly and did not care about "superficial" performance matters (though he was certainly an effective performer), but was obsessed about the quality of thought and reasoning.

It is not surprising, of course, that I would emphasize the cognitive and "understanding" aspects of education in general and artistry in particular. I am a committed cognitive psychologist who views art as a matter of the mind. I am a committed Westerner as well—and I remember a colleague's wry definition of the West as that place where Socrates is a cultural hero. Understanding, of course, is not inherently inconsistent with performance, and both societies clearly foster both practices, but understanding and performance do seem initially to pull in different directions. If one is to follow the direction of one's cognitive powers, and to focus on understanding and misunderstanding, one may well find oneself on a collision course with certain performance standards, which have survived for a long time but are not founded upon reason.

In putting forth this picture of China as a performing society, I am well aware of one criticism that could be directed at me. I was a high-level visitor to China; perhaps the performances I witnessed had little relation to what goes on in China normally, in the absence of observers from abroad. Of course, it's not possible for me to conduct the experiment of being in China without being there!

However, for two reasons, I feel that my characterization is not merely a function of the particular conditions under which our family visited China. First of all, the Chinese went to such great lengths to make sure that everything we saw was polished that they thereby revealed the great premium they placed on performance. (Despite enormous efforts, Americans could simply not have matched these performances.) Second, I am here describing what I take to be an ideal state, one that is striven for rather than one that is regularly achieved. Just as we in the West today value informality, casualness, and directness, the Chinese seem in comparison to value roles and rituals that are exquisitely realized.

IV. THE ARTS AS BEAUTIFUL AND GOOD

A focus on art as performance fits hand-in-glove with a view of art as entailing beauty and proper behavior. To be sure, in espousing this view of things, Chinese scarcely hold a monopoly. Most individuals anywhere in the world, when asked about the reason for the arts, would say that they are dedicated to, and indeed exemplify, beauty; and few would object initially to attempts to link the true, the beautiful, and the good.

But once again, just as the Chinese today take performance further than most other peoples, they also have a conception of beauty that is more precisely delineated, and more aggressively invoked, in artistic matters. We can see from an early age that Chinese parents and teachers convey to their charges very clear ideas about what a painting should look like, how a story should be told, an instrument should be played, a dance step executed, a calligraphic passage completed. There is one right way (or perhaps a small set of right ways) and many wrong ways; the right way is beautiful and should be enacted, while the wrong ways are ugly and should be spurned. So completely are students indoctrinated in these ways that they continue to exemplify them even when they are given free rein.

One sees these views in operation in the Benjamin key incident. There is a correct way to place the key in the slot, and that way is also beautiful. These canons of beauty need to be instilled early and completely so that a child is not tempted to carry out activities in an ugly or disruptive way (for example, by banging the key against the slot).

We also receive insight into why only certain forms of art are sanctioned in contemporary China. As long as art is representational, as long as music refers to identifiable content and circumstance, it is possible for censors to ensure that the works subscribe to evident canons. But if abstract art were allowed, how could one judge it and determine whether it was beautiful and good? Rather than open up that Pandora's box of normlessness, it is far better to restrict art to things that everyone can perceive and on which consensual beauty judgments can readily be rendered. Of course, not all artists in China endorse these views uncritically, but they entertain a risk if they challenge them publicly.

In contrast to a Chinese view of art as beauty, what do Westerners espouse? Consistent with my argument that we in the West have assumed an increasingly cognitive stance, I contend that art is now expected to be interesting, powerful, compelling—and that art exists in the first instance to allow individuals to see, to hear, to conceive of elements in new and perhaps initially unsettling ways.

What we seek (and find) in our most esteemed artists is not—or not merely—the exemplification of some form of beauty—and not beauty, certainly, in some fixed or preordained sense. Canons cannot be handed down. What, after all, is beautiful about a military scene from Goya or a bombed ruin by Picasso? Do T. S. Eliot and James Joyce write about beautiful subjects and use florid language in doing so? Are Stravinsky's *The Rite of Spring* or Bartok's string quartets conventionally beautiful?

When I put forth some of these ideas in China, I was called a formalist—someone only interested in abstract formal matters and unconcerned with connections to life. As one cadre put it, "In America you are interested in art for art's sake; in China we are interested in art for life's sake." I had a retort for this gentleman. "Actually," I pointed out, "we are not interested in art for the sake of art; we are interested in art for the sake of mind." I then explained that many Western observers regard art as a cognitive endeavor and as another way to expand our knowledge of what the world can be and what it might be—as in some ways closer to science than to nature. And I sought to explain as well our interest in joining, in education, the skills of producing, perceiving, and reflecting, as a better means of coordinating the various forms of knowledge that flow from artistic experience (see Essay 15).

The Chinese proclivity for linking art and morality—the beautiful and the good—lacks a parallel in the contemporary West. As Chinese colleagues have sought to explain it to me, involvement in the arts is part of being a good person. If you make beautiful paintings or beautiful sounds on an instrument, these performances contribute to your becoming a worthy person. Apparently there is a spillover from being involved in the arts to becoming a desirable kind of person: thus, in the past, the same Confucian gentlemen who painted and performed well were also good human beings.

Now, as a contemporary (and sometimes cynical) Westerner, I could not resist picking apart these claims. I pointed out that many individuals who are great artists were despicable and immoral individuals; and I pointed out that individuals without any aesthetic proclivities can be highly moral. While my Chinese colleagues listened patiently to my views, I soon realized that my remarks were beside the point. We are not dealing here with an empirical claim but rather with a belief system: a conviction that there is a certain notion of a good life, which includes art and morality, and that these things ought to—and do—go together. Indeed, much more so than Western intellectuals, and perhaps more like religious fundamentalists, Chinese believe that all good traits come together, and that if one is lacking on one dimension, one is unlikely to excel elsewhere. Education is supposed to develop as one piece of an individual's body, knowledge, sense of beauty, and morality; it fails if it does not accomplish all of these. Indeed, it is not even possible to develop one virtue without the others.

V: THE IMPORTANCE OF HIERARCHY

The next two conceptions convey the desired structure of society and the way of passing down information and performance standards from one generation to another. Any observer of Chinese society over the millennia has to be impressed with the extent to which it is hierarchically organized. Except during times of upheaval, it has always been clear who is at the head of the society—generally an emperor or a warlord—and where everyone else fits in relation to the center, and the apogee, of power. Hand-in-hand with this sense of organizational structure comes the educational conviction that individuals need to be carefully molded from the first to conform to societal values and practices.

In China, traditionally, "the people" must look in two directions: upward, toward those who hold authority; and backward, to the traditions of the past. This dual orientation is brought together neatly in the practice of ancestor worship, where one looks up to those who are higher than one in the family and back to those who are remote in time. The one direction in which

Chinese have not habitually looked is outward, since China has traditionally been considered to be the center of the world—the Middle Kingdom.

The structure of the school—both professionally and politically—reflects these notions. In the class, the teachers are considered the center of all activity, and students' behaviors and words are directed toward them. As I came to put it, the teacher is the sun and the students are the planets that revolve around that celestial body. All knowledge is assumed to exist in the Chinese past, and the teacher's job is to transmit that knowledge to her charges as faithfully and efficiently as possible. The ubiquitous proverbs, enumerated lists, and frozen phrases are simply efficient distillations of that knowledge. Sometimes, as a thought experiment, I asked teachers what they would do if they were not allowed to model behavior or to present the right answer; their difficulties in responding indicated how alien were these "progressive" notions of education in a non-Western context.

While Confucian classics no longer dominate the curriculum, parroting back the past remains a staple of most Chinese classrooms. The burden of the past is simply overwhelming. When I once had a protracted discussion with a teacher in which I challenged the rationales offered for some of the things she did, she effectively closed the conversation by asserting, "Well, we have been doing this for so long that we just *know* that it is right."

The existence in contemporary China of a single curriculum to which all must subscribe—and the extreme difficulty of introducing changes in it—reflects the fact that Chinese feel like members of one gigantic family or clan (the Han people, who constitute over 90 percent of the population). It is important for all members of this group to be able to share experiences and a common heritage. To some extent this commonality is impressive and allows all Chinese (at least in principle) to feel at one with their countrymen. (Today many Americans lament the absence, or loss, of a similar common culture in our country.) The situation is not, however, so pleasant for members of the 50-some minorities, nor is it palatable to individuals who might want to suggest some improvements or changes in the current social or educational order. Even to suggest changes is difficult because, as in some American paramilitary organizations, one is only allowed to address suggestions to the next level above and, accordingly, has no means of reaching people near the top. The options that we might have in America, of writing a public article or switching to another organization, are not readily available in China.

VI. SHAPING AND MOLDING FROM BIRTH ON

One of the most impressive accomplishments of the Chinese educational and training system has been its capacity to take even the most complex activity, break it down into its component parts, start the child out on the simplest part, have him perfect it, and then move on gradually but inexorably to more complex and more impressive performances. Every educational system uses this procedure, of course, but few have carried it through as relentlessly as the Chinese.

Thus, when our well-meaning Chinese observers at the Jinling Hotel came to Benjamin's rescue, they did not simply push his hand down clumsily, hesitantly, or abruptly, as I might have done. Instead they guided him with exquisite facility and gentleness in the desired direction. These Chinese were not just molding and shaping Benjamin's performance in any old manner; in the best Chinese tradition, they were *"ba je shou jiao"* (*"bazhishoujiao"*)—teaching by holding his hand—so much so that he would happily come back for more shaping. To borrow another Chinese phrase, they were inducing change through the chocolate offered in one hand—but if necessary, they would have used the whip that is traditionally clutched in the other hand.

Lurking behind and inspiring such shaping practices is the long-established procedure for mastering calligraphy—a dauntingly complex process that nonetheless has been mastered by millions—if not billions—of times over the centuries. Since this training course has worked so well for an invention about which the Chinese feel justifiably proud, it ought to be marshaled for as many other uses and in as many other circumstances as possible.

In general, childrearing in China proceeds as if following a chapter in the writings of behaviorists like B. F. Skinner. Reward, or positive reinforcement, is the preferred mode of training, though punishment (or negative reinforcement) is certainly not unknown. "The whip" is in fact inflicted quite brutally when older children do not study, fail to obey, or do not practice their musical instruments. (All of this punitiveness is very "backstage" and is certainly not part of the public Chinese performance.) Ultimately, after years of supervised study, Chinese individuals are expected to internalize these methods and to continue to study (more broadly, to cultivate themselves) on their own for the remainder of their lives.

According to an influential Western view, childhood is a very special time, and each child exhibits for a time a form of genius. Children are already born knowing certain things, and more importantly, they have been adequately equipped by nature to know how to figure things out, how to construct knowledge on the basis of their explorations. Children pass through a series of stages, also preordained; and at each stage they perceive the world in a different but intellectually respectable way. Those charged with rearing children should respect these stages and allow children to develop in their own way at their own pace.

Consistent with this psychology comes an educational regimen. Schools should supply and nourish, but they should not try to dictate or to mold. Such intrusions by civilization can be brutal and stultifying. The child has his own creative genius that should be allowed to flower. There is sufficient structure in the child's mind, enough chemistry in the contact between a child and an interesting material, that there is no need to intervene. Hence Benjamin can be left to play with the key—he will figure out the important things in due course.

These views—which I happen to cherish—are largely foreign to China. (I hasten to add that they are scarcely pervasive in America, either, but many good schools endorse and attempt to implement them.) Those artful scribbles and early metaphors for which I have remained alert in my own research are typically dismissed in China as mistakes that should be ignored or corrected. School is important precisely because it exorcises these mischievous, unpredictable, unproductive, and possibly pernicious elements as soon as possible. School is also important because it is society's most reliable way of assuring quality control and bringing about the Confucian treasure of a socially and politically harmonious society. The learning that takes place in America—from the examples of peers and at the hand of media like books, comic books, movies, and television—is considered much less trustworthy. And of course, whenever possible, these media materials are reworked by the state in China so that they will be consistent with, rather than antagonistic to, the lessons promulgated in school.

There are some signs that a way of teaching and molding that has worked, more or less well, for several thousand years may not be most appropriate for dealing with an uncertain future. Such a realization may have led to the interest among Chinese educators in the 1920s and 1930s in the works of John Dewey, to various experimental schools and programs over the years, and to the desire for the kind of exchange program in which I and others were privileged to participate. In 2024, alas, such openness is less evident.

VII. BASIC SKILLS BEFORE CREATIVITY

Attempts to change the basic structure of the Chinese classroom, or of Chinese society, touch directly on the issue that brought our family to China, and that remained centrally on our agenda throughout our stay: the relative importance of, and the relationship between, basic skills and creativity.

There are few issues about which attitudes have differed so sharply. In America, many aspects of the society are designed so as to encourage innovation and creativity. From its foundation, America has looked to its frontier and to its youth to forge new and unanticipated forms of living and types of knowledge. Though America's schools are not its most innovative institutions, the educational sector has long tolerated experiments of various sorts. And in the view of many Americans, schools are but one of the socializing influences, along with parents, siblings, peers, various media of communication, and life in the broader society—each of which may be transmitting its own idiosyncratic messages.

As the oldest continuing civilization in the world, China has witnessed innovations over centuries, rather than decades. Oriented to tradition, Chinese educators have generally striven to adhere to what has gone before. Even under a (in some ways) radical new political system, the continuities with the past are striking, and nowhere more so than in those inherently conservative institutions called schools.

To the extent that change occurs in each society, the preferred mode also differs. In America, as in other parts of the West, we place a premium on radical departures from the recent past and, at least over time, honor the Beethovens, Picassos, Joyces, and Einsteins who have within one lifetime radically altered our worldview. Interestingly, some of these same individuals are also revered in China, but the kind of iconoclasm they epitomize is not similarly prized and is actively discouraged during the frequent political swings to the left.

While no one would nominate Benjamin's session with the key as a prototype of creative behavior, this little incident captures something telling about attitudes toward creativity. The Chinese approach to this task is straightforward: for Benjamin to succeed, he needs to acquire basic skills of manipulation, orientation, and placement. Since the means for acquiring these are well-known and unproblematic, they ought simply to be passed onto him as efficiently and constructively as possible. Should he at some later date wish to make modest modifications in his form of attack, that's okay too. Indeed, this toleration of minor modifications comes close to my notion of how "creativity" is understood in China—as neither a massive dislocation nor a radical reconceptualization but rather as a modest alteration of existing schemes or practices.

One way of summarizing the American position: we value creativity more, and will readily postpone the acquisition of basic skills. Yet it can also be argued that for us, other skills are basic—skills like devising a new problem, looking at one's work critically, or drawing upon one's own feelings. One society's skills may be another society's residuals.

TOWARD A PRODUCTIVE SYNTHESIS

Assuming that the argument I have developed has some validity, and that the fostering of skills and of creativity are both worthwhile goals, the important question becomes this: Can we glean, from the Chinese and the American case studies, a superior way to approach education, perhaps striking an optimal balance between the poles of creativity and basic skills?

I'll begin my answer by suggesting that each country has proved that its way can succeed. There is ample evidence in the United States that one can begin by fostering creativity in a progressive environment and yet turn out individuals who master basic skills fully and go on to achieve in an innovative manner in some cultural domain. Based on my experiences in China, I can vouch for the fact that it is possible as well to follow a regimen of strict skill development and still end up with products that are highly distinctive and creative. I've observed this in the case of individual students and teachers, and many of us in the West rub shoulders with Chinese students who, while reared in a skill-oriented milieu, go on to become creative artists, scientists, or business executives.

A first answer, then, is that it is not essential to begin one way, as opposed to the other. As long as the society wants to develop *both* basic skills *and* creativity, it can have both. It is important that the alternative approach be kept in mind, lest an exclusive orientation toward creativity, or a total commitment toward skill development, preclude the possibility of developing the other facility. But as long as such extremes are avoided, there seems to be no necessary edge to one approach.

Yet I am not satisfied with a simple answer of "either approach will do." My own opinion, based on general studies in developmental psychology, and on my observations in these and other countries as well, is that there is a preferable or optimum sequence. I find it preferable to devote the early years of life—roughly speaking, up to the age of 7—to a relatively unstructured or creative orientation where students have ample opportunity to proceed as they wish and to explore media on their own, as long as they don't harm themselves or others. (In traditional China, some individuals apparently held similar views, but I never heard these referred to during my trips there.) Thereafter, given the child's increasing inclination toward the learning of rules, it is both appropriate and advisable to inculcate basic skills. This is a time when children readily acquire skills and have some appreciation of the reasons for doing so.

With the advent of adolescence, particularly in our society, youngsters want to be able to put their skills to a public, and possibly personal as well, use. By this time they have acquired sufficient skills so that they will not be disappointed or embarrassed by their own efforts. Building on the early experience with unhampered exploration, and in the light of the subsequent honing of skills, they should be in a favorable position to form novel products that make sense to them and that can also speak to others in their culture.

The idea of a shift in emphasis at some point in development is central to my case. It is possible, in fact, that the Chinese might want to begin with more of a stress on skill development (as they in fact do) and then shift to periods of more free-ranging explorations (which they rarely do). Least desirable is an *exclusive emphasis* on one end of the continuum. If there is too great a leaning in the direction of untrammeled creativity—the American risk—the child may end up without skills and thus able to communicate only with himself. On the other hand, if there is unrelieved focus on skill development—the Chinese danger—the child may end up unable to depart from the models that he has absorbed.

In seeking to acquire a more balanced pedagogical portfolio, each country can learn from the other. Too many efforts in creativity training in China are destined to fail because they are based on a superficial understanding of how to sustain a playful atmosphere, a willingness to challenge received wisdom, and a genuine receptivity to new ideas in an educational setting. And too many attempts to institute the training of basic skills in America fail because they underestimate the degree of drill and dedication needed on the part of both teacher and pupil if a complex skill is to be thoroughly mastered. If attempts are not to be caricatures, they need to be based on rigorous study and patient practice. Exchanges such as the one in which we were privileged to participate provide an excellent means for understanding the techniques of another culture and the reasons why they work as effectively as they do.

ACKNOWLEDGMENTS

Preparation of this chapter was made possible by support from the Rockefeller Brothers Fund to Harvard Project Zero and the Center for US-China Arts Exchange at Columbia University. I am indebted to numerous colleagues in the United States and China as well.

EDUCATIONAL PHILOSOPHY

PROGRESSIVISM—THE TRUE, THE BEAUTIFUL, AND THE GOOD

At Wyoming Seminary, my secondary school in northeastern Pennsylvania, there was a prominently displayed motto, "*Verum, Pulchrum, Bonum*"—Latin for "*Truth, Beauty, and Goodness.*" Until my 40th high school reunion in 2001, I had actually forgotten that this phrase had been the school's motto—though I had not forgotten the words.

Indeed, not only has the phrase remained with me, it has long been my tacit goal for education. As an aspiring scholar—first a historian, then a social scientist—I had always valued the pursuit of truth. *Veritas* is the slogan of Harvard University, where I've spent over 60 years. And Sissela Bok's 1978 book *On Lying*—a devastating critique of the notion that one should ever lie or prevaricate out of convenience—has had a considerable influence on my thinking.

As an investigator for many years at Project Zero—our research project that had begun as a study of "basic research in the arts and arts education"—I had formally studied the realm of beauty. Since early childhood, I have played the piano, and for a decade I taught piano—and I have worked extensively in art museums, and even served for decades on the board and various committees of New York's Museum of Modern Art. The pursuit and pondering of beauty has been in my blood, so to speak.

And then, the good. I come from a highly ethical family, one where doing the right thing was a watchword. It's up to others to determine whether I myself have behaved morally and ethically. But in the last decades, much of my thinking, research, and writing has focused on what is good in our complex contemporary world and how best to achieve it.

So here's my educational watchword—a primary aim for education: to inculcate in all individuals—and especially the young—a sense of and an aspiration for understanding and achieving these three virtues. Of course, this goal can be achieved—or undermined—in many different ways. Both Western democracies and long-lasting Asian civilizations (e.g., China, India, Japan) have distinctive notions of the three virtues and how to inculcate them. They also have conceptions of the correlative vices and how to avoid them. Much of education in the 21st century will constitute a struggle among these competing conceptions of virtue-based education.

There is also the question of "how" to educate—at least as controversial as "what" it means to be educated. My own educational background has been quite traditional and conservative; perhaps as a reaction, my own children (and now my grandchildren) have generally gone the route of a progressive, more liberal education. Of course, over time, it must be noted that the connotations of "conservative" and "progressive" change. As an example, in the United States, in the 20th century, being able to speak and write freely was a progressive virtue. In the 21st century, it is more likely to be defended by conservatives, while the "language police" are more likely to be individuals on the left. Needless to say, there are blends of attitudes across the political spectrum. The educational pendulum sways back and forth in ways that are rarely predictable.

I have a more complex relation to progressivism—admiring its goals, but questioning some of its core psychological assumptions, as well as some of its favored methods. Accordingly, in this chapter, co-authored with my valued students (now colleagues) Bruce Torff and Tom Hatch, I step back and talk about how to preserve and build upon the best aspects of progressivism—what we label "the new progressivism."

ESSAY 5

The Age of Innocence Reconsidered
Preserving the Best of the Progressive Traditions in Psychology and Education

Co-authored by Bruce Torff and Thomas Hatch

A CANONICAL VIEW IN PSYCHOLOGY AND EDUCATION AT MIDCENTURY

Both the passage of time and the exigencies of scholarly writing can conspire to yield a past that appears appealingly simple. Succumbing to those pressures, one can readily compose views of the child and of education that are optimistic in tone and in harmony with one another. While scarcely going unchallenged, such views associated with an earlier time have done much to frame current discussions of the nature of childhood and the preferred course of education.

From the discipline of developmental psychology—which arose in significant measure out of a Rousseauian tradition—there emerged a view of the child as a relatively free-standing spirit, one destined to pass in the fullness of time through a series of preordained stages. Assuming only a nonabusive environment, the Piagetian child would first learn about the world directly through spontaneous and natural actions upon the physical world; then, acquiring a set of more complex cognitive structures in a preordained fashion, that child could perform mental operations of increasing abstraction and power on the representations of the world that she had constructed. Moving along parallel lines, the Eriksonian child would confront in turn a set of psychosexual and psychosocial tensions; and again, assuming a relatively supportive environment, the child would emerge as trustworthy, autonomous, competent, and a viable member of the community.

A related intellectual tradition underlies that view of education that has been particularly celebrated among those with a deep interest in childhood. John Dewey and, perhaps even more, his progressivist successors saw the child as the centerpiece of the educational firmament. Children learned best through their explorations of the world around them; the opportunity to pursue their own interests at their own pace was a crucial ingredient. In a manner that drew on the developmental tradition, Dewey asserted that youngsters must construct their own meanings out of daily school and community experiences.

Armed with a more determinedly social vision than that of the prototypical developmentalist, Dewey emphasized the importance of the support of other human beings, especially well-trained teachers, and the desirability of learning about the roles and practices featured in one's community. Yet he did not fundamentally question the need to educate youngsters in the major disciplines; he assumed that there would be a natural and typically unproblematic progression from more project-centered activities in the community to the more scholastic regimen of academic disciplines.

Although these developmental and educational traditions evolved relatively independent of one another, it is important to underscore their compatibility. Both focused on children's interests and personally initiated activities; both expected relatively smooth progress toward scholastic mastery and full citizenship in the community. While each perspective acknowledged that children differed from one another—both in terms of their interests and their native intellectual potential—neither stance dwelled on these differences: "the child" was a more natural way of speaking than "the children." And perhaps not surprisingly, both of these traditions reflected the environments in which they were conceived, ones that from today's perspective can be seen as comfortably middle-class, and ensconced in a democratic society, be it a Piagetian Swiss canton or a Deweyian New England village.

Since we here assume a somewhat critical stance toward this canonical view, it is important to indicate the kinds of conceptions against which these progressive views were reacting. Within child study, scholars like Piaget and Erikson were critiquing strong forms of environmentalism, on the one hand, and biological determinism, on the other. Against the "blank slate" empiricists a la philosopher John Locke or psychologist B. F. Skinner, they were acknowledging organismic/biological constraints on the ways in which human beings develop. Against committed hereditarians, they were underscoring the need for interactions with a specific environment, as well as the possibility that development might not necessarily proceed at a proper pace or in a desired direction.

More positively, these 20th-century developmentalists saw the child as passing through a set of ordered but qualitatively different stages, each with its own organization and integrity. Children were not merely shorter or less intelligent adults; they embodied particular views of reality and engaged cognitive and emotional problems in ways that were appropriate for their life situation. Indeed, it was important to see the various facets of the child—cognitive, emotional, social—as working together to yield an integrated person.

"Child-centered" educators were analogously engaged in characteristic responses to previously prevalent perspectives. They opposed the view of so-called "faculty psychologists," who saw the child as a collection of separate mental abilities, each to be independently fostered. They equally rejected the atomistic views of pedants, who sought to present curricula as a set of isolated facts or disparate skills. Particularly problematic from their point of view was a factory model of education, where children were marched through their paces so that they could ultimately be sorted into their proper roles in an increasingly industrialized society. Progressivists rejected the classroom in which an adult—her head filled with information—sought to transmit as much information as efficiently as possible into the small but growing head of the child; in its place, progressivists sought to configure educational spaces in which children actively explored materials, working with other youngsters in a socially supported environment, rehearsing for life in a democratic society.

NEW INSIGHTS

It has been important to delineate the forces against which the psychological and pedagogical progressives were aligned; we (the authors) share the antipathy of the progressives to adultcentric views of children, on the one hand, and to a transmission view of education, on the other. We continue to cherish much of the vision that was forged in the last century by such scholars as Dewey and Piaget. Yet in the decades since the canonical "innocent" view was first consolidated, an ensemble of new perspectives has arisen (or, to put it less grandly, some earlier perspectives have received fresh attention).

In what follows, we first list the set of ideas that have emerged during recent decades. We then introduce a new approach—the "symbol systems approach"—one that purports to preserve the strengths of the canonical view while drawing upon the insights of more recent times. We examine the ways in which views of human development and approaches to education might be reformulated in the light of the "symbols systems approach," yielding a new and perhaps more powerful intellectual and practical synthesis.

Among the perspectives that have emerged in the past several decades, we single out for special mention six insights that have pointed the way toward a new perspective.

1. The Existence of Domains Beyond Universals

The broad spectrum of work in developmental psychology has, perhaps appropriately, begun by examining those conceptions and domains that are part and parcel of the experience of every human being. Thus Piaget focused on the development of conceptions in what might be termed the Kantian realms, such as time, space, and causality; and other scholars, like Lawrence Kohlberg and Rudolf Arnheim, have investigated other putatively universal domains, such as morality and the arts.

However, much of what is most valued within a culture is not necessarily esteemed or even shared by other cultures. That literacy that is virtually required within Western culture has until recently not been known in many indigenous cultures (Olson, 1994). And other activities, ranging from the playing of chess to the mastery of calculus to the execution of various dances and rituals, are restricted to specific cultures or subcultures. Thanks to the work of Feldman (1980), we are far more cognizant of those domains that, while of import in one or several cultures, are not valued universally; and may have quite distinctive courses of development.

2. The Importance of Specific Knowledge and Expertise

Just as there has been increasing recognition of the existence of domains that range beyond the universal, there is growing skepticism about the existence of general knowledge and general skills. Rather than there being "general thinking" and "general problem-solving" skills, it is now widely believed that most skills are far more task-specific, with ready transfer across contexts being questionable at best. Individuals acquire expertise by working regularly over long periods of time on tasks and skills in particular domains, and the attainment of high levels of skill in one domain is by no means a guarantor of any significant level of skill in other domains, unless they happen to be quite closely related to one another.

3. The Need to Explain Individual Differences

The concern with difference across domains and tasks has been paralleled by an interest in the differences among individuals. While differences among individuals have always been noted in both lay and scientific circles, of course, these differences have either been viewed along one dimension (more or less intelligent) or in a very general way (individuals have different personalities, temperament, styles, and the like).

Of special importance for our work is the possibility that individuals may differ in their profiles of intellectual strengths. The "theory of multiple intelligences" posits that individuals may foreground quite different sets of mental skills, having disparate strengths and weaknesses, and that these in turn are important for the ways in which individuals learn and the kinds of creative or expert achievements that they may ultimately realize.

4. The Existence of Potent, Enduring Misconceptions

Part of Piaget's enduring legacy was his demonstration that young children often exhibit quite distinctive conceptions of the world, including ones that are poignantly animistic, artificial, or otherwise egocentric. Because Piaget was concerned primarily with universal domains, he was able to document the spontaneous disappearance of these misconceptions.

Recent work on the acquisition of disciplinary expertise has established an unsettling phenomenon. Put succinctly, except for experts, most individuals continue to adhere to early misconceptions, even in the face of considerable tutelage and counterevidence. Thus, even college physics students often retain Aristotelian notions of force and agency, just as advanced students in the humanities and social sciences continue to adhere to the most simplistic forms of stereotypical thinking. The pedagogical moves needed to dissolve these misconceptions, and to place in their stead more well-grounded, complex, and comprehensive views, turn out to be quite demanding. (See Essay 18.)

5. The Critical Role of Contextual and Mediated Experiences

Every behavioral and cognitive scientist at least plays lip service to the importance of the surrounding context. However, in the progressive developmental tradition, such contexts were discussed only in the broadest terms for three reasons: universal properties were of primary interest; differences across context were thought to be (and perhaps were) of lesser consequence; and there did not exist a conceptual apparatus for analyzing contextual influences in any detail or with any precision.

Stimulated by the work of Lev Vygotsky and other contextualists, researchers have now provided convincing documentation that the society into which one is born, the styles and values of the family in which one lives, the procedures of the cultural and educational institutions of one's community, and perhaps especially nowadays the messages transmitted by the dominant media exert an enormous influence on the kind of person that each child becomes. To be sure, certain universal cognitive and emotional milestones may differ little across contexts. But once one begins to attend to the values held by individuals; the ways in which such individuals organize, reflect upon, and symbolize their experiences; and the manners in which individuals interact with others, the pervasive role played by contextual and mediated factors cannot be ignored.

6. The Application of Standards in the Judgment of Work

Amidst the welter of contextual factors and agents that surround every developing human being, one strand deserves to be singled out for separate mention. We refer here to those individuals and institutions—sometimes called "the surrounding field"—that render judgments about the acceptability and quality of human work. Every culture transmits explicit and implicit signals about the products and behaviors that it values, and these values permeate schools and other educational and cultural institutions. But within these institutions, there are specific individuals—ranging from master teachers to admissions officers to prize-givers to encyclopedia writers—who exert massive influence on who and what gets recognized. Indeed, the set of standards and values beheld by the next generation is determined largely by the actions of members of the field in the present generation. As one instance, a scholarly handbook represents an effort to control the signals or "memes" that will be available for digestion by the next generation of researchers and educators.

* * *

These six insights—along with others that could have been mentioned—amount to the legacy which a new generation of workers must encounter, master, and evaluate. To use a Piagetian analogy, it is possible to assimilate these lines of work to an existing educational or psychological framework. However, it is also possible to use these fresh insights as the basis for creating a new synthesis, one that may be better suited for the research and practical issues of today and tomorrow.

THE SYMBOL SYSTEMS APPROACH

We introduce here an approach to the study of human development that grows out of the canonical tradition sketched above—but that, in our view, is better able to make use of the new lines of investigation and better suited toward constructing an educational approach that is valid for our times. We term our approach the symbol systems approach, and we set forth here its basic assumptions and implications.

For over a century it has been recognized that a distinctive property—perhaps *the* distinctive property of human beings—has been the species' cognitive capacity to employ various kinds of symbol systems: physical or notional elements that refer, denote, express, or otherwise convey various kinds of information and various strands of meaning. Initially, the interest of scholars centered around the symbols of language and of logic—those coherent sets of systems that make possible everyday communication as well as the mastery of the crucial domains of mathematics and the sciences. But since the seminal writings of Ernst Cassirer, Susanne Langer, and Nelson Goodman, the existence of other kinds of symbol systems has also been recognized. While artistic symbol systems may lack the precision and unambiguity of more conventional symbol systems, their potentials to create and transmit powerful and otherwise inexpressible meanings is now appreciated within the scholarly community. Moreover, scholars have become attuned not only to the syntactic and semantic properties of symbol systems but to their uses—their pragmatics; and they have come to note both the potential of symbol systems to be combined with one another and the capacities of human beings to create new personal or even public symbol systems.

To mention symbol systems to developmental psychologists is to invoke a widely acknowledged phenomenon. Nearly all recognize the crucial milestone in the life of the child when that individual becomes able to capture and convey meanings not only through direct physical contact or through personal regard but through such mediated vehicles as words, pictures, numbers, and the like.

So much work has been done on the nature of symbolization in general, and on the ontogenesis and development of symbolization in particular domains, that one could virtually rewrite developmental psychology—or at least cognitive developmental psychology—in terms of the mastery of symbolic systems (See "Developmental Psychology After Piaget" in *The Essential Howard Gardner on Mind.*) And yet, strangely, the crucial nature of symbol systems and their implications for how we think about children, development, and education have not been sufficiently pondered.

A focus on symbolization makes profound sense from both a substantive and an analytic point of view. There is a sense in which one can speak of the infant as presymbolic: both her interactions with the physical world and her relations with the world of other human beings occur primarily in terms of direct, unmediated contact, using mechanisms that have presumably been programmed into the species. By the end of the first year of life, however, overtly symbolic processes begin to come to the fore, and they remain prevalent for the remainder of life. Some of these forms of meaning-making are distinctly personal: every child, every family can develop idiosyncratic ways of conveying messages and meanings. But the vast majority of symbolic forms are public, reflecting modes of meaning-making that have evolved over many centuries within and across cultures and that all children must gradually internalize.

Until the age of 5 or so, assuming a sufficiently rich environment, the development of competence within symbolic systems occurs without the necessity of much direct instruction or crafted mediation. Children are so constructed as species members that they readily pick up the various languages that are expressed around them, and also begin to use them productively and fluently. Researchers differ on the extent to which they endorse a single, comprehensive story of symbolization—a so-called "semiotic track"—as opposed to an account that invokes instructive and telling differences in the trajectories of different symbolic competence. (Our own view is that the developmental paths are quite distinct in matters of syntax but have stronger parallels in their semantic and pragmatic dimensions.) But whether one is a unitarian or a pluralist, the increasing domination by symbolic codes during the course of early childhood is difficult to dispute.

Symbolic development continues throughout childhood but takes on different colors after the first years of life, and particularly so in a literate culture. Education in the mastery of the most important symbol systems comes to take place in more formal settings—in apprenticeships, in craft learning, in religious training, and, of course, in those institutions called schools.

Some education consists in a refinement of the first-order symbol systems. But literate cultures are defined by their employment of second-order symbol systems—notations/marks that themselves refer to first-order symbolic codes. And in the reaches of higher education, ever more subtle and higher-order symbol systems come to be used, a phenomenon exemplified by complex mathematical and computational systems.

Until this point, we have ignored an important ambiguity in the use of our term "symbol systems." In fact, the term has two distinct meanings and disciplinary histories. Within the area of philosophy—and in such allied disciplines as semiotics and linguistics—a symbol system consists of a publicly examinable set of marks whose syntax and semantics can be identified and dissected by trained analysts. Codes ranging from written language to dance notation to scientific diagrams all function as external symbol systems.

In contrast, within psychology and various cognitively oriented disciplines, symbol systems are thought of primarily in internal terms—as cognitive representations in some kind of mentalese or language of thought. Fierce debate remains about the exact nature and specificity of this internal symbolic representation, but that there exists some kind of mental code has been a defining assumption of cognitive science.

In noting the internal/external contrast in any discussion of symbol systems, we segue to a discussion of the analytic role that can be assumed by a symbol systems perspective. Academic disciplines play an important—indeed indispensable—role in our inquiries and in our institutional life. Yet few would question the assertion that many important issues do not respect disciplinary boundaries; indeed, a key goal of research is to forge appropriate connections among disciplinary perspectives.

It's here, we claim, that a symbol systems approach exhibits special virtues. Any thorough understanding of the mind of the child and the process of education must span the gamut from human biological and evolutionary heritage, on the one hand, to the operation of human cultural institutions and practices, on the other. Yet the distance between genes and gods is simply too great to be casually bridged.

Consider, however, the role that can be played in such disciplinary conversation by the analytic construct of "symbol systems." As a species, human beings are programmed in their genes and equipped in their nervous systems to become symbol-using creatures. Rather than positing a single general cognitive capacity, however, we find it more useful to think of the nervous system as congenial to the development of a number of different cognitive systems that process different kinds of information; one can term these systems "multiple intelligences." (See Essays 8–12.)

The multiple intelligences commence as a set of uncommitted neurobiological potentials. They become crystallized and mobilized by the communication that takes place among human beings and, especially, by the systems of meaning-making that already exist in a given culture. It is the existence of spoken language, sung music, and communal number systems, respectively, that convert linguistic, musical, and numerical potentials into discretely operating and interacting intelligences. Here the encounter of the human brain with sounds, sights, or marks in the world brings about a dialectic between external symbol systems—present for all to behold—and internal symbol systems—the particular variants of mental language that allow individuals to participate in, make use of, and even come to revise the evolved symbol systems of their cultures.

Consider the following assertion: the functioning culture must ensure that it continues to exist—the survival of *memes* proves to be as important for the culture as the survival of *genes* is for the species. The culture cannot observe genes, brains, or even intelligences, but it can observe the presence and the use of external symbols. And indeed, the culture determines the extent of its survival by creating institutions that monitor whether, to what extent, and how appropriately symbol systems are being learned, absorbed, utilized, and transformed by the younger members of the society. Put more concretely, responsible adults note the appearance (or nonappearance) in growing children of the myths, adages, rituals, artworks, scientific practices, and philosophical systems of the community.

Here, then, we may begin to see the powerful analytical role that can be played by symbol systems in any comprehensive human science. Put directly, symbol systems serve as an indispensable *tertium quid* for the analyst—a safe, respected, and hallowed middle ground between the genes and the gods. To look at it schematically, consider the location of symbolic systems within the continuum of the human sciences:

Symbolization As Represented in Different Areas of Knowledge

Biology	Psychology	Sociology/Anthropology
Genes, brain (knowledge represented in the nervous system)	Mind operates on strings of symbols (e.g. reading words, musical notation, traffic signs)	Cultural roles that feature symbol use or that make judgments about how individuals deploy symbols (e.g., teachers, curators, judges of competitions)

THE VIEW FROM EDUCATION

From one vantage point, it has been argued that scientific findings—including those from psychology—are not strictly relevant to educational practice. Nearly every social scientific finding or perspective harbors within it a number of possible educational implications, not all of which are necessarily consistent with one another. Moreover, it is hardly the case that educational practitioners need to peruse scientific journals, avoiding the classroom until they have digested the latest finding from the theorist's study or the experimentalist's laboratory. Plato's Academy introduced quite powerful educational notions without any "research base"; neither John Locke nor Jean-Jacques Rousseau (the ancestors of current educational practice) ever conducted an experiment; and most educators rely as much on careful observation of their own (and others') practices as on lectures or monographs.

Yet, even if there is not (and perhaps should not be) a unidirectional path from psychological insights to educational practice, representatives of both lines of work do rightfully participate in constant conversations about principles and practices. We should think of both psychologists and educators as reflecting the predominant intellectual trends of their time. And in this spirit, many contemporary psychological ideas, including those about symbolization, have come to exert influence on the beliefs and practices of educators.

We have tried to forge an approach to educational practice that draws upon the strength of the progressive movement, while cherishing features of more traditional approaches, on the one hand, and being mindful of newly emerging insights about human cognitive functioning, on the other. These ideas have been worked out, in part, on the theoretical level. But they have been tested as well within schools—as embodied in experimental programs that we and our colleagues have set up; as parts of model school programs, instituted by practitioners in the field; and by collaborative work with other educational reformers, most especially in the ATLAS project, a collaboration of our research and development group with Theodore Sizer's Coalition of Essential Schools at Brown University, James Comer's School Development Program at Yale University, and the Education Development Center, directed by Janet Whitla.

Sketched in the ideal, what are the principal features of the "new progressivism" in education? To begin with, the goals and processes to be adopted by a school or school system need to be negotiated by the principal stakeholders—educators, families, and community members. Schools are unlikely to be effective unless they reflect the input and "stake" of those responsible for the life of the community. These parties—in this case the "field"—need to agree on what kinds of knowledge, skills, and understandings should be exhibited by students when they have completed their education. In our terms, there should be extended conversation and ultimately consensus about the symbolic competences to be achieved and exhibited. And "exhibition" is an operative work here. Students can be said to be educated when they are able to display *publicly* to an acceptable level of accomplishment what they have been able to understand and to master, whether it be performing a new composition on the piano or creating a map of an unfamiliar region of one's community. Of course, the adoption of exhibitions as occasions for assessment presupposes at least two conditions: the existence of a community that has developed a sense of what constitutes an acceptable performance, and the constitution of a group of judges who can apply standards in a reliable way. (See Essay 14 on projects at the Key School.)

What should be the focus of such an education? As we see it, all human beings are motivated to better understand certain basic issues and questions: Who are we? To what group do we belong? Where do we come from? Where are we headed? How does our group relate to others? What is the physical world made of? How about the biological and social worlds? What is true, what is beautiful, what is good? Youngsters bring versions of these questions with them to school—and both graduates and older individuals hope that they will be able to come up with satisfactory and satisfying answers to these essential questions.

Even the 5-year-old mind has constructed an approach to these questions, but, as we noted earlier, this approach is limited and flawed. Human beings have over the centuries devised more sophisticated approaches to these essential questions and have in a number of ways fashioned more comprehensive and satisfactory responses. The principal path to these privileged approaches is through the mastery of disciplines and domains—organized approaches to knowledge, devised over the centuries, that make use of the existing symbol systems and that, when necessary, revise those systems, or proceed to devise new ones.

A principal purpose of school—indeed, we would argue, *the* principal purpose of school—is to acquire facility and fluency in the use of the disciplinary symbol systems, moves, and understanding. Not for its own sake—though the cultivation of such skill can be rewarding; but rather because such accumulated wisdom represents human beings' hard-won efforts to gain leverage on deep and subtle questions and issues. Individuals demonstrate their education by exhibiting understandings of the approaches, and the resolutions, that have been arrived at over the centuries; and to the extent possible, by putting forth their own more personal (though still disciplinary-grounded) responses to these issues. In pursuing this path, they are mastering the symbolic processes and products wrought by those who have worked within and across the disciplines.

So far, this educational regime seems quite traditional—we make no apologies for that fact. To deny tradition is to turn one's back on the very best work done by countless individuals over many hundreds of years. And yet, while the program of disciplinary mastery is one to which we subscribe, we have little sympathy with many of the established pedagogical moves—for instance, strings of lectures, memorization of text, issuing of short-answer tests as a measure of one's learning.

Indeed, we gladly revisit some of the principal practices of the progressive movement, though with a newly cut key. To begin with, youngsters possess different interests; these must be taken seriously if one wants to involve them integrally in the crucial experiences of exploring the physical and symbolic worlds. Relatedly, they also subscribe to different belief and causal theories, held with varying degrees of explicitness, and these must be taken into account as well. Finally, youngsters also learn in different kinds of ways, exhibiting different profiles and blends of intelligences, which result in different representations of bodies of knowledge. In all of these senses, education must be personalized.

Following a period of initial romance, as philosopher Alfred North Whitehead termed it, a time when interests are first crystallized, there can be no substitute for years of disciplinary training. The classical apprenticeship, where an individual worked for several years at the foot of a master artist or craftsperson, remains an unequaled route toward mastery of a discipline. Still, there is no reason whatsoever why this experience of skill acquisition needs to be dull or dulling. Individuals can gain disciplinary (and interdisciplinary) skills through working with others; through engagement in rich projects; and through public exhibitions of their understanding, complete with informative and supportive feedback. Apprenticeships come in many flavors. There is at least as much to be learned from time spent within the institution of the children's museum as from hours at the traditional school, church, or factory. The power of personalization, the miracle of motivation, can be marshaled to the ends of disciplinary mastery.

Nor need mastery occur at the expense of creativity and individuality. Even as there are common elements that need to be mastered by every individual, there are alternative routes to mastery, as well as costs and benefits for every road taken and every road spurned. As long as both students and masters remain cognizant of these pluralities and these trade-offs, the goal of creativity can continue alongside the goal of skill development and disciplinary mastery.

Even well-set-up educational environments, with exciting materials and stimulating teachers, may not suffice to produce genuine understandings. Research on misconceptions has documented the robustness of early conceptions and the sometimes overwhelming obstacles to genuine disciplinary understanding. (See Essays 16–18.)

Neither we nor others have discovered a royal road to genuine understanding. But our research has suggested a number of pointers. To begin with, individuals must be brought face-to-face with their misconceptions and stereotypes—they have to be exposed repeatedly to the nonsensical implications of uncritically held beliefs. At the same time, they need multiple opportunities to develop more complex notions and to see the ways in which these conceptions more adequately address the questions and issues at hand. A combination of exposure to models of understanding, on the one hand, and regular opportunities to work out the consequences of one's own beliefs and conceptions, on the other, seems to be a necessary prerequisite for a deeper understanding.

In collaborative work with our colleagues at Project Zero, we have developed an explicit approach to teaching for understanding. (See Essays 16–17.) This approach begins with the recognition of "Understanding Goals" (of a general sort) and with the identification of specific "Performances of Understanding," which alone can reveal the extent to which understanding is actually evolving. Care is taken in selecting questions and issues that have proved generative for students and that can address students in ways that connect with their own sometimes idiosyncratic motifs and intellectual styles. Thus, young musicians can be asked to invent a notation for an exotic set of sounds, or budding geographers can be asked to create maps for outer space.

Along with publicly recognized instances of performances of understandings, we also call for assessment that is regular and ongoing. Both the symbolic products to be emulated and the symbolic means for assessing them need to permeate the educational milieu. Only under circumstances where all members of the community are aware of the standards that are being honored, of the various valid approaches to the achievement of these norms, and of the relative success of current performances relative to this standard is there a reasonable possibility of obtaining deeper understandings over time.

Should one wish to teach for understanding, one has to accept a painful truth: *It is simply not possible to cover everything.* Indeed, perhaps the greatest enemy of understanding is "coverage." Only to the extent that one is willing to choose certain topics as worthy of exploration, and then to devote the time that is needed to explore that topic in depth and from multiple perspectives, is there any possibility that genuine understandings will be widely achieved.

So far, it may appear that we have sidestepped the most nagging question of curriculum—which topics should be covered, which books should be read, which subjects are mandatory, which optional, which expendable? Particularly when we are calling for a sharp reduction of coverage, it may seem derelict to avoid the listing of the most important topics, subjects, and themes.

Here, we adopt a distinctly nontraditional approach. Once the basic literacies have been acquired, once individuals are comfortable in the crucial symbol systems of reading, writing, and reckoning, *we discern no necessity to place a special premium on one subject as opposed to another (biology vs. chemistry; American history vs. world history)*, let alone particular topics (light vs. gravity) or library works (Homer vs. *Hamlet*). Far more important, in our view, is the experience of approaching with depth some key topics or themes in the broadest disciplinary areas—math and science, history and philosophy, literature and the arts. Students need to learn how to learn and how to probe deeply into one or another topic. Once they have achieved these precious insights, they can then continue their own education as long as they'd like. And if they have not mastered these lessons, all the facts, factoids, and mandated tests will not save their souls. Assessment should look for evidence of deep understanding; the teacher and student should be afforded wide latitude in the topic that is to be assessed.

Progressive education, in its innocence, had too optimistic a view of education—giving rise to the belief that all students could learn, without much scaffolding; ignoring the conceptual obstacles en route; all too often minimizing the need for disciplinary mastery, skill-building, and milestones and markers along the way. For committing these sins of omissions, we may cast a critical eye on some of our predecessors. Yet, on the bigger picture—the need to establish interest, the openness to various ways of learning, the conviction that one can benefit from sustained work on rich projects set in context, the perceived relationship in a democratic society between the conditions of learning and the conditions of citizenship—John Dewey and his associates arrived at profound and enduring truths.

CLOSING THE LOOP: INNOCENCE RECAPTURED

At the end of the day, what do we hope to have achieved? Scholarship and practice are greatly indebted to the giants of our world: upon the life works of Jean Piaget and John Dewey, who inhabited the same century and adjoining intellectual spheres, there is much to build. While we have devoted at least as much energy to critique, we trust that such criticism has not masked our profound respect for their achievements.

Perhaps as penitence, perhaps as proof, we suggest that developmentalists and the pedagogues from more recent times would not reject the picture that we have put forth here. Modify perhaps, quibble here and there, raise a few objections and point in a few new directions—but not challenge it in a fundamental way. And that is because, by and large, the fresh insights about human nature and the keener sensitivities to educational complexity in no fundamental way contradict the picture forged at the middle of the 20th century—instead they deepen and complexify it in relatively congenial ways. Moreover, the emerging dialectic between researchers and school personnel is in its deepest respects congenial to the vision of society and knowledge that was embraced by Piaget, Dewey, and their associates.

In putting forth the symbol system approach—as a privileged perspective for the broad understanding of human development and as a central element in conceptualizing the purposes of education—we again make no claim for a revolutionary change of direction. Both the psychological and educational traditions have been sensitive to the importance of symbolic vehicles and systems. Yet we do believe that the picture of symbolization put forth here has the potential to bring about a greater degree of order and a more reliable synthesis of knowledge and practice than has been available heretofore.

It is our deepest belief that the human mind comes prepared—we might even say well prepared—to be open to new ideas. It is the obligation of any society in which we would choose to live to maintain that openness and to facilitate the routes to new insights and new understandings. We oppose those psychological and educational approaches that threaten that openness or presume to deny its importance and even its existence. The approaches that we choose to build on are those that share with us this fundamental theme, this "world hypothesis." It is because we believe that creativity is not possible in the absence of disciplines and discipline, and that new knowledge must be based upon a deep mastery of tradition, that we have sought to leaven the more innocent aspects of progressivism—the better to preserve its core vision.

REFERENCES

Feldman, D. (1980). *Beyond universals in cognitive development*. Ablex.

Gardner, H. (1979). Developmental psychology after Piaget: An approach in terms of symbolization. *Human Development, 22*(2), 73–88. http://www.jstor.org/stable/26764784

Olson, D. R. (1994). *The world on paper*. Cambridge University Press.

ESSAY 6

Educating for the True, the Beautiful, and the Good

> As noted in this introduction to this section, I have long been haunted by the idea of an education that cherishes the true, the beautiful, and the good. It's been almost a watchword, an article of faith. And yet, perhaps because it's so much in my bones, my bloodstream, my neural nets, it took decades before I could step back, draw on my knowledge and learning, and attempt to sketch out my beliefs about these three human virtues and how they could be made central for education across the ages and across the globe.

The prolific French anthropologist Claude Lévi-Strauss once quipped that in writing books, there are only three moments of unalloyed pleasure: (1) when the author gets the idea for the book; (2) when the manuscript is completed; and (3) when the author can hold the physical book in his or her hands. While endorsing Lévi-Strauss's testimony, I would also add a fourth moment: when the author has a chance to reintroduce the work to the public—in this case, introducing a new edition of the work.

In many ways, *Truth, Beauty, and Goodness Reframed* is my most personal book. I foreground issues with which I've wrestled and put forth the solutions at which I've arrived. It is also a very general book—I am dealing with issues that affect the lives of all individuals, though in many cases these are not issues with which they are consciously grappling.

On a daily basis, we all have to decide which statements to believe and which to question; which scenes, songs, and stories to value and which to spurn; how to behave toward others and how to judge others' behaviors toward ourselves.

Until May 2011, a month after the book had been published, I did not realize how personal the book was. My wife Ellen and I went back to my old school—Wyoming Seminary, a small private school in northeastern Pennsylvania—for my 50th reunion. We were walking through classrooms that I only dimly remembered when Ellen said, "Look, look, there it is." Displayed on a wall was the phrase "*Verum, Pulchrum, Bonum.*"

Though my Latin is rusty, I immediately recognized the words of my book's title: *Truth, Beauty, and Goodness.* If I had been asked for the motto of my school, I would not have remembered these words in either language. Indeed, for a while I was skeptical that they had even been codified in my time. But a little research confirmed that this was indeed a venerable motto. Whether or not I had been consciously aware of it at the time, it seems likely that it affected me. Perhaps I could even quip that the slogan was true, beautiful, and good!

I have no desire to alter the *title* of the book, but in the second edition of *Truth, Beauty, and Goodness Reframed*, I've elected to change the *subtitle*. In place of the colorless *Educating for the Virtues in the Twenty-First Century*, I've introduced the more vivid *Educating for the Virtues in the Age of Truthiness and Twitter*. My subtitle is far more "tweetable"—the term we may now use to describe phrases that are short and colorful and, one hopes, memorable.

Also, the new edition of this book helps me present more succinctly my definitions, key examples, and educational recommendations. And so here it goes. . . .

TRUTH

Truth is the property of statements. Any statement can be judged as true, false, or indeterminate. No truths—not even mathematical truths—can be considered secure for all time. But over time, and with the openness afforded by the Internet, we have a greater likelihood of establishing truths than during any previous era of human history.

Although truth is the property of statements, we can also speak of the truths of practice. In any skill area—ranging from reporting to microsurgery—individuals arrive at ways of operating that get the job done expertly. Often these are picked up by observation. But at least potentially they can be expressed as statements, and the truth value of those statements can be ascertained.

How do we help students, peers, or ourselves assess the truth of statements? By understanding the methods that the issuers of propositions use to support their statements.

Whether we are contemplating the work of a historian or an economist, a surgeon or a reporter, we need to understand how these professionals go about their daily occupation so that they can with some confidence put forth a proposition that they believe to be true. If we do not trouble to understand the method—say, that of a blogger versus a trained reporter, or a barber versus a board-certified surgeon—then our chances of ascertaining truth are sharply reduced.

BEAUTY

Beauty is the property of experiences. We tend to apply the descriptor "beautiful" to works of art or scenes of nature, but in fact almost any experience—be it a trip, a conversation, or a meal—can be considered beautiful.

To be deemed beautiful, an experience must exhibit three characteristics. It must be *interesting* enough to behold. It must have a form that is *memorable*, and it must *invite revisiting*. Many things that are initially interesting lose their interest quickly; many things that are interesting are simply stored as content and their form is quickly forgotten; and some experiences that are both interesting and memorable do not invite revisiting—either because they are too awful or because their content has been exhausted. For those beautiful experiences that survive all three tests, there is a special reward: a pleasurable tingle.

Truth is marked by convergence; over time, we should be increasingly confident about what is true and what is not. In contrast, beauty is marked by divergence; each person's collection of beautiful experiences is likely to become increasingly personalized, idiosyncratic, even unique. And in my view, that is a blessed situation.

Two educational implications follow from this characterization. First of all, it is useful for each person to keep a portfolio of his or her experiences of beauty. This portfolio can be physical, it can be virtual, it can even reside within one's head. But the purpose of the portfolio is to trace the way in which one's own most cherished experiences change over time. In principle, there is no reason why one's gallery of beautiful experiences needs to change, but in practice, life would be dull if we simply encountered the same experiences over and over again and never enlarged our personal canon. (Of course, if subsequent visits deepen or alter our conceptions and evaluations, these come to resemble new experiences.)

Second, we need to have reasons why we consider one experience beautiful and another not. It is not necessary that we put these reasons into words—indeed, much of beauty is ineffable or at least difficult to articulate in propositions. But in some legitimate way, we need to be able to demonstrate to ourselves—and, as necessary, to others—that there are palpable reasons, factors, that differentiate an experience that we consider beautiful from one that does not fulfill the three criteria that I've introduced.

Cuisine provides a useful analogy. Every 10-year-old has food preferences, and that is fine. Those likes could remain over the years—for instance, a life of devouring hamburgers, donuts, and milkshakes. But in a society of any complexity, individuals are exposed to a variety of cuisines from all over the world. Most of us welcome this experience: we search for new foods; we keep track of what we come to crave and what we no longer cherish. And at least in principle we should be able to point out the differences between a wine, a fruit, or a bread that we seek and one that we no longer desire.

GOODNESS

Good describes the relations among human beings. We should aspire to have good relations with others and vice versa—and we should spurn relations that are unequal, repugnant, toxic. We'd all like to live in a society composed of good persons, good workers, and good citizens, and we'd all prefer to flee from a society where persons are evil, workers promote only themselves, and citizens are selfish or oblivious.

In discussing the good, I introduce a distinction that is important for my argument and yet not immediately intuitive: the difference between *neighborly morality* and *the ethics of roles*. Courtesy of both human evolution and cultural evolution, we are prepared to be good neighbors. The Ten Commandments and the Golden Rule call on us to be kind to our neighbors, to help them out, to avoid stealing, adultery, lying, killing. These strictures are well known to almost every person, although of course that does not mean that all people are good neighbors.

In any reasonably complex modern society, individuals need to go beyond being good neighbors and good persons. Individuals—and that means *all of us*—need to be good workers and good citizens. Fulfilling these roles means that we are competent (we are excellent); that we care about these roles (we are engaged); and that we fulfill these roles in a responsible way (we are ethical).

Here's the key: Although we have considerable preparation for being good persons, we are less prepared as a species to be good workers or good citizens. Many of the roles that we fill today are relatively new, and nearly all roles require actions and understandings that were not needed in generations past. By the same token, while human beings have belonged to communities for thousands of years, the role of citizen is a relatively new one, experienced by a few in classical times and by increasing numbers in the light of the Glorious Revolution of the 17th century, the American and French revolutions of the 18th century, and their more recent incarnations in many emerging nations.

In a word, we have little preparation for fulfilling the ethics of roles. In the ideal case, we become good workers and good citizens by watching positive role models, becoming their apprentices, trying things out, learning from our mistakes, and striving to become better workers and better citizens. To help us achieve these desirable roles, I recommend the establishment of commons or common spaces—real or virtual territories where workers and citizens can speak candidly about their efforts, where they have succeeded, where they have erred, and how they might do better going forth. Since no individual has all the answers, the common spaces are ones where individuals draw on their own experiences and share them with others, in the hope that all will be enlightened by the exchange—even though they are unlikely to agree on particulars in all cases. Skilled moderating or curating of these is crucial.

* * *

These, then, in brief, are my executive summaries of the three virtues, and how I think of them. Much of my previous and much of my subsequent research and writing have been devoted to an exploration of these constructs and how they best can be nurtured in young persons and sustained throughout life.

Time now to introduce the two threats to the virtues, and the villains and heroes of this undertaking.

THREATS

In an earlier book, *The Disciplined Mind* (see Essay 17), I put forth a simple educational agenda: to help students understand, and act, on the basis of what is true, what is beautiful, and what is good. I believed, and still believe, in that agenda. However, in the intervening years, I became convinced that my treatment was naive.

In particular, the trio of virtues had come to be threatened by two forces. On the philosophical side, both postmodernism and relativism led many people to challenge the very notions of truth, beauty, and goodness. Either those concepts were so fuzzy that they ought to be abandoned; l or one could continue to use them but realize that individuals and groups might define them differently; it was either pointless or hopeless to challenge those alternative formulations.

On the technological side, there was the emergence of the new digital media: the Internet, the Web, multiuser games, social networks, epurchasing, smartphones, innumerable apps, large language instruments, and many other forms of hardware and software.

At the very least, these digital entities initially made it increasingly difficult to ascertain truth, beauty, and goodness. And perhaps the digital change was so revolutionary, so epochal, that these concepts had to be abandoned altogether, or completely reformulated.

Not so! In the end, I concluded that the core of truth, beauty, and goodness can—and, indeed, must—be preserved. Most of us would not want to live in a world bereft of the true, the beautiful, and the good any more than we'd want to live in a world marked by falseness, repulsive experiences, and evils of various sorts. Just how those cores can be reframed and reinvigorated is the heart of *Truth, Beauty, and Goodness Reframed*. It is a vital, dramatic story.

VILLAINS AND HEROES

Any drama worthy of its name has its villains and its heroes. For me, one villain comes from the field of biology—specifically, evolutionary psychology, which attempts to account for too much of human behavior in terms of our evolutionary past (which, in any event, is largely unknowable and therefore rich soil for self-serving speculation). The other villain comes from the field of economics—specifically, the assertions that individuals (and organizations) behave according to a rational calculus, and that, left to their own unregulated operations, markets will ultimately yield positive results. One might have thought that recent events throughout the world would cast severe doubt on market fundamentalism, but at least until now it appears to have no generally accepted successor.

To my mind, the pursuit of virtues has its heroes. These are the individuals, groups, organizations, and sometimes whole societies that—in the face of possible biological constraints or powerful economic forces—strive to do the right thing, the best thing; to serve the true, the beautiful, and the good. To be sure, these individual agencies do not always succeed. But when they do not, they try to regroup, to learn from their mistakes, and to continue to fight the good fight. One phrase of our time that we owe to anthropologist Margaret Mead cannot be repeated often enough: "Never doubt that a small group of committed people can change the world. Indeed, it is the only thing that ever has."

GOING FORWARD

I've now had the chance to make my case in brief (for detailed argument and educational implications, see *Truth, Beauty, and Goodness Reframed* and Essays 17–18 in this collection). My most fervent hope is that readers—individually or in groups—will engage with these issues. I hope to see groups of citizens establish the kind of "common spaces" that I have espoused here. In the essays in this collection I know that I have not provided the ultimate answers. But I remain confident that I have asked the right questions.

REFERENCE

Gardner, H. (2000). *The Disciplined Mind*. Simon and Schuster.

ESSAY 7

The Tensions Between Education and Development

With the positing of the theory of multiple intelligences, I began a gradual but lengthy transition: from being primarily a researcher in developmental psychology and neuropsychology to becoming an investigator and sometime "guru" in education as well as a teacher of students who had chosen education as a profession.

As it happens, my colleagues in the Harvard Graduate School of Education were largely psychologists or social scientists who were also making that transition (Kurt Fischer, Carol Gilligan, Gerald Lesser, Robert LeVine, Catherine Snow, and Sheldon White, to name a few), as well as possibly the most prominent, Lawrence Kohlberg, an expert on moral development, broadly speaking, in the Piagetian tradition. After Kohlberg's untimely death in 1987, I was asked to deliver an address in his honor. I used the occasion to reflect on the tension between the two fields that we had chosen . . . or, as he might have quipped, that had chosen us![1]

I. MEMORIES OF LARRY KOHLBERG

I had the honor and pleasure of knowing Larry Kohlberg for almost 20 years. There is little need to comment on my use of the word "honor." Larry was one of the most thoughtful, original, and incisive scholars of our era. His influence went well beyond the borders of psychology, even when those borders were defined in a generous way; and it went well beyond the United States, encompassing much of the world.

But there were countless meetings, and lunches, and interchanges in the hall or on elevators, in the intervening years; it was those that conveyed to me what was most special about Larry. He was an expert in moral development, an area about which I knew little; my major interest was in the area of the arts, an arena where Larry had some interest but little professional concern.

---

1. This is the text of the third annual Lawrence Kohlberg Memorial Lecture delivered to the 15th Annual Conference of the Association of Moral Education, Notre Dame University, November 9, 1990.

He used to joke that Piaget was concerned with the True, I (as a student and aficionado of the arts) was concerned with the Beautiful, and he (Larry) was concerned with the Good. Despite the distance between our principal research interests, we found it easy to talk about almost everything. Most people who knew Larry had the same experience with this gifted, genuinely curious, and concerned conversationalist.

One throughline of our conversations was developmental theory and its relation to practice, particularly in the area of education. It was understandable that we would gravitate toward this topic. We were both trained as developmental psychologists, yet found ourselves working at a graduate school of education and having increasingly practical concerns, in what some Harvard wags term "the real world." In these conversations Larry was clearly the teacher, the expert, while I was at most a chatterer. Yet Larry had the gift of making me a full partner in these conversations. And this ploy had a bracing effect; it made me think more deeply, work even harder, to carry off my end of the conversation; it was thus a Socratic learning experience, in the full sense of that overused term.

II. THE RELATION BETWEEN DEVELOPMENT AND EDUCATION

Stated in unadorned form, the classical issue of the relationship between development and education becomes a question of the relationship between human nature and cultural nurturance. As students of human development, we are concerned with the nature of human organisms: their initial endowment, their principal lines of growth, the options they confront at various stages, the potentials they can realize.

All but the most extreme genetic determinist acknowledges that development takes place in a cultural context and that the lines of development will reflect the regularities and idiosyncrasies of the culture in which it takes place. Yet at the same time, the peculiar burden of the developmentalist—as Piaget, Freud, Kohlberg, Werner, and their followers saw the role—has been to look beyond the accidentals of cultural diversity and to attempt to tease out the underlying principles built into the genome. In this analysis, the developmentalist looks for the principal stages and laws of cognition, of moral judgment, of aesthetic evaluation, and the like, in the hope that these will bear at least a family resemblance across the myriad of cultural milieus.

In contrast to the developmentalist following universalistic scientific dictates, educators must grapple with the challenges and opportunities afforded in the particular culture in which they find themselves. Necessarily accepting whatever constraints human nature may impose, educators must focus instead on the various forms of knowledge, understanding, skill, and values of importance in their culture. Their task is to determine the optimal ways in which those who grow up within the culture can master these understandings, bodies of knowledge, and skills; and to determine how these individuals can utilize their education in ways that make sense to them and to their culture.

Thus stated, there may appear to be no genuine tension between the developmentalist and the educator. The developmentalist, in her incarnation as the scientific researcher, provides the broad picture of development in specific domains—like science, morality, or aesthetics—with that picture marred as little as possible by the wrinkles of particular cultural settings.

The educator, in her incarnation as social engineer, helps to structure learning environments so that the individuals in her charge will attain the highest possible levels of competence in these domains. Superimposed upon these domain-specific trajectories may be a more general view of what it means to be a "developed person" and an "educated person." Partaking of the Dewey-Kohlberg tradition, some workers take it as their goal to nurture individuals so that they will be as fully developed and fully educated as possible.

While this harmonious relationship between development and education is one possible scenario, it is by no means the only one. Traditionally, one can tease out at least four other possibilities.

1. *Development as regnant.* In this position, clearly articulated by Jean-Jacques Rousseau, the genius of human nature is encoded in intrinsic laws of development. These principles are best allowed to unfold with as little interference as possible from the external society, a nefarious agency that provides chains rather than guide ropes. At most, the educator is a handmaiden who keeps the destructive society at bay, thereby allowing the natural processes of development to unfold.

2. *Education as regnant.* Classically arrayed against this position is the view of human nature as fundamentally insufficient, flawed, or even evil. In this Hobbesian or Lockean view, individuals left to their own inclinations will destroy themselves or others. The only hope for survival resides in an intelligently educating society. The wisest educator sketches the proficient student upon the youthful "blank slate" or attempts to reform the "fallen angel."

3. *Development as internalization of cultural inventions.* A popular view associated particularly with the Soviet psychologist Lev Vygotsky, this stance recognizes the basic principles of biological development in the organism. At the same time, however, this orientation stresses the many artifacts, tools, and cultural innovations that have been devised by human cultures over the millennia. In the Vygotskian view, much of development and education consists of the gradual internalization by the young organism of those techniques, strategies, and insights that have initially been encountered in interactions with other members of the species. At first, the young child needs considerable support in using these materials; but with time and experience, the growing child internalizes the understandings sufficiently so that he can exhibit them even in the absence of external scaffolding and eventually transmit them to his own offspring.

4. *Development as the end of education.* In a justifiably well-known paper, Kohlberg and Mayer (1972) articulate a novel and intriguing position on the relationship between development and education. Building particularly on the crucial writings of John Dewey, Kohlberg and Mayer argue that education ought to be so fashioned that it results in the fullest development of the human individual. In this analysis, we discover from open-ended, wide-ranging examinations of human development what it is like for the individual to achieve the highest stages in such areas as rationality, morality, and scientific understanding. These end states ought to serve as points of orientation for educators. The approaches most likely to achieve such apogees of development are ones that allow the developing organism to interact fully with the materials and persons of the culture. Rather than seeking to convey or impose "correct answers" or "bags of virtue" on the student, the teacher provides manifold and varying opportunities whereby the student can make discoveries and consolidate knowledge through rich interactions with his or her world.

Characteristic of each of these positions is that they detect no necessary conflict between development and education. Classically, they simply divide the labor between two complementary professional domains; or with Rousseau, they place all responsibility upon process of development; or with Locke, they place all responsibility upon the educator; or with Vygotsky, they look upon education to enrich and inform development; or with Kohlberg and Mayer, they see education as the means of realizing development.

My own studies suggest, however, that the relationship between development and education may not be as untroubled as earlier scholars have believed or wished. Indeed, considerable evidence suggests that developmental processes may pull in a direction quite different from those that usually characterize educational forces. There may be a strong tension between development and education; and if that tension is to be reduced, it is essential that it be understood well and confronted directly. An initial effort of identification, understanding, confrontation, and resolution undergirds the remainder of this chapter.

III. PARAMETERS OF THE PROBLEM

As David Feldman (1980) has pointed out, most classical developmental theory has been concerned with the positioning of end states, stages, and processes that are universal—such classical theory deals with those events that can be expected to occur in any reasonably normal individual who lives in any reasonably supportive culture. Nearly all of Piaget's work describes sensorimotor, symbolic, and concrete-operational understandings that will eventually come to pass for any human being. Excepting conditions of gross deprivation, it is difficult to think of a culture in which the overwhelming majority of individuals fail to achieve these milestones. Having object permanence, being able to play symbolically, appreciating conservation of liquid and number—by the end of the first decade of life, these accomplishments are virtually synonymous with being human.

While Piaget focused on logical-scientific thought, those who have looked at other domains of development—ones not treated in Kant's *Critique of Pure Reason*—are still concerned primarily with developmental universals. Thus the development of moral reasoning, graphic skill, language competence, or social negotiation are all conceived of as essentially universal accomplishments.

It is probably appropriate, and certainly justifiable, for a science of human development to begin with a portrait of these universal accomplishments. And yet, it would be most shortsighted to remain there. Much of what we value in contemporary culture consists of acquisitions that would have been inconceivable a few hundred, let alone a few thousand years ago: such nonuniversal competences as literacy, numeracy, skill in specific games, knowledge of cultural artifacts such as computers, their increasingly powerful programs, and the like.

In contrast to the virtual inevitability of universal acquisitions, it is not reasonable to expect most people to acquire nonuniversal competences on their own. Even skills as ubiquitous as reading and writing are difficult to acquire in the absence of some formal training.

Here, of course, those institutions called schools enter the picture. Schools have been created all over the world, for many purposes, during many eras. Nonetheless, in the first instance they are institutions that have proven successful in inculcating in children those habits of mind that allow the acquisition and use of literacies. Additionally, and particularly in the past century, schools have also served as the primary venue where children acquire formal disciplinary concepts, diverse notational systems, and the forms of reasoning and argument that are prized in disciplines ranging from physics to philosophy to literary criticism and historical analysis.

We may speak, then, of a rough division of labor. Universal forms of knowledge are acquired outside of school, and largely in the years before school; in contrast, nonuniversal forms of knowledge are acquired in communal institutions, and principally in schools, in the years following early childhood. At least in theory, this process could unfold quite smoothly, with the school simply taking over once the relatively universal competences have been achieved. However, I shall argue that the relation between "prescholastic" and "scholastic" knowledge is by no means devoid of tension.

IV. THREE PRINCIPAL WAYS OF REPRESENTING KNOWLEDGE

My recent work has suggested that human beings reared in a relatively complex, schooled society will be exposed to at least three different ways of representing knowledge. Each of these ways of knowing is powerful and worth acquiring; and in principle these ways of knowing can work together in a powerful way. My conclusion, however, is that in practice these forms of knowledge rarely work together; much of the tension between development and education, as conceptualized here, stems from this lack of harmony.

By virtue of her birthright, every normal human child comes to know the world in a certain way before the years of schooling. During infancy and thereafter, as Piaget has shown, the child acquires a great deal of knowledge from her several senses and from her motor activity. In the years following infancy, this sensorimotor knowledge is complemented by first-order symbolic knowledge—the capacity to know and describe the world in terms of words, pictures, gestures, numerals, and other common and readily learned symbolic vehicles.

By the ages of 5–7, the time at which "serious schooling" begins all over the world, the young child has achieved considerable competence in both sensorimotor and symbolic forms of knowledge. As I have sometimes put it, she has attained a "first-draft" mastery of stories, poems, drawings, dances, and other symbolic vehicles, being able both to appreciate and to create instances of these genres.

Also, as we have come to understand recently, the child will have developed robust (though not necessarily accurate) theories of the world—*theories of how the mind works* (people have intentions, they are usually but not always straightforward about them); *theories of matter* (objects float unless they are too heavy; something heavier will fall more quickly than something that is light; a ball will keep rolling until it runs out of the energy or force that is propelling it); *theories of life* (living things are entities that move; we survive because we can eat food); and *theories of the self* (I'm shy in new situations; I get angry a lot; I'll never be good at drawing).

Armed with these intuitive understandings and theories—some accurate, some misconceived—the young child enters school. In this new environment, over the course of the next decade or so, the child is exposed to a wholly new set of understandings and ways of knowing, which I shall here term "scholastic knowledge." In addition to the aforementioned notational skills, the child will learn about the precise meanings of terms that are usually bandied about loosely on the street: What do "hundreds more" or "dozens less" mean in strictly quantitative terms? How are time or distance computed with precision? What is a state or a country? The child will also learn about new concepts—gravity, mass, acceleration, evolution, revolution. And as noted above, the child will begin to appreciate that information and knowledge are culled and arrayed in different ways, depending upon the subject matter or discipline that is at issue.

In any culture, there exists a third set of knowledge structures as well, complementing the universal sensorimotor forms and the ensemble of scholastic ways of knowing. I call these *culturally valued skills*—those abilities and roles that are highly valued in a particular culture and that are transmitted by the most effective possible means to the younger generation. These roles encompass ones that are virtually universal, like a parent's; ones that are shared by a significant portion of the population (like hunters or farmers); and ones that are far more restricted (magic man, weaver, surgeon, geographer, pharmacist, therapist).

Two crucial points characterize culturally valued skills. First, their utility is manifest to an observer at the time when they are encountered. Second, expert practitioners who exhibit culturally valued skills make use of the range of ways of knowing that are extant in the society. Hence, in a preliterate society, the skilled weaver uses sensorimotor and first-order symbolic knowledge, whereas in a more advanced "schooled" society, the weaver will draw as well on notational, literary, pictorial, and graphic knowledge. In either case, younger individuals have the opportunity—seldom available within the school walls—of observing the competent adult at work and noting how the various forms of knowing are drawn on synergistically in the successful execution of the tasks associated with that role.

V. THE DISJUNCTIONS AMONG WAYS OF KNOWING

In the last few decades, educationally oriented researchers have surveyed the range of scholastic disciplines only to arrive at an astounding finding. Put directly, as long as students are examined in schools, in line with the ways in which they have been taught, they will appear well educated—that is, they will appear as if they had understood the lessons of school reasonably well.

Once, however, students are asked about the same kinds of issues in a somewhat different context, they reveal a much less happy picture. Specifically, school knowledge seems strictly bound to school settings. Once students are asked about the same kinds of issues elsewhere, they readily abandon the concepts and ways of reasoning apparently mastered in school and instead revert to their basic, universal ways of knowing and the aforementioned theories of mind and matter, which were apparently deeply entrenched. It is as if the new knowledge had simply been superimposed upon older forms of knowing. Once the props surrounding the new knowledge are removed, the students simply fall back on the older and apparently more robust understandings. (For details, see Essays 17–18.)

The most dramatic examples of disjunction between two forms of knowing come from the realm of physics. Students from first-rate universities like Johns Hopkins and MIT, who have received top grades in physics courses, reveal the same basic (mis)conceptions about physical phenomena as do much younger students who have never studied physics. It is as if the robust theories of matter, which congealed originally in early childhood, rush to the surface once physics class is over. Thus we find students exhibiting such misconceptions as a belief that an object that follows a curvilinear trajectory while rotating through a circular tube will continue to follow that same trajectory once it is allowed to fall freely; that an object resting on a table is subjected only to force from above and not an equivalent supporting force from below; and that an object will proceed in the direction in which it has just been kicked, irrespective of its prior velocity. It is as if students had learned to say, in response to a teacher's query in class, that the earth is round but continued to believe in actuality that it is as flat as it seems to a 5-year-old!

Every discipline has its own configurations, and so, perhaps not surprisingly, each discipline exhibits its own form of student misconception. In algebra, students perform adequately on word problems as long as the phrases mimic the syntax of the correct algebraic expression; but once the usual order has been altered, student ability to set up the equation correctly often reverts to chance, or even below chance, level. Graduate students in statistics exhibit the same proclivity of ignoring baseline rates as do individuals who have never heard of the concept of probability. Undergraduates at the finest universities evaluate poems on the same dubious criteria as unschooled individuals, rating rhyme and superficially cheerful subjects above skilled arrangement of words or profound ruminations about troubling life-and-death issues. Musical performers who have learned to read notations fail to capture the underlying rhythms and expressions to which untutored youngsters remain sensitive. And the very history students who receive an A for indicating the complex multicausal origins of World War I, invoke simple linear causal chains when trying to explain equivalently vexed events that have recently been reported in the daily newspaper. It's just easier to blame one tyrannical leader.

Why this dismal picture? It cannot simply be that our schoolteachers are failing. After all, at least some of the students are doing very well on the very instruments of achievement that our society endorses. Nor can the difficulties be attributed to a simple loss of knowledge, because much of the research occurs within the time frame when students are in school. It can perhaps be said that students experience severe problems in transferring scholastic knowledge outside the school setting, but this statement simply restates the problem. The issue: Why this problem in applying school-learned knowledge once one has left the classroom?

In my view, the key to this apparent ignorance lies in the uncontaminated persistence of separate forms of knowing. When students acquire new forms of knowing, new representations of knowledge in school, they prove able to use these in school settings. However, in general, these forms are presented in an entirely decontextualized way, which makes it difficult for students to discern when and where those ways of conceptualizing knowledge might be activated and deployed outside of school. For this and other reasons, students have never found it necessary to examine the possible contradictions or inconsistencies between school knowledge and the other forms of knowing that they brought to school or that they can observe at work in competent professionals outside of school. Without such confrontation, these forms of knowing co-exist under the same roof—comparable to two tenants who inhabit the same apartment house but have never spoken to each other in all the years of their cohabitation.

To put it differently: There is a 5-year-old mind struggling to get out and express itself in nearly every student. It is difficult to silence that mind, and yet much disciplinary mastery requires precisely such total silencing or complete transformation. I believe that the disjunctions to which I have referred here have been relatively invisible to teachers and administrators, and to educational and scientific researchers as well. In the past, the stunning disjunction between different ways of representing the world was simply unappreciated in the worlds of education and of educational psychology—as unnoticed and unremarked-upon as was the difference between scientific paradigms in the years before Thomas Kuhn published his important account about the origin of scientific revolutions.

Until this point, I have deliberately avoided reference to the domains of moral thought and moral action (hereafter abbreviated as the moral domain). As I indicated earlier, my own expertise is remote from that of Larry Kohlberg's; it would be presumptuous for me to claim that my analysis—even if appropriate for the aforementioned cognitive spheres—would necessarily obtain in the domain of morality.

That said, I hope that I will be permitted a few speculations.

It strikes me that the area of moral thought and moral action may represent a hybrid between universal domains, such as linguistic competence, and domains that are clearly nonuniversal, such as physics or chess. On the one hand, individuals in every culture must wrestle with issues of good and bad, and there appears to be a sequence that, at least in its early stages, is universal. Yet it is also the case that moral codes vary radically across cultures, and an individual's ultimate moral orientation will necessarily reflect the particular values and criteria implied in his or her culture.

If my analysis is on the mark, and if it could be extended to the moral sphere, I would expect a situation something like the following: During early life, youngsters develop very strong conceptions of morality, ones that are deeply constrained by neurobiological and universal-cultural factors. As they grow older, enter school, and are exposed to culturally elaborated moral codes, children find that they are expected to master more specific and culture-bound moral precepts. As long as the students remain within the context where these procedures and practices are propounded, they will be able to recite them and follow them (e.g., knowing the Boy Scout oath, not peeking at another's paper, speaking of rights and responsibilities); but once they have been removed from the scholastic setting, earlier, more robust, more deeply entrenched moral principles and practices quickly return.

As I can see, my account so far does not directly conflict with Kohlberg's portrait of moral development, since he was always suspicious of "bags-of-virtue" views of morality, of rote learning, of performances exhibited because of patterns of reward and punishment. Kohlberg called for regular, direct confrontations between alternative moral perspectives; he had confidence that, under such circumstances, the universal higher stages would ultimately emerge and triumph. Clearly, this view of moral development is remote from the scholastic approach to learning that I have criticized.

Still, it is possible that our ultimate views on these matters might have diverged. My analysis suggests that the early forms of morality are likely more robust, and more difficult to undermine, than one might have anticipated. It suggests, further, that the earlier forms of moral thought and action are never totally erased and that under the appropriate activating circumstances, they might well reemerge in full force. The mind of the 5-year-old moralist may be as enduring as the mind of the 5-year-old theorist of matter or mind. It may be that only true "experts" in the moral domain—only those individuals who regularly confront, wrestle with, and have to enact their moral principles in a consistent manner—ever fully transcend the morality of early childhood.

VI. POSSIBLE BRIDGES AMONG DISPARATE WAYS OF KNOWING

If my analysis of the difficulties of learning is even approximately correct, we confront a very unsettling picture of our schools. The deepest processes of human development, undergirded by millennia of evolution and thousands of years of development in a variety of human cultures, seem at basic odds with the forms of knowing that have been painfully constructed by scholars (and other practitioners) in the more recent past. Certainly, the success of our educational institutions, and the possibility of synthesizing educational and developmental factors, depends upon our being able to address this disjunction successfully.

A number of promising efforts have been made in recent years, efforts that could inspire a more developmentally cogent educational approach. In this "immersion" view, young students need to have extensive hands-on experiences with materials relevant to a scholarly endeavor before they are introduced directly to scholarly concepts, notations, and forms of argument. And so, rather than being instructed in musical notations, a youngster is encouraged to develop his or her own notation, and thereby to appreciate the considerations that enter into the creation of any notation. By the same token, students develop their own theories of weight and density, of heat and temperatures, before encountering the scientist's analysis of these concepts.

A second approach also permeated the writings of Larry Kohlberg. The salient notion in the "contradiction" perspective is that development is spurred by the encountering and constructive handling of conflict. According to this analysis, intellectual progress occurs when students are encouraged to make predictions, and then to confront directly those situations in which their predictions do not pan out; or when students put forth their own reasoned-out views and have to defend them against opinions espoused by more sophisticated peers.

While acknowledging both of these types of educational interventions, my own personal predilections lie in the implementation of student apprenticeships. In such an approach a young person has the opportunity to observe the range of relevant skills and knowledge as they are brought to bear within a discipline or domain valued in the culture. Assuming a competent master, the child or youth is gradually introduced to the skill at his or her current level of development and is allowed to advance at a comfortable rate.

In an effective apprenticeship, the disjunction between scholastic and universal forms of knowing should be effectively reduced. On the one hand, the young person witnesses a model who appreciates (indeed, embodies) the situations in which various forms of knowledge use and representation are appropriate. On the other hand, the youth herself has the opportunity to begin with universal forms of knowing, but then to perceive the ways in which more scholastically tuned forms can enhance, supplement, revise, or altogether replace the deeply entrenched forms of knowledge.

In view of the array of disturbing empirical findings to which I have adverted, it would be Panglossian to assume that any single approach to education can be a panacea. I expect that there will continue to be tensions between the universally based forms of knowing, on the one hand, and those tied to particular cultural institutions, preeminently schools, on the other. Still, if one could combine some of the strengths of the immersion, the contradiction, and the apprenticeship approaches, it might be possible to build an educational system that is far more compatible with developmental processes than has usually been the case, and that results in understandings that are both robust and accurate.

VII. CLOSING THOUGHTS

Since I have envisioned this talk as part of a continuing dialogue with Larry Kohlberg, I pause at this point. Whatever dialogue is to take place must do so either in my own mind or with those who are part of the enormous intellectual legacy he has bequeathed us. I suspect that Larry would find the results on misconceptions interesting but not terribly surprising. I suspect, further, that he would attribute them to the admittedly low quality of much schooling, both here and abroad.

He would perhaps point out that not all forms of knowledge are universal, and that these disciplinary understandings, while certainly important in certain cultures for certain purposes, are of a different order from the broad forms studied by Piaget and by Kohlberg himself. He would stress that development is a time-consuming process, one that cannot be jump-started by a single exposure to a new concept or paradigm. Finally, he would submit that in a fertile educational environment, one that strove to enhance human development in all of its varieties, we would cease to encounter the massive disjunctions that have exercised me. Knowing how persuasive Larry could be, and knowing that, after all, at least some individuals do succeed in bridging the gap, I am at least half inclined to agree with him and to let the matter rest.

But not quite. As Larry would be the first to agree, progress in scientific or philosophical matters is most likely to occur when contrasting positions are laid out clearly, defended as best they can be, and then subsequently analyzed, sorted out, and evaluated. It would be wrong, or at least premature, for me to withdraw my line of argument at this early moment.

And so, let me close this essay with the suggestion that, in every domain of life—be it science (the True), morality (the Good), or aesthetics (the Beautiful)—there are deeply held understandings that all individuals bring from early on to their maturing years. Part of the burden of our educational institutions is to challenge, when appropriate, these deeply held understandings; such institutions will seek to substitute for them more sophisticated forms of knowing, which may well clash with the more basic, more universal forms. Even when these institutions have been sensitively fashioned, they may not always succeed in transforming the earlier forms of knowing: the mind of the 5-year-old is a potent force. Nor is that failure to always transform an undesirable situation: after all, basic forms of survival, if not wisdom, are embodied in these initial takes on the world. Yet, when fully apprised of the obstacles and constraints that attend even ordinary forms of knowledge acquisition, educational institutions can do much to bring about a rapprochement among disparate forms of knowing. In that sense, they can help to realize the dream that Larry Kohlberg articulated so well—an education for the fullest human development.

ACKNOWLEDGMENTS

Several colleagues provided helpful comments on an earlier draft of this essay. I should like to thank Drs. William Damon, David Feldman, Deanna Kuhn, and Robert Selman.

REFERENCES

Feldman, D. (1980). *Beyond universals in cognitive development*. Ablex.
Kohlberg, L., & Mayer, R. (1972). Development as the aim of education. *Harvard Educational Review, 42*, 449–496.

INTRODUCING MULTIPLE INTELLIGENCES

CLAIMS, CRITIQUES, AND EDUCATIONAL IMPLICATIONS

Overview of MI Theory

Suppose you had spoken to me in the middle 1970s and asked about my professional identity, I would likely have said: "I am the co-director of Project Zero, housed at the Harvard Graduate School of Education; I am a researcher in developmental psychology and neuropsychology." At that time, my interests in education were largely personal—reflections on the strengths and weaknesses of my own education, and concern that our own children would have the best aspects of our education while avoiding the less positive facets.

A decade or so later, my response would have been entirely different. And that's because of the research that I had conducted for the Project on Human Potential and the book that had come out of that research, *Frames of Mind: The Theory of Multiple Intelligences*. In that book, now over 40 years old, I had challenged the hegemony in psychological research of the word "intelligence." And I had taken on as well the primacy, the hegemony, of the IQ test—an attempt to document, on the basis of responses to a few dozen short-answer questions, how smart/intelligent/educable a person is.

To be sure, the psychological concept of intelligence and the psychological instrument the IQ test have their place. But as an attempt to convey the full sweep and potential of human cognition, the "intelligence track" is remarkably narrow and shortsighted. Many people could have written a book about the human mind that pluralized its capacities; in fact, some others had. But I had made three crucial additions:

1. I proposed seven different human faculties. Featured were linguistic and logical capacities—the ones ordinarily tapped in intelligence tests. But alongside were at least five other "faculties": spatial, musical, bodily-kinesthetic, interpersonal, and intrapersonal. These other forms of intellect made sense to reflective individuals in many places with many pursuits.
2. I did not simply list these human faculties; I provided ample evidence of their existence and operation through studies from anthropology, developmental psychology, psychometrics, neuroscience, and genetics. Indeed, I had authored a book of nearly 400 pages, with hundreds of footnotes, issued by a reputable publisher, reviewed widely (and usually favorably) in both popular and professional media.

3. I decided to call these human faculties "intelligences," and I dubbed the collective "multiple intelligences." *This seemingly simply lexical choice made a huge difference.* This work would not have become as well-known had I used other descriptors like "talents" or "faculties" or "computational devices." To reinforce this point, Daniel Goleman would not have received renown had he not written about "emotional *intelligence*" (Goleman, 1995) and had *Newsweek* magazine not featured the evocative abbreviation of EQ (Brant, 2005).

Words and labels matter, perhaps excessively!

And so my life indeed changed. The purpose of *Frames of Mind* had not been avowedly educational—in the early 1980s I saw myself as addressing primarily fellow psychologists and the general educated public. But it was the immediate and wholly embracing reactions of educators all over the world that nudged me increasingly to think about educational issues, to initiate projects in education, and to write for educational audiences. And so, decades later, the "essential" readings collected here.

REFERENCES

Brant, M. (2005, June 13). Why emotional intelligence matters. *Newsweek*. www.newsweek.com/why-emotional-intelligence-matters-120505

Goleman, D. (1995). *Emotional intelligence*. Bantam Books.

Beyond IQ
Developing the Spectrum of Human Intelligences

Allow me to transport all of us to the Paris of 1900—La Belle Époque. Around 1900 the city leaders of Paris approached a psychologist named Alfred Binet with an unusual request: Could he devise some kind of a measure that would predict which youngsters would succeed and which would fail in the primary grades of Paris schools?

As is well known, Binet succeeded. He produced a set of test items that could predict with some accuracy a child's success or failure in school. In short order, his discovery came to be called the "intelligence test," his measure, the "IQ." Like other Parisian fashions, the IQ soon made its way to the United States, where it enjoyed a modest success until World War I. Then it was used to test over one million American military recruits, and it had truly arrived. From that day on, the IQ test has looked like psychology's biggest success—a genuinely useful scientific tool.

What vision led to the excitement about IQ? At least in the West, people had always relied on intuitive assessments of how smart other people were. Now intelligence seemed to be quantifiable. Of course, you could measure someone's actual or potential height, and now, it seemed, you could also measure someone's actual or potential intelligence. At last we had a single dimension of mental ability along which we could array everyone.

The search for the most perfect measure of intelligence has proceeded apace. Here, for example, are some quotations from an ad for a widely used test:

> *Need an individual test which quickly provides a stable and reliable estimate of intelligence in four or five minutes per form? Has three forms. Doesn't depend upon verbal production or subjective scoring. Can be used with the severely physically handicapped (even paralyzed) if they can signal yes or no. Handles two-year-olds and superior adults with the same short series of items and the same format. Only $16.00 complete.*

Now, that's quite a claim. Psychologist Arthur Jensen suggests that we could look at reaction time to assess intelligence: a set of lights go on; how quickly can the subject react? Psychologist Hans Eysenck suggests that investigators of intelligence should look directly at brain waves.

There are also, of course, more sophisticated versions of the IQ test. One of them is called the Scholastic Aptitude (or Assessment) Test (SAT). It purports to be a similar kind of measure, and if you add up a person's verbal and math scores, as is often done, you can rate him or her along that dimension. Programs for the gifted, for example, often use that kind of measure.

I suggest that along with this one-dimensional view of how to assess people's minds comes a corresponding view of school, which I will call the "uniform view." In the uniform school, there is a core curriculum—a set of facts and processes that everybody should know, and very few electives. The better students, quite likely those with higher IQs, may be allowed to take courses that call upon critical reading, calculation, and thinking skills. In the "uniform school," there are regular assessments, using paper-and-pencil instruments, of the IQ or SAT variety. They yield reliable rankings of people; the best and the brightest get into the better colleges, and perhaps—but only perhaps—they will also get better rankings in life. No question—this approach works well for certain people. Since this measurement and selection system seems meritocratic in certain respects, it has something to recommend it.

But allow me to present an alternative vision—one based on a radically different view of the mind, and one that yields a very different view of school. It is a pluralistic view of mind, recognizing many different and discrete facets of cognition, acknowledging that people have different cognitive strengths and contrasting cognitive styles. Let me as well introduce the concept of an individual-centered school that takes this multifaceted view of intelligence seriously. This model for a school is based in part on findings from sciences that did were unknown in Binet's time: cognitive science (the study of the mind), and neuroscience (the study of the brain).

One such approach I have called my "theory of multiple intelligences." I will now relate something about its sources, its claims, and its educational implications for a possible school of the future.

Dissatisfaction with the concept of IQ and with unitary views of intelligence has been fairly widespread—one thinks, for instance, of the works of L. L. Thurstone, J. P. Guilford, and other critics. From my point of view, however, these criticisms do not suffice. The whole concept has to be challenged; in fact, it has to be replaced.

I contend that we should get away altogether from tests and correlations among tests. We should look instead at more naturalistic sources of information about how populations around the world develop skills important to their way of life. Think, for example, of sailors in the South Seas, who find their way around hundreds, or even thousands, of islands by looking at the constellations of stars in the sky, sensing the way a boat passes over the water, and noticing a few scattered landmarks. A word for intelligence in a society of these sailors would probably refer to that kind of navigational ability.

Think of surgeons and engineers, hunters and fishermen, dancers and choreographers, athletes and athletic coaches, tribal chiefs and sorcerers. All these different roles need to be taken into account if we accept the way I define intelligence—"the ability to solve problems, or to fashion products, that are valued in one or more cultural settings."

For the moment I am saying nothing about whether there is one dimension, or more than one dimension, of intelligence; nothing about whether intelligence is inborn or developed. Instead I emphasize the ability to solve problems and to fashion products. In my work I seek the building blocks of the intelligences used by the aforementioned sailors and surgeons and sorcerers (and scholars).

The science in this enterprise, to the extent that it exists, involves trying to discover the right description of the intelligences. What is an intelligence?

To answer this question, I have, with my colleagues, surveyed a wide set of sources that, to my knowledge, have never been considered together before. One source is what we already know of the development of different kinds of skills in normal children. Another source, and a very important one, is information on the ways that these abilities break down under various conditions of brain damage. When one suffers a stroke or some other kind of brain damage, various abilities can be destroyed, or spared, in isolation from other abilities. This research with brain-damaged patients yields a very powerful kind of evidence; it seems to reflect the way the nervous system has evolved over the millennia to yield certain discrete kinds of intellectual competences

My research group looked at other special populations as well: prodigies, savants, autistic children, and children with learning disabilities, all of whom exhibit very jagged cognitive profiles—profiles that are extremely difficult to explain in terms of a unitary view of intelligence. We examined cognition in diverse animal species and in dramatically different cultures. Finally, we considered two kinds of psychological evidence: correlations among psychological tests of the sort yielded by a factor analysis of a test battery, and the results of efforts of skill training. When you train a person in skill A, for example, does that training transfer to skill B? So, for example, does training in mathematics enhance one's musical abilities, or vice versa?

Obviously, having examined all these sources—information on development, on breakdowns, on special populations, and the like—we end up with a cornucopia of information. Optimally, we would perform a factor analysis, feeding all the data into a computer and noting the kinds of factors or intelligences that are extracted. Alas, this kind of material didn't exist in a form that is susceptible to computation, and so we had to perform a more subjective factor analysis. (Note: Today, in 2024, I would call it a "synthesis," and I might feed it into a Large Language Instrument.) In truth, we simply studied the results as best we could, and tried to organize them in a way that made sense to us, and hopefully to critical readers as well. My resulting list of seven intelligences is a preliminary attempt to organize this mass of information.

Here are the seven intelligences we have identified, along with one or two examples of each. Linguistic intelligence is the kind of ability exhibited in its fullest form, perhaps, by poets. Logical-mathematical intelligence, as the name implies, is logical and mathematical ability, manifested especially by scientists and engineers. Jean Piaget, the great developmental psychologist, thought he was studying all intelligence; I claim that he was actually focusing on the development of logical-mathematical intelligence.

Although I name the linguistic and logical-mathematical intelligences first, it is not because I think they are the most important. In fact, I think all seven of the intelligences have equal claim to priority. In our society, however, we have put linguistic and logical-mathematical intelligences, figuratively speaking, on a pedestal. Much of our testing is based on this high valuation of verbal and mathematical skills. If you do well in language and logic, you will likely do well on IQ tests and SATs, and you may well get into a prestigious college. But whether you do well once you leave is probably going to depend as much on the extent to which you possess and use the other intelligences, those that I propose to give equal attention (and of course, how you deploy whichever intelligences you have—see Essays 26 and 28 on good work).

Spatial intelligence is the ability to form a mental model of a spatial world and to be able to maneuver and operate using that model. Sailors, engineers, surgeons, sculptors, and painters—to name just a few examples—all have highly developed spatial intelligence. *Musical intelligence* is the fourth category of ability we have identified: composer-conductor Leonard Bernstein had lots of it; Mozart, presumably, had even more. *Bodily-kinesthetic* intelligence is the ability to solve problems or to fashion products using one's whole body, or parts of the body. Dancers, athletes, surgeons, and craftspeople all exhibit highly developed bodily- kinesthetic intelligence.

Finally, I propose two forms of personal intelligence—not well understood, elusive to study, but immensely important. *Interpersonal intelligence* is the ability to understand other people: what motivates them, how they work, how to work cooperatively with them. Successful salespeople, politicians, teachers, clinicians, and religious leaders are all likely to be individuals with high degrees of interpersonal intelligence. *Intrapersonal intelligence*, a seventh kind of intelligence, is a correlative ability, turned inward. It is a capacity to form an accurate, veridical model of oneself and to be able to use that model to operate effectively in life. It's challenging to study; perhaps one's therapist is best equipped to rate a patient's understanding of self.

Note that the personal intelligences are closest to what Daniel Goleman has called "emotional intelligence." But Goleman adds a value component—emotional intelligence is desirable—while I see my intelligences as value-free; any intelligence can be used benignly or malevolently.

These, then, are the seven intelligences that we have described in our research. This is a preliminary list, as I have said; obviously, each form of intelligence can be subdivided, or the list can be rearranged. And later, I have added an intelligence and discussed the plausibility of yet more intelligences (see Essays 9 and 19 in *The Essential Howard Gardner on Mind*).

The essential point: to make the case for the plurality of intellect.

Additionally, I believe that individuals may likely differ in the particular intelligence profiles with which they are born, and that certainly they differ in the profiles they end up with. I think of the intelligences as raw biological potentials that can be seen in pure form only in individuals who are, in the technical sense, freaks. In almost everybody else, the intelligences work together to solve problems, to yield various kinds of cultural end states—vocations, avocations, and the like.

This, in capsule form, is my theory of multiple intelligences. In my view, the purpose of school should be to develop intelligences and to help people reach vocational and avocational goals that are appropriate to their particular spectrum of intelligences. People who are helped to do so, I believe, feel more engaged and competent, and therefore more inclined to serve the society in a constructive way.

These thoughts, and the critique of a universalistic view of mind with which I began, lead to the notion of an *individual-centered* school, one geared to optimal understanding and development of each student's cognitive profile. This vision stands in direct contrast to that of the uniform school I described earlier.

The design of my ideal school of the future is based upon two assumptions. The first is that not all people have the same interests and abilities; not all of us learn in the same way. (And we now have the tools to begin to address these individual differences in school.)

The second assumption is one that is sobering: It is the assumption that nowadays no one person can learn everything there is to learn. We might all like, as Renaissance men and women, to know everything, or at least to believe in the potential of knowing everything, but that ideal clearly is not possible anymore.

Choice is therefore inevitable. I contend that the choices that we make for ourselves, and for the younger persons under our charge, might as well be informed choices. An individual-centered school would be rich in assessment of individual abilities and proclivities. It would seek to match individuals not only to curricular areas, but also to particular ways of teaching those subjects. And after the first few grades, the school would also seek to match individuals with the various kinds of life and work options that are available at that time in their culture.

Let me propose a set of roles for educators that might make this vision a reality. First of all, we might have what I will call "assessment specialists." The job of these professionals would be to try to understand as sensitively as possible the abilities and interests of the students in a school. It would be very important, however, for the assessment specialists to use "intelligence-fair" instruments. We want to be able to look specifically and directly at spatial abilities, at personal abilities, and the like—*not* through the usual lenses of the linguistic and logical-mathematical intelligences.

Up until now nearly all assessment has depended indirectly on measurement of those abilities; if students are not strong in those areas, their abilities in other areas may be obscured. Once we begin to try to assess other kinds of intelligences directly, I am confident that specific students will reveal strengths in quite different areas, and the notion of general brightness will disappear or become greatly attenuated.

In fact, I have been involved with colleagues in two collaborations through which we are attempting to determine what assessment might be like in the future. One such effort is taking place at a local preschool with which we are working closely. We have richly equipped the school with materials that should engage the range of the students' intelligences, and in fact we call our effort "Project Spectrum." The children are allowed to gravitate naturally to a wide variety of games, puzzles, and other materials; they can show us, through their play activities, what their particular combinations of interests and strengths are. At the conclusion of the school year, we present what we call a "spectrum profile" for each child to his or her parents and teachers. This is a clearly worded description of a child's particular cognitive profile, together with some concrete suggestions of what might be done at home, in school, and in the wider community to help that particular child to develop his or her interests and abilities. (For details, see Essays 13 and 14.)

Our second research collaboration involves the teaching of the arts and humanities to preadolescent and adolescent students. In this project, named Arts PROPEL, in collaboration with the Educational Testing Service, we are developing ways of figuring out the strengths of junior and senior high school students in the arts and humanities. We agree that whatever use paper-and-pencil tests may have in other areas, they are not the optimal way to reveal students' latent or unfolding abilities in the arts and humanities. In Arts PROPEL, students are working instead in a much more holistic way on large-scale projects, which will then be collected in portfolios for us to assess. It is my hope that a student profile based on such assessments might serve at least as an adjunct to standardized testing, and that perhaps it may eventually even serve as an alternative to testing. (See Essay 15 and 19.)

In addition to the assessment specialist, the school of the future might have the "student–curriculum broker." It would be his or her job to help match students' profiles, goals, and interests to particular curricula and to particular approaches to learning. Interactive technologies offer considerable promise in this area:

There should also be, I think, a "school–community broker," who would match students to learning opportunities in the wider community. It would be this person's job to find situations in the community—particularly options not available in the school—for children who exhibit distinctive or unusual cognitive profiles. I have in mind apprenticeships, mentorships, internships in organizations, "big brothers," "big sisters"—individuals and organizations with whom these students might work to secure a feeling for different kinds of vocational and avocational roles in the society.

I am not worried about those youngsters—if they in fact exist!!—who are good at everything. (Leonardo da Vinci types are welcome, but they are not common!) They're likely to do just fine. I'm concerned about those who don't shine on standardized tests, and who, therefore, tend to be written off as not having gifts of any kind. The school–community broker could spot these youngsters and find placements in the community that provide chances for them to improve, and perhaps shine.

There is ample room in this vision for teachers as well, and also for master teachers. In my view, teachers would be liberated to do what they are supposed to do, which is to teach their subject matter in their preferred manner(s) of teaching. The job of master teacher would be demanding. It would involve, first of all, supervising the novice teachers and guiding them; but the master teacher would also seek to ensure that the complex student-assessment-curriculum-community equation is balanced appropriately. If the equation is seriously askew, master teachers would intervene and suggest ways to make things better.

Clearly, what I am describing is a tall order; it might even be called utopian. And there is a major risk to this program, of which I am well aware. That is the risk of premature billeting—of saying, "Well, Johnny is four, he seems to be musical, so we are going to send him to The Juilliard School in New York City and drop everything else." There is, however, nothing inherent in the approach that I have described that demands this early overdetermination—quite the contrary. Early identification of strengths can be very helpful in indicating the kinds of experiences children might profit from, but early identification of weaknesses can be equally important. If a weakness is identified early, there is a chance to attend to it before it is too late, and to come up with alternative ways of teaching or covering an important skill or content area.

We now have the technological and the human resources to implement such an individual-centered school. Achieving it is a question of will, including the will to withstand the current enormous pressures toward uniformity and unidimensional assessments. There are strong pressures now to compare students, to compare teachers, states, even entire countries, using one dimension or criterion, a kind of a crypto-IQ assessment.

Clearly, everything I have described today stands in direct opposition to that particular view of the world. Indeed, that is my intent—to provide a ringing indictment of such one-track thinking. I would refer readers to the *Finnish Lessons* books and articles of educator Pasi Sahlberg (2014), who describes a fundamentally different approach to K–12 education.

I believe that in our society we suffer from three biases, which I have nicknamed "Westist," "Testist," and "Bestist." "Westist" involves putting certain Western cultural values, which date back to Socrates, on a pedestal. Logical thinking, for example, is important; rationality is important; but they are not the only virtues.

"Testist" suggests a bias toward focusing upon those human abilities or approaches that are readily testable. If it can't be tested, it sometimes seems, it is not worth paying attention to. I believe that assessment can be much broader, much more humane than it is now, and that psychologists should spend less time ranking people and more time helping them.

"Bestist" is a not very veiled reference to a 1972 book by journalist David Halberstam called *The Best and the Brightest*. Halberstam referred ironically to figures such as Harvard faculty members who were brought to Washington in the early 1960s to help President John F. Kennedy and in the process launched the Vietnam War (which they proved unable to navigate successfully). Any belief that all the answers to a given problem lie in one certain approach, such as logical-mathematical thinking, can be very dangerous.

A message: Current hegemonic views of intellect need to be leavened with other points of view.

It is of the utmost importance that we recognize and nurture all of the varied human intelligences, and all of the combinations of intelligences. We differ from one another significantly because we have different combinations of intelligences. If we recognize this, I think we will have at least a better chance of dealing appropriately with the many problems that we face in the world. If we can mobilize the spectrum of human abilities, not only will people feel better about themselves and more competent; it is even possible that they will also feel more engaged and more readily able to join with the rest of the world community in working for the broader good. Perhaps if we can mobilize the full range of human intelligences, and ally them to an ethical sense, we can help to increase the likelihood of our survival on this planet, and perhaps even contribute to our thriving.

REFERENCES

Halberstam, D. (1972). *The best and the brightest.* Random House.
Sahlberg, P. (2014). *Finnish Lessons 2.0: What can the world learn from educational change in Finland?* Teachers College Press.

ESSAY 9

Reflections on MI Myths and Messages

Even after 40 years, most of my "over- the- transom" correspondence is about the theory of multiple intelligences. And in that cache, a favorite topic is the nomination of additional intelligences: religious, financial, technological, work, play, you name it.

Now, of course, anyone can play the "'name your intelligence" game. But anyone who has looked at Frames of Mind *or other writings knows that I had a strict set of criteria for what counts as an intelligence, and what does not. And it took me several years to sift through various candidate intelligences and choose ones that qualify.*

That said, I think it is legitimate to contemplate additional intelligences. And indeed, in a sabbatical year (1994–1995), I concluded that there was sufficient evidence to add the "naturalist intelligence." I was not convinced that there is a "religious"; or "spiritual" intelligence, though there may be an: "existential intelligence"—the intelligence of "'big questions.'" (See Essay 19 in The Essential Howard Gardner on Mind.*)*

I have not had the time (or, to be straightforward, the motivation) to review evidence for candidate intelligences—though others are welcome to engage in that demanding and time-consuming activity. I do believe that a case could be made for pedagogical intelligence—*the capacity to teach others and to adjust the content and the mode accordingly. And I've given license to others to speak informally of other intelligences—since the concept has entered the public domain, I have neither the right nor the need to be the ultimate arbiter. That said, before declaring a new intelligence, I encourage people to see whether the thoughts and actions can be adequately accounted for by the existing set of eight distinct intelligences.*

In the decade following the publication of Frames of Mind, *there was considerable discussion of the advantages of the approach, especially from educators, as well as considerable critique, especially from the psychological and psychometric community. But I was also struck by a number of recurring misunderstandings about what I had claimed and what it meant.*

Accordingly, I stepped back to consider the major problems—I called them "myths"—and to correct these misunderstandings by presenting what I called the complementary "realities." I indicated a few areas in which I myself bear some of the blame and would rephrase some of the claims. In addition, I provided some educational implications. I believe that this is my most reprinted, and possibly most translated and most cited, article.

I. BREAKING A DECADE OF SILENCE

A silence of a decade's length is sometimes a good idea. I published *Frames of Mind*, an introduction to the theory of multiple intelligences (MI theory), in 1983. Because I was critical of current views of intelligences within the discipline of psychology, I expected controversy among my fellow psychologists. I was not disappointed!

I was unprepared for the large and mostly positive reaction to the theory among educators. Naturally, I was gratified by this response and was stimulated thereby to undertake some projects in which the implications of MI theory were explored. I also took pleasure from—and was occasionally moved by—the many attempts to institute an MI approach to education in schools and classrooms. By and large, however, except for a few direct responses to criticisms, I did not speak up about new thoughts concerning the theory itself.

In the years since *Frames of Mind* was published, I have heard, read, and seen several hundred different interpretations of what MI theory is and how it can be applied in the schools. (See *Howard Gardner Under Fire*, Schaler, 2006.) Until now, I have been content to let MI theory take on a life of its own. As I saw it, I had issued an ensemble of ideas (or "memes") to the outer world, and I was inclined to let those memes fend for themselves. Yet, in light of my own readings and observations, I believe that the time has come for me to issue a set of new memes of my own.

In what follows, I discuss seven myths that have grown up about multiple intelligences; by putting forth seven complementary "realities," I attempt to set the record straight. Then, reflecting on my observations of MI experiments in the schools, I describe three primary ways in which education can be enhanced by a multiple intelligences perspective.

I make no attempt to isolate MI theory from MI practice. Multiple intelligences began as a theory but was almost immediately put to practical use. The back-and-forth between theory and practice has been ready, continuous, and, for the most part, productive.

II. MYTHS OF MULTIPLE INTELLIGENCES

Myth #1: Now that several intelligences have been identified (as of 1995), one can—and perhaps should—create several tests and secure seven scores.

Reality #1: MI theory represents a critique of psychometrics as usual. A battery of MI tests is inconsistent with the major tenets of the theory.

Comment: My concept of intelligences is an outgrowth of accumulating knowledge about the human brain and human cultures—it is not the result of a priori definitions nor of factor analyses of test scores. As such, it becomes crucial that intelligences be assessed in ways that are "intelligent-fair," in ways that examine the intelligence directly rather than through the lens of linguistic or logical intelligence (as ordinary paper-and-pencil tests typically do).

Thus, if one wants to look at spatial intelligence, one should allow an individual to explore a terrain for a while and see whether she can find her way around it reliably. Or if one wants to examine musical intelligence, one should expose an individual to a new melody in a reasonably familiar idiom and see how readily the person can learn to sing it, recognize it, transform it, and the like.

Assessing multiple intelligences is not a high priority in every setting. But when it is necessary or advisable to assess an individual's intelligences, it is best to do so in a comfortable setting with materials (and with cultural roles) that are familiar to that individual. These conditions are at variance with our general conception of testing, as a decontextualized exercise using materials that are by design unfamiliar; but there is no reason in principle why an "intelligence-fair" set of measures cannot be devised. The production of such useful tools has been our goal in various projects described elsewhere in this book.

Myth #2: An intelligence is the same as a domain or a discipline.

Reality #2: An intelligence is a new kind of construct, and it should not be confused with a domain or a discipline.

Comment: I must shoulder a fair part of the blame for the propagation of this myth. In writing *Frames of Mind,* I was not as careful as I should have been in distinguishing intelligences from other related concepts. As I have now come to understand, largely through interactions with my colleagues Mihaly Csikszentmihalyi and David Feldman, an intelligence is a biological and psychological potential; that potential is capable of being realized to a greater or lesser extent as a consequence of the experiential, cultural, and motivational factors that affect a person.

In contrast, a domain—one can also call it a discipline—is an organized set of activities within a culture, one typically characterized by a specific symbol system and its attendant operations. Any cultural activity in which individuals participate on more than a casual basis, and in which degrees of expertise can be identified and nurtured, should be considered as a domain. Thus, physics, chess, gardening, and rap music are all domains in Western culture. Any domain can be realized through the use of a variety of intelligences; thus the domain of musical performance involves bodily-kinesthetic and personal as well as musical intelligences. By the same token, a particular intelligence, like spatial intelligence, can be put to work in a myriad of domains, ranging from sculpture to sailing to *Minecraft* to neuroanatomical investigations.

Finally, the field consists of the set of individuals and institutions that judge the acceptability and creativity of products fashioned by individuals (with their characteristic intelligences) within established or new domains. Judgments of quality cannot be made apart from the operation of members of a field, though it is worth noting that both the members of a field and the criteria that they employ can and do change over time.

Myth #3: An intelligence is the same as a "learning style," a "cognitive style," or a "working style."

Reality #3: The concept of style designates a general approach that an individual can apply equally to every conceivable content. In contrast, an intelligence is a capacity, with its component processes, that is geared to a specific content in the world (like musical sounds or spatial patterns). (For further explication, please see Essay 10.)

Myth #4: MI theory is not empirical.

Variant of Myth #4: MI theory is empirical and has been disproved.

Reality #4: MI theory is based wholly on empirical evidence and can be revised on the basis of new empirical findings.

Comment: Anyone who puts forth Myth #4 cannot have opened—let alone read—*Frames of Mind*. Literally hundreds of empirical studies were reviewed in that book, and the actual intelligences were identified and delineated on the basis of empirical findings. The seven intelligences described in *Frames of Mind* represented my best-faith effort to identify mental abilities of a grain size that could be readily discussed and critiqued.

No empirically based theory is ever established permanently. All claims are at risk in the light of new findings. In the last decade, I have collected and reflected upon empirical evidence that is relevant to the claims of MI theory, 1983 version. Thus, work on the development in children of a "theory of mind," as well as the study of pathologies in which an individual loses a sense of social judgment, has provided fresh evidence for the importance and independence of interpersonal intelligence. In contrast, the findings of a possible link between musical and spatial thinking has caused me to reflect on the possible relations between faculties that have previously been thought to be independent. Many other lines of evidence could be mentioned here. The important point is that MI theory is—and should be—regularly reconceptualized in terms of new findings from the laboratory and from the field (see also Myth #7).

It is true that MI cannot be proved or disproved by experiments. It is a work of synthesis. (See Essays 24 and 26 in this volume, as well as Essays 17–21 in *The Essential Howard Gardner on Mind*.)

Myth #5: MI theory is incompatible with "g" (the technical term for general intelligence), with hereditarian accounts, or with environmental (cultural) contents.

Reality #5: MI theory questions not the *existence*, but the provenance and explanatory power of "g." By the same token, MI theory is neutral on the question of heritability of specific intelligences, instead underscoring the centrality of gene-environmental interactions.

Comment: Interest in "*g*" comes chiefly from those who are probing scholastic intelligence and those who traffic in the correlations among test scores. (Recently there have been interests in the possible neurophysiological underpinnings of "*g*," as well as the possible social consequences of "low *g*.") While I have been critical of much of the research in the "*g*" tradition, I do not consider the study of "*g*" to be scientifically taboo, and I am willing to accept the utility of "*g*" for certain theoretical purposes. My interest, obviously, centers on those intelligences and intellectual processes that are not covered by "*g*."

While a major animating force in psychology has been the study of the heritability of intelligence(s), my inquiries have not been oriented in this direction. I do not doubt that human abilities, and differences among humans, have a genetic base. Can any serious scientist question this in the era of the genome? And I believe that behavioral genetic studies, particularly of identical twins reared apart, can illuminate certain issues. However, along with most biologically informed scientists, I reject the "inherited versus learned" dichotomy and instead stress the interaction, from the moment of conception, between genetic and environmental factors.

Myth #6: MI theory so broadens the notion of intelligence that it includes all psychological constructs and thus vitiates the usefulness, and the usual connotation, of the term.

Reality #6: This statement is simply wrong. In my view, it is the standard definition of intelligence that *narrowly constricts* our view; it treats a certain form of scholastic performance as if it encompassed the range of human capacities and leads to disdain for those who happen not to be psychometrically bright. Moreover, I reject the distinction between talent and intelligence; in my view, what we call "intelligence" in the vernacular is simply a certain set of talents in the linguistic and/or logical-mathematical spheres.

Comment: MI theory is about the intellect, the human mind in its cognitive aspects. I believe that a treatment in terms of a number of semi-independent intelligences presents a more sustainable conception of human cognition than one that posits a single bell curve of intellect.

Note, however, that MI theory makes no claims to deal with issues beyond the intellect. MI theory is *not*, and does not pretend to be, about personality, will, morality, attention, motivation, and other much-bandied-about psychological constructs. Note, as well, that multiple intelligences theory is not connected to any set of morals or values. An intelligence can be put to an ethical or an antisocial use. Poet and playwright Johann Wolfgang von Goethe and Nazi propagandist Joseph Goebbels were both masters of the German language, but how different were the uses to which they put their linguistic prowess!

Myth #7: There is an 8th (or 9th or 10th) intelligence.

Reality #7: Not in my writings, as of now. But I am working on it.

Comment: For the reasons suggested above, I thought it wise not to attempt to revise the principal claims of multiple intelligences theory before the 1983 version of the theory had been debated. But recently, I have turned my attention to possible additions to the list. If I were to rewrite *Frames of Mind* today, I would add an 8th intelligence—the intelligence of the naturalist. (See Essay 19 in *The Essential Howard Gardner on Mind*.) It seems to me that the individual who is able to readily recognize flora and fauna, to make other consequential distinctions in the natural world, and to use this ability productively (in hunting, in farming, in biological science) is exercising an important intelligence not adequately encompassed in the initial list. Individuals like Charles Darwin and Barbara McClintock embody the naturalist's intelligence, and in our consuming culture, youngsters exploit their naturalist's intelligence as they make fine-grained discriminations among cars, sneakers, and/or hairstyles.

I have read in several secondary sources that there is a spiritual intelligence and, indeed, that I have endorsed a spiritual intelligence. That statement is not true. But there may indeed be an existential intelligence—the intelligence that enables human beings to pose and ponder big questions.

III. MESSAGES ABOUT MI IN THE CLASSROOM

If one were to continue adding myths to the list, a promising one would read:
There is a single educational approach based on MI theory.

I trust that I have made it clear that I do not subscribe to this myth. On the contrary, MI theory is in no way an educational prescription. There is always a gulf between psychological claims about how the mind works and educational practices and such a gulf is especially apparent in a theory that was developed without specific educational goals in mind. Thus, in educational discussions, I have always taken the position that educators themselves are in the best position to determine the uses to which MI theory can and should be put.

Indeed, contrary to much that has been written, MI theory does *not* incorporate a "position" on tracking, gifted education, interdisciplinary curricula, the layout of the school day, the length of the school year, or many other hot-button educational issues. I have tried to encourage certain "applied MI efforts," but in general my advice has echoed the traditional Chinese adage "Let a hundred flowers bloom." And often I have been surprised and delighted by the fragrance of some of these fledgling plants—for example, the use of a "multiple intelligences curriculum" in order to facilitate communication among youngsters drawn from different cultures, or the conveying of pivotal principles in biology or social studies through a dramatic performance designed and staged by students.

I have become convinced, however, that while there is no "right way" to conduct a multiple intelligences education, some current efforts go against the

Reflections on MI Myths and Messages

spirit of my formulation and embody one or more myths sketched above. Let me mention a few applications that have jarred me:

- *The attempt to teach all concepts or subjects using all the intelligences.* As I indicate below, most topics can be powerfully approached in a number of ways. But there is no point in assuming that every topic can be effectively approached in at least seven ways, and it is a waste of effort and time to attempt to do this.
- *The belief that it suffices, in and of itself, just to go through the motions of exercising a certain intelligence.* Thus, I have seen classes in which children are just encouraged to move their arms, or to run around, on the assumption that exercising one's body represents in itself some kind of MI statement. Don't read me as saying that exercise is a bad thing: it is not. But random muscular movements have nothing to do with the cultivation of the mind . . . and perhaps not even of the body!
- *The use of materials associated with an intelligence simply as background.* In some classes, children are encouraged to read or to carry out math exercises while music is playing in the background. Now, I myself like to work with music in the background. But unless I focus on the performance (in which case the composition is no longer serving solely as background), the music's function is unlikely to be different from that of a dripping faucet or a humming fan.
- *The use of intelligences primarily as mnemonic devices.* It may well be the case that it is easier to remember a list if one sings it, or even if one dances while reciting it. I have nothing against such aids to memory. However, these uses of the "stuff" of an intelligence are essentially trivial. What is not trivial—as I argue below—is to think musically, or to draw on some of the structural aspects of music in order to illuminate concepts like biological evolution or historical cycles.
- *The conflating of intelligences with other desiderata.* This practice is particularly notorious when it comes to the personal intelligences. *Interpersonal intelligence* has to do with understanding other people—but it is often misinterpreted as a license for cooperative learning or applied to individuals who are extroverted. *Intrapersonal intelligence* has to do with understanding oneself—but it is often distorted as a rationale for self-esteem programs or applied to individuals who are loners or introverted. Individuals who use the terms in this promiscuous way seem never to have read my own writings on intelligence.
- *The direct evaluation (or even grading) of intelligences, without regard to context or content.* Intelligences ought to be seen at work when individuals are carrying out productive activities that are valued in a culture or subculture. And that is how reporting of learning and mastery should take place, in general. I see little

point in grading individuals in terms of how "linguistic" or how "bodily-kinesthetic" they purportedly are; such a practice is likely to introduce a new and unnecessary form of tracking and labeling. As a parent (and as a supporter of education in the community in which I reside), I am interested in the uses to which children's intelligences are put; reporting should have this focus.

Note that it is reasonable, for certain purposes, to indicate that a child seems to have a relative strength in one intelligence and a relative weakness in another. However, these descriptions should be mobilized in order to help students perform better in meaningful activities and perhaps even to show that a labeling was premature or erroneous.

Having illustrated some problematic applications of MI theory, let me now indicate three more positive ways in which MI can be—and has been—used in the schools:

1. The cultivation of desired end-states. Schools should cultivate those skills and capacities that are valued in the community and in the broader society. Some of these desired roles are likely to highlight specific intelligences, including ones that have often been given short shrift in the schools. If, say, the community believes that children should be able to perform on a musical instrument, then the cultivation of musical intelligence toward that end becomes a value of the school. Similarly, emphasis on such end-states as considering the feelings of others, being able to plan one's own life in a reflective manner, or being able to find one's way around an unfamiliar terrain are likely to result in an emphasis on the cultivation, respectively, of interpersonal, intrapersonal, and spatial intelligences.

2. Approaching a concept, subject matter, or discipline in a variety of ways. Along with many other reformers, I am convinced that schools attempt to cover way too much material; superficial understandings (or non-understandings) are the inevitable result. It makes far more sense to spend a significant amount of time on key concepts, generative ideas, and essential questions, and allow students to become thoroughly familiar with these notions and their implications.

Once the decision has been made to dedicate time to particular items, it then becomes possible to approach those topics or notions in a variety of ways. Not necessarily in 7, let alone 70, ways, but in a number of ways that prove pedagogically appropriate for the topic at hand. Here is where multiple intelligences comes in. As I argue in "The Unschooled Mind" (Essay 16 in this volume), nearly every topic can be approached in a variety of ways, ranging from the telling of a story through a formal argument, to an artistic exploration, to some kind of hands-on experiment or simulation. Such pluralistic approaches should be encouraged.

When a topic has been approached from a number of perspectives, three desirable outcomes ensue. First of all, because children do not all learn in the same way, more children will be reached—I term this desirable state of affairs "multiple windows leading into the same room."

Second, students secure a sense of what it is like to be an expert when they observe that a teacher can represent knowledge in a number of different ways and that they, still students, are also capable of more than a single representation of a specified content.

Finally, since understanding can also be demonstrated in more than one way, a pluralistic approach opens up the possibility that students can demonstrate their new understandings—as well as their continuing difficulties—in ways that are comfortable for them and accessible to others.

Performance-based examinations and exhibitions are tailor-made for the foregrounding of a student's multiple intelligences.

3. The personalization of education. Without a doubt, one of the reasons that MI theory has attracted attention in the educational community is because of its ringing endorsement of an ensemble of propositions: we are not all the same; we do not all have the same kinds of minds; education works most effectively for most individuals, if these differences in mentation and strengths are taken into account rather than denied, deplored, or ignored.

I have always believed that the heart of the MI perspective—in theory and in practice—inheres in *taking extremely seriously the cognitive differences among human beings*. At the theoretical level, one acknowledges that all individuals cannot be profitably arrayed on a single intellectual dimension. At the practical level, one acknowledges that any uniform educational approach is likely to serve only a minority of children.

When I visit an "MI school," I look for evidence of personalization: evidence that all involved in the educational encounter take such differences among human beings extremely seriously; evidence that they construct curricula, pedagogy, and assessment insofar as possible in the light of these differences. All the MI posters, indeed all the references to me personally, prove of little avail if the youngsters continue to be treated in homogenized fashion. By the same token, whether or not members of the staff have even heard of MI theory, I would be happy to send my children or grandchildren to a school with the following characteristics: differences among youngsters are taken seriously; knowledge about differences is shared with children and parents; students gradually assume responsibility for their own learning; and materials that are worth knowing are presented in ways that afford each learner the maximum opportunity to master those materials and to show others (and themselves) what they have learned and understood.

* * *

I am often asked for my views about schools that are engaged in MI efforts. The implicit question may well be, "Aren't you upset by some of the applications that are carried out in your name?"

In truth, I do not expect that initial efforts to apply any new idea are going to be stunning. Human experimentation is slow, challenging, and filled with zigs and zags. And so I fully expect that the initial applications of any set of innovative ideas will sometimes be halfhearted, superficial, even wrong-headed.

For me the crucial question concerns what has happened in a school (or class) in the years after it's made an initial commitment to an MI approach. Often, the initiative will be long since forgotten—the fate, for better or worse, of most educational experimentation. Sometimes the school will get stuck in a rut, repeating the same procedures initiated on the first days, without having drawn any positive or negative lessons from this exercise. Needless to say, I am not happy with either of these outcomes.

I cherish an educational setting where discussions and applications of MI have catalyzed a more fundamental consideration of schooling: its overarching purposes, its conceptions of what a productive life will be like in the future, its pedagogical methods, and its educational outcomes, particularly in the context of the values of that specific community. Such discussions generally lead to more thoughtful schooling. Exchanges with other schools, and more extended forms of networking among MI enthusiasts (and critics), constitute important parts of this building process. If, as a result of these discussions and experiments, a more personalized education is the outcome, I'll conclude that the heart of MI theory has been embodied. And if this personalization is fused with a commitment to the achievement of worthwhile (and attainable) educational understandings for all children, then the basis for a powerful education has indeed been laid.

The MI enterprise is a continuing and changing one. There have emerged over the years new thoughts about the theory, new understandings and misunderstandings, and new applications, some very inspired, some less so. Especially gratifying to me has been the demonstration that this process is dynamic and interactive: no one, not even its creator, has a monopoly on MI wisdom or MI foolishness. Practice is enriched by theory, even as theory is transformed in the light of the fruits and frustrations of practice. The burgeoning of a community that takes MI issues seriously is not only a source of pride to me but also the best guarantor that the theory will continue to live in the years ahead

REFERENCE

Schaler, J. (Ed.). (2006). *Howard Gardner under fire: The rebel psychologist faces his critics*. Open Court.

ESSAY 10

"Multiple Intelligences" Are Not "Learning Styles"

It's been decades since I developed the notion of multiple intelligences. I have been gratified by the interest shown in this idea and the ways it has been used in schools, museums, and businesses around the world. But one unanticipated consequence has driven me to distraction—and that's the tendency of many people, including some whom I cherish, to credit me with the notion of "learning styles" or to confuse "multiple intelligences" with learning styles. It's high time to relieve my pain and to set the record straight.

Even before I wrote and spoke and wrote about "MI," the term "learning styles" was being bandied about in educational circles. The idea, reasonable enough on the surface, is that all children (indeed, all of us) have distinctive minds and personalities. Accordingly, it makes sense to find out about learners and to teach and nurture them in ways that are appropriate, that they value, and—above all—that are effective.

Two problems. First, the notion of "learning styles'" is itself not coherent. Those who use this term do not define the criteria for a style, nor where styles come from, nor how they are recognized/assessed/exploited/altered. Say that Johnny is said to have a learning style that is "impulsive." Does that mean that Johnny is impulsive about everything? How do we know this? What does this imply about teaching—should we teach "impulsively," or should we compensate by "teaching reflectively"? What about a learning style that is "right-brained" or visual or tactile? The same sorts of issues apply.

Problem #2: When researchers have tried to identify learning styles, teach consistently with those styles, and examine outcomes, there is no persuasive evidence that the learning style analysis produces more effective outcomes than a one-size-fits-all approach. Of course, the learning style analysis might have been inadequate. Or, even if it is on the mark, the fact that one intervention did not work does not mean that the concept of learning styles is fatally flawed; another intervention might have proved effective. Absence of evidence does not prove nonexistence of a phenomenon; it signals to educational researchers: "Back to the drawing board."

Here's my considered judgment about the best way to parse this lexical terrain:

Intelligence: We all possess the multiple intelligences. But we single out, as a strong intelligence, an area where the person has considerable computational power. Your ability to win regularly at a game highlighting spatial thinking signals strong spatial intelligence. Your ability to speak a foreign language well after just a few months of immersion signals strong linguistic intelligence.

Style or Learning Style: A style is a hypothesis of how an individual approaches the range of materials. If an individual has a "reflective style," he is hypothesized to be reflective about the full range of materials. We cannot assume that reflectiveness in writing necessarily signals reflectiveness in one's interaction with others. But if reflectiveness truly obtains across the board, educators should take that style seriously.

Senses: Sometimes people speak about a "visual" learner or an "auditory" learner. The implication is that some people learn through their eyes, others through their ears.

This notion is incoherent. Both spatial information and reading occur with the eyes, but they make use of entirely different cognitive faculties. Similarly, both music and speaking activate the ears, but again these are distinct cognitive faculties.

Recognizing this fact, the concept of intelligences does not focus on how linguistic or spatial information reaches the brain—via eyes, ears, hands, it doesn't matter. What matters is the power of the mental computer, the intelligence, that acts upon that sensory information once picked up.

These distinctions are consequential. My goal here is not to give a psychology or a physiology or a physics lesson, but rather to make sure that we do not fool ourselves and, just as important, that we do not shortchange our children. If people want to talk about "an impulsive style" or "a visual learner," that's their prerogative. But they should recognize that these labels may be unhelpful at best, and ill-conceived at worst.

In contrast, there is strong evidence that human beings have a range of intelligences and that strength (or weakness) in one intelligence does not predict strength (or weakness) in any others. All of us exhibit jagged profiles of intelligences. There are common sense ways of assessing our own intelligences, and if it seems appropriate, we can take a more formal test battery. And then, as teachers, parents, or self-assessors, we can decide how best to make use of this information.

As an educator, I draw three primary lessons for educators:

1. Individualize your teaching as much as possible. Instead of one size fits all, learn as much as you can about each student and teach each person in ways that seem comfortable and allow effective learning. Of course, this is easier to accomplish with smaller classes. But apps make it possible to individualize for everyone.

2. Pluralize your teaching. Teach important materials in several ways, not just one (e.g., through stories, works of art, diagrams, role-play). In this way you can reach students who learn in different ways. Also, by presenting materials in various ways, you convey what it means to understand something well. If you can only teach in one way, your own understanding is likely to be thin.
3. Drop the term "styles." It will confuse others, and it won't help either you or your students.

ESSAY 11

The Crystallizing Experience
Discovering an Intellectual Gift

Joseph Walters and Howard Gardner

One of the most rewarding aspects of new lines of research is the questions that they spawn. Since MI theory is well conveyed by the cases of individuals who are outstanding in a domain (the rare Pablo Picasso or Toni Morrison), the questions arises about the origins of these talents: were they inborn, prompted easily by early opportunities, or due to the pressures of avid parents or teachers?

To gain some clarity on this issue, with my colleague and friend the late Joseph Walters, I explored the notion of crystallizing experiences—the time and circumstances under which a talent emerges. We look at this issue both biographically (looking at esteemed creators in music, mathematics, and drawing) and contemporaneously (through interviews of master teachers). The resulting picture was complex, but pointed to the integral interaction of multiple factors.

According to standard mathematical history, Évariste Galois (1811–1832) was initially tutored at home by his mother and entered public school at the age of 11. Because his unpredictable disposition and stubborn attitude precluded any formal success as a student, he had to make the personal discovery of the world of mathematics on his own. Quite by chance, he came across a geometry textbook written by Legendre: "The book aroused his enthusiasm; it was not a textbook written by some hack, but the work of art composed by a creative mathematician. A single reading sufficed to reveal the whole structure of elementary geometry with a crystal clarity to the fascinated boy. He had mastered it" (Bell, 1965, p. 364).

Galois next turned to algebra and, finding no suitable textbook, began studying the works of master mathematicians Abel, Legrange, and Gauss in the original. After high school, Galois twice failed the entrance examination for the Polytechnique Institute in Paris (presumably for reasons other than mathematical ability); he was killed in a duel at the age of 21. Up to the day of his death, he pursued mathematics on his own. His collected papers, many of them published posthumously, served as the basis for a new field of mathematics now called Galois Theory.

The Crystallizing Experience

Composer Claude Debussy (1862–1918) began his formal study of music at the Conservatory in Paris at the age of 10, and by 14 he had won the prize for piano. During these first years he did not show any interest in composition, and in fact he hated his harmony class. This changed, however, when he began studying music theory with the young instructor Lavignac:

> Lavignac introduced Debussy to the music of Wagner. We read in the memoirs of [a fellow student] that one winter evening, after class time, the score was set out on the piano of the Overture to *Tannhauser*, the work which had recently created a notorious scandal at the Paris Opéra. Here is [Debussy] confronted for the first time with the work of the composer who was soon to exert the most powerful influence on his creative life. The experience was overwhelming.
>
> The young professor and his eager pupil became so absorbed in the novel Wagnerian harmonies that they forgot all sense of time. When they eventually decided to leave, they found themselves locked in and were obliged to grope their way out, arm in arm, down the rickety stairs and the dark corridors of the crumbling scholastic building. (Lockspeiser, 1962, p. 32)

As an apprentice porcelain decorator, Pierre-Auguste Renoir (1841–1919) demonstrated a facility with a paintbrush that earned him an adult's wages at the age of 12. Despite this useful technical proficiency, he showed little interest in or sensitivity to the aesthetic qualities of the visual arts. During his apprentice years he made regular trips to the Louvre to sketch the masterworks, but only with the intention of using these sketches in designing porcelain.

One day during his apprenticeship he had this experience:

> He made a momentous discovery, the sixteenth-century *Fontaine des Innocents*. "I stopped spell-bound," he said afterward. He gave up the idea of lunch in a restaurant, and instead bought some sausage at a nearby shop and returned to the fountain. He walked round and round it slowly, studying the group of statues from every angle. From that moment he felt a particular affinity with the sculptor Jean Goujon; his work possessed everything he loved: grace, solidity, and elegance, with the feeling of living flesh. "Goujon knew how to make drapery cling to figures. Until then I hadn't realized how drapery brings out the form." (Hanson, 1968, p. 15)

These three events—each crucial to the life of a particular creative individual—share a number of common features. In each case, the individual discovered an important and hitherto unappreciated aspect of a particular field of endeavor. In reading Legendre, Galois chanced upon a world of mathematical discovery, filled with challenges. Through Wagner's opera, Debussy came to realize the creative potential of composition in contrast to musical performance. Renoir's experience at the *Fontaine des Innocents* crystallized a notion of the power of sculpture to transcend the limited world of decoration.

The three anecdotes also share the fact that each event occurred in relative isolation, either apart from or prior to formal instruction. Galois read Legendre outside mathematics class. Debussy's discovery of Wagner occurred only after his first systematic study of composition. Renoir began art instruction when he was 18, several years after his experience at the Fontaine. In each case, these young individuals brought certain expectations, skills, or predispositions to the three events, something apparently not acquired through previous experiences with the domains, as if they had been "prepared" for those domains in some special way.

Following the work of our colleague David Feldman, we will designate these unusual encounters between a developing person and a particular field of endeavor as "crystallizing experiences." As we define them, such experiences involve remarkable and memorable contact between a person with unusual talent or potential and the materials of the field in which that talent will be manifested. As illustrated in our three examples, these crystallizing experiences may appear in advance of formal training. In any case, their dramatic nature focuses the attention of the individual on a specific kind of material, experience, or problem. Moreover, the individual is motivated to revisit these occasions for the indefinite future and to reshape his self-concept of the basis of these experiences.

Our interest in the existence and structure of these so-called crystallizing experiences has grown out of multiple intelligences theory (hereafter MI theory). According to this view all normal individuals are capable of at least seven independent forms of intellectual accomplishment. Initially, these intelligences exist as biological potentials; they are manifested in the opening years of life as the capacities to process certain kinds of information (e.g., patterned sounds) in certain kinds of ways (e.g., pitch analysis, phonological analysis). When the individual becmes capable of symbolic behavior, the intelligences are manifested in the deployment of various symbol systems (like natural language, drawing, mapmaking, religious customs, and the like). Still later in development, the intelligences form the core capacities involved in all cultural roles, ranging from parenting to toolmaking to the practice of science. (For further details about MI theory, see Essays 8–10.)

Under normal or reasonably enriched conditions, a human being can be expected to become involved with or achieve some measure of competence in each of these intellectual realms. Ultimate achievements, however, will vary greatly across individuals and across specific intelligences or groups of intelligences. One source of variance is probably genetic proclivity, but the earliness of exposure to a field and the amount of practice and training clearly make equally decisive contributions. One may achieve high skill in music through strong biological heritage (consider the example of some autistic children), through intensive training (the Suzuki method) and, most happily, through the epigenetic interaction of these features, as in the case of Mozart.

A crystallizing experience, then, is the overt reaction of an individual to some quality or feature of a domain: the reaction yields an immediate but also a long-term change in that individual's concept of the domain, his performance in it, and his view of himself. We restrict the term "crystallizing experience" to those experiences that exhibit the set of indices just described. Of course, it is not possible to identify a crystallizing experience at the moment of its occurrence. Only retrospectively, after the individual's behavior in the postcrystallizing period has been observed, is it possible to single out an experience as having crystallized ensuing activities.

In our view, crystallizing experiences can take various forms. For example, some crystallizing experiences, which we term "initial," occur early in life and signal a general affinity between an individual and some large-scale domain in his culture. An example would be Galois's discovery of the excitement involved in mathematical proof. Other crystallizing experiences, which we term "refining," occur well after an individual has undergone an initial attraction to a domain. In these refining cases an individual discovers a particular instrument, style, or approach within a field to which he or she is especially attuned. Both the Renoir and the Debussy episodes might be thought of as refining crystallizing experiences.

The theory of multiple intelligences does not prescribe the existence or the importance of crystallizing experiences. But it does suggest that such experiences may well occur across a variety of domains; moreover, it provides an explanation for why they may exert powerful, long-term effects on the individual. It is consistent with the theory that many (if not most) individuals will experience the affective phase of such experiences; however, unless an individual is "at promise" within a particular intelligence or domain, it is unlikely that the experiences will have a lasting effect and result in an ultimate redefinition of self.

In short, then, crystallizing experiences are neither necessary nor sufficient for ultimate achievement within the field; yet at the same time, they are a useful construct for explaining how certain talented individuals may first discover their area of giftedness and then proceed to achieve excellence within the field. Our present investigation of the construct of crystallizing experiences thus helps to assess the utility of multiple intelligences and brings that theory into contact with such broader issues as the nature of giftedness and the achievement of talent.

Several empirical questions can be asked of the construct of crystallizing experiences. One set of questions concerns the commonness of such experiences: For example, are they typical, or quite atypical? And if they are typical, are they restricted to those with intellectual gifts, or are they found throughout the population? Another set of questions concerns the possible explanations for such crystallizing experiences: Why do they occur, how do they occur, and what are their consequences?

Finally, a set of questions arises from the perspective of multiple intelligences. We are interested in determining how crystallizing experiences may differ across the various intelligences; for instance, do they appear in childhood?

In this essay, we undertake an empirical investigation of the phenomenon of crystallizing experiences and then offer our own thoughts about why this singular kind of event may unfold in the manner that it does.

Of course, there are other possible approaches to the issue of crystallizing experiences. One is to challenge the legitimacy of these reports. For example, to researchers who believe that the differences in achievements are due primarily to the amount of training received (cf. Bloom, 1985), the crystallizing experiences, as in the vignettes of Galois or Renoir, might be treated as anomalies, exaggerations, or retrospective justifications or rationalizations. In this view, the example taken from Debussy begs the question of talent versus training, because here the crystallizing experience appears after a considerable amount of training.

To illustrate this point, we can contrast the multiple intelligences (MI) perspective with a strict training theory. According to the training explanation, highly talented children like Mozart are anomalies. One cannot diagnose talent in a child until he has received a reasonable amount of training; and even then, what appears in the child's behaviors are manifestations not of inborn "talent" or "gift" but rather of the effectiveness of a particular set of training experiences.

In the MI view, on the other hand, gifted children are a special variety of human beings: children with a high degree of "raw" or unmediated intelligence in a specific field should under certain circumstances demonstrate evidence of that intelligence even before they are engaged in any kind of training regimen. In contrast to the training account, MI predicts a small but measurable number of such gifted children in each of the fields identified.

With our own approach to crystallizing experiences and these alternative views as a background, we undertook an empirical investigation designed to assess the commonness of crystallizing experiences and to cull information on the ways in which they may occur.

We used two sources of data in our study. First, we reviewed the biographical and autobiographical literature in the three aforementioned domains: mathematics, music, and the visual arts. A total of 25 people in these three fields were chosen, and the available biographical materials were reviewed for each subject. We recorded the experiences that we considered crystallizing, as well as any other evidence documenting a subject's unusual talent as a child. Finally, any information about the nature of talents outside the domain, including success or failure in school or other areas, was noted as well. In the second part of the study, we included interviews with teachers of especially talented students in the same three areas.

THE BIOGRAPHIES

Musicians

Our study indicates that 10 of the 11 distinguished musical composers and performers included in this review were either very talented as children or demonstrated crystallizing experiences. Three subjects who were recognized

The Crystallizing Experience

as talented while still young did not have crystallizing experiences: Mozart, Beethoven, and Mendelssohn announced their talent very early, but the crystallizing of that talent apparently occurred without fanfare or self-recognition.

Mozart and Beethoven came from musical families, and their total immersion in the world of music can be attributed to the efforts of others, but this is not always the case. For example, Mendelssohn's parents provided the opportunity for private music lessons, but they had him tutored in other subjects as well. Later he studied law at university and pursued music only as a sideline. Indeed, for the affluent and privileged Mendelssohn Bartholdy family, musicianship and the life of the stage were considered degrading.

Pianist Arthur Rubinstein also came from a nonmusical family. He announced his talent in what might be considered a crystallizing experience at the age of three, when the family purchased a piano:

> The drawing room became my paradise. Half in fun, half in earnest, I learned to know the keys by their names and with my back to the piano I would call the notes of any chord, even the most dissonant one. From then on it became mere "child's play" to master the intricacies of the keyboard, and I was soon to play any tune that caught my ear. (Rubinstein, 1973)

The family recognized the extraordinary talent of their son and obtained an audition with Joseph Joachim, a renowned 19th-century musician, who guided his career and obtained patron support for him. It appears, then, that childhood talent, as exemplified by Mendelssohn and Rubinstein, can be recognized even by parents who are untrained in music.

The crystallizing experiences that appear in the biographies of the musicians are of two distinct types. First, there are the earliest experiences with music, experiences that reveal a raw talent. For instance, violinist Yehudi Menuhin's reaction at age 3 to the violin sound of Louis Persinger or composer Stravinsky's response to Glinka's orchestra both fall into this category. The anecdote reported in the Rubinstein quotation might also be considered as an illustration, although it does not have the same sense of immediate insight. Finally, opera composer Richard Wagner's reaction as a teenager to the singing of *Fidelio* can be included in this category as well, even though he was appreciably older. These experiences suggest that the minds of these musicians were prepared in some way for the experience of hearing the violin, the orchestra, or the voice.

A second type of crystallizing experience occurs later in development and presupposes an individual who is already attuned to the area of music. In this particular case, the "refining crystallizing experience" guides the individual to *that area of the musical domain* in which his strongest talents or deepest inclinations may lie.

In the cases we studied, individuals who were already musically inclined discovered that composition—or a certain kind of composition—was the appropriate form of involvement in music. The experience of Debussy in transcribing the opera of Wagner and the reaction of Stravinsky to harmony and counterpoint are good examples of this form of crystallizing experience. In each case, the crystallizing experience involves the recognition of the complexities of composition. The reaction is not that of the initiating experience of early youth, in which the raw intelligence encounters the domain itself for the first time. Rather, one sees at work a more mature problem-solving faculty that perceives subtle distinctions or potentials in the materials of the domain. This refining experience also serves as a revelation to the artist, but in a way that is more sophisticated than the earlier initiating experience.

As a young adult, composer and conductor Pierre Boulez recognized in the music of Messiaen a "new language": "Here was the music of our time, a language with unlimited possibilities. No other language was possible. It was the most radical revolution since Monteverdi, for all the familiar patterns were now abolished. With it music moved out of the world of Newton and into the world of Einstein" (Peyser, 1976, pp. 25–26). Boulez had been trained in standard analyses of harmony and counterpoint, but his understanding of these dimensions changed when he heard Olivier Messiaen's compositions. In this case, we see the reaction of the relatively mature artist to the more serious and profound deliberations characteristic of the art form. According to our analysis, these insights reflect not the raw intelligence or even manipulation of the symbol system, but rather the skills central to the domain or subdomain of the adult culture.

It appears, then, that all crystallizing experiences are not the same. Instead, they reflect the level of development in the artist (or scientist) in the particular domain(s) to which they are attracted.

The developmental gap between the young Menuhin and the older Boulez provides a picture of a spectrum of experiences that range from first contacts in childhood—the more dramatic crystallizing experience of the untrained but extremely talented individual—to the more gradual decisions and reflections of young adult artists and scientists.

On several counts, composer Franz Joseph Haydn emerges as an anomaly. He received no individual training. He sang in the Vienna Boys Choir, but during that time he received no systematic instruction. His talent for musical composition developed over a period of many years. Indeed, his brother Michael was initially considered to be the better composer. However, unlike Michael, Franz Joseph became one of the titans of the classical era and greatly influenced both Mozart and Beethoven.

Mathematicians

Note: A similar analysis was performed for young mathematicians and visual artists. Here we just present a few highlights.

The Crystallizing Experience

Born to a poor family in India, mathematician Srinivasa Ramanujan showed his facility with numbers and interest in mathematics in elementary school. His obsessive devotion to mathematics, however, made him a poor student overall. He failed to complete even one year at university, even though he had received a scholarship for his mathematical skills. Leaving university, he took up a job as a clerk and continued his mathematical research on his own, publishing several papers and receiving some encouragement from local mathematicians. At the age of 25, he wrote a letter to the leading English mathematician G. H. Hardy in which he announced several of his discoveries. Hardy was so impressed with the originality and insight of the work that he secured a scholarship for Ramanujan at Cambridge, and they collaborated there until Ramanujan's tragic death at the age of 32. Ramanujan was the first Indian elected to the Royal Academy, receiving that accolade at the age of 28. Ramanujan's crystallizing experience occurred while reading a mathematics textbook.

It was in 1903 on a momentous day for Ramanujan, that a friend of his secured for him the loan of a copy of Carr's Synopsis of Pure Mathematics. Through the new world thus opened to him, Ramanujan went ranging with delight. It was this book that awakened his genius. He set himself to establish the formulae given therein. As he was without the aid of other books, each solution was a piece of research so far as he was concerned.

He first devised some methods for constructing magic squares. Then he branched off to Geometry, where he took up the squaring of the circle and succeeded so far as to get a result for the length of the equilateral circumference of the earth which differed from the true length only by a few feet. He (then) turned his attention to Algebra, where he obtained several new series.

These feats are even more remarkable when considered in the light of the text that Ramanujan was working with. G. H. Hardy noted:

> I suppose that the book is substantially a summary of Carr's coaching notes. If you were a pupil of Carr, you worked through the appropriate sections of the *Synopsis*. It contains the enunciations of 6165 theorems, systematically and quite scientifically arranged, with proofs that are often little more than cross-references and are decidedly the least interesting part of the book. All this is exaggerated in Ramanujan's famous notebooks (which contain practically no proofs at all), and any student of the notebooks can see that Ramanujan's ideal of presentation had been copied from Carr's. (Hardy, 1940, p. 7)

Ramanujan's experiences with Carr's text prove relevant to our discussion in two ways. First, despite its unusual pedagogical style and a minimum of explanation, this book revealed to Ramanujan the world of mathematics; his intellect filled in the gaps. Second, the book had a profound impact on the manner in which Ramanujan pursued the field as an adult. In other words, Ramanujan's interest in mathematics was "crystallized" via Carr's *Synopsis* and can be said to have been stunted by it as well.

Hardy's own crystallizing experience was as different from Ramanujan's as was his cultural background and schooling. Whereas Ramanujan was self-educated in a small village in India, Hardy was thoroughly trained in the English elite school system. Although an excellent mathematics student throughout school, he did not develop a passionate devotion to the subject until he worked with a particular professor at Cambridge. That experience crystallized his sense of the subject matter as well as his view of himself as a "real mathematician with sound mathematical ambitions" (Hardy, 1967, pp. 23–24).

The aforementioned relationship of crystallizing experience to developmental level reappears in mathematics. The earlier "initiating" crystallizing experiences ushered in the rapid development of certain talented subjects in which they reached adult levels at an earlier age (Ramanujan, Rubinstein, and Menuhin). With the older children and young adults, on the other hand, the "refining" crystallizing experiences reflect an interaction between an already blossoming talent and a set of more subtle, but crucial, distinctions within the domain (Debussy and Boulez). In some cases, a prodigious talent together with a highly supportive initial environment removes the opportunity (or the need) for a crystallizing experience in childhood (Mozart). One finds examples of autodidacts in mathematics as well as music (Haydn; Ramanujan).

Finally, in both domains, the nature and extent of crystallizing experiences appears closely related to the environment in which the talented child is raised. Crystallizing experiences prove more likely in those environments in which the domain is not stressed or where it is underutilized—Ramanujan serves as an illustration.

But Hardy and Debussy suggest a more complex explanation. In these two cases, the domain was thoroughly supported in childhood—Hardy in the elite English schools and Debussy at the Conservatoire—and consequently the crystallizing experiences occurred closer to adulthood, as the subjects developed new insights into their respective domains. For instance, Debussy's crystallizing reaction to the "scandalous" music of Wagner was in part a response to the conservative and perhaps uncreative atmosphere that permeated his theory and composition instruction. Finally, those environments that provided strong, immediate experiences in the domain from an early age (Mendelssohn, Mozart) were least likely to produce crystallizing experiences.

Visual Artists

The pattern of childhood talent and crystallizing experiences that cuts across the domains of music and mathematics does not recur in the domain of the visual arts.

One possible reason for this distinction between the visual arts and the other two domains arises from this consideration: It is much more likely for an artist to take up the career during young adulthood than for a musician

The Crystallizing Experience

or mathematician. Van Gogh and Matisse come to mind as examples. In our interviews with teachers, we asked a distinguished and extremely knowledgeable college mathematics professor if he knew of any students who entered the mathematics program after a career in another field. He answered, "It probably happened twice in the history of mathematics. I really don't know of any examples of that." We asked the same question of the director at a college of art. His response was quite different:

> In this school this year we only took 23 students out of high school in the whole student body of about 600 students. We tend to have older students. It is a tough school to get into out of high school, simply because if we let them in they flounder . . .
>
> (Do you find people who quit a job in order to come to school for art training?) Yes, all the time. One of my staff members was an attorney. He is now an artist. He was in his 30s or early 40s and he made a complete turnaround. It took him a long time of real struggle to get anywhere. But now he is an artist of real merit.

From one perspective, it might appear that our view of crystallizing experiences is invalidated by these findings from the visual arts. Yet, paradoxically, we believe that *these findings may reinforce a principal tenet of MI theory*. Our survey suggests the following: Rather than development occurring in a parallel fashion in every domain, an experience critical in certain domains—for example, the early emergence of the talented mathematician or the musician—proves relatively unimportant in another cultural domain, the visual arts.

Just why this is so is difficult to say. It may be that these three domains are viewed in a particular way by Western culture and may, in fact, be viewed differently by other cultures. For example, in Bali it might turn out that the visual arts are heavily stressed in early life, and that consequently there are more crystallizing experiences and more examples of prodigious behavior in that domain. It is also possible to imagine a society in which logical-mathematical precocity is of no relevance, or even actively discouraged, in which case one would not expect to find rapid development in that domain.

Another quite different explanation suggests that the mental processes involved in the visual (or plastic) arts develop at a different rate and hence are less susceptible to the one-time crystallizing experiences than are the quickly developing and more digitalized processes entailed in other domains. Mathematics and music, for example, are both more self-contained, more likely to develop in relative isolation from the real world, and relatively digital and notational. In contrast, according to this analysis, the visual arts relate from the first to the external world, and are not in any sense self-contained; also, digital or notational processes do not play any role in the visual arts, which inherently entail symbol systems that are not discrete but rather continuous and "non-notational." (Comment in 2024: Of course, the previous statement is no longer true—much of contemporary art involves digital production and display.)

THE INTERVIEWS

As a source of data, the biographies have several significant shortcomings. First, biographies are often derived from the reminiscences of the subject and the subject's friends after a successful career. The biographies also restrict our exploration in that they provide no opportunity for cross-examination.

It was for these reasons, then, that we supplemented the investigation of biographies with interviews of master teachers in these three domains. We hoped that intensive conversations with master teachers would provide an important supplement (and perhaps a needed corrective) to information culled from the genre of written biography.

During the interviews, we posed a large set of questions. We sampled broadly for two reasons: (a) our interest in the issues surrounding the discovery and development of talent in general; and (b) our desire not to focus directly on crystallizing experiences. (As will become evident, we succeeded quite well in masking our goal of eliciting crystallizing experiences from these teachers!) Among the questions we posed were whether or not teachers perceived some of their students to be more talented than others; if they could recognize that talent quickly and easily; what skills co-occurred with the talent in question; and, of course, whether or not the teachers had observed or been informed of any crystallizing experiences.

We spoke to teachers who had worked with gifted students. The music and art teachers were affiliated with private schools or colleges for music and art. The two teachers of mathematics were professors at a university. The interviews lasted about 1 hour; they were recorded and later transcribed. The quotations here are taken from those tapes with only minor editing to maintain continuity. Because the teachers responded to the interview candidly—even when the questions concerned their own development—we refer to them only through their specialties: violin, cello, piano, photography, number theory, and topology.

CRYSTALLIZING EXPERIENCES

The teachers did not report crystallizing experiences on the part of their students. Although this finding was unanticipated, we can offer an explanation in retrospect. In the biographies, crystallizing experiences were most frequent in precisely those cases where there was little or no teaching or where there was an early discovery of the domain before teachers had been contacted. Even in cases where crystallizing experiences occurred relatively late, the individuals were frequently alone and engaged in self-instruction at the time of their occurrence. It may also be that individuals themselves do not recognize a crystallizing experience fully at the time it happens; only in retrospect do individuals become aware of it. Finally, crystallizing experiences are by their

The Crystallizing Experience

nature intensely personal and private: adolescent students may be reluctant to share these with others, even trusted parents and teachers.

Although the teachers did not observe crystallizing experiences in their students, most reported them in discussing the development of their own careers:

> *Photographer:* When I was growing up I had very little exposure to art; we visited the Metropolitan Museum maybe once. Then, in the Navy, I was lying in my bunk reading the book *Lust for Life,* the novelization of Van Gogh's life, and I noticed that the pictures in the back were in the Museum of Modern Art in New York, and since we were in dry dock in the Brooklyn Navy Yard at the time, I jumped up and went to see them.
>
> I remember that day like yesterday—the weather, the people on the street. I guess you could say it was an "epiphany." When I left the Navy, I tried to get a job as a guard in an art museum because I had been a payroll guard in the Navy.
>
> *Topologist:* My father was an interesting person mathematically. He had a great deal of facility, although he was no mathematician. He had worked out for himself a number of interesting "tricks" and I can give you an example of one. You would write a number and he would write after it immediately another number. When you added the two, the answer was divisible by 37. I remember him doing this kind of trick and being very impressed by it and being very curious about how it could work. I was attracted to this because it was a completely unposed problem, not a problem in a book. He did this trick, and he didn't have any training—how did he figure it out? I think that kind of experience was probably very important to me at the time.

Though quite different, these two experiences share a common quality—they serve as a reference point in the individual's perception of his development as an artist or mathematician. For the photographer, the situation involved the first contact with the world of art. Its impact was quite immediate and profound, and we might suppose that he was "prepared" in some way for this experience.

In the second case, what was crystallized was the topologist's appreciation of mathematics as a field of inquiry. As a field, mathematics contains many problems that have no apparent solution; problems posed in texts, on the other hand, inevitably do have solutions, and their study is not representative of the highest and most creative aspects of the field.

The teachers also discussed a phenomenon that might also be interpreted along crystallizing lines—choosing the instrument in the domain (e.g., violin, photography, or topology). We learned that the teachers described this choice as if it were predetermined in some way—as if they had to discover the instrument most appropriate for them. This finding suggested that talent may be tuned not only to a domain but, more specifically, to a particular approach or instrument within that domain.

These early experiences of "choosing an instrument" can be considered fine-tuning in the domain—finding a niche within the field. In this case, the teacher serves as an important aid in this search for the instrument. In fact, the teachers report that an important part of the job is to provide the right kinds of experiences that help their students choose wisely.

At the same time, however, several of these experiences sound very much like crystallizations as we have formulated them. In these cases, the teacher does not play an important role. Both Yehudi Menuhin and the violinist in our interviews reported that the sound of the violin was different for them as young children, before any formal instruction. In these cases, hearing the violin crystallizes the sense of the individual as a musician at a time antecedent to formal training. We consider these types of revelations to be legitimate examples of crystallizing experiences.

These examples of choosing an instrument recall our distinction between initiating crystallizing experiences and refining experiences. That is, the choice of the instrument does not serve to crystallize the youngster to the domain per se, but rather points to the way in which that child is likely to enter the domain. So it is a crystallizing experience at the time that we usually find the initiating experiences, but it has more of the flavor of the refining experiences generally found later on.

THE ISSUE OF TALENT

As a part of our interest in crystallizing experiences, we talked to teachers about how they judged the talents of their students—what specific things made some students special, how quickly the teachers could make such a distinction, what specifically marked the differences among students, and so on. We were particularly interested in determining whether the teachers would report simply that children are talented, or whether such differences were merely a matter of hours of practice.

The answers prove quite instructive. On the one hand, the teachers described, quite articulately, differences among their students that may be attributed to differences in talent. At the same time, those teachers *often denied outright that there was such a quality that operated independent of their teaching*. For example:

> *Violinist:* You can notice the very great musical feeling sometimes from the very beginning. A student can play a little Bach duet, just beautifully, with such grace and taste and (still) be quite elementary

(in terms of technique). I heard a tape recently of an 8-year-old girl who plays so beautifully, so musically. Now, she is not particularly advanced for 8 years old by our standards today, but in her playing there is such a feeling of her whole being; and just so free, and such expression in it, that I thought on hearing the tape, "Hmm, this is a remarkable child."

Here's the testimony of another musician:

Cellist: I think that one of the most important things is cultivating a love of music in the young person. If you start them very young and train and develop them slowly, then you have the time to set up the technique but at the same time to develop the love of playing and the love of music, and that in the long run will make for a child who wants to play well who will develop a musical soul from that.

Number theorist: (Question: In mathematics, what can't be taught?) Anything can be taught! The difference is strictly in terms of motivation. To be a mathematician you have to "do math" 16 hours a day.

These quotations suggest contrasting perspectives on eventual success in a domain—a special quality, aptitude, or predilection in the learner versus a disciplined motivation derived in part from well-managed teaching. But we found several teachers who reported both perspectives in the same interview. Of course, the two perspectives are not logically contradictory; success in a field could result from a combination of natural aptitude and good teaching. However, most teachers did not appear to embrace this compromise position and maintained instead either one pole or the other.

There is an explanation for the apparent inconsistency in the teachers' point of view. Good teachers have a high investment in the act of teaching and in its role in the process of the development of the mature artist or mathematician. They believe—perhaps they must believe—that teaching makes a difference. At the same time, however, they may well actively seek out those students who display unique qualities or talents within the field, even before the instruction has begun. This is equally important to the teaching process: for one thing, students with these special qualities are more likely to achieve success, but perhaps more importantly, they are more likely to continue the development of their talent over a longer period of time.

The teachers, and perhaps especially those in music, consider the time they spend an investment in a particular student, and they are very careful to select those students who will not squander that investment. They make this choice on the basis of motivation and aptitude. Consequently, the teachers can discuss aptitude in detail, and they can articulate specific skills and behaviors that they look for as indicators of aptitude. These concerns lead to a paradoxical situation: the teacher can, on the one hand, claim that anything can be taught to anyone who is properly motivated, while at the same time actively seeking out certain kinds of students to receive that teaching.

In choosing students, the teachers look for several very specific traits that in their experience are related to eventual success. Consider this testimony:

> *Number theorist:* Yet another interesting trait is "artful dodging." Some people, when they run into a problem, persistently remain there even if they are getting no closer to a solution. This is counterproductive. Others, if they are "artful dodgers," know enough to try something else, or to drop the problem, or to contrive the skill that they lack. This is much more adaptive and productive.

And a cellist who described the need for "love of playing" also looked for the following skills in young children:

> The talented generally have strong, flexible fingers. This is a real key to the whole of playing. The child has to be strong enough to push the string down, but at the same time the hand is still flexible so that you can get a beautiful sound. I can just tell when a student comes in, in the first month of lessons, I can tell by the feel of their hand whether it is going to be easy or hard for them.

The music teachers also mentioned the ability to handle different kinds of problems (e.g., key, rhythm, fingering) at the same time, as well as the ability to process information quickly (especially in sight-reading). The mathematicians mentioned the ability to identify and focus on one particular quality of a problem. So, even as they talked in general terms about "lyricism" or "insightfulness" or "vulnerability," the teachers also talked about specific skills like intonation, craft, and problem-solving. It does not appear that talent as described by these teachers resides strictly in either the mysterious intangibles, nor does it reside in the technical faculties. Rather, talent comprises both factors; and perhaps they cannot and should not be separated.

Motivation is yet another feature to which teachers pay careful attention—the love of playing in a young musician, or the desire to do mathematics 16 hours a day. To some degree, motivation is outside the direct control of the teachers, and so they are very careful to evaluate this trait in their students; but at the same time, they feel that motivation can be instilled, and to some degree they can affect it. In contrast, talent as defined in our culture is entirely outside the control of the teachers, and again, this probably is responsible in part for the unenthusiastic response of the teachers to the construct of "talent."

Although teachers claim it is important to have motivation, and that this is within the students' (if not the teachers') control, *the theory of multiple intelligences suggests a different perspective*. Specifically, turning the usual formula on its head, we propose that individuals are, or become, motivated to the extent that they have (or can readily acquire) some facility within a particular domain. That is, a talented mathematician would be more likely to do mathematics 16 hours a day because of a basic understanding of the domain and the intriguing problems that it presents than the person who does not have that talent and does not understand the domain in that way. Motivation, then, would be the consequence of talent rather than the explanation of it.

IN CONCLUSION

In the biographies, we found that crystallizing experiences do occur frequently, but there are noticeable and probably important differences across individuals and across domains. For one thing, the nature of a crystallizing experience depends on the age of the subject. The experiences of younger subjects are closely related to unmediated or "raw" intelligence; we called these "initiating crystallizing experiences." With older children and young adults, the crystallizing experience reflects a mediated contact with the domain, in which some training in the materials of the domain is presupposed—Debussy's reaction to Wagner or Hardy's response to his Cambridge mathematics professor illustrate what we have called "refining crystallizing experiences."

Our results also suggest that crystallizing experiences differ across domains as well. They are more prevalent in mathematics and music than in the visual arts. Perhaps in the visual arts individuals are "crystallized" over a longer period of time, through repeated visits to museums, for instance. In that case, the memorable experience of Renoir stands as an exception and the more gradual development of Cézanne as the rule. Or it may be that visual artists are less willing to share their experiences with teachers and appreciate the crystallizing experience only in retrospect.

The domains also differed with respect to the early appearance of talent. Music and mathematics were both characterized by a large number of talented children, whereas the visual arts were not. Similarly, music and mathematics appear to require disciplined training during childhood, whereas the visual arts typically do not. We have considered the possibility that these differences may reflect contrasting cultural values about the various domains (e.g. early mathematics being valued more than early visual art in Western culture), but they may also reflect the differences intrinsic to the domain (the degree to which the domain is cut off from others and can be negotiated in a manner independent of real-world experiences).

Some of these findings from the biographies were affirmed by our interviews with the teachers: the requirement of early training or learning in mathematics and music but not the visual arts; the personal experiences of the teachers in discovering their own talents; the manner in which training keeps pace with the general move from raw intelligence to mediated intelligence.

However, other points emerged during the interviews that did not appear in the biographies. Tellingly, *the teachers spoke a great deal about motivation in contrast to talent*. This perspective can be seen as either a challenge to the theory of multiple intelligences or, as we have suggested, a call for supplementary data. Also, aside from the choice of the particular instrument, the teachers reported no observations of crystallizing experiences in their students, although they did report them from their personal development. We have offered several retrospective explanations for this apparent discrepancy.

How, then, does our perspective fare in accounting for the phenomenon of crystallizing experiences? Our analysis strongly suggests that crystallizing experiences are a genuine phenomenon, although one that also confirms revealing differences across domains. It would be difficult to maintain that these experiences are accidental or artifactual, because this implies that they should occur in the same fashion and with the same frequency across domains and across developmental levels.

Second, it appears that the crystallizing experience is a fragile phenomenon that occurs principally when circumstances combine inborn talent, self-teaching, and proper exposure to a set of materials in a particular way.

Finally, in those circumstances where there is a strong predisposition to excel with a given material, and where there are some but not exceptional opportunities, crystallizing experiences are most likely to occur.

In this essay, we have stressed the kinds of experiences that may befall individuals of indisputable talent and that help to set them on their life course. In conclusion, we raise the question about whether crystallizing experiences are indeed just a purview of the most gifted, or whether they may occur in more mundane ways with individuals who are closer to the norm.

The present study fails to cast light on this question. Still, it would seem to be good pedagogy—if not just good common sense—to treat all children as if they have the potential for crystallizing experiences, and to expose them at an early age to materials that may motivate them to explore a domain. It may turn out that there are far more gifted" children than could have been anticipated from the unplanned encounters that until now have been the chief locus for crystallizing experiences.

REFERENCES

Bell, E. (1965). *Men of mathematics*. Simon & Schuster.
Bloom, B. (1985). *Developing talent in young people*. Random House.
Hanson, L. (1968). *Renoir: The man, the painter, and his world*. Dodd, Mead.
Hardy, G. (1940). *Ramanujan*. Cambridge University Press.
Hardy, G. (1967). *A mathematician's apology*. Cambridge University Press.
Lockspeiser, E. (1962). *Debussy: His life and mind*. Cassell.
Peyser, J. (1976). *Boulez*. Schirmer.
Rubinstein, A. (1973). *My young years*. Knopf.

EDUCATIONAL EXPERIMENTS IN THE SPIRIT OF MULTIPLE INTELLIGENCES

ESSAY 12

MI Around the World

After decades of considering the educational implications of MI theory, I have concluded that two are paramount. First, educators who embrace MI theory should take differences among individuals seriously; as much as possible, they should craft education so that each child can be reached in the optimal manner. The advent of personal computers makes such individuation easier than ever before; what was once possible only for the wealthy (personal tutoring) is now available to millions of learners around the world.

Second, any discipline, idea, skill, or concept of significance should be taught in several ways. These ways should, by argument, activate different intelligences or combinations of intelligences. Such an approach yields two enormous dividends. First, a plurality of approaches ensures that the teacher (or teaching material) will reach more children. Second, a plurality of approaches signals to learners what it means to have a deep, rounded understanding of a topic. Only individuals who can think of a topic in several ways have a thorough understanding of that topic; those whose understanding is limited to a single instantiation have a fragile grasp.

THE MI MEME

But, of course, I do not own MI theory. To borrow Richard Dawkins's term, MI is a meme—a unit of meaning, created at a certain place and time, that has spread widely in the past decades. Initially it spread around educational circles in the United States. But soon it ventured abroad, and it became an item of discussion and application not only in schools, but in homes, museums, theme parks, places of worship, the workplace, and the playground.

Once the meme of MI was created and began to spread in the United States, the question was whether it would be short-lived, like so many educational fads, or whether it would have a longer half-life, and if so, how broadly and in what forms.

I was both surprised and gratified to see the extent to which the meme spread. The MI meme was probably spread chiefly by books—translations of my books and more practically oriented books like those authored in English by Thomas Armstrong, Linda and Bruce Campbell, Tom Hoerr, Mindy Kornhaber, David Lazear, and many others.

In 1995 the publication of Daniel Goleman's book *Emotional Intelligence* catalyzed an unexpected turn of events. Goleman's book, which generously cited my work, had a worldwide influence unequaled by any similar work in recent memory—and qualitatively greater than any of my writings. His ideas were more accessible than mine, and often our works were confused with each other. In fact, sometimes we ourselves were confused with each other. In Latin America, I was frequently asked to sign copies of Dan's book! A whole industry developed around the assessment and training of what came to be called "emotional intelligence," or EQ. In the subsequent decade, the writings about multiple intelligences were complemented by books on a dizzying array of candidate intelligences: sexual intelligence, business intelligence, spiritual intelligence, and financial intelligence, to name just a few. Indeed, once the MI and EQ genies had been let out of the bottle, there was no way to limit the written works, training sessions, and media presentations done under the umbrella of a pluralistic view of intelligence. (If you doubt this claim, test it out on a search engine.)

Going beyond the United States, an indigenous coterie of authors arose. In China, for example, there are dozens of books about multiple intelligences by persons unknown to me. Other writings, such as popular articles in journals and, eventually, doctoral theses (by 1999, according to Clifford Morris, a Canadian scholar and archivist, there were over 200 theses), also spread the wisdom. Note that there was discussion in psychology and other scholarly disciplines, but by far the bulk of the dissemination occurred in educationally oriented writings, even as criticism was heavily skewed to academic outlets.

In addition to the influence of authors or individual promoters, memes can be spread by charismatic institutions or powerful practices. Self-declared "MI schools" in the United States and abroad can prove to be a powerful petri dish for spreading the ideas. Over the course of their existence, the Key Learning Community in Indianapolis and the New City School in St. Louis had thousands of visitors, many from abroad. These visits can have a powerful effect. When visitors from Norway attended the opening of the MI library at the New City School, they pledged to open an MI library in their country and carried through on their pledge. Media that carry MI stories can exert great influence. When ABC news and *Newsweek* featured the Key Learning Community, millions of persons learned about MI educational experiments. Happy Cheung's publications and broadcasts have had similar reverberations in China. The existence of institutions based on MI ideas, such as the Explorama in the theme park Danfoss Universe, has exposed families and businesspeople to MI ways of thinking—even if these individuals never encounter the MI meme per se. Assessment instruments—qualitative ones, like Spectrum in Scandinavia, and quantitative ones, like the MIDAS in East Asia—spread the MI meme as effectively as books or soapbox speakers.

It is relatively straightforward to do a travelogue, to mention the places where MI ideas have taken hold and where they have not, and to speculate about the carriers of the ideas. But this "tour of the horizon" raises two related and more searching questions: Why are certain regions more receptive than others, and what messages is MI bringing to these disparate soils?

THE NATURE OF THE SOIL

It is useful to think of MI as a new plant (all the while being careful not to stretch the analogy too far). Having blossomed on its home soil, its seeds can now be borne to distant terrains. The new soil, however, may be so resistant, so alien, that the seed cannot take hold, and it simply dies.

It may be that the soil is already so stocked with other seeds and plants that there is no room for any additional flora. Often schools and institutions are so busy, or so self-confident, or so beleaguered, that they show no interest in any new ideas or practices.

Or the soil may be so impoverished, so lacking in nutrients, that it cannot absorb any new living matter. I suspect that there are some institutions, regions, and even entire societies that lack resources to attempt anything new, nor to attend to any new ideas or practices.

At the opposite end of the continuum, some seeds grow naturally and easily in a rich but hitherto sparsely stocked terrain. An MI seed has little trouble in sprouting in a well-resourced environment that has long been receptive to ideas like individual differences, teaching in multiple ways or styles, a focus on arts and creative activities, and so on. These institutions can embrace MI ideas, but they may not be much affected by them. They can rightly say, "We are already doing this, we are happy to wear the MI banner, but [to coin a phrase!] you have simply brought tulips to Holland."

Of course, there are also false positives. As Mindy Kornhaber and colleagues have observed, many places claim to be carrying out MI practices and may even feature banners, slogans, and the like. And yet shorn of such appurtenances, these institutions look indistinguishable from ones that have never heard of MI and ones that are in effect "uniform schools" (featuring a single way of teaching and assessing). These places may believe that the soil is receptive, but in fact the soil cannot, for whatever reason, actually absorb the seed. The seed dies on the vine, so to speak, but somehow continues to cling there, deceiving those who cannot see the difference between pseudo- and genuine MI practices.

Of most interest are those places, institutions, and leaders who initially resist MI or initially understand MI in the most superficial way. Using our analogy, these places at first prove quite resistant to the MI seed. And yet, over time, either the ground becomes friendlier to the seed, or a mutant version of the MI seed proves able to take hold and eventually flourish in the initially hostile environment. I am reminded of a poignant anecdote featuring Pat Bolanos, the charismatic founder of the Key Learning Community. At the 15th anniversary of the school, she addressed a large supportive audience gathered in a concert hall in downtown Indianapolis. After thanking the many who had supported Key over the years, she declared, "And finally, I'd like to thank the six superintendents who have been in office in Indianapolis since we first thought of the school. Without your steadfast opposition, we would never have achieved anything!"

WHY MI TAKES HOLD IN CERTAIN SOILS

As the progenitor of the idea of multiple intelligence, I'd like to think that its intrinsic power, beauty, and truth have accounted for its success in various venues. And in fact, I'd like to think that many advocates of MI are attracted to the idea on the basis of its merits. Yet for an idea like MI to spread in various regions, to go beyond the advocacy of a precious few, there have to be reasons that appeal to a wider group. In reviewing my own experiences and observations over the past decades, I have identified four factors that stand out.

Rediscovery of Traditions. In some cultures, there is a belief that certain norms or practices, valued in the past, have been ignored or minimized in recent years. In Japan, for example, the formal schools and apprenticeships of an earlier era featured many practical arts and crafts. By the same token, the Confucian tradition in China recognized a whole gamut of competences that distinguished the educated person. The Dine group in the American Southwest used to honor various craft traditions, and approaches like the DISCOVER method devised by June Maker allow a recognition of these practices and their associated cognitive and sensory faculties.

Sometimes this renewed embrace of traditional values can lead to unexpected and even humorous effects. In China in 2004, I attempted to discover the reasons that MI theory had taken such hold. The mystery was cleared up by a journalist in Shanghai who said to me, "Dr. Gardner, in the West, when people hear about the idea of multiple intelligences, they go directly to what is special about their child, to discover his or her 'unique genius.' In China, by contrast, the multiple intelligences are simply eight talents that we must nurture in every child!" (Exclamation point added.)

A Desire to Broaden Curricula, Pedagogy, and Assessments. In many regions of the world, there has been a steady narrowing of the curriculum, so that it highlights STEM subjects (science, technology, engineering, and mathematics); short shrift is given to the arts, physical education, and certain of the humanities and social sciences. MI can be a useful vehicle for broadening the remit of education: to include subjects that address the several intelligences and ways of thinking, as well as teaching methods that speak to individual differences, and assessments that go beyond standard, short-answer language-and-logic instruments.

A Desire to Reach Underserved Students. Even as the mandated curriculum has tended to narrow in recent years, in many regions curricula are addressed to average or typical students; there has been relatively little effort to help students who fall outside the mainstream. Accordingly, MI ideas have been used widely in special education, gifted education, and the education of traditionally underserved students. Alas, this laudable aim can be abused. Too often have I heard a specific ethnic or racial group described as "having" certain intelligences and "lacking others." There is no scientific warrant for such a statement, and considerable damage can be done in its wake.

An Affirmation of Democratic Practices and Values. Nowadays, few countries in the world would declare that they are opposed to democratic values. Even the most authoritarian of countries call themselves democracies, indeed even incorporate the word "democracy" into the country's current name. Yet truly democratic practices are often elusive. Schools are often authoritarian institutions that stifle debate, controversy, and individual points of view—light-years away from democratic communities whose members participate in decision-making and governance.

THE POLICY LEVEL

Many times these goals are put forth by individuals or single institutions that simply want to make changes at the local level. But as some educators document, more ambitious efforts have been launched to alter practices on a wider scale. In England, Scotland, China, and Norway, for example, MI approaches are explicitly promoted as an alternative to practices that are currently regnant but are seen by some as shortsighted, counterproductive, or even destructive. At times, even in these countries, policies are announced that seem more congenial to MI approaches. Not surprisingly, supporters of MI are quick to embrace these reformist inclinations (China, Korea, Scotland, Turkey). As long as ministers of education around the world are focused largely on the comparative performance of countries on the Programme for International Student Assessment (PISA) examinations, we can expect that supporters of MI will mount counterefforts. And in the event that these supporters find themselves in policymaking positions, they will attempt to institute policies that are more "MI- friendly."

I am still mystified by one development. Some years ago, a colleague visited Pyongyang, the capital of North Korea. In a major library there, he saw only two books in English. One was Michael Moore's *Stupid White Men.* The other was *Frames of Mind: The Theory of Multiple Intelligences.* I cannot help wondering why—and how—these two memes managed to plant themselves in such seemingly resistant soil.

CONCLUDING NOTE: THE PERSONAL AND THE POLITICAL

The theory of multiple intelligences was developed by a psychologist; it was initially a proposal of how we should conceive of individual minds. This way of thinking initially proved most congenial to individuals who themselves have a psychological perspective on the world and who are excited rather than threatened by the idea of a plurality of individual differences.

I was surprised to see how this "inside psychology" meme spread quickly to education, first in the United States and then abroad. I was surprised by the staying power of the meme. And I am surprised that this meme has begun to be of interest to those in the policy realm, thus melding the personal and the political. It is striking that an idea that arose as an account of how the human brain/mind evolved and how it is organized today could end up joining forces with movements that give more voice to individuals and promote more democratic classes, schools, and perhaps even societies. I would like to think that this combination would please John Dewey, an American philosopher and psychologist who was perennially rooted in both the personal and the political.

Still, it is salutary to remember that the idea of multiple intelligences remains a minority view in psychology and that most schools around the world remain so-called "uniform schools," where a narrow group of topics is taught in the same way to all children and where modes of assessment are unadventurous, to say the least. My own view—or perhaps, to be more accurate, my own hope—is that digital media will allow so much individualized education in the future that the meme of multiple intelligences will be taken for granted. Should that be the case, my colleagues in many corners of the world will deserve considerable credit for sustaining and enriching MI ideas and practices in the interim.

IDENTIFICATION AND NURTURING OF INTELLIGENCES IN EARLY LIFE

Once the educational community had learned about and embraced MI theory, applications were soon forthcoming—some expected (schools that claimed to develop all intelligences), some exotic (schools that served food and drink that purportedly developed the intelligences).

For the most part, I thanked these educational pioneers but remained largely on the sidelines. But a few times, opportunities arose at Project Zero to carry out some modest educational experiments. In the following Essays 13–15, my colleagues and I describe three such experiments—all collaborations, each addressing different age groups—and doing so in distinctive ways.

As a kind of a teaser, here's a brief summary:

Project Spectrum arose out of the question: "If multiple intelligences indeed, exist, can they be discovered and nurtured early in life?" My colleague David Feldman and I were both interested in this question—and we were eventually joined in this effort by Jie-Qi Chen, Mara Krechevsky, Janet Stork, Julie Viens, and other colleagues.

Perhaps many of our colleagues would simply have developed half a dozen tests, given them to a representative group of young people, and reported our findings. But we were more ambitious—and perhaps more foolhardy!

Instead, we set up an entire classroom at the Eliot-Pearson Children's School, a preschool affiliated with nearby Tufts University. The classroom was equipped with many games, exercises, corners, and activities—all designed to evoke the expression (and the power) of the several intelligences. And over the course of a couple of years, we devised a variety of ways in which to identify and nurture the gamut of multiple intelligences.

STUDENT PROJECTS IN THE PODS AT THE KEY SCHOOL

The Key School was the first school in the world built around the idea of multiple intelligences.

Described broadly, the goals of the Key School were to recognize and legitimate the range of human intellectual strengths; to help students discover their strengths and preferences; and to give them ample opportunity—within and beyond school—to nurture and develop their intelligences.

Where might I, and my colleagues at Project Zero, be helpful? In addition to being frequent visitors to Indianapolis, and willing "thought partners," we selected one area where our expertise might be helpful.

An important building block of the school was the devising and carrying out of projects by the students. Projects are an excellent way in which to exhibit one's interests, strengths, and challenges. But while projects are easy to assign, and (unlike standard tests) lend themselves to public display, they are not as easy to assess and evaluate, let alone give letter grades and make consequential decisions about what passes muster and what does not. That's where we made use of our research and analytic skills—seeking to help Key create, nurture, and evaluate projects that drew on various intelligences, alone or in combination.

THE ARTISTIC INTELLIGENCES: CAN THEY BE MASTERED AND MEASURED IN ADOLESCENCE?

Given my interests and those of Project Zero, it's not surprising that we developed rough-and-ready assessments of the intelligence profiles at a preschool in the Boston area (Project Spectrum), or that we helped a K–8 public school in Indianapolis assess the projects of their students.

Arts PROPEL was somewhat of a surprise—we might say a far bigger stretch. To begin with, it focused on secondary school—a time when the competition for class time and homework time is fierce. Second, it focused on an area of the curriculum—the arts—that has not been much valued in American public education. Third, and most surprisingly, it involved an intensive and extensive collaboration with the Educational Testing Service in Princeton, New Jersey.

Yet as one who can chronicle many unsuccessful collaborations (see Barendsen et al., 2011), our work on Arts PROPEL was one of our best collaborative efforts in educational research. This was due to our ETS colleagues (especially Drew Gitomer and Alice Sims-Gunzenhauser); our PZ team (especially Lyle Davidson, Steve Seidel, Seymour Simmons, Ellen Winner, and Dennie Wolf); and our farsighted and supportive program officer at the Rockefeller Foundation, Alberta Arthurs.

An explanation of the name: Arts PROPEL is an acronym of the three skills we deemed most important in the arts: production, perception, reflection. should mention that our approach was developed—quite deliberately—in contrast to a more academic approach to the arts, one that highlighted traditional disciplines—historical, analytic, biographical. That seemed more American high school -typical than our artistic stance.)

Our PROPEL approach entailed ample aspects, and took several handbooks to outline. In Essay 15 I present the highlights—and I am happy to say that facets of Arts PROPEL continue to be drawn on in various schools both in the United States and abroad.

REFERENCES

Barendsen, L., Farrell, K., Fischman, W., & Waltrous, C. (2011). *Collaboration in non-profit education: Emerging findings*. Interim report submitted to John Abele and the Argosy Foundation.

Winger, P. (1991, December 1). The best schools in the world. *Newsweek*.

ESSAY 13

The Spectrum Approach to Assessment
Nurturing Intelligences in Early Childhood

Co-authored With Mara Krechevsky

Standardized tests of intelligence have been used to identify unusual talents, and such instruments are certainly capable of revealing prodigies. But consider the individuals who do not perform well on such assessments.

How can we assess their strengths, and what would it mean to do so?

Jacob is a 4-year-old boy who was asked to participate in two forms of assessment at the start of the school year: the Stanford-Binet Intelligence Scale (4th ed.) and a new approach to assessment called Project Spectrum. Jacob refused to be tested on the Stanford-Binet. Three subtests were attempted and partially completed, after which Jacob ran out of the testing room, left the building, and climbed a tree.

Consider, as a striking contrast, Jacob's reaction to the Spectrum battery, which includes 15 different tasks spanning a wide range of domains. Jacob participated in most of the activities, and he demonstrated outstanding strength in the areas of vsual arts and numbers. He revealed a consuming love of different materials and worked with every possible medium in the art area. On other activities, even when he resisted engaging in the task at hand, he nearly always expressed interest in the materials from which the games were made—for example, the small figures on a storytelling board and the metal of the bells for the music activity. This passion for the physicality of materials extended to almost every area: Jacob's exploration of the discovery or natural science area focused at one point on an examination of bones and how they fit together, and led to a remarkably accurate sculpture of a bone fashioned from clay.

Of all the activities in the Spectrum battery, Jacob was least interested in movement and music. At first he also resisted participating in a numbers task embedded in a bus game. However, when he at last became engaged, he seemed to take special delight in figuring out the correct number of people boarding and leaving the bus. Tapping Jacob's understanding of numbers in a context that was meaningful and familiar to him seemed to help elicit abilities that might otherwise have remained hidden.

While the Spectrum and Stanford-Binet (or IQ) assessments can reveal similar qualities, there are distinct advantages to an assessment conducted over time with rich materials in the child's own environment. The example of Jacob indicates four ways in which the Spectrum assessment system might benefit children:

First, Spectrum engages children through games that are meaningful and contextualized.

Second, Spectrum blurs the line between curriculum and assessment, thereby integrating assessment more effectively into the regular educational program.

Third, the Spectrum approach to assessment makes the measures "intelligence-fair" by using instruments that look directly at the intelligence in operation, instead of through an intermediating linguistic or logical-mathematical lens.

Fourth, Spectrum suggests how a child's strengths may provide access to more challenging areas in which the child shows less promise.

Here we consider the possibility that children's exceptional talents can be identified at an early age and that the profile of abilities exhibited by preschoolers can be clearly distinguished from one another. We also consider some of the educational implications of an approach that focuses on the early identification of areas of strength and weakness. After a brief introduction to the theoretical background of the Spectrum approach to assessment, we discuss some of the research findings and offer some preliminary conclusions.

THE SPECTRUM APPROACH TO ASSESSMENT

Project Spectrum is an innovative attempt to measure the profile of intelligences and working styles of young children. It has been undertaken by several researchers at Harvard Project Zero with our colleague David Feldman at Tufts University (we thank Jie-Qi Chen, Elise Iseberg, Valerie Ramos-Ford, Janet Stork, and Julie Viens).

Spectrum began with the assumption that every child has the potential to develop strength in one or more areas. The project's focus on preschool children has both a scientific and a practical thrust. On the scientific side, we address the question of how individual differences can be reliably detected in early life as well as the predictive value of such early identification. On the practical side, parents and teachers are likely to benefit most from information about their children's cognitive competences during this stage of childhood, when the young child's brain is relatively plastic, when schools are likely to be less rigid, and when a free-choice component is typically built into most curricula.

Rather than attempting to look at intelligences in pure form, we looked at the domains of accomplishment of the culture through which those forms are taken up by children. For example, we address both production and perception in music; invented and descriptive narrative in language; and expressive and athletic movement in the bodily-kinesthetic realm. We also used the notion of adult end-states to help us focus on the skills and abilities that are relevant to achieving significant and rewarding adult roles in our society, rather than just on those skills that are useful in the school context. Thus, instead of looking at logical-mathematical skills in the abstract, we examined competences that may culminate in scientific inventiveness; instead of examining competence at repeating a series of sentences, we look at the child's ability to tell a story or provide a descriptive account of an experience.

In order to capture fully a child's approach to a task, we found it important to look at cognitive or working styles as well as sheer intellectual capacities. Working style describes the way a child interacts with the materials of a content area, such as ability to plan an activity and to reflect on a task, and level of persistence. Whereas some individuals exhibit working styles that determine their approach to any task, no matter what the content area, others have styles that prove much more domain-specific.

IMPLEMENTATION OF THE SPECTRUM APPROACH

In a Spectrum classroom, children are surrounded each day by rich and engaging materials that evoke the use of a range of intelligences. We do not attempt to stimulate intelligences directly, with materials that are labeled "spatial" or "logical-mathematical." Rather, we use materials that embody valued societal roles or end-states and that draw on relevant combinations of intelligences. So, for example, there is a naturalist's corner, where various biological specimens are brought in for students to examine and compare with other materials; this area draws on sensory capacities as well as naturalistic and logical intelligences. There is a storytelling area, where students create imaginative tales using an evocative set of props and designing their own storyboards; this area evokes linguistic, dramatic, and imaginative faculties. There is a building corner, where students can construct a model of their classroom and manipulate small-scale photographs of the students and teachers in the room; this area draws on spatial, bodily-kinesthetic, and personal intelligences.

It is highly desirable for children to observe competent adults or older peers at work or at play in these areas. With such observation, youngsters readily come to appreciate the reasons for the materials as well as the nature of the skills that enable a master to interact with the materials in a meaningful way. Because it is not always feasible to provide such an apprentice–master setting, learning centers have been constructed in which children can develop some facility from regular interactions with the materials by themselves or with only other novice-level peers. In this sense, our entry-level environment is a self-sustaining one that harbors the potential for cognitive and personal growth.

Over the course of a year or more spent in this nourishing environment, children have ample opportunity to explore the various learning areas, each featuring its respective materials and its unique set of elicited skills and intelligences. Reflecting the resourcefulness and curiosity of the mind of the 5-year-old, most children readily explore the majority of these areas. Children who do not cast their nets widely are encouraged to try out alternative materials or approaches. For the most part, the teacher can readily observe a child's interests and talents over the course of the year, and no special assessments are needed. For each domain or craft, however, we have also devised specific games or activities that allow a more precise determination of a child's intelligences in that area.

At the end of the year, the information gathered about each child is summarized by the research team in a brief essay called a Spectrum Report. This document describes the child's individual profile of strengths and weaknesses and offers specific recommendations about what might be done at home, in school, or in the wider community to build on strengths as well as to bolster areas of relative weakness.

Such informal recommendations are important. In our view, psychologists have traditionally been far too concerned with norming or ranking. Instead, efforts comparable to the Spectrum Report made throughout the school years should help students and their families make informed decisions about their future course, based on a survey of their capacities and options.

What of the actual measures that we devised? In order not to confound competences, we tried as much as possible not to rely exclusively on logical and linguistic measures. Instead we used measures that were "intelligence-fair"—measures that tap the intelligence directly and in a holistic manner. We also tried to avoid hypothetical situations and abstract formulations; we provided children with something concrete to manipulate no matter which domain was being assessed. For example, the classroom model described above provides children with small figures of their peers and teachers, offering a tangible structure through which to consider children's knowledge of friends, social roles, and classroom dynamics. The music perception task provides children with Montessori bells with which they can play a pitch-matching game or create their own melody.

Spectrum measures range from relatively structured and targeted tasks (for example, in the number and music domains) to relatively unstructured measures and natural observations (in the science and social domains). These measures are implemented throughout the course of a year—the classroom is equipped with engaging materials, games, puzzles, and learning areas. Documentation takes a variety of forms, from score sheets and observation

The Spectrum Approach to Assessment

checklists to portfolios and tape recordings. Although most teachers do not find it practical to formally administer all 15 measures to each child, we have used such a procedure for research purposes.

In addition to the Spectrum Report, parents are provided with a Parent Activities Manual with suggestions for activities in the different domains addressed by Spectrum. Most of the activities use readily accessible and affordable materials. A cautionary note to parents is included regarding the premature streaming or fast-tracking of a child. The idea is not to make each child a prodigy in his or her area of greatest strength. Rather, Project Spectrum stresses the notion that every child is unique: parents and teachers deserve to have a description faithful to the child as well as suggestions for the kinds of experiences appropriate to the child's particular configuration of strengths and weaknesses.

INITIAL RESULTS

What of the results of our initial research? We posed three questions:

1. Do young children have domain-specific as well as more general strengths?
2. Is there any correlation between performances in different activities?
3. Does a child's strength in one domain facilitate or hinder performance in other domains?

The Spectrum battery was administered in two preschool classrooms at the Eliot-Pearson Children's School. We restricted our analyses to twenty-three 4-year-olds.

We looked at each child's strengths and weaknesses, both in relation to the group and to the self. Children who scored one standard deviation or more above the mean on the Spectrum measures in a domain were considered to have a strength in that domain, whereas children who scored one standard deviation or more below the mean were considered to demonstrate a weakness.

The majority of the children revealed a strength in at least one domain and a weakness in at least one domain. A few children exhibited one or more strengths across Spectrum activities and no weaknesses, and a few children exhibited no strengths and one or more weaknesses. Finally, every child exhibited at least one strength and one weakness relative to performance on the majority of tasks.

To determine the degree of correlation between performances on the different activities, we created a matrix of the correlations between pairs of the 10 activities. The results indicated very little correlation between the activities, reinforcing the notion that the Spectrum measures identify a range of nonoverlapping capabilities in different content areas. Only one pair was significant at the $p < 0.01$ level: the two number activities—the dinosaur game and the bus game ($r = 0.78$). In contrast, the two music and the two science activities were not significantly correlated ($r = -0.07$ and $r = 0.08$, respectively).

There was also some evidence that a child's strength in one area might facilitate performance in another. For example, one child exhibited a keen sensitivity to color and demonstrated both interest and ability in the area of visual arts. While playing the treasure hunt game, which focuses on logical inference skills, this child's attentiveness to colors apparently helped her identify the rule governing the placement of treasures under color-coded flags. Another child, who was identified as having a strength in music production (singing), found it easier in the creative movement sessions to synchronize his movements to the underlying rhythm of a piece of music if he sang while he moved. His musical talents also characterized his performance on the invented narrative task: he created both a theme song and a death march for the characters in his story.

A third child, who exhibited outstanding ability in storytelling, yet remained motionless in the creative movement sessions, moved with uncharacteristic expressiveness when storyboard props were used as a catalyst in one of the exercises. She also transformed tasks in visual arts, social analysis, and mathematics into occasions for further storytelling. Her drawings in art often served to illustrate accompanying narratives. Her mother reported that she often made puppets and dolls at home, modeling them on characters from the books she was "reading." She also used the classroom model as a reality-based storyboard, creating vignettes with the figures of her classmates. On the bus game, however, she became so involved in the motivations for the different figures boarding and leaving the bus that she was distracted from recording the correct numerical information.

It seems that pronounced strength in one area can also interfere with a child's performance. One child exhibited outstanding strength in visual arts, demonstrating an unusual sensitivity to line, color, and composition. However, his sensitivity to visual cues led him to misinterpret directional signs when using dice that had a + and a – on their sides. He interpreted the crossing lines (+) to mean that the player could move in two directions and the single horizontal line (–) to mean that the player could proceed in only one direction.

WORKING STYLES

Note: While Howard critiques the notion of "learning styles" in two essays in this volume, because they are not the same as multiple intelligences, we found this concept useful for our Spectrum project.

The Spectrum Approach to Assessment

As noted earlier, in addition to recording a child's performance, we also recorded working style or the way in which the child approached each activity. We were primarily interested in two issues:

1. Do children utilize distinctive working styles when solving problems from different domains? If so, what is the nature of the differences in a child's areas of strength and weakness?
2. Are some working styles more effective than others in particular domains?

It seemed that for the majority of children, while one or two working styles usually obtained across domains, other working styles depended more on the content of the area being explored. Approximately three-quarters of the children in the sample exhibited general working styles that, in specific instances, combined with one or two others to yield domain-specific configurations. For example, one girl displayed attention to detail only on the classroom model activity, her one area of strength, and was impulsive only in the music perception activity, her area of weakness. Another child was easily engaged and confident, even in areas of weakness, as long as the task involved a performance aspect.

Not surprisingly, performances in an area of strength were typically characterized by "easy to engage," "confident," and "focused" working styles. In contrast, weak performances were characterized by "distractible," "impulsive," and "reluctant to engage" working styles. "Playfulness" characterized both strengths and weaknesses. Also, a number of children showed reflectiveness and attention to detail in their area of strength. Three of the five children who exhibited no strengths relative to their peers never reflected on their own work, and eight children reflected only on their work in areas of strength.

Five of the children demonstrated working styles that were highly domain-specific. Jacob, the boy described at the beginning of this essay, exhibited confidence, attention to detail, seriousness, planning skills, and reflectiveness only in the visual arts and numbers domains—his areas of strength. Another child found it very difficult to remain focused on most of the Spectrum and classroom activities. However, when she was presented with the materials for the assembly activity, she worked in a focused and persistent manner until she had completely taken apart and reassembled the objects. This result gave the teacher valuable information about how she might use this child's strength to engage her in focused work in the classroom.

With regard to the second question, some of the children who exhibited a consistent working style were clearly helped by their content-neutral style, whereas others were probably hindered by it. One child worked in a *serious and focused manner* across domains; this approach helped him complete activities in which he experienced difficulty as well as those in which he exhibited competence. Every child exhibited *confidence* in at least one activity. One girl who revealed no strengths relative to her peers nonetheless demonstrated *pride in accomplishment* on more tasks than any other child, perhaps indicating a *resilience* that augurs well for her scholastic prospects. Ironically, it may be that too pervasive a confidence inhibits successful performance across tasks. The child who was identified as having the most weaknesses of the five children and no strengths relative to her peers never showed any *tentativeness*, whereas all but three of the rest were tentative in their approach at least once.

One child brought his own agenda to every Spectrum activity. Although his ideas were often compelling, his unwillingness to attend to the task caused him to perform poorly on many of the activities. On the music perception activity, for example, he was most interested in how the metal bells, all of which looked exactly the same, could nonetheless produce different sounds. To explore this phenomenon, he examined the differences in their vibrations after hitting them with the mallet. He also invented new rules for the dinosaur game, and he tried to fashion tools out of the parts of the two food grinders in the assembly activity. Because he was so interested in exploring his own ideas, he often resisted exploring the ideas of others. When he experienced difficulty with an activity, he would become frustrated and rely on his sense of humor to distract the adult from the task at hand.

It also appeared that the structure of the tasks (or sometimes their lack of structure) served to inhibit the performances of some children. In the less structured environment of the Spectrum classroom, the boy just described demonstrated notable experimental ability and constantly formulated and tested hypotheses to find out more about the world around him. Jacob was another child who required very little structure, so immersed in the materials did he become. Unfortunately, his intense focus on materials to the exclusion of other people—whether child or adult—might present problems for his future scholastic performance.

A COMPARISON OF VIEWS: PARENTS, TEACHERS, AND SPECTRUM

While the Spectrum measures clearly identified domain-specific strengths in the children, it also seemed important to determine whether we were uncovering abilities hitherto unrecognized by teachers and parents. To address this question, we asked parents and teachers to fill out a questionnaire indicating the level of ability shown by each child in a number of different areas. We also sent response forms to parents to solicit their reactions to the Spectrum profiles.

Seventeen sets of parents returned a completed questionnaire. In general, parents were quite generous in identifying their child as demonstrating outstanding ability in an area. The average number of areas checked by parents for their child was eight out of 30. On the other hand, the teachers rarely scored a child as exhibiting outstanding ability in any area, identifying on average one out of 30. This discrepancy between parent and teacher ratings presumably reflects the broader frame of reference available to teachers, who see children in the context of their peer group. While parents may understandably be biased, they also have fewer opportunities to view the strengths of a large number of children. These factors should be kept in mind in the comparison.

A child was considered by Spectrum to have an outstanding strength only if the score in a given domain activity was at least one standard deviation above the mean. Spectrum identified outstanding strengths that had not otherwise been identified in eight of the 17 children—12 strengths in all, in the domains of science, visual arts, music, and social understanding. Seven children were identified by parents and teachers as exhibiting outstanding strengths, but not by Spectrum. In most of these cases, although Spectrum identified relative strengths, the performances were not considered outstanding in relation to the group. For a number of other children, strengths scoring close to but less than one standard deviation above the mean were identified by Spectrum, but not by parents or teachers.

Finally, parents, teachers, and Spectrum identified the same areas of outstanding ability in nine of the 17 children in the comparison.

It appears that some areas, such as language and numbers, can be relatively easily identified regardless of whether the child is at home or at school; but other areas, such as music perception, mechanical skills, and social analysis, are not so easily noticed. In fact, Spectrum never identified language or numbers as outstanding strengths where they had not already been identified by parents or the teacher. However, even in a commonly recognized area of ability like language, Spectrum provides a breakdown of the area into component skills (vocabulary, sentence structure, use of descriptive language, and so on) employed in the service of a meaningful endeavor (storytelling).

Of course, even the most competent preschool teachers simply cannot provide experiences in all areas, especially areas with which they may be relatively unfamiliar, such as music perception and logical inference tasks. The object assembly activity in particular helps break down gender preconceptions by providing girls with the same opportunity as boys to reveal a strength and become engaged in an area traditionally considered masculine. The profile response forms also revealed that the areas in which parents were most surprised to learn of strengths included music perception, mechanical ability, and creative movement. Because the information in the profiles is generated from contextualized tasks (rather than one-off tests), it may be easier for parents to translate it into meaningful follow-up activities.

A COMPARISON OF SPECTRUM RESULTS WITH THE STANFORD-BINET INTELLIGENCE SCALE

A trained diagnostician administered the Stanford-Binet Intelligence Scale to 19 of the 20 children in one class. Two of the 19 children did not complete the measure and are therefore not included in the analysis. The results from this sample, while useful for providing a very general sense of how the two measures compare, should be read with caveats in mind.

First, Spectrum addresses seven domains of ability through 15 activities, 10 of which are included in the analysis, whereas the Stanford-Binet focuses on four areas or factors (verbal reasoning, abstract/visual reasoning, quantitative reasoning, and short-term memory) through eight subtests. Second, the battery of Spectrum activities is administered in a series over the course of a year, whereas the Stanford-Binet is administered in a 1-to-2-hour session. Finally, the Stanford-Binet is a standardized measure, and Spectrum is not.

The 17 children in the sample who completed the Stanford-Binet assessment scored in the range of low-average to very superior, with composite scores ranging from 86 to 133. The average score was 113. As with the preceding analysis, a child was considered to demonstrate a strength or weakness on a Spectrum activity only if he or she scored one standard deviation or more above or below the mean of the group.

To determine whether Stanford-Binet composite scores were predictive of performance on some or all Spectrum activities, we ranked the composite scores of the children to see how the top five children (with composite scores from 125 to 133) and the bottom five children (with scores from 86 to 105—the low-average to average range) performed on the Spectrum battery.

Of the five children with the highest Stanford-Binet composite scores, one demonstrated a strength on three of the 10 Spectrum activities in the analysis, three displayed strengths in two activities, and one child exhibited one strength. The areas Spectrum identified as strengths for these children were as follows: two in narrative language, four in music perception and production, two in the visual arts, one in social understanding, and one in science (logical inference).

The movement, numbers, and mechanical component of the science domains were not identified as strengths for any of the children, and, in fact, movement and numbers were identified as areas of weakness for two of them. Moreover, only one of the three children who displayed three or more strengths on the Spectrum measures was among the top five scorers on the Stanford-Binet. One of the top three Spectrum scorers was also the top scorer on the combined Spectrum numbers activities.

Overall, it seems that the Stanford-Binet Intelligence Scale did not predict successful performance either across Spectrum activities or on a consistent subset of them. One qualification to be made in that regard is the possibility of a connection between the Stanford-Binet composite scores and performance on the Spectrum music tasks. Four of the five strengths in music identified by the Spectrum measures were displayed by the children who received the highest Stanford-Binet composite scores. However, in general, no correlation was found between Stanford-Binet subscores and the individual Spectrum activities. Of course, without a much larger sample, no firm conclusions can be drawn.

The Stanford-Binet also did not seem to predict lack of success across Spectrum tasks, although it did identify three of the lowest-scoring children (children with no strengths and 0 to 5 weaknesses on the Spectrum activities). Of the five children with the lowest Stanford-Binet composite scores, one exhibited one strength (social understanding) and one weakness (music perception), and another exhibited no weaknesses and three strengths (mechanical ability, language, and music perception). The remaining three children displayed no strengths on the Spectrum activities and zero to five weaknesses.

The child who received the lowest composite score in the group (86) was also identified by the Spectrum battery as the lowest-scoring child across tasks: she exhibited no strengths and five weaknesses on the Spectrum activities (two more weaknesses than any other child). However, Spectrum did identify two relative strengths displayed by this child in the domains of social understanding and creative movement. The Stanford-Binet subtests also revealed some scatter (the verbal reasoning skills and memory for sentences subscores were in the 53rd and 49th percentiles, respectively, while bead memory and pattern analysis scores fell into the 39th and 40th percentiles).

Conclusion: Whereas the Stanford-Binet Intelligence Scale yielded a range of factor scores and subtest variability within factors, the Spectrum measures produced more jagged profiles. Part of this difference can be attributed to the number of domains addressed by each measure: eight tasks in four content areas for Stanford-Binet versus 15 tasks (10 in our analysis) in seven areas for Spectrum.

But Spectrum does more than simply expand the areas addressed by the Stanford-Binet. All of the Stanford-Binet subtests can be considered either good or fair measures of g, the general intelligence factor. The Spectrum model, however, does not postulate g as a general intelligence factor that is present in a wide range of mental abilities and that accounts for children's performances in different content areas. Rather, the Spectrum model suggests that the jagged profiles represent domain-specific abilities that reflect real-world problem-solving in the context of meaningful activities—for example, analysis of one's own social environment, assembling a mechanical object, telling a story, and so on. The information gained from the Spectrum inventory may therefore be potentially more useful in designing appropriate educational interventions for children.

Clearly, this study has limitations. Because of the small sample that received the Spectrum battery, the study should be regarded as useful for generating hypotheses rather than providing any conclusive findings. However, we can identify some of the potential benefits of Spectrum in comparison with other assessment approaches, such as the Stanford-Binet.

First, Spectrum provides an opportunity to involve children more actively in the assessment, giving them a chance to reflect on their experience and their own sense of their interests and strengths. Children also become actively involved in helping collect and document their work in the Spectrum model—for example, saving their work for the art portfolios, taping stories and songs, and bringing in items for the discovery or natural science area. Such involvement conveys to children the sense that their products are being taken seriously, and it includes them in the process of monitoring their own growth.

For children who are unusually sensitive about performance issues, Spectrum may have information to offer that a one-session, decontextualized, heavily verbal measure does not. For example, as part of the intrapersonal component of the social analytic activity, children are shown pictures of the different Spectrum activities and asked which activities they consider their favorite, their best, and the hardest. One boy who had remained unengaged in Spectrum activities (as well as the Stanford-Binet subtests) showed a surprising degree of interest in answering questions about his reactions to the different activities. He seemed to have an accurate sense about his areas of relative interest and strength. He identified the storyboard as his best activity and, indeed, it was the only one of the eight tasks he completed for which his score was above the group mean. He selected the water activity as his favorite. And although he was reluctant to try out his ideas for sinking and floating experiments during the task, he became so excited about a discovery he made at one point that he called his teacher over to the area in an uncharacteristic display of enthusiasm.

Of course, the Stanford-Binet Intelligence Scale has advantages as well. It is a standardized measure with excellent internal consistency and high reliability. The measure is easily and efficiently administered, and the areas examined map readily onto the standard school curriculum. While we do not yet know whether a Spectrum assessment can predict scholastic success with the reliability of standardized forms of assessment, the Spectrum measures do identify distinctive areas of strength, with immediate implications for further avenues to explore, both inside and outside of school. The Spectrum battery also allows teachers and parents to perceive individual differences in areas traditionally considered important only with regard to passage through universal stages of development or as a reflection of general intelligence.

The Spectrum approach contains its own risks. The danger of premature streaming of children must be weighed against the benefits of giving every child a chance to do well. There is also the potential for achievement-oriented parents to push their children to excel not just in the traditional academic areas but in all domains, increasing an already powerful pressure on children to achieve. Moreover, families outside the mainstream culture may quite properly be less concerned with performance in elective domains like visual arts and music, and more concerned with those areas that continue to be valued most by the broader society—language and logic.

Clearly, family environment will determine in part both the use and the usefulness of the information contained in the Spectrum profile. As one parent reported, because the family members were either not interested in music or were simply not musical, her child's musical capabilities might never have surfaced without Spectrum, and even if they had, they would not have been recognized as talent. This result can be contrasted with the case of a mother who considered music to be an important part of her son's life and greatly encouraged his interest in it. During follow-up a year later, she reported that he loved watching musical and operatic performances, and would sit through them attentively, without talking or moving. While no one really knows the exact relationship between early talents and later achievements (see Essay 11), the identification of strengths early on may become a self-fulfilling prophecy.

Although Spectrum reflects in part a value system of pluralism associated with the middle class, it may also have something to offer children from less privileged backgrounds. The Spectrum assessment system has the potential to reveal unsuspected areas of strength and bring about enhanced self-esteem, particularly for children who do not excel in the standard school curriculum.

Over time, Spectrum evolved from serving as a means of assessing strengths to constituting a rounded educational environment. In collaboration with classroom teachers, we developed curricular materials in the form of kits that draw on the range of intelligences as they may figure in the development of a broad theme, such as "Night and Day" or "About Me." With younger children, these materials are used primarily in an exploratory mode. With older children, they are tied more closely to the traditional goals of school, promoting preliteracy or literacy attitudes, approaches, and skills. Thus, children encounter the basics of reading, writing, and calculating in the context of themes and materials in which they have demonstrated interest and an emerging expertise. As they gain proficiency in a board game, for example, children can be introduced to numerical tally systems, and as they create adventures at the storyboard, they can begin to write them down as well as recite or dramatize them.

The adaptability of Spectrum has proved to be one of its most exciting features. Teachers and researchers from several regions of the country have used Spectrum as a point of departure for a variety of educational ends. The Spectrum approach has been adapted with children ranging in age from 4 to 8 for purposes of diagnosis, classification, and teaching. It has been used with average students, gifted students, disabled students, and students at risk of school failure, in programs designed for research, for compensatory purposes, and for enrichment. It was made the center of a mentoring program in which young children have the opportunity to work with adults from their neighborhood who exemplify different combinations of intelligences in their jobs. As researchers-turned-implementers, we have had the privilege of sitting in on discussions among people who have never met each other but who have adapted Spectrum to their varied needs. It seems clear from such conversations that the Spectrum school-museum blend is appropriate for young children of diverse interests, backgrounds, and ages.

In a number of respects, Project Spectrum epitomizes the way the theory of multiple intelligences catalyzed the creation of effective educational interventions—in this case, with young children. Beginning with a scholarly interest in the existence and identification of talents in very young children, we have seen Spectrum evolve naturally over time into a full-scale approach to early education. This approach was inspired by aspects of MI theory, but in no way did MI theory dictate the exact contents or the precise steps in the implementation of Spectrum. We altered the program considerably in response to our own observations, to feedback from parents, teachers, researchers, and students, and to the changing conditions within which we attempted to implement the approach. Add to that the very different uses made of Spectrum ideas by researchers and practitioners in different parts of the country, and a picture emerges of a family—indeed a spectrum—of variations of Project Spectrum. It is fitting that a program rooted in the celebration of individual differences among young children should itself generate a family of highly individualized approaches.

ESSAY 14

Projects During the Elementary Years

A few years after *Frames of Mind* was originally published, I was scheduled to give a talk in Kutztown, Pennsylvania. Shortly before I left Boston to make the trip there, I received a phone call from a teacher in Indianapolis. She said that she and some of her fellow teachers had read *Frames of Mind* and wanted to speak with me about some of the ideas in the book. Was I available for a meeting in Kutztown?

Unbeknownst to me, a group of eight teachers from the Indianapolis public school system had driven for 14 hours in order to have a relatively brief meeting with me in Kutztown. At that eventful meeting they showed me a videotape they had recently completed and told me that they were interested in starting their own K–6 elementary school, inspired in part by the ideas of MI theory. I was as surprised as I was delighted.

While I was becoming increasingly interested in educational applications of the theory, it had never dawned on me that someone might take these ideas so seriously as to actually plan a school based on them. I told the "Indianapolis 8" quite frankly that I would be happy to help them but that I knew little about schools. "You are the school people," I insisted, "and it will have to be your school."

AN MI SCHOOL

Few groups of teachers anywhere can have worked harder than the Indianapolis 8 did over the next 2 years. Under the guidance of the energetic nd visionary Patricia Bolanos, who eventually became the school principal, they raised funds, lobbied, and planned curricula, and after many moments of suspense and some disappointments, they were eventually allowed to have their own inner-city public "options" school in downtown Indianapolis, the Key School. While I deserve no credit for the launch of this project, I met regularly with the teachers to talk with them about what they were doing, and, in the way of these things, received excessive credit in the popular media for having inspired the Key School. After the death of principal Bolanos and a series of political perturbations in the Indianapolis educational system, the school finally closed. But in 2023, the Teacher of the Year in Indianapolis turned out to have been a student at the Key School—and credited her experiences there with her choice of career and her distinctive approach to teaching. In this spirit, I have retained a description of the Key School as an enterprise of our time.

Later called the Key Learning Community, the Key School proved to be a remarkable success in many ways. One of its founding principles is the conviction that each child should have his or her multiple intelligences stimulated each day. Thus, every student at the school participates regularly in the activities of computing, music, and bodily-kinesthetics, in addition to mastering theme-centered curricula that embody standard literacies and subject matter.

While an MI curriculum is the Key Learning Community's most overtly innovative aspect, many other facets of the school suggest an education that strives toward diverse forms of understanding.

Three practices are pivotal. First, each student participates every day in an apprenticeship-like "pod," where students work with peers of different ages and a competent teacher to master a craft or discipline of interest. Because the pod includes a range of ages, students can enter into an activity at their own level of expertise and develop at a comfortable pace. Working alongside a more knowledgeable person, students have what may be a rare opportunity to see an expert engage in productive work. At any one time, there are perhaps a dozen pods in a variety of areas ranging from architecture to gardening, from cooking to "earning money." Because the focus of the pod falls on the acquisition of a real-world skill in an apprenticeship environment, the chances of securing genuine understandings are enhanced.

Second, complementing the pods are strong ties to the wider community. Once a week, an outside specialist visits the school and demonstrates an occupation or craft to all the students. Often the specialist is a parent, and typically the topic fits into the school theme at that time. For example, if the current theme is "Protection of the Environment," visitors might talk about sewage disposal, forestry, or the political process of lobbying. The hope is that students will not only learn about the range of activities that exist in the wider community, but will also have the opportunity to follow up in a given area, possibly under the guidance of the visiting mentor.

One way of achieving this end is through participation in a Center for Exploration at the Indianapolis Children's Museum; students can enter into an apprenticeship of several months, in which they can engage in such sustained activities as animation, shipbuilding, journalism, and monitoring the weather.

The final—and to my mind the most important—avenue for growth at the Key Learning Community involves student projects. During any given year, the school features a number of different themes, introduced at approximately 10-week intervals. The themes can be quite broad, such as "Patterns" and "Connections," or more focused, such as "The Renaissance Then and

Now" and "Mexican Heritage." Curricula focus on these themes, and whenever possible, desired literacies and concepts are introduced as natural adjuncts to an exploration of the theme.

As part of school requirements, each student is asked to carry out a project related to the theme. Thus, students execute three or four new projects each year. These projects are placed on display at the conclusion of the theme period, so that students can examine what everyone else in the school has done (students prove to be very interested in monitoring the work of friends and peers). Students present their projects to their classmates, describing the project's genesis, purpose, problems, and future implications; they then answer questions raised by classmates and by the teacher.

Of special importance is the fact that all project presentations are videotaped. Each student thus accumulates a video portfolio in which his or her succession of projects has been recorded. (At the time, in the mid-1980s, this form of recording was quite innovative.) The portfolio may be considered an evolving cognitive model of the student's development over the course of his life in the Key Learning Community. On graduating, students receive a copy of their entire video portfolio—an amazing record of personal and intellectual development. Our research collaboration with the Key Learning Community has weighed various uses that might be made of these video portfolios.

PROJECT ASSESSMENT

Most students in the United States, in the course of their scholastic careers, take hundreds, and perhaps thousands, of tests. In the process, they develop skill—often to a highly calibrated degree—in an exercise that will essentially become useless immediately after their last day in school.

In contrast, when one examines life outside of school, projects are ubiquitous. Some projects are assigned to the person, and some are carried out strictly at the person's initiative, but most projects represent an amalgam of personal and communal needs and ends. Although schools have sponsored projects for many years—indeed, the Progressive Era of the 1920s and 1930s featured an educational approach called the "project method"—such involvement in projects over the years has been virtually invisible in records of a child's progress.

Here our research team has endeavored to make a contribution. We believe that projects are more likely to be taken seriously by students, teachers, parents, and the wider community if they can be assessed in a reasonable and convenient way. We have therefore sought to construct straightforward ways of evaluating the developmental sophistication and the individualized characteristics of student projects. We view projects and student portfolios in terms of the following five separate dimensions, each of which can be assessed (Camp et al., 1993; Seidel, 1989, 1992).

Individual Profile

At issue here is what the project reveals about the specific cognitive strengths, weaknesses, and proclivities of the student. The profile includes the student's disposition toward work (taking risks, persevering) as well as the student's particular intellectual propensities (linguistic, logical, spatial, interpersonal, and the like).

Mastery of Facts, Skills, and Concepts

Projects can be quite marvelous to behold and yet be remote from—or directly at odds with—what is being taught in school. When invoking this dimension, we are able to look at the students' capacity to showcase their command of factual knowledge, mastery of concepts, and skills in deploying the standard curriculum. Customarily a bargain is struck between student and teacher: the teacher can ask the student to draw on school knowledge and understanding in creating a project, and the student can select the facts, skills, and concepts to draw on in the project.

Quality of Work

Each project is an instance of a certain genre—a comic play, a mural, a science experiment, a historical narrative. These genres harbor within them certain specific criteria of quality that can be invoked in their evaluation—skits are not assessed in the same way as lectures. Among the aspects of quality that are customarily examined are innovation and imagination, aesthetic judgment and technique, the development of a project in order to foreground a particular concept, and the execution of a performance. As a student continues to create in a genre, he or she gains greater familiarity with the criteria of that genre and learns increasingly to think in the symbol system of that domain.

Communication

Projects offer an opportunity for students to communicate with a wider audience: with peers in collaborative efforts, with teachers and other adults, and with their own prior goals and concerns. Sometimes the communication is quite overt, as in a theatrical or musical performance. But even in a more "desktop" science or history project, students have to communicate their findings skillfully, and that process is distinct from the work of conducting the experiment or the library research.

Reflection

One of the most important but most neglected features of intellectual growth is the capacity to step back from one's work, to monitor one's goals, to assess what progress has been made, to evaluate how one's course can be corrected and how to make use of knowledge that has been obtained in the classroom or from others, and the like.

Projects provide an excellent occasion for such metacognitive or reflective activity. Teachers and students can review work together, and ponder how it relates to past work, longer-term goals, working styles, and so on. Equally important, students can come to internalize these reflective practices, so that they are able to evaluate their work even in the absence of outside agents.

* * *

It should be stressed that there is nothing magical or final about these dimensions. They reflect a distillation of much discussion in our research group and can be expected to evolve further. Despite our belief that these dimensions constitute a powerful set of lenses for the examination of student work, we do not believe that it would be efficacious simply to impose them on a school or a school system. Rather, we believe that a consideration of such dimensions will arise naturally, as teachers (and students and perhaps even families) learn to look at work together and think about projects' distinctive qualities and their evolution over time.

Still, there is a distinct place for a research team in such an effort. As researchers, we can present teachers with rich examples for discussion and help guide the discussion—for example, avoiding terminological dead ends or confounding of dimensions. We believe that groups of teachers who are engaged in serious evaluation of student efforts will eventually come up with an ensemble of dimensions much like the one I described above. In that sense, the five dimensions can serve as a kind of supermatrix—what we have humorously dubbed "the mother of all scoring systems." Should such a system be adopted, it will be possible for schools to compare the works of students with one another—a desirable outcome if such scoring systems are to achieve a more enduring stature in American assessment.

Naturally, part of the evaluation of student projects focuses on the quality of the projects. But we are also interested in two other facets. One is the extent to which the project reveals something about the individual student—his or her own particular strengths, limitations, idiosyncrasies, and overall cognitive profile. The other is the extent to which the project involves cooperation with other students, teachers, and outside experts as well as the judicious use of other kinds of resources, such as libraries and computer databases.

Students are not graded up or down if projects are more individualistic or more cooperative. Rather, we describe projects in this way because we feel that these features represent important aspects of any kind of project in which a person will ever participate, aspects that should be noted rather than ignored. In particular, in working with others, students become sensitive to the varying ways in which a project can be conceived and pursued; moreover, in reflecting on their own particular styles and contributions, students receive a preview of the kinds of project activities in which they are most likely to become involved after they finish school.

PROJECT SCAFFOLDING

As researchers, we have also become involved in reflection on what it takes to plan and execute projects. Somewhat naively, researchers and teachers originally thought that students could readily create and present projects on their own. In the absence of help at school, however, most projects either are executed by parents or, if done by children, are pale imitations of projects already carried out before or observed elsewhere. Particularly common are book reports or television-style presentations in front of displays resembling weather maps. If students are to conceptualize, develop, and present their own projects effectively, they need to be guided—"scaffolded" is the educational term of art—in the various phases and aspects of this activity.

Far from undermining the challenge of making one's own projects, such support actually makes participation in projects possible and growth in project-execution abilities likely. Just as students benefit from apprenticeships in literacy or in a craft, discipline, or pod, they also benefit from an apprenticeship in the formulation and execution of projects. Some students are fortunate enough to have had this apprenticeship at home or in some community activity, such as organized sports or music lessons or scouting. But for the vast majority who have not had such opportunities, elementary school is the most likely place where they can be apprenticed in a project way of life—unless they happen to go to graduate school 15 years later!

The course of project construction facilitates new understandings. A project provides an opportunity for students to marshal previously mastered concepts and skills in the service of a new goal or enterprise. The knowledge of how to draw on such earlier forms of representation or understanding to meet a new challenge is a vital acquisition. Planning the project, taking stock along the way, rehearsing it, assembling it in at least a tentatively final form, answering questions about it, and viewing the videotape critically afterward should all help enhance the student's understanding of the topic of the project as well as his or her own contributions to the project's realization.

These features of the Key Learning Community point up some aspects of effective education during the period of middle childhood. To an immersion in a richly furnished environment, one now adds a more or less formal apprenticeship. Skills are acquired in a domain-appropriate form, and the purposes and uses of these skills remain vivid in the consciousness of the apprentice. At the same time, disciplines are encountered not in an isolated form that provides little motivation, but rather as part of encompassing themes that reverberate throughout the curriculum of the school.

The student's emerging knowledge and skills are mobilized in the course of executing a project of his or her own devising, one that has meaning for the student, for his or her family, and within the wider community. Such skills and projects are assessed as much as possible within the context of daily school activities; the assessment involves not only the teacher but also peers and, increasingly, the student him- or herself. The student comes to view the project from a variety of perspectives as it speaks to a variety of audiences and as he or she observes it evolving, often in unpredictable ways.

It would be a mistake to consider projects a panacea for all education ills or as the royal road to a nirvana of knowledge! Some materials need to be taught in more disciplined, rote, or algorithmic ways. Some projects can become a license for fooling around, whereas others may function as a way of hiding fundamental deficiencies in the understanding of vital disciplinary content.

Still, at their best, projects can serve a number of purposes well. They engage students over a significant period of time, spurring them to produce drafts, revise their work, and reflect on it. They foster positive cooperativeness in which each student can make a distinctive contribution. They model the kind of useful work that is carried out after the completion of school in the wider community. They allow students to discover their areas of strength and to put their best foot forward; they engender a feeling of deep involvement or "flow," substituting intrinsic for extrinsic motivation. Perhaps most important, they offer a proper venue in which to demonstrate the kinds of understandings that the student has (or has not) achieved in the course of the regular school curriculum.

Although the project method has a long history within American educational circles, I am not alone among my contemporaries in being in debt to the Key Learning Community for clarifying these possibilities. Alas, projects are under siege in American education circles today, and they are vulnerable elsewhere in the world as well.

The reason is simply stated: Various national and international tests now occupy center stage in nearly all educational systems. Indeed, I would go so far as to say that improvement (or, in the happy instance, maintenance) of a country's standing in international comparisons drives curriculum and pedagogy everywhere. To the extent that scores on such instruments hold sway over educational regimes, it is difficult to carry out well-rounded projects.

The demise of projects, especially in the secondary school years, would be tragic. Through well-designed project work, students learn invaluable lessons of in-depth research, clear expression, use of media, and cooperation with peers. Projects are highly motivating and can be memorable; many students remember best those projects in which they invested much time and much effort. The challenge to those of us who value projects is clear: We must make the best case we can for continuing to feature them in the curriculum.

REFERENCES

Camp, R., Seidel, S., Wolf, D., Zessoules, R., and Winner, E. (Eds.), (1993). *Arts PROPEL: A handbook for imaginative writing*. Educational Testing Service and Harvard Project Zero.

Seidel, S. (1989). Even before portfolios: The activities and atmosphere of a portfolio classroom. *Portfolio*, December, 6–9.

Seidel, S. (1992). Looking Carefully Together: *A Comparative Analysis of Four Models of Collaborative Investigation of Children's Work*. [Qualifying Paper]. Harvard Graduate School of Education, Cambridge, MA.

Winger, P. (1991, December 1). The best schools in the world. *Newsweek*.

ESSAY 15

Arts PROPEL

DISCIPLINED INQUIRY IN HIGH SCHOOL: AN INTRODUCTION TO ARTS PROPEL

In the early 1990s, I noted the renaissance of interest in education in the arts. And indeed, for a variety of reasons, the arts had gained—or regained—a place in the American curriculum in the 1980s.

Alas, those days seem distant. With the hegemony of high-stakes testing in the first decades of the 21st century, quality arts education seems under siege in all but the most well-resourced public schools. Nonetheless, those of us who believe that an education bereft of the arts is, so to speak, "half-brained" will continue to advocate for the arts and will try to do so on the basis of sound arguments and quality curricula.

At the rhetorical level it is easy to find areas of consensus among the various participants in the national arts education movement. Nearly everyone would call for more class time spent on the arts, better-trained teachers, and some kind of graduation requirement. Yet lurking beneath the surface agreement are vexed issues that engender sharp controversy.

In this chapter I introduce an approach to curriculum and assessment in the arts, principally at the high school level, called Arts PROPEL. While a number of the features of Arts PROPEL are shared with other contemporary initiatives, the approach differs both in terms of its intellectual origins and its particular mix of components. This chapter thus also serves as an introduction to the general approach to arts education devised over the past decades at Project Zero at the Harvard Graduate School of Education and to a particular form it has currently assumed in the practical arena.

BUILDING ON THE THEORY OF MULTIPLE INTELLIGENCES

In my own work, various insights came together in MI theory (see Essays 8–12). In light of a pluralistic view of the intellect, the question immediately arises as to whether there is a separate artistic intelligence. According to my analysis, there is not.

Rather, each of these forms of intelligence can be directed toward artistic ends; that is, the symbols entailed in a domain of knowledge may, but need not, be marshaled in an aesthetic fashion. Thus, linguistic intelligence can be used in ordinary conversation or for the purpose of authoring legal briefs; in neither case is language employed aesthetically. The same intelligence can be used for writing poems or creating dialogue in plays, in which case it is deployed aesthetically.

By the same token, spatial intelligence can be used by sailors or sculptors, and bodily-kinesthetic intelligence can be exploited by dancers, mimes, athletes, or surgeons. Even musical intelligence can be used nonaesthetically (as in a communication system based on bugle calls), just as logical-mathematical intelligence can be directed in an aesthetic vein (for instance, when one proof is favored because it is judged more elegant than another). Whether an intelligence is mobilized for aesthetic or nonaesthetic ends turns out to be an individual or a cultural decision.

ALTERNATIVE ACCENTS IN ARTS EDUCATION

Over the course of history, human intelligences have been trained or cultivated primarily in one of two contrasting ways. On the one hand, individuals have become participants from an early age in activities that mobilize and channel their intelligences. This process occurs in traditional apprenticeships as well as in informal scholastic activities that feature observation, demonstration, and coaching in context.

On the other hand, human intelligences have been trained in formal scholastic settings and formats. Students attend lectures or read textbooks on various subjects and are expected to memorize, understand, and draw from this material for homework, examinations, and "later life." According to my analysis, the scholastic approach has come to dominate our thinking about learning and to exercise a near stranglehold on school activities. Yet people can also nurture and train intelligences—including a much wider band of their intelligences—through informal or non-scholastic regimens.

In few areas of knowledge has the distinction between these two forms been more salient than in the field of arts education. For hundreds if not thousands of years, students have learned much of artistry through apprenticeships. They observe artistic masters at work. They are gradually drawn into these activities. They at first participate in simple, carefully supported ways, then gradually tackle more difficult assignments with diminishing support from their coach or master. Certainly this was the procedure of choice in the ateliers of the Renaissance; versions of it persist in private art and music lessons today. Artists-in-the-schools programs are efforts to exploit the power of these traditional learning schemes. In such instances, appropriate intelligences are mobilized directly, without the need for extensive linguistic, logical, or notational interventions.

Over the past few hundred years, a second front has opened in arts education. With the emergence of fields such as art history, art criticism, aesthetics, communications, semiotics, and the like, an ensemble of scholastic understandings about the arts has gained importance in the academy. Rather than being acquired through observation, demonstration, or apprenticeship, these "peri-artistic" bodies of knowledge are mastered primarily through traditional scholastic methods: through lectures, texts, and writing assignments, in a manner akin to history, economics, and sociology.

Now there is no necessary link between these aspects of the arts and the modes of teaching. Art history could be taught through observation or demonstration, just as painting or playing the violin could be taught (if not learned!) through lecturing or reading a textbook. And yet, for evident reasons, each of these artistic disciplines has tended to favor one form of pedagogy over its rival.

DISCIPLINED INQUIRY IN HIGH SCHOOL: AN INTRODUCTION TO ARTS PROPEL

In a few school systems, efforts have been made to train children in "peri-artistic" activities like cultural history or connoisseurship. Traditionally there has been little constituency in the community for this activity; only with the advent of discipline-based arts education, an approach developed in the early 1980s by the Getty Trust, has there been a call for training in artistry outside the production sphere.

Within the professions of arts education, however, a consensus has emerged over recent decades that production alone will not suffice. While arts educators differ in their assessment of the importance of artistic production—and its putative connection to creativity, more broadly framed—they concur that for the majority of the population, such an exclusive emphasis no longer makes sense. Thus, nearly all reform efforts call for an arts education that encompasses some discussion and analysis of artworks themselves as well as some appreciation of the cultural contexts in which artworks are fashioned.

THE PROJECT ZERO APPROACH TO ART EDUCATION

Given our cognitive approach to artistic education, these general trends have been applauded within Project Zero. (Indeed, in our more chauvinistic moments, we claim a bit of credit for the recent reorientation in arts education.) We believe that students need to be introduced to the ways of thinking exhibited by individuals involved in the arts: practicing artists and those who analyze, criticize, and investigate the cultural contexts of art objects.

Yet, in contrast to some advocates of discipline-based arts education, we nuance this position. Consider the following points:

1. Particularly at younger ages (below, say, age 10), production activities ought to be central in any art form. Children learn best when they are actively involved in their subject matter; they want to work directly with materials and media. In the arts, these strengths and inclinations almost always translate into the making of something. Moreover, young children have considerable gifts for figuring out the crucial components or patterns in an artistic object, and they should have the opportunity to do such ferreting out on their own. This accent is a legacy of the Progressive Era that deserves to endure, even in a more "disciplinary epoch."
2. Perceptual, historical, critical, and other peri-artistic activities should be closely related to and, whenever possible, emerge from the child's own productions. That is, rather than being introduced in an alien context to art objects made by others, children should encounter such objects in relation to the particular artistic products and problems with which they are themselves engaged—and, whenever possible, in intimate connection to the child's own art objects. (Older students and adults can also benefit from such contextualized introductions to peri-artistic activities.)
3. Arts curricula need to be presented by teachers or others with a deep knowledge of how to think in an artistic medium. If the area is music, the teacher must be able to think musically—and not merely introduce music via language or logic. Likewise, education in the visual arts must occur at the hand—and through the eyes—of someone who can think visually or spatially. To the extent that teachers do not already possess these skills, they ought to enroll in training regimens that can develop these cognitive capacities.
4. Whenever possible, artistic learning should be organized around meaningful projects that are carried out over a significant period of time and that allow ample opportunity for feedback, discussion, and reflection (see Essay 14). Such projects are likely to interest students, motivate them, and encourage them to develop skills; and they may well exert a long-term impact on the students' competence and understanding. As much as possible, one-shot learning experiences should be spurned.
5. In most artistic areas, it will not be profitable to plan a strict K–12 sequential curriculum. (I have in mind here simple-minded but all too frequent curricular goals: can provide four color names; can sing three intervals; can recite two sonnets.) Such a formula may

sound attractive, but it flies in the face of the holistic, contextually sensitive manner in which people customarily gain mastery in crafts or disciplines. Artistry involves a continuing exposure, at various developmental levels, to certain core concepts, such as style, composition, and genre, and to certain recurrent challenges, such as performing a passage with feeling or creating a powerful artistic image.

6. Curricula need to be rooted in this "spiral" aspect of artistic learning. A curriculum may be sequential in the sense that it revisits concepts and problems in an increasingly sophisticated way, but not in the sense that one set of problems, concepts, or terms is addressed in 2nd grade and another set in 3rd grade, and so on.

7. Assessment of learning is crucial in the arts. The success of an arts program cannot be asserted or taken on faith. Assessments must respect the particular intelligences involved—musical skill must be assessed through musical means and not via the intervening screens of language or logic. Assessments also must probe those abilities and concepts that are most central to the arts. Rather than crafting the curriculum to suit the assessment, we must devise assessments that do justice to what is most pivotal in an art form.

8. Artistic learning does not merely entail the mastery of a set of skills or concepts. The arts are also deeply personal areas through which students confront their own deepest feelings as well as the feelings of others. Students need educational vehicles that allow them such exploration; they must see that personal reflection is a respected and important activity, and be assured that their privacy will not be violated.

9. In general, it is risky—and, in any case, unnecessary—to teach artistic taste or value judgments directly. However, it is important for students to understand that the arts are permeated by issues of taste and value that matter to anyone who is seriously engaged in the arts. These issues are best conveyed through contact with individuals who care about these issues and are willing to introduce and defend their values, but who also are open to discussion and countenance alternative views.

10. Arts education is too important to be left to any one group—even that group designated as "art educators." Rather, arts education needs to be a cooperative enterprise involving artists, teachers, administrators, researchers, and the students themselves.

11. While ideally all students would study all art forms, this is not a practical option. There are simply too many subjects—and, in my terms, too many intelligences—competing for space on the calendar—and the school day is already excessively fragmented. In my view, no art form has any intrinsic priority over others.

Thus, at the risk of offending aficionados of a particular art form, I assert that students should all have extended exposure to some art form—but it need not be one of the visual arts. Indeed, I would rather students be well versed in music, dance, or drama than have a smattering of knowledge across the several lively arts. Then they would at least know what it is like to "think" in an art form, and they would retain the option of assimilating other art forms in later life, rather than be forever consigned to dilettante status, or even to drop out of the world of arts altogether.

ARTS PROPEL

The above points could give rise to any number of programs in arts education. For us at Project Zero, they contributed to an approach called Arts PROPEL. In 1985, with encouragement and support from the Arts and Humanities Division of the Rockefeller Foundation, Project Zero joined forces with the Educational Testing Service and the Pittsburgh Public Schools in a 5-year project. Our goal: to devise a set of assessment instruments that could document artistic learning during the later elementary and high school years.

As anyone involved in educational experiments can readily appreciate, it proved easier to state our goal than to implement it. We began by attempting to delineate the kinds of competences that we sought to measure in our students. We decided to work in three art forms—music, visual art, and imaginative writing—and to look at three kinds of competences: *production* (composing or performing music; painting or drawing; engaging in imaginative or "creative" writing); *perception* (effecting distinctions or discriminations within an art form—"thinking" artistically); and reflection (stepping back from one's own perceptions or productions, or those of other artists, and seeking to understand the goals, methods, difficulties, and effects achieved). PRoPeL captures acronymically this trio of competences in our three art forms, with the final L emphasizing our concern with learning.

Ideally, we would have liked simply to devise adequate assessment instruments and administer them to students in the target age groups. However, we soon arrived at a simple but crucial truth: There is no point in assessing competences or even potentials unless the student has had some significant experience in working directly with relevant artistic media. Just as baseball scouts look at students who are already playing baseball, it is necessary for educational assessors to examine students who are already engaged in artistic activities. Similarly, just as baseball rookies need well-trained and skilled coaches, so, too, do art students require teachers who are fully acquainted with the goals of an educational program and able to exemplify the requisite artistic skills and understandings.

To bring about these goals, therefore, we devised curriculum modules and linked them to assessment instruments. We implemented a careful procedure of curriculum and assessment development. For each art form, we assembled an interdisciplinary team (with teachers playing an indispensable role) charged with defining the central competences in that form. In writing, we looked at students' capacities to create instances of different genres—for example, writing a poem and creating dialogue for a play. In music, we examined the ways in which students learn from rehearsals of a work-in-progress. And in the area of visual arts (from which I draw most of my examples here), these competences focused on sensitivity to style, appreciation of various compositional patterns, and ability to plan and create a work such as a portrait or a still life.

TWO EDUCATIONAL VEHICLES

For each of these nominated competences, we generated a set of exercises called a "domain project" that had to feature Perceptual, Productive, and Reflective elements. Domain projects do not in themselves constitute an entire curriculum, but they must be curriculum-compatible; that is, they should fit comfortably into a standard art curriculum.

The domain projects are first explored and critiqued by teachers. After revision, they are administered in pilot form to students. A preliminary assessment system is then tried out by the teachers. An iterative process is invoked until the domain project is considered adequate from the perspective of each of its audiences. Once the project has been completed, it can be used as is by teachers or adapted in various ways to fit a particular curriculum or the teaching style or goals of a specific teacher. Part of the assessment procedure is rough-and-ready—simply giving students and teachers a feeling for what the student is learning. However, it is also possible to make more fine-grained analyses (for research purposes) as well as to produce a summary score for use by the central school administration.

An example—the "composition" domain project. This project is designed to help students notice how arrangements and interrelationships of shapes affect the composition and impact of artistic works. Students are given an opportunity to make compositional decisions and to reflect on the effects of such decisions in their works and in works created by acknowledged artistic masters.

In an initial session, students are given a set of 10 odd, black, geometric shapes. They are asked simply to drop those shapes on a piece of white paper. The exercise is then repeated, although this time students are asked to put together a set of shapes that they find pleasing. They are then asked to reflect on the differences between the "random" and the "deliberate" work. In a notebook they record the differences they see and state the reasons that motivated their own deliberate choices. Most students find this exercise fun, although at first they may not quite know what to make of it.

In a second session, students informally encounter certain principles of composition. The teacher introduces the students to a number of artistic works of different styles and periods that differ significantly from one another in the kinds of symmetry or balance they epitomize or violate. Students are asked to describe the differences among these works and to develop a vocabulary that can capture these differences and convey them effectively to others. Achievements (or violations) of harmony, cohesion, repetition, dominant forces, radial patterns, surprise, or tension in the works are noted. At the conclusion of the session, students are asked to jot down in their notebooks similarities and differences in a contrasting set of slides. They are also given an assignment: During the next week, they should search their daily environment for instances of different compositions—both compositions already achieved by an artist and those that the students can create by "framing" a scene in nature.

In a third session, students report on the compositions they observed in their own environment and discuss them with reference to those observed in the art class. The students then return to the deliberate composition of session one. Now they are asked to make a final work. Before proceeding, however, they are asked to indicate their plans for this work. Then they go about realizing and, if they wish, revising their final composition. On a worksheet they indicate what they found most surprising about their composition and which further changes they might want to make in a future work.

In addition to the student's own compositions, perceptual discriminations, and reflections, the teacher also has his or her own assessment sheet. The teacher can evaluate students in terms of the kinds of compositions attempted or achieved. Other kinds of learning—for instance, the students' success in discovering interesting compositions in their environments or their ability to connect their own compositions with those of well-known artists—can also be assessed. This domain project can be repeated, in its initial or an altered form, to determine the extent to which the students' grasp of compositional issues has developed over time.

The composition domain project works with a traditional element of the visual arts—the arrangement of form—and seeks to tie this element to students' own productive and perceptual experiences.

A quite different approach is taken in a second domain project called "the biography of a work." In this instance our goals are much broader. We want to help students synthesize their learning from previous domain projects in composition, style, and expression, and to do so through tracing the development of a complete work.

In the biography of a work, students first observe a large set of sketches that Andrew Wyeth prepared before he completed *Brown Swiss*. They survey a companion set of sketches and drafts of Picasso's *Guernica*. After these perceptual explorations of the roots of masterworks, students are asked to draw their room at home in a way that expresses something about themselves. They are given a range of media (paper, pencil, charcoal, pen and ink, and so on) as well as some pictorial material, such as magazines and slides. In an initial session, students are asked to choose any element(s) of their room, to add whatever props or objects might be revealing about themselves, and to use these in preparing a preliminary sketch. Their focus should be on composition, but they are encouraged as well to think about how the range of artistic elements can reveal themselves and not just what is represented literally in the picture. A few examples are given of how aspects of form can convey metaphorically a property of an individual.

In a second session, students begin by examining slides that show how artists have used objects metaphorically in their work and how particular objects or elements can carry a multiplicity of meanings. They are also shown slides of artists' studios or rooms and asked how these rooms might bring out something about the artists' view of their particular world. Students then return to their own preliminary sketches and are asked to make provisional decisions about the media that they wish to use and the style, color, line, texture, and so on that they plan to employ. As in the earlier session, students fill out worksheets in which they are asked to reflect on the choices they made, the reasons for these choices, and their aesthetic consequences.

In a third session, students review all of their preliminary sketches and "trial sheets," think about whether they are satisfied with them, and then begin their final work. Students discuss their works-in-progress with other students. Then, in a final session during the following week, the students complete their works, critique one another's efforts, and review their sketches, trial sheets, and reflections. The activities in this final week serve as a model for the kinds of reflections that are used as well in the student portfolio compilations (described below).

In Arts PROPEL we sought to create an ensemble of domain projects for each art form. These prototypes should encompass most of the important concepts in an art form. Over the long haul, one should be able to develop a model of domain projects: which set of exercises qualifies as a domain project, which kinds of learning one can expect to take place, and how best the student can be assessed within and across domain projects.

In addition to the ensemble of domain projects, we introduced a second educational vehicle. While this vehicle is often called a portfolio, I prefer the term process folio—or "processfolio."

Most artists' portfolios contain only their very best works, the set by which the artist would wish to be judged in a competition. In contrast, processfolios are much more like works-in-progress. In their processfolios, students include not just finished works but also original sketches, interim drafts, critiques by themselves and others, and artworks by others that they admire or dislike and that bear in some way on their current project. Sometimes students are asked to present the whole folder of materials; at other times they are asked to select those pieces that appear particularly informative or pivotal in their artistic development.

The maintenance of high standards—so crucial to the success of any arts education program—is dependent at the outset on the stance the teacher takes vis-à-vis artistic performance and productivity; with time, students' effects on one another may well become a powerful means of conveying and maintaining standards. The teacher's role in a processfolio environment differs from the role of the master in a classical apprenticeship in that no single model of progress—no set of discrete levels—underlies the instruction. Still, in the sense that the teacher serves as an exemplar of productive artistry and as an embodiment of the standards of the community, an Arts PROPEL classroom does resemble a classical atelier.

Given our initial charge, much of the energy in Arts PROPEL went into the construction of assessment systems. Each domain project features a set of self-assessment procedures that can be used during the life of that project.

In the case of the composition project, students have the opportunity to step back and reflect on the strengths and weaknesses of each composition; the expressive effects achieved in each composition; and just how these effects are (or are not) fully realized.

In the case of the biography of a work project, students reflect on the changes they have made; the reasons motivating the changes; and the relationship between the early and late drafts. The students' drafts and final products, along with their reflections, are then assessed on a variety of qualitative dimensions, such as engagement, technical skills, imaginativeness, and critical evaluative skills. While the primary assessment for the domain project occurs within the class, it is also possible to assess these projects off-site; such assessment sessions have been carried out with reasonable success by external arts educators brought together under the auspices of ETS.

Whereas domain projects lend themselves to a number of familiar forms of assessment, the assessment of processfolios is a more challenging and delicate operation. Processfolios can be assessed on a large number of dimensions. Some are straightforward, such as the regularity of the entries, their completeness, and the like. Others are more complex and subjective, but still familiar: the overall quality of the final products, on technical and imaginative grounds.

Of special interest to us are those dimensions that help illuminate the unique potential of processfolios: students' awareness of their own strengths and weaknesses; capacity to reflect accurately; ability to build on self-critique and to make use of critiques of others; sensitivity to their own developmental milestones; ability to use lessons from domain projects productively; capacity to find and solve new problems; ability to relate current projects to those undertaken at earlier times and those that one hopes to undertake in the future;

and capacity to move comfortably and appropriately from one aesthetic stance or role to another and back again. The goal is not only to assess along a variety of potentially independent dimensions, but also to encourage students to develop along these dimensions. Such an assessment system has the potential to alter what is discussed—and what is valued—in the classroom.

Under the direction of Ellen Winner, the Arts PROPEL team set down dimensions of production, perception, reflection, and "approach to work" that can be applied to student processfolios and the projects contained therein. The four dimensions are presented in the accompanying table.

Even to list these dimensions is to convey something of the difficulty of the assessment task and the extent to which it breaks new ground. It would be misleading to suggest that we have solved the problems involved in any of these facets of assessment; indeed, as we sometimes jest, we simply have several years' more experience than others in recognizing what does *not* work! It is sobering to note that it took a century for standardized tests to reach their present, hardly glorious status; it is unreasonable to expect assessment of domain projects and from processfolios to mature in just a few years. Still, our progress to date, and our belief that we are assessing in a way that is worthy of the subject matter, has emboldened us to continue his work.

Processfolio Assessment System

(Based on art, music, and writing. Can be expanded to other artistic domains.)

I. PRODUCTION: Thinking in the Domain

Evidence: The evidence for assessing work on the dimension of production lies in the work itself. Thus, these dimensions can be scored by an outsider looking at drafts and final works as well as by the classroom teacher.

- A. Craft: The student is in control of the basic techniques and principles of the domain.
- B. Pursuit: The student develops works over time, as evidenced by revisions that are productive and thoughtful. She pursues the problem in depth. She returns to a problem or theme from a variety of angles.
- C. Invention: The student solves problems in a creative manner. She experiments and takes risks with the medium. She sets her own problems to solve.
- D. Expression: The student expresses an idea or feeling in the work (or in the performance of the work, as in music).

II. REFLECTION: Thinking About the Domain

Evidence: The evidence for assessing reflection comes from the student's journals and sketchbooks and from observations of the kinds of comments the student makes in class. Thus, these dimensions need to be scored by a classroom teacher who knows the student.

- A. Ability and proclivity to assess own work: The student can evaluate her own work. She can articulate and defend the perceived strengths and weaknesses of her own work. She can engage in "shop talk" about her own work.
- B. Ability and proclivity to take on role of critic: The student has developed the ability to evaluate the work of others (peers, published artists). She has a sense of the standards for quality work in the domain. She can engage in shop talk about others' work.
- C. Ability and proclivity to use criticisms and suggestions: The student can consider critical comments about her own work and can incorporate suggestions where appropriate.
- D. Ability to learn from other works of art within the domain: The student can use work by artists for ideas and inspiration.

E. Ability to articulate artistic goals: The student has a sense of herself as an artist, as evidenced by the ability to articulate goals for a particular work, or more general artistic goals.

III. PERCEPTION: Perceiving in the Domain

Evidence: The evidence for assessing a student's perceptual skills comes from the student's journal entries and from observations of the student's comments made in critique sessions. Thus, only a classroom teacher can assess a student on this dimension.

A. Capacity to make fine discriminations about works in the domain: The student can make discriminations in works from a wide variety of genres, cultures, and historical periods.
B. Awareness of sensuous aspects of experience: The student shows heightened sensitivity to physical properties of the environment related to the domain in question (for example, she responds to visual patterns made by shadows, to sounds of cars honking in different pitches, to patterning of words on a grocery list, and so on).
C. Awareness of physical properties and qualities of materials: The student is sensitive to the properties of the materials that she is working with as she is developing a work (for example, textures of different papers, timbres of instruments, sounds of words).

IV. APPROACH TO WORK

Evidence: The evidence for assessing a student's approach to work lies in observations of the student in classroom interactions and from the student's journal entries. Thus, a student's approach to work can be assessed only by the classroom teacher.

A. Engagement: The student works hard and is interested in what she is doing. She meets deadlines. She shows care and attention to detail in the presentation of the final project.
B. Ability to work independently: The student can work independently when appropriate.
C. Ability to work collaboratively: The student can work collaboratively when appropriate.
D. Ability to use cultural resources: The student knows where to go for help: books, museums, tools, other people.

Even if we should fall short of our goal of adequate psychometric measures of processfolios, our effort has utility. As noted earlier, an important aspect of artistic learning is the opportunity for students to become involved in meaningful projects in which their own understanding and growth can come to the fore. It is already clear to us that both students and teachers find these processfolio activities engaging, exciting, and useful in their own right. Teachers find that their classrooms come alive. By encouraging the development of processfolios, and by looking at them sympathetically and systematically, we may be able to increase the use of these materials and activities in schools. While it may be too much to expect that colleges will ever base admissions decisions chiefly on such processfolio information, we hope that such educational vehicles may allow students to recognize and develop their own cognitive strengths.

Educators and educational critics frequently lament the gap between theory and practice—and between theorists and practitioners. It is no doubt true that the professional goals of the two groups are different—the theorist's triumph often leaves the practitioner untouched; the practitioner's pleasures seem uninteresting to the theorist.

Those of us at Project Zero believe that it is important to look at "natural" development before contemplating interventions; and we believe that it is important to establish the psychological facts and to develop one's educational philosophy before attempting to influence practice—especially since it is always possible that one might influence practice for the worse!

But having had the luxury of decades-long exploration of artistic development, it has certainly been opportune for us to become more directly involved in educational experimentation. The fact that arts educational practice is being widely discussed only heightens the need for us to get our feet wet. Arts PROPEL represents one concerted effort to do just that.

It is too early to know how successful this effort will prove to be and, if it is successful in its "hothouse" atmosphere, whether it can be successfully transported to more remote soils. Still, it is not premature to indicate that researchers can learn a great deal from attempting to implement their ideas in a school setting. As long as we are on the alert for any disruption that we may cause, this intermingling of theory and practice should redound to the good of all those involved in arts education. (As I write these words, in 2024 Arts PROPEL investigator Ellen Winner is deeply into a study of the impact of Project Zero ideas around the world—stay tuned!)

As for immediate impact, Arts PROPEL received a tremendous accolade in the early 1990s, when it was selected by *Newsweek* magazine as one of only two "model educational programs" in the United States—the other being graduate education at the California Institute of Technology.

Especially gratifying is the fact that the ideas undergirding PROPEL have proved attractive to educators in other subject matters. Although the notion of projects and processfolios has a long history in the arts, teachers and curriculum supervisors in domains ranging from history to mathematics have come to appreciate the usefulness of rich and engaging projects and the desirability of the systematic cast of thought involved in reflecting on one's work and keeping a regular journal. As a longtime arts educator who is used to seeing his field treated as a backwater, I gain special satisfaction from the present circumstance: our ideas and practices may actually provide inspiration to areas of the curriculum that have traditionally been more prestigious.

CURRICULUM, PEDAGOGY, AND ASSESSMENT

My early work in education drew on two very different sources. On the one hand, there were my own experiences with educational research. As a member of Jerome Bruner's "instructional research group," I had studied the development and impact of the middle school curriculum "Man: A Course of Study"; and as a founding member of Project Zero, I had surveyed the theories and research in arts education. I was also a sometime teacher of piano and an observer of education in other art forms. (See Essays 1 and 2.)

On the other hand, I was deeply steeped in developmental psychology. My studies in that area formed my thoughts about the human mind. And yet, from the start, I was skeptical about two prevalent assumptions. (See Essays 5 and 6.)

To begin with, development was universally seen as culminating in the capacity to think, and to proceed as a scientist. While sympathetic to the importance of science, I believed that this was a limited perspective. After all, science as we know it is basically an invention of Europe in the 17th century—think Galileo, think Newton. This seemed quite shortsighted. On the other hand every known society has engaged in the arts—storytelling, pictorial craft, making music, dance—and most human societies have a clear sense of the difference between a master, a participant, and a consumer—a mere member of the audience.

In addition, while I was deeply sympathetic to the American pragmatic tradition—as embodied by the great philosophers William James and John Dewey and my own teacher Jerome Bruner—I saw its limitations. I did not believe that educational materials could be mastered easily or naturally or easily. I did not agree with Bruner's often-cited assertion "we begin with the hypothesis that any subject can be taught effectively in some intellectually honest form to any child at any stage of development." Indeed, I thought that many of children's natural ways of thinking, conceptualizing, and problem-solving were deeply antithetical to disciplinary learning, and had to be dissolved or eliminated. (After all, we evolved as a species to survive in the savannahs of East Africa—not to master calculus or to interpret the deeper meaning of poetry.)

Relatedly, while I endorsed the importance of communal and of social bonds as well as the desirability of democratic processes in Dewey's philosophy, I believed that Dewey had also underestimated the challenges involved in learning to think well in and across the scholarly disciplines. What Dewey and Bruner almost took for granted was the heart—if not the soul—of what it meant to become an educated person.

Accordingly, in my own studies, I detailed the misconceptions widely held by young children that had to be dissolved or overcome in order for genuine disciplinary thinking to occur. And by the same token, I personally valued and felt comfortable in carrying out interdisciplinary work. Yet, with Veronica Boix-Mansilla, I delineated the challenges entailed in carrying our work, which genuinely merits the descriptor "interdisciplinary."

In 1983 the U.S. government issued a major report critical of K–12 education: *A Nation at Risk*. Shortly thereafter. I was drawn into ambitious efforts to define more broadly the goals of education and how best to achieve them. An ambitious initiative, ATLAS, took up lots of time and resources, but, in my view, it was not successful. But our work on ATLAS led to Teaching for Understanding—often shortened to TFU—my largest collaborative effort to indicate what it means to understand, to master—what one has been exposed to, what one has learned.

Contrary to its common connotation, "understanding" emerges not as something that just occurs in your mind or just between your ears. Rather, understanding emerges as a performance—something you do, you act out, you run through, so that you and, importantly, others can determine whether you have actually mastered and can make use of the material that you observed or studied or committed to memory.

Teaching (or Education) for Understanding is part of an interconnected set of four ideas: you need appropriate entry points; opportunities to practice; an arena for performing your understandings; and ways of evaluating the quality of the performances. Over the decades, colleagues at Project Zero and other educational institutions have developed these ideas with various materials and in various contexts—you can read about some of these applications at http://pz.harvard.edu.

I happen to live in a nation that is obsessed with testing and measurement of just about everything. (In a strange way, we share this property with China—both traditional and contemporary.) Sometimes the assessments are quite imaginative, but in education there is a long tradition—alive and well—of going for the shortest, most readily administered, and most easily scored tests. As a counterpoint, I've pondered the kinds of assessments that work best in real life—the medical resident taking a hand in surgery, the young reporter covering the state house along with a veteran, the junior lawyer on a legal defense team, the fledgling teacher alongside the master teacher. This has led to a broader essay on "Assessment in Context" (Essay 19 in this volume).

As I turned from empirical research in developmental psychology to the study of education, I pondered what we know about young children as they begin to enter school (rather than preschool). My own studies and my survey of the research cast doubt on two widely held views: (a) 5-year-olds are a blank slate onto which one can sketch all of human knowledge; and (b) young children have the capacity to master the core and the methods of the several disciplines.

I reached a different conclusion. Young children have worked out views on many topics and puzzles; they are not blank slates! But few of those views withstand deep scrutiny; that's why we had to create disciplines and methods. In this chapter, I describe the content and approaches of an "unschooled mind" and suggest ways in which to begin to school it. As is often the case, I begin with a conversation—a set of affectionate arguments—with Jean Piaget.

ACKNOWLEDGMENT

This chapter was first presented as the Peterson Lecture to the International Baccalaureate Organization. The transcript of the talk was published in *IB World* in April 2003. An edited version of this talk was published as Chapter 2 of Howard Gardner's *Development and Education of the Mind* (2006), which appears here with some further revision by the author. © Howard Gardner. Reprinted with the author's permission.

REFERENCES

Bruner, J. (1960). *The process of education*. Harvard University Press.
United States Commission on Excellence in Education. (1983). *A nation at risk*.

ESSAY 16

The Unschooled Mind
Why Even the Best Students in the Best Schools May Not Understand

I'm trained in developmental psychology, a field in which the contributions of Jean Piaget are unequaled. I have had quite a full career during which I nonetheless challenged Piaget on several issues. My three principal arguments with him are as follows.

First of all, Piaget believed that if you studied children, you had to know what they were going to become—to identify the "end state" of development. Piaget thought it was to be a scientist; after all, that's what Piaget was.

However, in my own training I had spent a lot of time working in the arts. I felt that there was something deficient with a theory that only talked about the mind of the scientist as being the end-all of a child's development. So I began to explore what development would be like if one thought of *participation in the arts* as an artist, or a critic, or a performer, or a connoisseur, as being a viable end-state. This is not to say that all human beings should develop to become artists any more than they all should develop to become scientists, but rather that we can develop many different kinds of human beings.

The second argument I had with Piaget—and the one that I gained recognition for—was with respect to the notion that there is a single thing called intelligence that can be measured by an intelligence test. Now, it's not widely known that Piaget studied in Alfred Binet's laboratory, specifically with Théodore Simon, who had worked with Binet. Brilliantly, Piaget became interested in children's minds because of the mistakes the children made on the intelligence tests. Piaget explored the general intelligence that all human beings share.

In my work, I define intelligence as the ability to solve a problem, or to fashion a product that is valued in at least one culture or community. (See Essays 8–11.) Psychologists of intelligence concede that solving problems is important, but they shy away from any concern about making something, like writing essays, staging plays, designing buildings, and other human feats. Moreover, psychologists get upset when you talk about an ability being valued in a culture; that is because it suggests that unless a culture provides certain opportunities, a person might not seem to be smart. Many—if not most—psychologists believe that intelligence is completely in the brain...

and that if you know exactly where to stick the measurement device and how to "read" it, you can figure out how smart that person is.

In my view, intelligence is always an interaction between potentials and what's available in a culture. For example, Bobby Fischer was one of the greatest chess players in the history of the world. But if Bobby Fischer had been born in a culture where there was no chess, he would likely have been just an awkward geek; he had a brain that was perfectly matched to something in his culture, namely chess, but seemingly mismatched to just about everything else.

It is worth pointing out that Piaget thought he was studying all of intelligence. But I believe he was actually studying logical-mathematical intelligence. In contrast, I talk about the intelligence that artists have as well as those intelligences that are crucial in the human sphere—something of great concern to educators as we are expected to deal—and perhaps *should* deal—with global issues, moral quandaries, questions of value, and the like.

My third argument with Piaget concerns the most interesting claim that he made. If you remember your studies of Piaget, you will recall his claim that children pass through stages of cognitive development. So infants "know" the world in one way, 5-year-olds in another way, 10-year-olds in another way, and 15-year-olds in still another way. When you go from 9 to 11 or from 13 to 16 years old, not only do you see the world in a very different way, but you can't even remember how you used to construe the world.

An example: At age 7 or later, you don't believe that you ever embraced certain ideas: that if a ball of clay were squished, there would be less clay there; or that if water were poured into a different kind of vessel, there would be more or less water, depending on the shape of the receiving vessel.

Yet every 4-year-old in the world believes those things. Where Piaget was wrong, I believe, was in his argument that when people get older, they see the world in a different way and they no longer have access to earlier ways of knowing. I argue that except in areas where we are expert, *most of us continue to think the way we did when we were 5 years old*. We continue to think the way we did before we went to school. That's a pretty radical thesis.

So my remarks focus on the subject of education for understanding. If I said to you, "What is understanding and how can we determine whether understanding has been achieved?," those are much more difficult questions.

I define understanding as the capacity to take knowledge, skills, concepts, and faces learned in one context—usually the school context—and draw on that knowledge in a new context, in a place where you haven't been forewarned to make use of that knowledge. If you were only asked to use knowledge in the same situation in which it was introduced, you might understand, but you might not; we can't tell. But if something new happens out in the street or in the sky or in the newspaper, and you can draw on your earlier knowings, then I would infer that you understand. Let me introduce my "problématique" with three quite commonsense examples.

In the first 5 years of life, children all over the world, with very little formal tutelage, learn to speak, to understand, to tell stories, to tell jokes, to draw, to sing, to invent new tunes, to engage in pretend play—all the things that Piaget and other investigators have demonstrated. Even though nobody knows how to teach these things, young people still learn them all. Then they go to school and suddenly, in the very place where we are supposed to know how to teach them, it's very hard and many of them don't do well. That's a paradox.

One more example: Students at the very best universities in the United States (places like MIT and Johns Hopkins), with very high grades in physics, ultimately leave their class and are given a problem to solve on the street, or a game to play, each of which involves various physical principles. Not only do the students fail to make use of what they learned in school, but they actually answer in essentially the same way that 5-year-olds do.

Ask almost anybody what happens, what forces obtain, when you flip a coin. Most people will come up with the following answer (even people who have taken physics courses): you've got a certain amount of force in your hand and you transfer that force to the coin; for a while that force makes the coin go up and then, when the force kind of gets spent, the coin is tired and kind of flips to the ground. However, physics teaches us that the second you release the coin, the only force that obtains on the coin is gravity. That authoritative account goes against a very powerful intuition that you develop when you're young. And it's not the intuition that's abandoned. It's Newton's and Galileo's laws of motion that prove very difficult to master and draw upon appropriately.

A third vignette is a personal one. My daughter, a very good student, telephoned me when she was a sophomore in college, crying. I said, "Why are you crying?" She said, "It's my physics; I don't understand it." I said, "Well, you know," (and I was telling the truth), "I really respect you for taking physics because it's difficult and I wouldn't have taken it in college." I then added, "I don't even care what grade you get, but it's really important that you understand your physics." So I said, "Go to your instructor and have him or her explain to you what it is you don't understand." And she said, "Dad, you don't get it! I've *never* understood."

This exchange had a profound impact on me. My daughter was not saying that she was a faker or a poseur. Believe me, Kerith is not! What she was saying is what I think most of us experience: We know the moves to make in school, to get good grades, and even to be successful; but we know as well that if people put the questions to us in another way, if they push to see how much we have really understood, the whole house of cards might fall.

At least in the United States, there are formidable obstacles to understanding:

1. Short-answer assessments, or what I call a "text/test context." You read a textbook. The test is based on the textbook, and the textbook tells you the answers you have to give.

2. The correct answer compromise is an entente between the teacher and the student. No matter how you respond, nobody should ask any further questions. No one is made uncomfortable, but deeper understanding is avoided.
3. The pressure for coverage, which means that there are 37 chapters in the book and you *must* get through all 37 chapters by the end of the term.

So, three vignettes. The young child learns so easily; the school child has difficulty. The students who get A's at the best universities in the world are still typically Aristotelians (or pre-Aristotelians!) in their models of the physical world. And then, of course, the most powerful evidence from my own daughter. What's going on here? I've dubbed it "cognitive Freudianism."

Freud convinced many of us that as adults, we continue to have the same personality traits as we did when we were children. We fight the same battles that we fought in the nursery with our parents and our siblings. Most people who live in a modern Western society believe this. (If you don't believe it and you pay me $150 an hour, I will convince you that it's true.) That's what psychoanalysis is all about.

I'm making the claim that Freud was correct in an area that he wasn't expert in, and where Piaget was allegedly the authority; namely, except in areas where we *are* experts, most of us continue to think in much the same way we did when we were 5 years old.

An expert is a person who comes to understand the world differently. But that is very difficult to do, and I'm going to argue today that it's not done very often. This is the thesis of my remarks.

I'm going to provide evidence that no matter where you look in the curriculum, you will find students who don't understand: physics, mathematics, biology, literature, art. It's ubiquitous. Later I will chronicle things we can do about this situation. It *is* possible to educate for understanding.

My analysis of the potency of the 5-year-old mind has three foci, which I have already introduced to you. There is the *young natural learner*: the 3-, 4-, or 5-year-old who absorbs and constructs so much about the world without formal tutelage. There is the *student in most schools who* basically masters what school requires so that he or she can get to the next level. But I will argue the student doesn't *really* understand. Then there's the individual we want: the person who can use knowledge in new situations. That's my definition of an *expert*.

A form of knowing (a theory of knowledge) goes with each of these three foci. The expert is a person who can use the skills that are valued in his or her culture. So when a historical example comes up, he can draw on history; when a mechanical example comes up, she can draw from physics; and so on. That's what we want; that's why we go to school. If people are not going to be able to use the knowledge acquired, then we may as well close schools down.

The Unschooled Mind

Scholastic knowledge is what we are very good at doing in school, but unless that scholastic knowledge can be activated in new circumstances, it remains inert and essentially useless.

We teach people notations, squiggles on a paper, formal concepts—what is gravity, what is density, what is force. People who have no sense of what it's like in the world can nonetheless give you a formula and a definition if that's what is called for in class. Then, if you're lucky and you attend an excellent college preparatory school, you get *epistemic forms*. Epistemic forms constitute the ways in which people think in the different disciplines. To think like a historian is not the same as to think like a literary critic or to think like a biologist.

In the first years of life, a natural learner benefits from what Piaget so brilliantly described: *sensorimotor knowledge,* learning about the world using your hands and your eyes, exploring the world of objects, the world of liquids poured from one container to another, and what I call *first-order symbolic competence*. People use words, pictures, and gestures to communicate meanings. That's what every 5-year-old can do.

That's the good news. However, 5-year-olds do one thing that is troublesome: They form *intuitive conceptions or theories*—theories of matter, theories of mind, theories of life. Every normal 5-year-old develops these theories. And those theories can prove serviceable for getting along in the world. However, all too often the theories are wrong. School—indeed, any formal education—is supposed to replace the erroneous theories with better theories.

So what's a *theory of matter*? Here's one: If l have a heavy object in this hand and a light object in that hand and I release them at the same time, the heavier one will fall more quickly. That's what you learn intuitively. Heavy things fall more quickly. However, Galileo went to the top of the tower of Pisa and dropped two objects, and since then, well-informed individuals have understood that that's not in fact what happens. We understand that the laws of acceleration are independent of weight (density). But as children we develop a very powerful theory of matter, and that's very hard to shake.

Here's a *theory of life*: every 5-year-old believes if it's moving, it's alive; if it's not moving, it's dead. This is a very useful theory. However, it doesn't help for sleeping dogs, and computers pose a real problem. Are computers that display moving images alive or dead? It's very hard to say.

Here's a *theory of mind*: I've got a mind; you've got a mind. If we look the same, our minds are the same. If we look different, our minds are different. If you look like me, you've got a good mind; if you look different, you've got a bad mind.

This is a very powerful theory that is very entrenched. It shows up in all kinds of places. Just turn on the television for evidence. It's a conception like this that education is supposed to deal with, and it's this, I maintain, that education has, by and large, failed to deal with.

Why do these misconceptions arise and endure? I claim that it happens because there are different kinds of constraints operating on us.

The first constraint has to do with the *kind of species* we are. We learn certain things very easily. We develop certain theories very readily, and other ones prove very hard for us to acquire. It's an interesting evolutionary question *why* that should be the case.

There are *institutional constraints*. If you put 30 to 50 people in a room like this and one (typically taller) person in front of them, it's very hard to explain things so that all who are present can understand. For every person who is nodding, three are nodding off.

There are also *disciplinary constraints*. The moves that have been developed over the centuries for analysis in one discipline are very different from the moves in other disciplines. Physical causality is not like historical causality or literary causality.

Anticipating what we might do, there is some hope. The hope lies in two institutions. One of them is very old: *the apprenticeship*. There are many powerful clues about how to educate for understanding contained in the apprenticeship. The other is a new institution, more familiar in the United States than in many other countries, but it is spreading rapidly: *the children's museum,* the science museum, the discovery museum, or the San Francisco Exploratorium. Very powerful educational implications lurk in those two institutions.

Let me try to summarize this argument. The *natural learner* displays what I call intuitive understanding. He or she is very promiscuous with the theories already developed in the young mind. Whenever anything happens, the young child draws on the theories of mind, matter, and life to explain them, whether or not those theories are appropriate at all.

In contrast, the *scholastic learner* never tries to apply the theory anywhere, except where he or she is told to. So the scholastic learner gives a ritualized performance. The teacher asks the question, the student gives the prescribed answer or is told that she is wrong, and you go on to the next student.

The *disciplined learner,* the expert, produces a discipline of understanding. Not only can he or she draw on knowledge when it's appropriate but, equally importantly, doesn't draw on that knowledge when it's not appropriate. The 5-year-old is too cognitively promiscuous and uses it always. The 10-year-old is repressed (the opposite of being promiscuous) and never uses it. But the person with disciplined understanding has good judgment and uses the knowledge just when it's appropriate.

There are some deep—if you will, some epistemological—reasons why it's very difficult to teach for understanding. These limitations cover every discipline. I've already mentioned physics. Most people remain 5-year-olds or Aristotelians even though they may well have studied physics.

Here is a wonderful real-life example, taken from education in astronomy. Twenty-five Harvard students have just graduated, all wearing their gowns and their mortarboards. An interviewer says to the students, "Tell me, why is the earth warmer in the summer than it is in the winter?" Twenty-three out of the 25 students immediately came up with the same answer, the answer you would come up with if you didn't know what I was speaking about, namely the answer that the earth is closer to the sun in the summer than it is in the winter.

Now, if we think about it, that doesn't make any sense because it wouldn't account for the seasons in different parts of the earth. The right explanation has to do with the angle of the earth on its axis as it spins around. But 23 out of 25 students forget to apply what they have learned in their astronomy classes and give the same 5-year-old kind of answer.

You might say, "Physics is hard." How about biology? Research shows that students who have taken not one but two or three courses in biology focusing on the topic of evolution still do not understand the basics of evolution. They still believe that something in one generation can be passed on to the next, even if it was acquired in the former generation. They are also still perfectionists. They think that each organism is trying to get more perfect; that counter to Darwin, there is an unseen hand that's guiding that perfection rather than simply variation and selection within a particular ecological niche. So problems encountered in physics extend to biology and the other sciences as well.

What about mathematics? Mathematics is all abstract. It presumably has nothing to do with the real world. So maybe people don't have misconceptions in the area of mathematics. What they have instead is what I call *rigid algorithms*. They learn to fill numbers into a formula.

Consider this problem: There are six times as many students as professors. If there are 10 professors, how many students are there? Anyway, that is quite a simple problem. The answer is 60. If I ask you to capture the above information in a written equation where S stands for students and P stands for professors, most people will write the following equation: $6S = P$. This is because if you parse the sentence, it says there are six times as many students as there are professors. However, what they are *actually writing* is "6 times 60 equals 10"—clearly an absurd result.

What happens in mathematics is that students learn how to plug numbers into formulas, thereby solving equations. As long as the information is presented to them in a certain canonical order, they will get the answer right. If, however, the problem is presented in a new way—in a way which actually requires understanding of the formalism—most people will not get it right because they will not truly interrogate the formalism.

I think back to my own education. I studied the quadratic equation, and I must have solved 500 problems with the quadratic equation. I'm sure by the time I finished school, I could do the quadratic equation in my sleep. Never did anybody give me any explanation of what a quadratic equation stood for or be drawn upon. Nowadays, if I ran into a problem, I wouldn't have a clue that it called for the quadratic equation, even though I might, on a dark and stormy night, remember what a quadratic equation was. But I got very good grades in mathematics because I wasn't expected to know where and when to activate this kind of formalism.

So, the problem in science is *misconceptions*. The problem in mathematics is *rigidly applied algorithms*. How about in the arts, in the humanities?

In the arts and the humanities, the problem is different. It's what I call *scripts* or *stereotypes*. Early in life, children develop very powerful theories about the world. A favorite script is the restaurant script. In the developed world, every 4-year-old knows that if you go to a restaurant, somebody comes and seats you. You are given the menu; you order. Food comes. You eat it and then you call for the check, and you leave.

If you go to McDonald's, you pay first, but that's an exception to the script. Four-year-olds in such societies also know about birthday parties: who comes, what you serve, that kind of thing. The rules are different in different cultures, but everybody knows about birthday parties or analogous celebrations in their neighborhood.

Another script that you develop when you are very young is the *Star Wars* script—named both after the movie of that name and after President Reagan's strategic defense initiative. *Star Wars* says: "It's good to be big; you should be big yourself; if you' re not big, align yourself with somebody who is big." If you look like that person, you will be good and people who look different will be bad. That's the *Star Wars* script, and it's very powerful!

Now, gather people who've studied world history, and ask them about the causes of World War I. They say: "Oh, it's very complicated. There was colonialism, imperialism, ethnic strife, and long-term rivalries," and they give you a very nuanced response. Then you say to them: "Well, what happened in the Gulf War of 2003?" They will say: "Well, there was this bad guy named Saddam Hussein and if we got rid of him, everything would be okay." Now, that's a *Star Wars* type of explanation.

Perhaps the best example of the unschooled mind in the arts comes out of the University of Cambridge in the United Kingdom. In the 1920s a literary critic and poet named I. A. Richards (1956/1929) did a study of Cambridge undergraduates. He approached Cambridge undergraduates who were the best and brightest literary students. He gave them poems and he asked two questions about the poems:

- What do they mean?
- Are they any good?

He performed one manipulation on the poems: He removed the names of the poets. (It's like touring the Louvre or the National Gallery without the labels.)

What did Richards find? He found that the students didn't have a clue about which poems were good (according to the critics) and which were bad. They rejected John Donne. They rejected Gerald Manley Hopkins.

They embraced a Sunday poet who couldn't get published in the *Cambridge Chronicle*. And, when asked what accounted for the quality, they replied: If a poem rhymed, scanned, dealt with a pleasant subject, but was not too sentimental, it was good. But if it dealt with philosophy or anything tragic or anything abstract, it was bad.

So, here you have good students who have studied literature. When the authorial clue is removed (namely that this is by a good poet, this is by a bad poet or by a non-poet), these elite students essentially display the same taste that someone with no education in literature would exhibit.

I've argued that in every area of the curriculum you have real cognitive challenges, revealing how difficult it is to educate for understanding. You have misconceptions in the sciences, rigidly applied algorithms in mathematics, and scripts and stereotypes in social studies, humanities, and the arts. That said, I'm going to argue that there is some hope after all.

One source of hope entails taking some lessons from the venerable institution of apprenticeships and the new institution of children's museums.

Now I want to be very clear about this point. People misunderstand me as calling for seven-year legalistic agreements between the apprentice and the master, where the apprentice is indentured and has to sweep the floor and that kind of thing. Or that we should close schools down and put everybody in children's museums. That's *not* what I mean.

Rather, I contend that there are very powerful educational messages and lessons in these two institutions. In the case of the apprenticeship, a young person works for someone who is the master of his or her discipline or craft, and who uses that discipline or craft every day in the course of genuine problem-solving (and problem-finding). The master poses the problems and requires products from the apprentice at his or her level of competence; when the apprentice becomes more competent, the standards are raised accordingly. The master never has to take kids and test them at the end of the week, or the end of the year, because essentially he and the student are assessing every day. Moreover, the master embodies the learning that he or she wants the child to acquire.

In the United States every teacher can read and write, but too few of our elementary school teachers actually do read and write regularly. In fact, the average American schoolteacher reads one book a year. (Happily, many teachers read many more.) People who live in a literate world who read and write and talk about what they are reading and writing will have youngsters who do the same. People who simply say you should read but turn on the TV for several hours a day give a very different message.

Until some decades ago, there were almost no children's museums. These locales contain very lively demonstrations of many of the principles that students learn about in school. Museums allow children to explore those principles, those ideas, at their own pace and in ways that are comfortable for that child. Frank Oppenheimer, who founded the Exploratorium in San Francisco, said, "Nobody flunks museum."

I became a devotee of children's museums because when I took kids to children's museums, I sometimes found that kids who were called bright in school could not engage with the hands-on opportunities. They were very unschooled. But kids who were not considered bright in school could often learn very well in those contexts.

For each of the areas of the curriculum in which I have diagnosed a problem, there is a move that we as educators can make that can be helpful.

In the case of misconceptions: I recommend Christopherian encounters, named after Christopher Columbus. If you believe that the world is flat, but every month or every year you travel around the world and you come back to where you started, that tends to belie the notion that the world is flat. In a Christopherian encounter, you expose your theories to disconfirmation. If your theories are consistently disconfirmed, you will slowly abandon them and, hopefully, construct better theories.

Most schoolkids believe that the reason that you are warm when you put on a sweater is because that sweater has warmth in it. If every year in school during the winter you put a sweater outside and you come in the morning and find that item of clothing is freezing cold, that tends to disconfirm the notion that warmth inheres in the sweater.

Christopherian encounters need to happen over and over again. Think about the brain/mind as a surface that, earlier in life, becomes engraved with these primitive theories. What school usually does is simply to put some powder over that engraving so you can't readily see it any longer. And as long as you're in school, the powder is what the observer notices. When you leave school and you slam the door, the powder disperses and *the engraving is still there*, the early theory. What happens in the Christopherian encounter is that you slowly abrade that early engraving and slowly but firmly install a new and better one in its place.

But note that it doesn't happen in one time. Let me tell you what's wrong with the "one time" thing. If you had asked my son Benjamin at age 7 what's the shape of the world, he would have told you "it's round." This makes you think he's very smart. But if you had asked Benjamin where he was standing, he would have said, "That's easy. I'm on the flat part underneath." His naïve theory has been totally unaffected, but he has absorbed the powder that is required: namely, if you want to satisfy your father, you say that the world is round because that's what grown-ups say, but who could actually believe it?

Christopherian encounters challenge such notions every day. In mathematics the cure for a rigidly applied algorithm is what I call rich *exploration of the relevant semantic domain.* You must know what the equation stands for. You have to understand the formalism. So if you are going to do "distance, rate, and time" problems—a common algebra exercise—you do a lot of experimenting. You try to predict how long it will take for something to get from one point to the other. You develop an intuition so that when you learn the formalism, it actually refers to something that you already have an intuition for, that you already have an understanding for.

This has been done quite brilliantly with calculus. Before any of the formalism is introduced, students learn to make predictions about their bodies moving at various speeds, the kind of graphs that would be produced over the course of time, and procedures like that.

A mathematician is not somebody who *remembers* all the formalisms. Mathematician are persons who *don't care* if they remember because, if necessary, they can derive it again because they *understand* what it stands for. That's why most of us are not mathematicians!

In the case of the humanities, the cure for stereotypes is the regular adoption of multiple stances. If it becomes a regular habit of mind to look at things from many different points of view, you will gradually abandon stereotypical thinking.

During the 1991 Gulf War, one of my sons went to school where there were youngsters from many different countries. The teacher had a very good idea: Rather than everybody just affirming what a cable news network reported, he had a student from Iran, a student from Kuwait, a student from Israel, and so forth each convey his or her understanding of what was happening every day. Then, a few weeks after that, the teacher asked the kids in the school: "What do you think Moshe will think about this and what do you think Omar will think about this?" That's giving students the opportunity to put themselves into other people's minds. (Early in 2024, I think immediately of the clash between Israelis and Palestinians.)

If you study any revolution from the point of view of the vanquished as well as the victors, you get a very different story. If you study the American Revolution from the point of view of the British—where it was seen as a colonial uprising—and from the point of view of the French—where it was seen as a welcome opportunity to "get at" the rival British—it's a very different story than if you just read the average triumphant American textbook. That's how you break down stereotypical thinking, but it has to become a regular habit of mind. Otherwise, it won't work at all.

Let me, in conclusion, describe a project that I'm involved in to educate for understanding. It is based upon three core ideas that I have worked out in conjunction with colleagues at Harvard:

1. The identification of rich, generative ideas—nutritious topics on which it's worth spending a lot of time
2. The development of different kinds of teaching languages—multiple ways to approach those topics so we can be sure that students have maximum access to those ideas
3. The installation of "ongoing assessment"

"Ongoing assessment" means *that* assessment is taking place regularly, frequently by students and by peers as well as by the teacher.

We believe that if you can identify rich ideas, explore them in multiple ways, and give students ample opportunity to assess their own learning, there is a reasonable chance for education for understanding.

Let me flesh out those ideas.

First of all, *the greatest enemy of understanding is coverage.* If you are determined to cover everything in the book, you virtually guarantee that very few students will understand. So if you want to educate for understanding, you've got to make tough choices about what to focus on. And obviously you should focus on those themes and topics that have the biggest payoff. If you're teaching a course in history or social studies and you decide, say, to focus on democracy, or if you're teaching a course in biology and you choose to focus on evolution, you can cover a lot of the important material in those subjects by focusing on those generative topics.

It will mean, however, that if you're doing history, you're not going to get through every decade. If you're doing biology, you're not going to get through every cycle, or every part of the cell, every protein, or every branch of the tree. It's a hard choice, but it's a choice worth making. If you have rich concepts and you spend time on them, you can approach them in different ways.

Growing out of my theory of multiple intelligences, I claim that almost any topic worth spending time on can be approached from at least six different "windows" into the same room:

1. Narrational: The story mode.
2. A quantitative, logical rational way of dealing with numbers, principles, and causality.
3. A foundational way, asking basic kinds of questions such as: Why is this important? How does it relate to what came before? How is it related to our lives today?
4. Aesthetic: What does it look like? What does it sound like? What appearance does it make? What patterns and configurations? How does it strike or impress you?
5. Hands-on: What is it actually like to *be* this thing, to *do* this thing? If you're studying evolution, what is it like to breed *Drosophila*? If you're studying democracy, what's it like to be in a group—such as members of a classroom—that decides by consensus as opposed to one that decides by autocracy, oligarchy, or some other political principle?
6. Personal: Can you integrate facets of this topic through debate, role-play, projects, jigsaw participation, and other joint interactions?

There are two advantages of using these multiple entry points. First of all, you're more likely to reach every child, because not every child learns most readily in the same way. That's one of the consequences of the theory of multiple intelligences. Second, and equally important, if you approach a topic from many different vantage points, you're modeling for a student what it is like to be an expert.

An expert is somebody who can readily represent knowledge in more than one way. No expert is restricted to thinking about his or her topic in only one way. Experts have very flexible ways of thinking about their topics. You're modeling as a master to your apprentices if you approach a topic in a number of different ways.

That leaves assessment. In authentic assessments we get far away from short-answer examinations. We move toward what I call performance-based exams, where you actually demonstrate what it is that you're supposed to be able to do. Projects, exhibitions, portfolios, and processfolios provide good ways of assessing whether the students are really understanding (see Essays 14, 15, and 19).

In working with teachers, we ask them first to define "understanding goals"—these are the broad things that we want to achieve in a course. They will be very familiar things to you, like having a sense of the scientific method or understanding something about the nature of revolution. (For more on authentic assessment, please see Essays 14, 15, and 19.)

At this point we define a whole family of "performances of understanding"—performances that, if a student can carry them out, will count as evidence for understanding.

This entails a play with language, but I think it's an important play, because people tend to think of understanding as something that happens in the head. Perhaps it does, but we don't know if you understand unless you can *perform* your understanding publicly. So your performance involves analyses, critiques, debates, projects that you create, exhibitions that you put on, and so forth.

Finally, given "understanding goals" and the "performances of understanding," how are those performances going to be assessed? You make the assessment criteria absolutely clear. People know exactly what they are going to have to be able to do in order to perform an understanding. There are no surprises, no mysteries, no key to the answers, but rather abundant examples of what a good performance is and what are not such good performances, from apprentice level all the way to that of a master.

A few closing thoughts:

- After working for decades in psychology and education, I realized that I've been particularly interested in two things. The first: how to observe students carefully, and MI theory is a way to look at students more carefully. The second: how to observe student work more carefully. And that is done by having assessment that looks at student performances very carefully.

- In most of the schools that I visit, not much time is spent watching the students and developing a model of how particular students learn; nor is nearly enough time spent on looking at student work. This is what I call the teacher's fallacy: I taught a great class, therefore the students understood. *I* teach, therefore *you* understand. The only way you can find out if students are understanding is to have them actually do some work and then examine it critically.
- One technique that has become popular in the United States is the *minute paper*. At the end of a topic, and sometimes at the end of every session, you ask the student to write down one thing that he or she learned in the period and one question that he or she still has. It's a revelation! I never cease to learn when I assign the minute paper. And the misconceptions are revealing. But unless misconceptions get out in the open, they sit there underneath accumulating that powder.
- "Portfolios are great, but I don't have time to look at my students' work! I'm too busy, too much pressure for coverage, too many faculty meetings. I have a second job."

    If you don't have time to look at students' work, perhaps you shouldn't teach. Because if you don't look at your students' work, you have little idea whether they are learning anything.
- I used to think that if we simply change the assessment, everything else will be fine. But if the curriculum isn't good, the assessment is worthless. You can have wonderful assessment and curriculum, but if the staff isn't well instructed and teachers aren't educated even before or during the experience, the assessment and curricula are worthless.
- Finally, school doesn't have to be the way you remember it. Unfortunately, the "unschooled mind" even applies to parents and teachers; we have a stereotype formed by the age of 5 or 6 about what school is like. Namely, somebody at the front of the room is talking just as I am, and you're sitting or squirming in your seat, trying to be quiet, and all the knowledge is in the teacher's head and the purpose is to put it into your head. That's a very powerful idea. Whether people love school or hate school, most have that stereotype.

Unless we can help people think differently about what school can be like, what can be studied, how it can be taught, how it can be learned, then the opportunity for education for understanding is not going to be seized.

Final thought: Piaget said one valuable thing—which I haven't adhered to. He said that developmental psychologists should not try to be educators. And for the most part, he steered clear of proposing educational theory or pedagogical nostrums.

I have stepped into the lion's den today and offered you an educational theory that comes out of developmental psychology. Only time will tell whether I should instead have adhered to Piaget's admonition.

REFERENCE

Richards, I. A. (1956/1929). *Practical criticism.* Harper Perennial.

ESSAY 17

Understanding Through the Disciplines

In the largest research project I've undertaken in education, I collaborated with over a dozen researchers to illuminate what it means to understand a concept, issue, or topic of some complexity. Our singular insight: Understanding is not an event that happens inside one's mind-brain (between the ears, so to speak). Rather, understanding is a performance that one carries out publicly, enabling both oneself and others to ascertain whether one can actually apply, make use of, what one believes one has learned.

There is now a virtual industry of thinking, teaching, and learning for understanding. I don't know how much credit our own research team deserves for this line of work, but it's good to have been associated with an educational approach that in an era of short-answer tests gets at much deeper forms of knowledge.

Moreover, and importantly, our analysis of understanding allowed me to develop the notion that our multiple intelligences can be mobilized to aid in the understanding of complex materials—and I do so with reference to three gritty topics: the music of Mozart, the evolutionary theory of Charles Darwin, and the Holocaust of World War II.

THREE PUZZLES

During the 1830s, while Charles Darwin sailed around the world on the *Beagle*, most biologists, including Darwin himself, believed in the immutability of species. The species had been created, presumably by God, and they remained in the same pristine form forever, unless (like ancient mastodons) they perished.

Darwin began to question his convictions after he had visited the Galapagos Islands off the coast of Ecuador. He was struck by the wealth of flora and fauna that he encountered on just a few islands not distant from one another. In particular, he became intrigued by the incidence of finches; there turned out to be 13 different varieties in close proximity. Darwin pondered the reasons that the finches had different colors as well as beaks of varying shapes and sizes. And he reflected on the distributions of other birds, land animals, and plants on these islands, and across the many other exotic sites that he had visited.

Darwin devoted the succeeding decades to related questions: Why are there so many species throughout the world? Why such a variety on just a few islands? Why does one rarely see the same varieties in environments that differ ecologically from one another? What causes certain species to die out and others to flourish? How do new species come to be? Why are offspring always slightly different from their parents? Do species that closely resemble one another necessarily come from the same single parental stock? What happens where there are too many organisms for a given space and not all can survive?

In raising these questions, Darwin was touching on the then (and in some places, still today) hypersensitive topic of the evolution of species. This subject had engaged earlier thinkers, including his own grandfather Erasmus Darwin. But Charles Darwin came up with a set of answers that forever changed how informed individuals thought about the origins of species, and, most controversially, about the niche of human beings within the family of organisms.

* * *

In late 1785 and early 1786, Wolfgang Amadeus Mozart and his librettist, Lorenzo Da Ponte, composed an opera based on Pierre Beaumarchais's play *The Marriage of Figaro*. This French play about the Spanish aristocracy, a great success in the latter part of the 18th century, also proved controversial. Previously, most dramatists had portrayed a nobility that sat comfortably atop a stable social hierarchy; Beaumarchais created a more complex (and realistic) set of social relations, with a servant class that was enterprising, and an aristocracy that was not only flawed but that, eventually, could be undone by its own foibles.

The general plot of *Figaro* is a recognizable, typically convoluted member of the opera buffa genre, though the specifics were adventurous for the time. Figaro, a shrewd and upwardly mobile barber, is scheduled to marry the attractive Susanna. However, the domineering Count Almaviva, Figaro's boss, has his own designs on Susanna, who serves as the Countess's maid; and by tradition, the Count has seigneurial rights over her, at least until she marries Figaro.

Almaviva woos Susanna, going so far as to place encumbrances on the young couple's marital designs. To thwart the Count, Figaro concocts a scenario in which the Count will be led to believe that he will be able to meet with Susanna and that his wife, the Countess, will meet a lover. This scenario is not fully realized, because the Count interrupts while the plot is still being hatched.

Later Susanna pretends to accede to the Count's wishes for an amorous rendezvous. But then she and the Countess switch identities. With Figaro himself ignorant of the switch (and thus believing that Susanna is betraying him), the Count ends up wooing his wife and at the same time believing that his wife is being unfaithful.

At the end, "all is righted" in the world created in the work. Figaro and Susanna get married; Figaro's parents (of whose identity he had been unaware) are happily reunited; Cherubino and Barbarina, a young couple who became ensnared in the imbroglio, are also married; and the Count and Countess accept their fates as the authorized protectors of the realm. In this story, true love is celebrated and, in a rare (if prescient) reversal of the social order, the servant class triumphs over the aristocracy.

The opera consists of four acts, arranged in 27 scenes. No single scene encapsulates the entire drama. Just as I use Darwin's finches to represent the themes of evolution, I use the seventh scene of Figaro's first act to convey the atmosphere of the opera. I've dubbed that powerful scene, featuring Count Almaviva, the maiden Susanna, and the music master Basilio, the "Trio of Colliding Agendas." The three protagonists engage in exceedingly complex interaction and repartee that is not only amusing in itself but also moves the plot along briskly.

The opera created by Mozart and Da Ponte was not well received upon its original presentation in Vienna in 1786, but it soon came to be recognized as a masterpiece in many parts of the world. *The Marriage of Figaro* stands out by virtue of its beautiful score, its fast-moving dramatic action across several subplots, and its poignant combination of romance, slapstick, intrigue, and pathos.

To the naive ear, opera may sound like a bunch of people screaming at one another, sometimes alone, sometimes in ensemble. Indeed, though as a child I appreciated classical instrumental music, I remember my distinct antipathy for most of the operas broadcast on national radio on Saturday afternoons.

But once one has the opportunity to see a live performance, to understand an often-convoluted plot, and to appreciate how the singers accomplish actions through words and melodies, opera can become fascinating. Pieces like the trio in the first act of *Figaro* convey past and anticipate future events, a wide range of feelings, a collection of personalities, people's innermost thoughts, and their subtle (and not so subtle) interactions. Moreover, in an effective performance, one also beholds supreme artists—the performers as well as the creators—using their chosen medium to express feelings and convey actions with finesse, elegance, and power. Finally, though it is not the sort of thing that can be proved to an unhearing audience, the melodies, harmonies, and orchestration in the Mozart piece have struck millions of people as beautiful.

* * *

On January 20, 1942, leaders of the Nazi Third Reich gathered at a villa on the Wannsee in Berlin—Number 56–58 Am Grossen Wannsee, to be precise.

In the preceding years, the German military had conquered much of Western Europe and had also made inroads into the Soviet Union. Meanwhile, the German leadership had been trying out various approaches in an effort to solve what they termed the "Jewish problem."

Ever since Nazi leader Adolf Hitler began his rise to power in the early 1920s, he had made no secret of his antipathy to the Jewish people and his desire to be rid of them. During 1933–1939, the first years of his regime, Hitler and his disciples had pressured Jews to leave Germany and had mistreated or killed them in countless ways. Once World War II had begun, in September 1939, more severe measures were taken against the Jews. Many were sent to concentration camps; many others were simply killed or left to die of starvation.

But Hitler and his colleagues continued to search for what they termed the "Final Solution to the Jewish Question" in Europe. A number of radical measures were considered, including the mass deportation of the Jews to the island of Madagascar, off the east coast of Africa, and the creation of giant ghettos or reservations—for example, in the southeastern Polish city of Lublin.

But with the invasion of Russia and the capture of land that housed millions of additional Jews, none of these halfway measures seemed sufficient. By a series of steps still being pondered by historians, the Nazi leadership arrived at the fateful so-called Final Solution—the systematic, as opposed to the haphazard, murder of all European Jews. The meeting at Wannsee was designed to share this decision with those officials whose fateful job it would be to translate into action a plan for the execution of millions of people. Yet the records of the meeting never actually mention the genocide.

VANTAGE POINTS: FROM PUZZLES TO CONCEPTS

Each of my opening examples can be set forth as straightforward puzzles: Why do the finches of the Galapagos Islands look the way they do? And what does this tell us about the origins and varieties of species since the beginning of time?

How did Mozart and Da Ponte manage to convey so much about their protagonists' motivation and dramatic action in the course of a 4-minute trio? What resources are available to creating and performing artists? And why is this music of centuries ago so treasured today?

When and how did the Nazis arrive at the decision to begin the Final Solution, the elimination of European Jewry? How did they convey that sensitive information to those who would implement the policy? And why did so many German nationals participate—willingly and even enthusiastically—in mass murder?

Each of these puzzling entry points is designed to be intriguing in its own right—enough so that students (or readers) become curious about possible resolutions. Students wonder, for example, whether the same variety of finches could be found on a single landmass that spanned the same geographical distance as the Galapagos do; whether one could appreciate the personality traits and motivations of the characters in *Figaro* if one did not understand the language being sung or were unfamiliar with Western musical scales; and how specifically Hitler and/or his closest associates were orchestrating the events at Wannsee and thereafter.

While the interest of students can be engaged in many ways, the presentation of dilemmas—or their cousins, essential questions and generative ideas—has proved an especially effective means of attracting attention.

I've used these lures to introduce our "triplet" of central examples. The finches of the Galapagos (now often called Darwin's finches) offer a concrete way in which to raise the question of the evolution of species, and, ultimately, to introduce Darwin's ideas about variation and natural selection. These ideas, inevitably modified in the many decades since they were enunciated, represent an important set of scientific truths about the world.

The study of *The Marriage of Figaro*, featuring its "Trio of Colliding Agendas," serves to introduce the music of Mozart and the genre called opera. Most students have heard of Mozart, and many of them also have a notion—often quite dismissive—of classical music, including opera. Through analysis of how a single composition works, I hope to unravel some of the mysteries of classical music and to engender appreciation of a beautiful artifact in our world—a work of Mozart.

While organized killing has, alas, been a staple of human history, the Holocaust stands out in terms of the clarity of its aims as well as the thoroughness of its enactment. The Nazis aimed to eliminate an entire people—including women and children—and came very close to fulfilling their goal. They embarked upon genocide not because the Jews constituted any conceivable kind of military threat but rather because the Jews were seen as a "species" or "sub-species" that was hardly human and whose continued existence posed a threat to the "pure" Aryan race.

Particularly because there are some who deny the existence of the Final Solution, and many who question its frightening dimensions, it is important for students to learn just what happened and why. This is a question of historical truth. The decisions and events of the Holocaust must be understood in their own right; insights drawn from the Holocaust might be useful in preventing repetition of such horrific actions committed by one group of human beings against another. More generally, the actions of the Germans, and the reactions of the rest of the world, raise the most profound moral questions.

In attempting to understand these three phenomena, one is drawn into the approaches taken by different disciplines. Let me first sketch out some general considerations and then turn to specific features of the three scholarly spheres with which we are concerned here: science, art, and history.

As far as we can determine, human beings have always been interested in questions of the true, the beautiful, and the good.[2]

These questions are addressed in the myths of prehistory; they can be discerned in the ritualistic mourning behaviors of Neanderthals and in the early well-crafted artifacts of *Homo sapiens*; and they are raised as well in the play and the words of young children.

Over the years, cultures have evolved systematic ways of thinking about these issues. Folk science and folk wisdom are attempts to capture insights about what is true, and, of course, religions have mandated their own conceptions of truth. Explicit codes, systematic punishments, and implicit norms express what is morally acceptable and what is not. Artists and craftsmen (and, for that matter, mathematicians) create tangible or symbolic objects of beauty, and other knowledgeable members of the community bring to bear criteria of judgment on the relative aesthetic merits of particular creations.

There is no simple one-to-one mapping from questions to disciplines. Indeed, most questions can be approached from the perspectives of a variety of disciplines, even as a specific discipline can be brought to bear on a variety of questions and concerns. Still, the ensemble of fundamental questions, as a whole, helps to circumscribe and give direction to the family of disciplines.

Dating back at least to the time of the Greeks in the West, and to the school of Confucius in the East, organized disciplines have grown up around issues of the true, the beautiful, and the good. These disciplines harbor assumptions and mandate certain practices. For example, in Greece Socrates presented a model of how to practice philosophy; then Plato and Aristotle laid out the means whereby select others could become philosophers in quest of truth. Sophocles and Aristophanes wrote compelling tragedies and comedies; Aristotle set forth these rules explicitly for future dramatists, thereby proposing a set of standards of artistic beauty. By the same token, within Confucian societies, deliberate rules were set out about how to become a keen archer, a skilled calligrapher, a performer of music, a gentleman. Taken together, these constituted a range of definitions of a good person and a good life.

Disciplines have endured over the ages, even as their identities and boundaries have shifted. At any given moment, the disciplines represent the most well-honed efforts of human beings to approach questions and concerns of importance in a systematic and reliable way.

Nowadays, when it comes to questions of truth, most practitioners, Eastern as well as Western, turn to the sciences. Methods dating back to the Greeks, Romans, and Babylonians, and brought to a new level of precision in Europe in the 17th and 18th centuries, constitute our most trusted means of determining what is true about the physical world (physics and chemistry);

---

2. There is an awkwardness in using the term "good" in connection with the Holocaust. More precisely, one should always use the phrase "good/evil."

the biological world (biology, genetics, botany, zoology); the worlds of remote space and time (astronomy, cosmology); and the world of human beings (social and behavioral sciences). Methods become refined, and specific theories and claims are often replaced by more sophisticated ones.

When it comes to issues of beauty, there is a division of labor. We look to artistic creators and performers (and, to a certain extent, critics) for an evolving sense of what is beautiful and, by implication, what is not. Their works constitute replenishable wellsprings of instances of beauty; and, unlike ideas in the sciences, notions of beauty are not regularly supplanted. We think of Greek science as quaint; we continue to admire Greek vases and sculpture, even as our contemporary view of beauty extends and broadens the Greek ideal.

In addition, modes of analysis help us to understand how such objects are created and why they affect many of us in the way that they do. Complementing artists, aestheticians help us to discover the common properties, as well as the differentiating features, of ancient literary and plastic arts, and those wrought in more recent times: Greek vases, Chinese scrolls, contemporary jazz and performance art. During periods like ours, when elite aesthetic standards veer away from traditional concepts of the beautiful, aestheticians help us to understand what's going on in the several arts.

The discipline of mathematics proves instructive in this context. At first blush, mathematics represents a search for truth—indeed, for the identification of the most permanent truths that human beings can know. Yet the simplicity and the elegance of the truth, and the actual form in which the truth is presented, are of great import to mathematicians. In this sense, mathematics is akin to music, entailing its own sense of the beautiful, and averting what seems unwieldy.

Turning finally to the area of morality, each culture puts forth its own standards of behavior—some unique, some closely resembling those of other cultures. Even the Nazis had their own morality, twisted though it seems to us today. (The historian Daniel J. Goldhagen [1997] tells the incredible story of a German officer named Hoffmann who had presided over the deportation and killing of tens of thousands of Jews. Hoffmann refused to sign an order agreeing not to steal from or plunder those Gentiles who came under his jurisdiction. He was insulted by the request: he believed that he and his men would never stoop to such dastardly acts.) Various disciplines, ranging from philosophy to literature, touch on issues of morality, each in characteristic ways. Historians play an important role in our understanding of morality, for they can help us to understand the sources of morality at a particular place and time, why certain choices were made, and what consequences flowed from those choices.

There has been a close association between the development of disciplines and the rise of civilizations. This link is in no way inevitable; after all, the Nazis practiced many disciplines at a high level, yet their expertise did not prevent them from ushering in a new and perhaps unprecedented barbarism. Still, the disciplines are civilizing in that they offer practiced methods for dealing with issues and questions. Shorn of the disciplines, one is driven back to common sense and its inevitable undersurface, common nonsense (see Essay 16).

Nowadays, in a postmodern era, one incurs risks in praising the disciplines. Some question the validity of the disciplines altogether, while others rail against the undue power of those reactionary bastions—the academic disciplines. I do not agree with these critiques, yet I do not want to engage in a full-scale debate here about where the disciplines have fallen short and where they still have value. Suffice it to say that, as an introduction to systematic thought about perennial human puzzles, virtues, and vices, I know of no reasonable alternative to the several scholarly disciplines.

The phrase "human puzzles" harbors a valuable pun, for the disciplines respond to human challenges in two senses. First of all, the questions they address have always been important to human beings. Second, they also focus on issues of what it means to be human.

My three areas of investigation readily reveal their human dimensions: the place of *Homo sapiens* in the evolutionary galaxy; the foibles of aristocrats (and nonaristocrats); and the stench of prejudice yoked to absolute power. But even those disciplines that seem less directly concerned with human experience—say, the physical sciences and mathematics—cast light on human beings. After all, we humans are also entities in the physical world, and the discovery of mathematical truths underscores the power of the human mind to somehow fathom the most profound regularities in the universe.

Whatever the power—even the necessity—of the disciplines, in the end, questions never stop at the boundary of a discipline. Efforts to develop decisive and personal ideas of the true, the beautiful, and the good necessarily take us beyond specific disciplines and invite syntheses. The scientists investigating Darwin's theory, the musicologists who analyze Mozart's works, and the historians of the Holocaust are all attempting to answer questions about truths, though they are truths of different epistemological status.

And without stretching a point too far, one can also see these disciplinarians engaged in efforts to touch on other fundamental concerns: Darwinians looking for the sources of beauty and morality in the principles of evolution (such as natural selection); analysts of *Figaro* (and the society portrayed therein) raising issues about standards of morality, political truth, and artistic truth; and students of the Holocaust pondering standards of truth and beauty in the Nazi regime.

Let's look briefly at these disciplinary lenses.

THE PATTERNS OF THE SCIENTIST . . . AND THE MATHEMATICIAN

Scientists attempt to explain the regularities of the world. In this undertaking, they are aided by their own observations, which themselves may depend upon quite complex measurement devices; and by the earlier efforts of empirically oriented thinkers to pose questions and secure systematic answers.

This dialectic between observational data and theoretical frameworks is crucial to the working scientist. If the scientist only makes observations, he or she may be a keen observer or naturalist, but will not have entered fully into scientific practice. That is because observations can focus on an infinite number of details culled for a variety of unspecified ends. Indeed, all of us make observations most of the time, and yet few of us are practicing scientists.

The other element of scientific thinking is a concern with placing observations within a systematic framework; in the most developed form, the framework is a scientific theory. Many people were as impressed with the variety of plants and animals as Darwin was, and not a few had attempted to group and regroup them. Darwin relied heavily on the observations of the finches made by other travelers, but it was he who placed these observations into an explanatory framework, thus crossing the threshold into scientific theorizing.

On the other hand, people interested only in theoretical issues are not scientists, either. They may be theorists or philosophers, but their claims will lack grounding in concrete reality—often dubbed "data." Indeed, it has rightly been said that most sciences begin in philosophy—in the raising of provocative questions and in the sketching out of possible answers while sitting in one's armchair. Philosophy turns into science when relevant observations are fitted into the current theoretical framework or an improved one. As we now appreciate, science places a special premium on observations that undermine a current theory. Progress is made not by establishing permanent truths, but rather by calling into question a provisional truth and substituting one that is more firmly grounded in the evidence. This, in turn, may be replaced by yet another, better grounded claim.

Mathematics plays an important role in the more developed sciences. Initially, science grows out of systematic observation and features theories that can be expressed in lay language. However, these approaches engender a science mired at a level of description that is approximate at best. For science to be precise, for all practitioners to agree about the facts of a matter, it is important for claims and predictions to be stated as unambiguously as possible. This is the insight expressed by Galileo Galilei when he famously declared that the book of the universe was written in mathematics and that its alphabet consisted of triangles, circles, and geometrical forms.

But mathematics is not merely an aid for the working scientist. Quite independently, it represents the efforts of human beings to discover (or, if you prefer a more active description, to make) and lay out with precision the abstract relationships among idealized quantities and forms in the world. Mathematicians crave patterns in the realms of number and form; they seek to demonstrate, preserve, and explain the reasons for these patterns to all who find them of interest. Mathematicians are as compelled by the beauty of these patterns as by their truth value.

And yet, paradoxically, while scientific truths are fated to be temporary, mathematical ones, once verified, remain true. That is why mathematician G. H. Hardy declared that the most marvelous experience a human being can have is to discover a mathematical truth, because it will remain forever. One can quibble here, because new mathematical discoveries or systems may reconfigure earlier truths; as an example, in a non-Euclidean universe, parallel lines *do* meet. But within the bounds of a given system, mathematical truths are permanent: the square of the hypotenuse of a right triangle will always equal the sum of the squares of the other two sides of that triangle.

Most students will not become scientists, and many will only need elementary arithmetic in their daily and work lives. And yet, to deprive students of scientific and mathematical ways of thinking is to consign them to ignorance about the world in which they live. Only with adequate exposure to these disciplines will students have any understanding of the forces that govern the physical and natural world (as opposed, say, to accepting astrological explanations); the kind of thinking that has led to current world pictures (as opposed, say, to accepting magical thinking) and that will lead to valid revisions thereof; and the role of mathematical language in fixing these truths so that all may confirm them for themselves (as opposed to arguments based on slippery language, ambiguous images, or mere authority).

Indeed, rather than focusing on Darwinian evolution, I might well have used a mathematical example—say, the power of zero, the meaning of infinity, the quest to prove Fermat's last theorem. These are legitimate targets for understanding. Through the pondering of rich examples, I would like all students to gain a feeling for the regularities and beauties of mathematics and the fact that numbers and patterns can be exquisitely organized.

Students have no need to work through copious examples; at least through secondary school, a few well-understood examples should convey the power of mathematical thinking. Other curricular choices ought to be guided by the kinds of mathematical performances that are most likely to be useful for the world in which students will live. I must admit my discomfort that so much of what we (as school children) learn in mathematics is drawn on only decades later, when we are helping our own children carry out the same lessons.

THE BEAUTY OF THE ARTIST

The artist creates works in a genre. Usually the genre exists prior to the artist: like their predecessors, writers today create novels or poems, visual artists create paintings or pieces of sculpture. However, on occasion, artists will create new genres or reconfigure old ones. In the wake of Mozart's unsurpassable achievements, Beethoven changed the rules of classical music; a century later, in the aftermath of Brahms and Wagner, Arnold Schoenberg created a new system of atonal or 12-tone music.

Like the scientist, the artist moves between two worlds, but the realities of these worlds are quite different. On the one side, there are the artists' thoughts, feelings, beliefs, visions, and imagination: the content of his or her conscious (and unconscious) experiences. (And of course, as was the case with Mozart and Da Ponte, there can be multiple artists.) On the other, there are the materials or media available to artists, the techniques with which they and others work in order to fashion a work of art.

Neither base alone suffices. If an artist is filled with ideas or inspirations but lacks mastery of a medium, she will not be able to express herself (or her intended meanings) in an accessible way. Either she will be addressing only herself, or she will use a medium in a way that bewilders others. If, on the other hand, the artist has mastered a medium but lacks ideas or inspiration, then her work can at best be derivative; it will not sustain the interest of others.

Mozart illustrates well the working realms of the artist. In the collaboration on *Figaro,* Mozart's goal was to create (with Da Ponte) a musical work that captured the spirit and the meanings of Beaumarchais's play; in addition, Mozart had many ideas, feelings, and observations—some personal, some drawn from the general language of comic opera—that he hoped to capture in his own *Marriage of Figaro.*

Enter the mastery of technique. To produce a work, Mozart drew on the general principles of classical composition as they had evolved in Europe during the 17th and 18th centuries. With respect to the creation of a musical score, there were procedures for developing themes in a key, for modulating from one key to another, for using instruments alone or in combination, for altering rhythm and dynamics in order to achieve surprise, irregularity, or contrast. Individual and choral singers, the choice and arrangement of lyrics, a stage with its settings, costumes, lighting, acoustics—each introduced new elements that could be drawn upon in composition; in each case technical mastery of the relevant medium was necessary if a coherent and effective work were to result.

Mozart's technical knowledge may have been explicit, but explicitness is not of the essence. What was most important was that Mozart had the requisite skills to draw upon relevant techniques as needed. In contrast, the critic or aesthetician does need explicit knowledge of the artist's toolkit, and how the artist has drawn upon it to create certain effects.

While the target instance here is musical, the same line of analysis obtains for other art forms. Take, for example, the paintings of Picasso, the novels of Virginia Woolf, and the dances of Martha Graham. In each case, one beholds an artist with a distinct vision of the world, and one recognizes a set of techniques—graphic in the case of Picasso, linguistic in the case of Woolf, choreographic in the case of Graham—that allow the artist to bring this vision to reality. Moreover, each of these modern artists had a vision sufficiently original to change the practices of succeeding generations of artists.

Note, again, that neither the artists nor their followers required an explicit "language" or "metalanguage" to characterize their activities; it sufficed that they did their work well. But if we are to communicate about the effects these artists achieved, and the resources on which they drew, we (and that plural most definitely includes teachers) must draw on the language of the critic or philosopher of the relevant art form.

It would be wonderful if each growing individual had some opportunity to create in an art form. There is no substitute for drawing a portrait or a still life, composing a song or a sonnet, or choreographing and performing a dance. Education early in life ought to provide such opportunities to think and perform in an artistic medium.

As future citizens grow, it is equally important that they gain access to the most remarkable works fashioned by artists. These masterworks convey the ideas and feelings of different times and places, express a range of emotions, and embody a sense of beauty and harmony that enriches the experiences of all who can appreciate them. Indeed, our sense of beauty and taste comes chiefly from those works of art that we (as a culture over the centuries) have made our own. And the vocabularies and concepts created by students of the arts allow students and teachers to make explicit their understandings and their sometimes-idiosyncratic preferences. In this respect, languages of art play a role roughly analogous to that of mathematics in the sciences.

I must emphasize: works of art are quintessentially individual—each is different from every other. One cannot hope to enter into a work, let alone understand it, unless one engages its particular materials. To be specific, we cannot begin to appreciate the Mozart trio unless we heed the particular characters, events, melodies, harmonies, and orchestration of that particular Mozart-Da Ponte invention. Concreteness is also where science begins; however, in the case of the sciences, one always has one's vision primed for the general pattern, the set of rules that apply to all finches, all animals, all living matter. In this distinction between individual work and scientific principle lies the deepest gulf between science and mathematics, on the one hand, and art and the humanities, on the other.

THE ACCOUNTS OF THE HISTORIAN

The historian begins with an event (as large as a war, as limited as a treaty)—a setting and a number of participants. In rare cases, the historian was present as an observer or a recorder; sometimes the historian has access to eyewitnesses whom he or she can interrogate; but most often the historian must deal with documents—primary sources (as in the case of letters, journals, and minutes of meetings) or secondary sources (other written interpretive accounts by participants, journalists, or earlier historians). Recently, the written record has been complemented—and enhanced—by film and video sources as well; no doubt it will be similarly enriched by electronic and digital records and even by DNA fingerprinting.

Using these sources of data, the historian creates an account of what happened, in most cases venturing beyond simple narrative to offer explanations of why events happened in the ways that they did. Indeed, many would say that, like the scientist, the scholar enters into the discipline of history only when he or she goes beyond a mere recording of the data and becomes an interpreter of events.

The decisions that created the Holocaust throw these issues into sharp relief. Only naive or malevolent people who ignore the copious evidence question whether the Holocaust happened: the reports of those who survived the camps; the records kept by the Nazis themselves; the postwar testimony of certain Nazi leaders; the grisly photographs of the camps, with their gas chambers, and their piles of gold teeth, eyeglasses, and mud-caked shoes taken from victims; convince all rational individuals that mass extermination of millions of Jews—and members of other groups as well—took place in the death camps.

But when and how the Final Solution was arrived at remains a historical problem. In a way analogous to the challenge faced by other scholars, the historian must draw on two contrasting considerations. On the one hand, there is the documentary evidence: which orders were issued and by whom, what was said at Wannsee and elsewhere, and how veiled messages were apparently understood by those in attendance.

On the other hand, there are different ways to interpret human behavior. "Intentionalists" see the Holocaust as a direct consequence, dating back to plans stated in *Mein Kampf* (from the 1920s) of Hitler's resolution to rid Europe of the Jews. To intentionalists, the Nazis were only biding their time until an auspicious moment appeared for them take good on their threats.

"Functionalists" see a less rational, more chaotic process at work. In the opinion of these scholars, the Nazi leadership was casting about for ways in which to remove Jews from European society. Deportation to either Madagascar or the Lublin Reservation might have worked, in which case the phrase "Final Solution" might now be applied to one of those ploys.

However, neither alternative proved practical. At the same time, the Nazis saw that their command units were capable of massacring large numbers of Jews, generally avoiding unwanted side effects. In casting about for ways to make the process more efficient, and to distance Germans from the need to pull the trigger and stash the corpses, the idea of death camps gradually arose. Once the idea arose, it still had to be tried out; had it proved too unwieldy, other "final solutions" might have been considered.

In some ways, the methods used by historians resemble those adopted by other social scientists—psychologists, economists, or sociologists. Donning one or more of these disciplinary lenses, the analyst begins with an intriguing example of human behavior but then moves to a more general explanation of the phenomenon—for example, in terms of the explicit intentions of a certain class of persons or in terms of more general principles of group behavior.

But historians are also humanists, and they share features with the artistic critic as well: the historical event is unique, and so it must be explained in its own terms. Moreover, because historical events are unprecedented and nonreplicable, proposed explanations cannot be tested in the scientific laboratory. The patterns discerned by historians can be suggestive at best; historical accounts retain their singularity.

Nearly all humans are curious about their origins and their fate, and in that sense, the study of "our (individual and species) story" requires little justification. However, an appreciation of the discipline of history transcends personal curiosity. Only when they gain a sense of the diverse and often competing inputs to historians, and the conflicting ways of making sense of texts and other forms of evidence, do students begin to understand that history is not a given. Any historical account must be constructed, and those who do the construction help us to define ourselves, our allies, our enemies, and our options (including our moral choices).

The disciplined thinking of the historian is crucial—if individuals are to draw their own inferences about what happened in an event, decide which historical analogies are apt and which are not, and express opinions and cast votes on issues of import in terms of reasonable criteria rather than sheer whim.

The historical enterprise sheds light on issues of both truth and goodness. To establish as accurately as possible what happened in a given place at a given time represents an effort to attain truth. Historians never tire of quoting Leopold von Ranke's dictum that the historian's burden is to describe the past "as it actually happened." At the same time, however, historical accounts offer perennial opportunities to consider moral options and to render moral judgments: Was Columbus a hero or a villain? Should the United States have bombed Hiroshima and then Nagasaki? Which side actually provoked the "guns of August" in 1914, and were its actions justifiable? Judging the Nazis' actions in World War II is not a historical act but one of moral evaluation. And yet, in the absence of sound historical data, such judgments deservedly command little attention.

IN THE SHOPPING MALL OF THE DISCIPLINES

Even those of us who are not expert in the respective disciplines can appreciate the differing aims and perspectives of the scientist, the mathematician, the artist, and the historian. We contrast the data collected systematically by the scientist; the abstract patterns that intrigue the mathematician; the imaginative thoughts and feelings that inspire the artist; the reflective language of the critic; and the historian's struggle to figure out which documents are important and how to evaluate human motives and "extra human" forces as they play out among a particular set of characters at a particular historical moment.

Students face a formidable task. The questions that they themselves pose, or that are posed by an engaging teacher or text or video, are genuine. However, at the start, students do not know about the disciplines, nor are they in a position to recognize their utility (though they may be intimidated by their rigors). Moreover, students lack the rough-and ready intuitions that most adults have developed in a society that honors the scholarly and practical disciplines.

It is easy for students (and teachers and parents) to be confused about the disciplines. They are often seen simply as "subjects": courses to take, with discrete texts and teachers, in order to pass certain requirements. To the extent that disciplines are simply presented as sets of facts, concepts, or even theories to be committed to memory, students may remain innocent of their powers. After all, facts themselves are discipline-neutral; they acquire their disciplinary colors only when they have been pieced together in a certain (hopefully coherent) way and placed in the service of a particular theory, framework, or sequence.

For the disciplines do not inhere primarily in the specific facts and concepts that make up textbook glossaries and indexes, compendia of national standards, and, all too often, weekly tests. Rather, the disciplines inhere in the ways of thinking, developed by their practitioners, that allow those practitioners to make sense of the world in quite specific and largely nonintuitive ways. Indeed, once mastered and internalized, the disciplines become the principal ways—in our earlier image, the engravings—in which experts construe the phenomena of their world.

For the sake of argument, let us consider the contrasting stances taken by three hypothetical practitioners with respect to Darwin's finches. The biologist asks why the finches on a few neighboring islands differ from one another in appearance. He may love (or loathe) finches, but his focus is really on more general questions: Why do closely related species (or, indeed, any species) manage to survive, and how does their survival relate to the fact that they are segregated geographically? His goal is to come up with truths, general principles that obtain with respect to the evolution of species.

Our next example: While evolutionary biology is not generally considered to be a laboratory science, a practitioner of that discipline could test her claims empirically. For example, following the practices of E. O. Wilson and Robert MacArthur and their colleagues, such an investigator could actually observe what happens on a small island after it has been denuded of species either through a natural disaster, like a hurricane, or through fumigation. It proves possible to observe the way in which such islands are repopulated, and how the new range of species survive, or fail to survive, subsequent disasters.

The artist wants to capture her own experience in the company of finches. She observes the finches as much as possible and perhaps examines other sources of data about birds, islands, evolution, and Darwin's story. Her goal, however, has nothing to do with explanation or prediction. Rather, she wants to utilize a particular medium—it could be music, or dance, or drawing—to capture certain aspects of her own experiences, including her immediate and longer-term reactions to the finches. Members of an audience will judge the resulting work by their own criteria, among which beauty is likely to be a significant one. Critics will indicate how the artist achieved her effect and which aspects of her rendering were most likely to have impressed (or irritated) an audience.

Finally, the historian is likely to focus on what actually happened when Darwin encountered the finches. And it turns out that there is more to this encounter than meets the eye. To begin with, Darwin did *not* have an "Aha!" experience when he first saw the birds. On the contrary, while struck initially by the plethora of species in general, he simply made some notes about the finches and moved on. Only months later did he begin to think about the contrasting beaks on neighboring islands; and eventually, his colleague John Gould showed him that there were actually four separate species of finches among the 13 varieties that he had gathered.

Establishing "the facts" about Darwin's finches turns out to be a nontrivial exercise for historians, particularly in light of various legends and rival plausible accounts. However, even more difficult challenges are posed by another question: How large a role did the finches play, immediately and eventually, in Darwin's development of the theory of evolution? Indeed, were they necessary at all? This question prompts the historian of science to consider different models of creativity: inspirational, intentional, accidental, overdetermined. And then the historian must mount arguments about which model best fits what happened in the case of Darwin's finches. Whether the same explanation might apply to other cases of scientific discovery is a strictly empirical matter. In any event, a predictive model of scientific creation seems out of the purview of the historian—unless he hankers to create a new social-scientific discipline.

Darwin's finches may seem remote from issues of morality, especially in contrast with the issues that swirl about the Holocaust. Yet Darwin would not have felt such remoteness. He hesitated to reveal his findings publicly (and he suffered privately) because they ran completely counter to the religious ethos of his society—and, indeed, of his wife. Even today, few scientific issues cause as much moral tumult as the theory of evolution. While the historian may not possess special tools for making moral judgments, his accounts are indispensable ingredients in any evaluation by professional or amateur moralists.

In sum, disciplines all deal with impressions, observations, "facts," theories, and competing explanatory models. But each discipline has its characteristic observations and inferences; moreover, each discipline has developed its own means, its own "moves," for making sense of initial data. Teachers of the disciplines have a formidable task. How, in a way that is comprehensible, can one convey to students that the world as they know it is really a collection of worlds? Just as the cobbler and the surgeon perceive the "man on the street" in quite different lights, so, too, do the scientist, the artist, and the historian bring their own lenses and instrumentation to the experiences of every day, and to the phenomena that form the foundation of their work.

Education cannot fit every student with a full set of lenses; indeed, we are doomed to fail if we aim to make each youngster into a historian, a biologist, or a composer of classical music. Our goal should not be to telescope graduate training; rather we should seek to grant students access to the "intellectual heart" or "experiential soul" of a discipline. Education succeeds if it furnishes students with a sense of how the world appears to individuals sporting quite different kinds of glasses.

From ideas that are formed intuitively, and that are often misconceptions, students need to move toward a more sophisticated set of concepts and theories. In place of engravings that do not make much sense to sophisticated observers, they must acquire new tools—those of the several key disciplines—and they must use these tools to make better engravings. At the end of the day, they should be able to emulate some scientific, artistic, and historical ways of thinking, not simply because these are exciting, but because they constitute three of the most powerful ways human beings have devised for making sense of our world.

What is equally important is that the disciplines serve as points of entry for considering the deepest questions about the world—questions about truth, beauty, and goodness. Evolution tells us where we came from and how we got to be the way we are; Mozart shows us what humans can aspire to, as creators and performers; the Holocaust reminds us of the evil that members of our species have sometimes committed. There is never one-to-one mapping between the disciplines, on the one hand, and issues of truth-beauty-goodness, on the other. Neither the life of the mind nor the cartography of experience is that clear-cut. But the disciplines serve as our best, our indispensable handmaidens, as we seek to negotiate this trio of precious virtues.

In mounting this argument, I realize that I'm running risks. I have presented the disciplines as more consolidated and more schematic than they really are. Historians and scientists do not agree about the best way to describe what they are doing; there are historians of science as well as scientists (like geologists) who think of their work as historical; and artists and aestheticians live in uneasy proximity to one another, at best. Each of these disciplines is itself evolving, and the descriptions I give today differ from those that would have been offered 50 years ago or will be offered 50 years from now . . . especially in a world that is likely to be suffused with powerful computational systems.

Still, unless we are to cordon off students from the disciplines—a terrible prospect, in my view—we must begin with a picture of each. And using examples that I hope are clear and accessible, that's what I have sought to do in this essay.

REFERENCE

Goldhagen, D. J. (1997). *Hitler's willing executioners.* Vintage.

ESSAY 18

Teaching for Understanding Within and Across the Disciplines

Howard Gardner and Veronica Boix-Mansilla

Let's assume that the unschooled mind is the starting point for formal education (see Essay 16). We educators wish to proceed to a mind that is able to think in terms of the major scholarly disciplines and—as warranted—to begin to use disciplines together, as appropriate.

Veronica Boix-Mansilla and I worked extensively on this issue. In what follows, we put forth both our notions about how to develop disciplined knowledge and then distinguish among three more sophisticated stances: multidisciplinary work, interdisciplinary work, and metadisciplinary work.

Starting points: The disciplines are the most useful means for illuminating those issues that have perennially engaged the curiosity of thoughtful human beings. As they enter middle and high school, students are expected to understand central concepts in several disciplines.

While students may succeed in parroting back phrases from lectures and texts, they often falter when asked to apply their understanding to new situation. What does it take to demonstrate understanding within and across disciplines?

Consider the many different ways to approach the following hypothetical but plausible situations:

- *The New York Times* announced that the Queen of England has stepped down from her throne and at the same time has dis-established the House of Windsor. The English monarchy is at an end. (Note: We could update this to focus instead on King Charles III!)
- *The New England Journal of Medicine* has published a study in which two groups of elementary school students were randomly assigned to two after-school programs: indoor gymnasium sports and personal computer work. Twice as many students in the first group contracted colds. The speculation is that after-school athletics may be injurious to one's health.

Wearing the hat of the disciplinarian, we can consider our first example to be drawn from history or social studies and the second from biology or general science. Either account could serve as the point of departure of a set of lessons in appropriate high school classes. If reworded, they could be used with students at virtually any grade level.

The first account—which could also refer to the death of a president or the deposing of any kind of leader—raises questions such as "What makes a boss a boss?" and "Why do all civilizations have hierarchies of authority?" The second account could be reformulated to describe any source of disease and to encourage reflection about what keeps us healthy, what is illness, and how to prevent it.

Here we attempt to place current efforts at teaching for understanding into a sharper perspective by considering the way in which this performance view plays out in different disciplines.

UNDERSTANDING WITHIN THE DISCIPLINES

The framework developed by our Teaching for Understanding group is deliberately broad enough to cover the range of disciplines. (See Essay 16.)

At the same time, however, all disciplines are not equal. In fact, distinct disciplines have developed over the ages precisely because they allow scholars and students to take different kinds of perspectives and actions in order to elucidate specific kinds of phenomena.

Consider our opening examples. In each case, we are dealing with a central concept: (1) injury to the body politic, and (2) injury to the physical body. Analysis and evaluation of concepts are legitimate tacks in both examples.

While disciplines can blind or sway, they become, when used relevantly, our keenest lenses on the world.

In other respects, however, the disciplinary terrains prove quite different. For instance, to gain relevant expertise in our abdication situation, students might draw on knowledge about English history and its current form of government, as well as the legal and symbolic implications of the abolition of monarchy. Students can perform their understandings in any number of ways, ranging from a comparison of the situation at the time of the beheading of King Charles I or the abdication of Edward VIII, to a hypothetical argument in a local pub about the abolition, to the creation of a diagram of the new governmental organization.

By their very nature, historical phenomena are unique. One can compare abdications and beheadings, but they are never exactly the same. When dealing with individual personalities, varying contexts, and dynamic events, the complexity of the events can never be mastered, nor the consequences predicted. Finally, events in this sphere take on symbolic as well as literal/legal importance. While in practice the English monarchy has little authority, in actuality it assumes significant symbolic power. A disciplinary understanding of the possible impacts of dis-establishment on British public life is grounded in these specific features of historical events.

In contrast to the historical example, the realm of health and illness, at least in principle, should be open to explanation and prediction. This realm lends itself to the development of models of what causes illness and the testing of the models through experimentation. A well-founded model is able to predict results across diverse populations. Moreover, explicit methodologies exist for mounting experiments and for analyzing data, ones that can be used by anyone schooled in science. Consequently, in the case of colds among athletes, students might gain relevant expertise by drawing on knowledge about health and illness, including bacterial and viral theories of infection, as well as understandings of the nature of scientific hypotheses, experimental designs, and inferences from data. To demonstrate their understanding, students might conduct similar experiments. They could, for example, perform retrospective examinations of the incidence and plausible causes of their own recent colds or construct rival models of disease.

FROM COMMON SENSE TO INTERDISCIPLINARY STUDY

So far, we have dealt with might be called "normal" disciplinary work at the secondary level. We have assumed that there are classes that deal with historical-political studies, those that deal with scientific inquiry, and a set of roles and performances appropriate to students in those respective classes.

But we have also argued that younger students could approach the questions raised in appropriate ways. To illustrate, we single out four stages, corresponding roughly to different points in the growth patterns of students.

1. Common Sense

Novices fruitfully consider generative questions by relying on their intuitive theories of the world—their natural theories of mind, matter, and life. Students as young as 5 or 6 can consider what it means to be a leader and then to voluntarily or involuntarily renounce one's position as boss. They can consider what would happen if the teacher or the boss stepped down and no one took his or her place. Adults can ask young students to draw on their own theories of power—the person who is strongest, loudest, or bossiest, or the person chosen by someone even more powerful—to debate these issues.

These same students can also be guided into discussions of health. Nearly all youngsters are interested in their bodies—what makes them strong, weak, sick, or healthy. They can apply their own naive theories—you are sick because you were bad, because you sat near someone who was sick, because you did not wash your hands—to new events, including the appearance of a new sickness or a new cure or something enigmatic called COVID-19. Note that in these cases, it is not important that students espouse the "right theories," but that they draw fully on their own ideas in an effort to make sense—as it were, to "perform" their understandings—of intriguing phenomena.

2. Protodisciplinary Knowledge

Even in the absence of formal disciplinary study, students in our culture pick up certain moves that are made by systematic thinkers—through, for example, the media, debates among peers, and partial understanding of texts. Long before they have heard of college catalogues, and despite the cinematic and literary biographies, students in the late primary or early middle grades begin to appreciate the difference between a historical account (what actually happened) and a literary or cinematic account (a description contrived for aesthetic purposes). By the same token, they begin to distinguish claims that are based on conviction or prejudice from claims based on empirical evidence, which itself can be confirmed or questioned.

At this stage, youngsters can proceed in a more sophisticated way. They can read historical or scientific accounts, summarize them, conduct further research, and debate the validity of various claims. And they can engage in projects—such as holding a mock trial or conducting a survey—that introduce them naturally to the tools of the disciplines.

3. Disciplinary Knowledge

By late middle school and thereafter, students work mostly under the rubric of classical disciplines, such as history, literature, and the several physical and biological sciences. Because it has become fashionable to look askance at the disciplines, we feel it is important to make two points.

First, disciplines are not the same as subjects. Disciplines constitute the most sophisticated ways yet developed for thinking about and investigating issues that have long fascinated and perplexed thoughtful individuals; subject matters are devices for organizing schedules and catalogues.

Second, disciplines represent the principal ways in which individuals transcend ignorance. While disciplines can blind or sway, they become, when used relevantly and appropriately, our keenest lenses on the world.

When well taught, students are introduced to the disciplines in several ways. First, they observe teachers or experts who embody the practices of the disciplines. Second, students behold and create exhibitions that capture the accumulated wisdom of the discipline. Third, students encounter the concepts, theories, and methods that disciplinarians have evolved over the years, and receive ample opportunities to put them into practice. Only through such sustained work—work that is "disciplined" in both senses of the term—may students acquire the expertise that we have described.

4. Beyond Disciplinary Knowledge

Even as it is now fashionable to critique the disciplines, it is trendy to advocate interdisciplinary work. At its best, interdisciplinary work is indeed vital and impressive. However, such work can be legitimately attempted only if one has already mastered at least portions of the specific disciplines involved. Unfortunately, much of what is termed interdisciplinary work is actually predisciplinary work—that is, work based on common sense, not on the mastery and integration of two or more component disciplines.

Those who have slogged through a number of specific disciplines are in a privileged position. They can conduct multidisciplinary work in which, for example, they look at the abdication of King Edward VIII as portrayed in art, literature, history, and philosophy. They can undertake interdisciplinary work, in which they consider the concept of health in terms of both medicinal factors and individual psychology, and then synthesize these perspectives as they come up with a more general account. They can carry on so-called metadisciplinary work, in which they compare the practices of particular disciplines. And they can engage in transdisciplinary work, where they examine a concept, like "body," as it appears in political and in physical discourse.

Students should encounter individual benchmarks on the trail from novice to expert, as well as road maps of how to get from one milestone to the next.

DISCIPLINARY POWERS AND LIMITATIONS

In our view, the disciplines remain the most useful means for illuminating those generative issues that have perennially engaged the curiosity of thoughtful human beings. What in the past was approached first through common sense, and later through art, mythology, and religion, can now be approached as well—or even preferably—through systematic studies, such as political science or medical experimentation.

While we should be respectful of disciplines, we should remain aware of at least three limitations:

1. *Far from being ends in themselves, the disciplines are means for answering generative essential questions.* Indeed, armed with the disciplines and with the possibility of interdisciplinary work, individuals are in the best position to revisit these essential questions and to arrive at their own, often deeply personal answers.

2. *Disciplines are differently transfigured depending on purpose and developmental levels.* For elementary education, it may be enough to separate out the arts and humanities, on the one hand, and the experimental sciences on the other. At the high school level, a distinction into three or four disciplinary terrains probably suffices. And at the college or university level, a fine differentiation and articulation among disciplines is appropriate.

3. *All disciplinary boundaries are tentative.* Disciplines have not been, and probably never will be, marked in stone. Rather, they develop out of specific conditions, and as these conditions change, boundaries are redrawn. Moreover, even within the most established disciplines, serious disagreements exist with respect to content, methods, and scope. The dynamism of disciplines reflects the always growing, ever-changing nature of knowledge.

ASSESSMENT WITHIN AND ACROSS THE DISCIPLINES

Some aspects of assessment are appropriate for all disciplines, while others turn out to be far more specific to particular disciplinary priorities and practices. At the generic level, each discipline features certain characteristic roles—the historical analyst, the designer of experiments—and certain characteristic performances or exhibitions—a historical account, an experimental write-up. Students at the more sophisticated levels of education need to be immersed in instances of these roles and performances of understanding, particularly as they are practiced by proficient individuals.

Different disciplines call on different analytic styles, approaches to problem-solving and findings, temperaments, and, in fact, different intelligences.

But even the best instances do not suffice. It does not greatly benefit the rookie pianist to hear Arthur Rubinstein or the novice tennis player only to witness Martina Navratilova. (Reader: Feel free to update this with your examples from hip-hop or multiple martial arts.) Rather, students must encounter individual benchmarks on the trail from novice to expert, as well as road maps of the ways to get from one milestone to the next. Given these landmarks, along with ample opportunities to perform their understanding with appropriate feedback, most individuals should be able to steadily enhance their competence in any discipline.

Of course, disciplines lend themselves to different kinds of roles and performances. To read texts critically, in the manner of a historian, is a quite different matter than to design a crucial experiment and analyze data relevant to competing models of an infectious process. Different disciplines call on different analytical styles, approaches to problem-solving, and findings, temperaments, and intelligences. Therefore, a keen assessment must be alert to these disciplinary differences. By the same token, an effective teacher should help youngsters to appreciate that what counts as cause and effect, data and explanation, and use of language and argument varies across the disciplines.

FROM DISCIPLINARY TO PERSONAL KNOWLEDGE

Individuals the world over, not just knowledgeable experts, ask generative questions. Children do not ask about the meaning of life and death or good and bad in their own words merely because others talk about these issues. Rather, in many cases these questions arise spontaneously, prompting children to pose them in their own way and to come up with imaginative answers. The disciplines, individually and jointly, offer the best current efforts to approach, and to supply, provisional answers for these enduring questions. As we saw in our initial examples about abdication and illness, just as questions come from different perspectives and lead to different kinds of answers, the disciplines themselves have disparate roots and lead, by varying routes, to different kinds of accounts.

Drawing on the disciplines, we should find it possible to mount increasingly comprehensive approaches to generative questions—approaches that are appropriate to particular contexts and populations. In the end, however, we need to keep in mind that the disciplines are just the means for tackling these questions. The most important answers are those that individuals ultimately craft for themselves, based on their disciplinary understandings, their personal experiences, and their own feelings and values.

ESSAY 19

Assessment in Context
The Alternative to Standardized Testing

A familiar scene almost anywhere in the United States today (or at least at the start of the 21st century): Several hundred students file into a large examination hall. They sit nervously, waiting for sealed packets to be handed out. At the appointed hour, booklets are distributed, brief instructions are issued, and formal testing begins. The hall is still as students at each desk bear down on number 2 pencils and fill in the bubbles that punctuate the answer sheets. A few hours later, the testing ends and the booklets are collected; at a later moment, a sheet bearing a set of scores arrives at each student's home and at the colleges to which the students have directed their scores. The results of a morning's testing become a powerful factor in decisions that will affect the life trajectories of each student.

Now of course, much of this can be done online, so long as the procedure does not allow cheating of any sort.

An equally familiar scene in most preindustrial societies over the centuries: A youth of 10 or 11 (typically, if lamentably, a boy) moves into the home of a man who has mastered a trade. Initially, the apprentice is asked to carry out menial tasks as he helps the master prepare for his work or clean up the shop at the end of the day. During this initial phase, the lad has the opportunity to watch the master at work, while the master monitors the youth to discover his special talents or serious flaws. Over the months, the apprentice slowly enters into the practice of the trade. After initially aiding in the more peripheral aspects of the trade, he eventually gains familiarity with the full gamut of skilled work. Directed not only by tradition but also by the youth's particular skills and motivation, the master guides his charge through the various steps from novice to journeyman. Finally, after several years of supervised training, the youth is ready to practice the craft on his own.

While both these scenarios are idealized, they should be readily recognizable to anyone concerned with the assessment and training of young people. Indeed, they may be said to represent two extremes. The formal testing model is conceived of as an objective, decontextualized form of assessment that can be adopted and implemented widely, with some assurance that similar results will be obtained. The apprenticeship model is implemented almost entirely within a naturally occurring context in which the particularities of a craft are embedded. The assessment is based on a prior analysis of the skills involved in a particular craft; but it may also be influenced by subjective factors, including the master's personal views about his apprentice, his relationship with other masters, and his need for other kinds of services.

It should be evident that these two forms of assessment were designed to meet different needs. Apprenticeships made sense when the practice of various crafts was the principal career path for nonrural youths. Formal testing is a contemporary means of comparing the performance of many thousands of students who are being educated in schools. Yet these forms of assessment are not limited to the two prototypical contexts described earlier. Despite the overwhelmingly agrarian nature of Chinese society, formal tests have been used there in selecting government officials for over 2,000 years. And in many art forms, athletic practices, and areas of scientific research, apprenticeships and the concomitant ongoing, context-determined forms of assessment continue to be used in our highly industrialized society.

Thus, the choice of formal testing as opposed to apprenticeship is not dictated solely by the historical era or by the primary means of production in the society. It would be possible in our society to utilize the apprenticeship method to a much greater extent than we do. Very few people today lament the passage of the obligatory apprenticeship system, with its frequent excesses and its blatant sexism and racism. From several points of view, contemporary formal testing represents a fairer and more easily justifiable form of assessment. And yet aspects of the apprentice model are consistent with current knowledge about how individuals learn and how their performances might best be assessed.

Our society has embraced the formal testing mode to an excessive degree. I contend that aspects of the apprentice model of learning and assessment—described as contextualized learning—could be profitably reintroduced into our educational system. In this essay after presenting an account of the origins of standardized testing and the one-dimensional view of mentation typically implied by such testing methods, I suggest the need for a far more capacious view of the human mind and of human learning than that which informed earlier conceptions.

My task here is to envision forms of education and modes of assessment that have a firm rooting in current scientific understanding and that contribute to enlightened educational goals. In the latter half of the chapter, I will sketch the nature of an "assessing society."

BINET, THE TESTING SOCIETY, AND THE "UNIFORM" VIEW OF SCHOOLING

The widespread use of formal testing can be traced to the work on intelligence testing carried out in Paris at the dawn of the 20th century by Alfred Binet and his colleagues (see Essay 8). So great was the appeal of the Binet method that it soon became a dominant feature of the American educational and assessment landscape. To be sure, some standardized tests—ranging from the California Achievement Tests to the SAT—are not direct outgrowths of the various intelligence tests. And yet it is difficult to envision the proliferation of these instruments over just a few decades without the widely esteemed examples of the Stanford-Binet, the Army Alpha, and the various Wechsler intelligence instruments.

Especially in the United States, with its focus on quantitative markers and its cult of educational efficiency, there has been a virtual mania for producing tests for every possible social purpose. In addition to tests for students, we have standardized tests for teachers, supervisors, soldiers, and police officers; we use adaptations of these instruments to assess capacities not only in standard areas of the curriculum but also in civics and the arts; and we can draw on short-answer measures for assessing personality, degrees of authoritarianism, and compatibility for dating.

The United States is well on the way to becoming a "complete testing society," with automatic registering of the whole gamut of "data, including a range of physiological measures." We could encapsulate this attitude as follows: If something is important, it is worth testing in this way; if it cannot be tested in this way, then it probably should not be valued. Few observers have stopped to consider the domains in which such an approach might not be relevant or optimal; most have forgotten the insights that might be gained from modes of assessment favored in an earlier era.

It is risky to attempt to generalize across the thousands of formal instruments that are described in books such as the *Mental Measurements Yearbooks*. Yet, at the cost of doing some violence to certain instruments, it is worth specifying the features that are typically associated with such instruments.

There is within the testing profession considerable belief in "raw," probably genetically based, potential. The most highly valued tests, such as IQ tests and the SAT, have long been thought to measure ability or potential performance. There is no reason why a test cannot assess skills that have been learned, and many achievement tests claim to do this. Yet for tests that purport to measure raw ability or potential, it is important that performance cannot be readily improved by instruction; otherwise, the test would not be a valid indicator of ability. Most authorities on testing believe that performance on ability and achievement tests reflects inherent capacities.

Adherents of testing also tend to embrace a view of human development that assumes that a young organism contains less knowledge and exhibits less skill than a more mature organism but that no qualitative changes occur over time in human mind or behavior. Making such assumptions enables test-makers to use the same (or at least similar) kinds of instruments for individuals of all ages; and they can legitimately claim that descriptions of data at a certain point in development can be extended to later ages because one is dealing with the same kind of scale and the same property of mind or behavior.

Reflecting general American technological pressures as well as the desire for elegance and economy, most test-makers and buyers place a premium on instruments that are efficient, brief, and easy to administer. In the early days of testing (including in the Parisian laboratory of Alfred Binet), assessment typically took hours and was individually administered; now, group-administered instruments—often administered online—are desired. Virtually every widely used test has spawned a "brief" version. Indeed, some of the staunchest supporters of formal intelligence tests hope to strip them down even further—say to simple psychometric measures, or patterns of brain waves, or the examination of genes. (See Essay 8.)

Accompanying a fealty to formal testing is a view of education that I have termed the "uniform view of schooling." In this view, progress in school should be assessed by frequent formal tests administered under uniform conditions, and students, teachers, and parents should receive quantitative scores that detail the student's progress or lack thereof. These tests should be nationally normed for maximum comparability. The most important subject matters are those that lend themselves readily to such assessment, like mathematics and science. In other content areas, value is assigned to the aspects that can be efficiently assessed (grammar rather than voice in writing; facts rather than interpretation in history). Accordingly, or lamentably, those disciplines that prove most refractory to formal testing, such as the arts, are least valued in the uniform school.

In presenting this picture of Binet, the testing society, and the uniform view of schooling, I am aware that I am overemphasizing certain tendencies and lumping together views and attitudes in a way that is not entirely fair to those who are closely associated with formal testing. Some of those intimately involved with testing have voiced similar reservations (refer to *Howard Gardner Under Fire: The Rebel Psychologist Faces His Critics* by Jeffrey Schaler). That said, the trends in education in the last decades bear a strong resemblance to the views I have just sketched. At the very least, these views serve as a necessary contrast case to the picture of contextualized and individualized assessment and schooling limned here.

SOURCES FOR AN ALTERNATIVE APPROACH TO ASSESSMENT

The scientific ideas on which the testing society has been based derive from an earlier era in which behaviorist, learning-theoretical, and associationist views of cognition and development were regnant. According to these views, it made sense to believe in "inborn" human abilities, a smooth and probably linear curve of learning from infancy to old age, a hierarchy of disciplines, and the desirability of assessing potential and achievement under carefully controlled and maximally decontextualized conditions.

Over the past few decades, the various assumptions on which this testing edifice was based have been gradually undermined by work in developmental, cognitive, and educational studies; a quite different view has emerged.

THE NEED FOR A DEVELOPMENTAL PERSPECTIVE

Thanks to the pioneering work of Jean Piaget, it is widely recognized that children are not simply miniature versions of adults. The infant or the toddler conceives of the world in a way that is internally consistent but that deviates in important particulars from a more mature conception. Children pass through a number of qualitatively different stages, called sensorimotor, preoperational, concrete operational, and formal operational. A child at one stage in one area of knowledge will necessarily be at the same stage in other domains of experience.

Few investigators still hold to a literal version of this structured-stage perspective; too many findings fail to support it. But most developmental psychologists continue to subscribe to the view that the world of the infant or toddler has its own peculiar structures; many developmentalists believe that there are stage sequences within particular domains of experience (for example, language, moral judgment, understanding of physical causality); and nearly all emphasize the need to take into account the child's perspective and level of understanding.

Another feature of this approach is its assumption that development is *neither smooth, nor unilinear, nor free of perturbations*. While details differ, most researchers believe that there may be critical or sensitive periods during which it is especially easy—or especially difficult—to master certain kinds of materials. Similarly, since youngsters tend to improve in most areas with age, there will be periods of more rapid growth and periods of stasis. And a minority of researchers believe that in some domains there may actually be regressions or performances that exhibit a U-shaped curve: younger children and adolescents perform in a more sophisticated or integrated fashion than students in middle childhood.

THE EMERGENCE OF A SYMBOL-SYSTEM PERSPECTIVE

At the height of the behaviorist era (in the midde of the 20th century), there was no need to posit any kind of mental entity, such as an idea, a thought, a belief, or a symbol. Psychologists identified and observed behaviors or actions of significance as scrupulously as possible; so-called thoughts were considered simply to be "silent" movements of vocal musculature.

Over the past several decades, psychologists have recognized the importance of the capacity to use various kinds of symbols and symbol systems (see Essays 2, 5, and 7). Human beings are deemed the creatures par excellence of communication; we garner meanings through words, pictures, gestures, numbers, musical patterns, and a whole host of other symbolic forms. The manifestations of these symbols are public; all can observe written language, number systems, drawings, charts, gestural languages, and so on. However, the mental processes needed to manipulate such symbols must be inferred from the performances of individuals on various kinds of tasks. Unexpectedly potent support for the belief in internal symbol manipulation has come from the development and widespread use of computers; if these human-made machines engage in operations of symbol use and transformation, it would seem ludicrous to withhold attribution of the same kinds of capacities from the humans who invented them.

Considerable effort has been expended in various branches of science to investigate the development of the human capacity for symbol use. It is widely (though not universally) agreed that infants do not use symbols or exhibit internal symbolic manipulation and that the emergence of symbol use during the second year of life is a major hallmark of human cognition. Thereafter, human beings rapidly acquire skill in the use of the symbols and symbol systems that are featured in their culture. By the age of 5 or 6, most children have acquired a "first-draft" knowledge of how to create and understand stories, works of music, drawings, and simple scientific explanations.

In literate cultures, there is a second level of symbol use. Children must learn to utilize the invented symbol (or notational) systems of their culture, such as writing and numbers. With few exceptions, this assignment is restricted to school settings, which are relatively decontextualized. Mastering notational systems can be difficult for many students in our society, including those whose mastery of practical knowledge and first-order symbol systems has been unproblematic. Even students who prove facile at acquiring notational systems face a nontrivial challenge: They must mesh their newly acquired second-order symbolic knowledge with the earlier forms of practical and first-order symbolic knowledge they brought with them to school.

Nearly all formal tests presuppose that those taking them will be literate in the second-level symbol systems of the culture. These tests thus pose special challenges for individuals who, for whatever reason, have had difficulty in attaining second-level symbol knowledge or cannot map that knowledge onto earlier forms of mental representation. Moreover, it is my belief that those with well-developed second-level symbolic skills can often "psych out" such tests, scoring well even when their actual mastery of the subject matter that is ostensibly being assessed is modest. At any rate, the exact relations among practical, first-order, and second-order symbolic knowledge and the best way to assess these remain difficult issues to resolve.

EMERGENCE OF A MULTIPLE INTELLIGENCES PERSPECTIVE

When intelligence tests were first constructed, there was little attention paid to the underlying theory of intelligence. But soon the idea gained currency that the different abilities being tapped all fed into or reflected a single general intelligence. This perspective has remained the view of choice among most students of intelligence, although a minority have been open to the idea of different "vectors of mind" or "products, content, and operations" of intellect. This group has based its conclusions on the results of factor analyses of test results; however, it has been shown that one can arrive at either unitary or pluralistic views of intellect, depending on which assumptions guide specific factor-analytic procedures.

In recent years, there has been a resurgence of interest in the idea of a multiplicity of intelligences. Mental phenomena have been discovered that some researchers construe as evidence for mental modules—fast-operating, reflex-like, information-processing devices that seem impervious to the influence of other modules. The discovery of these modules has given rise to the view that separate analytic devices may be involved in tasks such as syntactic parsing, tonal recognition, and facial perception. (For an elaboration of the MI perspective, see Essays 8–11.)

Various multiple intelligences perspectives, including my own, concur on the following proposition: Instead of a single dimension called intellect, on which individuals can be rank-ordered, vast differences obtain across individuals in their intellectual strengths and weaknesses as well as their styles of attack in cognitive pursuit. Our own evidence suggests that these differences may be evident even before the years of formal schooling (see Essay 13).

The literature on different individual strengths, as well as the findings on diverse cognitive styles, has crucial educational implications. To begin with, it is important to identify strengths and weaknesses at an early point so that they can be incorporated into educational planning. Striking differences among individuals also call into question whether all students should be taking the same curriculum and whether, to the extent that there is a uniform curriculum, it needs to be presented in the same fashion to all students.

Formal tests can be an ally to the recognition of different cognitive features, but only if the tests are designed to elicit—rather than mask—these differences. It is particularly important that instruments used in for gatekeeping purposes (such as college admissions) be designed to allow students to show their strengths and to perform optimally. Thus far, little effort has been made in this regard, and tests are used more frequently to point up weaknesses than to designate strengths.

A SEARCH FOR HUMAN CREATIVE CAPACITIES

And what of human creative capacities or skills?

Recent studies have yielded two major findings. On the one hand, creative individuals do not seem to have at their disposal mental operations that are theirs alone; they make use of the same cognitive processes that others do, but they use them in a more efficient and flexible way and in the service of goals that are ambitious and often quite risky (Perkins, 1981). On the other hand, highly creative individuals seem to lead their lives differently than most others. They are fully engaged in and passionate about their work; they exhibit a need to do something new and a strong sense of their purpose and ultimate goals; they are extremely reflective about their activities, their use of time, and the quality of their products.

Except rhetorically, the quest for creativity has not been a major goal of the American educational system. However, to the extent that fostering creative individuals is a desirable goal for an educational institution, it is important that this goal be pursued in a manner consistent with current analyses of creativity (see Essays 24 and 25 in *The Essential Howard Gardner on Mind*).

THE DESIRABILITY OF ASSESSING LEARNING IN CONTEXT

When standardized tests and paradigmatic experimental designs were first introduced into non-Western cultural contexts, they led to a single result: People from preliterate cultures and others from non-Western societies appeared to be much less skilled and much less intelligent than Western control groups.

An interesting phenomenon was then discovered: Simple alterations of materials, test settings, or instructions frequently elicited dramatic improvements in performance. The performance gap between the subjects from other cultures and those from our own culture narrowed or even disappeared when familiar materials were used; when knowledgeable and linguistically fluent examiners were employed; when revised instructions were given; or when the same cognitive capacities were tapped in a format that made more sense within the non-Western context.

Now a huge body of experimental evidence indicates that assessment materials designed for one target population cannot be transported directly to another cultural setting; there are no purely culture-fair or culture-blind materials. Every instrument reflects its origins. Formal tests that make some sense in a Western context do so because students are accustomed to learning about quite abstract materials at a site removed from the habitual application of such materials. However, in unschooled or lightly schooled environments, most instruction takes place *in situ*, and so it only makes sense to administer assessments that are similar in context.

Building on this cross-cultural research, investigators have also generated findings about the cognitive abilities of experts in traditional societies. It has been shown that experts often fail on decontextualized measures of their calculating or reasoning capacities; but they can exhibit precisely those same skills in the course of their ordinary work—such as tailoring clothes, shopping in a supermarket, loading dairy cases onto a truck, or defending their rights in a dispute. In such cases, it is not the *person* who has failed, but rather the *instrument* that purported to measure the person's level of competence.

LOCATING COMPETENCE AND SKILL OUTSIDE THE
HEAD OF THE INDIVIDUAL

This avenue of research yields another novel conceptualization. In many cases it is erroneous to conclude that the knowledge required to execute a task resides completely in the mind of a single individual. This knowledge can be "distributed." That is, successful performance of a task may depend on a team of individuals; no single person possesses all of the necessary expertise, but, working together, members of a team can accomplish the task in a reliable way. Similarly, it is too simple to say that an individual either has or does not have the requisite knowledge; he or she may demonstrate that knowledge reliably in the presence of the appropriate human or mechanical triggers, but the knowledge might be otherwise invisible to probing or cuing.

Building on the analyses of my colleague Mihaly Csikszentmihalyi, it makes sense to think of human cognitive competence as an emerging capacity, one likely to be manifest at the intersection of three different constituents: the *individual*, with his or her skills, knowledge, and aims; the structure of a *domain of knowledge* within which these skills can be aroused; and a set of institutions and roles—*a surrounding field*—that judges when a particular performance is acceptable or even constitutes a creative breakthrough, as well as when it fails to meet specifications. The acquisition and transmission of knowledge depends on a dynamic that sustains itself among these three components. Particularly beyond the years of early childhood, human accomplishment presupposes an awareness of the different domains of knowledge in one's culture and the various "field forces" that affect opportunity, progress, and recognition. By focusing on the knowledge that resides within a single mind at a single moment, formal testing may distort, magnify, or grossly underestimate the contributions that an individual can make within a larger and supportive social setting.

The foregoing research findings point to a differentiated and nuanced view of assessment that, at least in certain ways, might more closely resemble traditional apprenticeship measures. Any assessment initiative being planned today should, in light of these findings, be sensitive to developmental stages and trajectories. Such an initiative should investigate human symbolic capacities in an appropriate fashion in the years following infancy and investigate the relationship between practical knowledge and first- and second-level symbolic skills. It should recognize the existence of different intelligences and of diverse cognitive and stylistic profiles. It should incorporate an awareness of these variations into assessments. It should be built on an understanding of those features that characterize creative individuals in different domains. Finally, any new assessment initiative should acknowledge the effects of context on performance and provide the most appropriate contexts in which to assess competences, including contexts that extend beyond the individual being assessed.

It is a tall order to meet all of these needs and desiderata. Indeed, an attraction of formal testing is that one can bracket or minimize most of the features that I have just outlined. However, if we seek an assessment that is both true to the individual and reflective of our best understanding of the nature of human cognition, we cannot afford to ignore these lines of thinking. And in an era of increasingly smart computers and artificial intelligence programs, this goal should be easier to accomplish.

GENERAL FEATURES OF A NEW APPROACH TO ASSESSMENT

If one were to return to the drawing board today and lay out a fresh approach to assessment, one might attempt to incorporate eight principal features.

1. Emphasis on Assessment Rather Than Testing

The penchant for testing in America has gone too far. While some tests are useful for some purposes, the testing industry has taken off in a way that makes little sense from the point of view of a reflective society. Many who seek to understand the underlying theoretical or conceptual basis of findings are disappointed. It seems that many tests have been designed to create, rather than to fulfill, a need.

While I have ambivalent feelings about testing, I have little ambivalence about assessment. To my mind, it is the proper mission of educated persons, as well as those who are under their charge, to engage in regular and appropriate reflection on their goals, the various means of achieving them, their success (or lack thereof) in achieving them, and the implications of the assessment for rethinking goals or procedures.

I define assessment as the obtaining of information about a person's skills and potentials—with the dual goals of providing useful feedback to the person and useful data to the surrounding community. What distinguishes assessment from testing is the former's favoring of techniques that elicit information in the course of ordinary performance, as against its general uneasiness with the use of formal instruments administered in a neutral, decontextualized setting.

In my view, those in the psychological and educational communities charged with the task of evaluation ought to facilitate such assessment. We should be devising methods and measures that aid in regular, systematic, and useful assessment. In some cases we would end up producing formal tests, but in most cases we would not.

2. Assessment as Simple, Natural, and Occurring on a Reliable Schedule

Rather than being imposed by external authorities at odd times during the year, assessment ought to become part of the natural learning environment.

As much as possible, it should occur on the fly—as part of an individual's natural engagement in a learning setting. Initially, the assessment would probably need to be introduced explicitly; but after a while, much assessment would occur naturally on the part of student and teacher, with little need for explicit recognition or labeling on anyone's part.

The model of the assessment of the cognitive abilities of the expert is relevant here. On one hand, it is rarely necessary for the expert to be assessed by others unless competitive conditions obtain. It is assumed that experts will go about their business with little external monitoring.

However, it is also true that the expert is constantly in the process of assessing; such assessment occurs naturally, almost without conscious reflection, in the course of working. When I first began to write scholarly articles, I was highly dependent upon waves of detailed criticism by teachers and editors; now most of the needed assessment occurs at a preconscious level as I sit at my desk scribbling, or typing a first draft, or editing an earlier version of the material.

As assessment gradually becomes part of the landscape, it no longer needs to be set off from the rest of classroom activity. As in a good apprenticeship, the teachers and the students are always assessing. There is also no need to "teach for the assessment" because the assessment is ubiquitous; indeed, the need for formal tests might atrophy altogether.

3. Ecological Validity

According to standard psychometric theory, a problem with most formal tests is their *validity*—that is, their significant correlation with some consensually valued criterion. As noted, creativity tests are not widely used because their validity has never been adequately established. The predictive validity of intelligence tests and scholastic aptitude tests is often questioned in view of their limited usefulness in predicting performance beyond the next year of schooling.

Returning to our example of the apprenticeship, it would make little sense to question the validity of the judgments by masters. They are so intimately associated with their respective novices that they can probably predict each novice's behaviors with a high degree of accuracy.

When such prediction does not occur reliably, trouble lies ahead. I believe that the assessments used today have moved too far away from the territory that they are supposed to cover. When individuals are assessed in situations that more closely resemble actual working conditions, it proves possible to make much better predictions about their ultimate performance. It is odd that most American schoolchildren spend hundreds of hours over their scholastic careers engaged in a single exercise—the formal test—when few if any of them will ever encounter a similar instrument once they have left school.

4. Instruments That Are Intelligence-Fair

As already noted, most testing instruments are biased heavily in favor of two varieties of intelligence—linguistic and logical-mathematical. People blessed with strengths in this particular combination are likely to do well on most kinds of formal tests—even if they turn out to be not particularly adept in the domain actually under investigation. By the same token, those with problems in either or both linguistic and logical-mathematical intelligences may fail at measures that purport to sample other domains, just because they cannot master the particular format of most standard instruments.

The solution—to be sure, easier to describe than to realize—is to devise instruments that are *intelligence-fair*, that focus *directly* on the intelligence in operation rather than proceeding via the *detour* of linguistic and logical faculties. Spatial intelligence can be assessed by having a person navigate around an unfamiliar territory; bodily intelligence by seeing how the person learns and remembers a new dance or physical exercise; interpersonal intelligence by watching him or her handle a dispute with a sales clerk or navigate an agenda through a fractious committee meeting. These homely instances indicate that intelligence-fairer measures could be devised, although they cannot necessarily be implemented in the psychological laboratory or the testing hall.

5. Uses of Multiple Measures

Few practices are more nefarious in education than the drawing of widespread educational implications from the composite score of a single test—like the Wechsler Intelligence Scale for Children or the Scholastic Assessment Test. Even intelligence tests contain subtests, and, at the very least, recommendations ought to take into account the differences among these subtests and the strategies for approaching particular items.

Attention to a range of measures designed specifically to tap different facets of the capacity in question is even more desirable. Consider, for example, the admission standards of a program for gifted children. Conservatively speaking, 75 percent of the programs in the United States simply admit solely on the basis of IQ—if the cutoff is 130 and you have only 129, then you do not qualify. How unfortunate!

I have no objection to the use of IQ as one consideration; but why not attend as well to the products that a child has already fashioned, the child's goals and desire for a program, performance during a trial period alongside other gifted children, and other unobtrusive measures? I often feel that enormous educational progress would be made if the Secretary of Education simply appeared in front of the television cameras, not accompanied by a single one-dimensional chart, but against the backdrop of a half-dozen disparate graphic displays, each monitoring a distinct aspect of learning and productivity.

6. Sensitivity to Individual Differences, Developmental Levels, and Forms of Expertise

Assessment programs that fail to take into account the vast differences among individuals, developmental levels, and varieties of expertise are increasingly anachronistic. Formal testing could, in principle, be adjusted to take these documented variations into account. But it would require a suspension of some of the key assumptions of standardized testing—such as uniformity of individuals in key respects (for example, in developmental level) and the penchant for ever more cost-efficient instruments.

Individual differences should also be highlighted when educating teachers and assessors. Those charged with the responsibility of assessing youngsters need to be introduced formally to such distinctions; one cannot expect teachers to arrive on their own at empirically valid taxonomies of individual differences. Such an introduction should occur in education courses or during teaching apprenticeships. Once teachers are introduced to such distinctions and given the opportunity to observe and work with children who exhibit different profiles, these distinctions come to life for them. (See Essay 13.)

It then becomes possible to take these differences into account in a tacit way. Good teachers—whether they teach writing to 2nd-graders, piano to toddlers, or research design to graduate students—have always realized that different approaches prove effective with different kinds of students. Such sensitivities to individual differences can become part of the teacher's competence and can be drawn on in the course of regular instruction as well as during assessment. It is also possible—and perhaps optimal—for teachers to season their own intuitive sense of individual differences with judicious occasions of assessment crafted with the particular domain of practice in mind.

7. Use of Intrinsically Interesting and Motivating Materials

One of the most objectionable, though seldom remarked upon, features of formal testing is the intrinsic dullness of the materials. How often does anyone get excited about a test or a particular item on a test?

It was probably only when, as a result of "sunshine" legislation, it became possible for test-takers to challenge the answer keys used by testing organizations that discussion of individual test items ever occupied space in a publication that anyone would voluntarily read.

It need not be that way. A good assessment instrument can—and perhaps should—be a learning experience. But more to the point, it is extremely desirable to have assessment occur in the context of students working on problems, projects, or products that genuinely engage them, that hold their interest and motivate them to do well. Such exercises may not be as easy to design as the standard multiple-choice entry, but they are far more likely to elicit a student's full repertoire of skills and to yield information that proves useful for subsequent advice and placement.

8. Application of Assessment for the Student's Benefit

A lamentable aspect of formal testing is the use made of scores. Individuals receive the scores, see their percentile ranks, and draw conclusions about their scholastic, if not their overall, merit. As I've often quipped, psychologists spend far too much time ranking individuals and not nearly enough time helping them.

Assessment should be undertaken primarily to aid students. The assessor should provide feedback to the student that will be helpful immediately: identifying areas of strength as well as weakness; giving suggestions on what to study or work on; pointing out which habits are productive and which are not; indicating what can be expected in the way of future assessments; and the like. It is especially important that some of the feedback take the form of concrete suggestions and indicate relative strengths to build on—independent of the student's ranking in a comparable group of students.

Armed with findings about human cognition and development, and in light of these desiderata for a new approach to assessment, it should be possible to begin to design programs that are more adequate than those that exist today. Without having any grand design to create a "new alternative to formal testing," my colleagues and I at Project Zero have become engaged in a number of projects over the last several years that feature new approaches to assessment (see Essays 13–15).

TOWARD THE ASSESSING SOCIETY

I have presented a brief in favor of regular assessment occurring in a natural fashion throughout the educational system and across the trajectory of lifelong learning. I have reviewed a sizable body of evidence that, by and large, points up problems with standard formal testing as an exclusive mode of assessment. Many of these findings point to two conclusions: (1) it would be fruitful to create environments in which assessments occur naturally, and (2) it would be desirable to devise curricular entities, like domain projects and processfolios, that lend themselves to assessment within the context of their production. It would be an exaggeration to say that I have called for a reintroduction of the apprentice method. Yet I do claim that we have moved too far from that mode of assessment; contemporary assessment might well be informed by some of the concepts and assumptions associated with traditional apprenticeships.

Indeed, if one considers formal testing and apprentice-style assessment as two poles of assessment, it could be said that America today has veered too far in the direction of formal testing without adequate consideration of its costs and limitations. Even outside the realm of physics, an excessive action calls for a reaction—one reason that this essay stresses the advantages of more naturalistic, context-sensitive, and ecologically valid modes of assessment. Standard formal tests have their place—for example, in initial screening of certain at-risk populations—but users should know the limitations of such tests as well.

Some objections to the perspective introduced here can be anticipated. One is the claim that formal testing is, as advertised, objective and that I am calling for a regression to subjective forms of evaluation.

I reject this characterization for two reasons. First, there is no reason in principle to regard the assessment of domain projects, processfolios, or Spectrum-style measures as intrinsically less objective than other forms (see Essays 13–15). Statistical reliability can be achieved in these practices as well. The establishment of reliability has not been a focus of these projects; however, the conceptual and psychometric tools exist to investigate and achieve reliability in these cases. Moreover, these assessment measures are more likely to possess ecological validity.

A second rebuttal of this characterization has to do with the alleged objectivity or non-bias of standard formal tests. In a technical sense, it is true that the best of these instruments avoid the dangers of subjectivity and statistical bias. However, any kind of instrument is necessarily skewed toward one or a few kinds of individuals and one or a few intellectual and cognitive styles. Formal tests are especially friendly to those who possess a certain blend of linguistic and/or logical intelligences and to those who are comfortable in being assessed in a decontextualized setting under timed and impersonal conditions. Correlatively, such tests are biased against individuals who do not exhibit this blend of intelligences or whose strengths show up better in sustained projects or when they are examined *in situ* or without time limits.

Especially when resources are scarce, everyone should have the opportunity to exhibit strengths. There is no objection to a high scorer being able to show off a string of College Board 800s to a college admissions staff. By the same token, individuals with other cognitive or stylistic strengths ought to have their day as well.

Some observers might be in sympathy with the line of analysis pursued here and yet would reject its implications because of considerations of cost or efficiency. According to this argument, it is simply too inefficient or expensive to mobilize a society around more sustained forms of assessment; hence, even if formal testing is imperfect, we will have to settle for it and simply try to improve it as much as possible.

Despite its superficial plausibility, I reject this stance as well. To be sure, formal testing is now cost-effective, but it has taken millions, perhaps billions, of dollars expended over many decades to bring it to its current, far-from-perfect state. Spending more money on it, I believe, could improve it only marginally, if at all.

The major obstacle I see to assessment in context is not shortage of resources but lack of will. There is in the United States (and likely elsewhere) an enormous desire to make education uniform, to treat all students in the same way, and to apply the same kinds of one-dimensional metrics to all. This trend is inappropriate on scientific grounds and distasteful on ethical grounds. The current sentiment is based in part on an understandable disaffection with some of the excesses and limitations of earlier educational experiments.

But, to a disturbing degree, it is also based on a lack of respect—and sometimes even general hostility—for students, teachers, and the learning process. In other countries in which the educational process is held in higher regard—for example, Finland—it has proved possible to have higher-quality education without subscribing to some of the worst features of one-dimensional educational thinking and assessment.

It is not difficult to sketch the reasons for the tentative national consensus on the need for more testing and more uniform schools. Understandable uneasiness with poor student performance in the latter half of the 20th century resulted in a general indictment of contemporary education, which was blamed for a multitude of societal ills. Government officials entered the fray; the price paid for increased financial support was more testing and more accountability based on the results of these tests. The fact that few experts in education were entirely comfortable with the diagnosis or the purported cure was not relevant. After all, political officials rarely pore over the relevant literature or consult informed researchers; they almost reflexively search for scapegoats and call for the quick fix.

If significant forces or interest groups in this country were to dedicate themselves to a different model of education—for example, the assessment and schooling philosophy outlined here—I have every confidence that they could implement it without breaking the bank. It would be necessary for a wider array of people to pitch in; for college faculty to examine the processfolios that are submitted; for community members to offer mentorships, apprenticeships, or "special pods"; for parents to find out what their children are doing in school and to work with them (or at least encourage them) on their projects. These suggestions may sound revolutionary, but they are daily occurrences in excellent educational settings in the United States and elsewhere. Indeed, it is hard to imagine quality education in the absence of such a cooperative ambience.

To my way of thinking, the ultimate policy debate is—or at least should be—centered on competing concepts of the purposes and aims of education. As I have intimated above, the formal standard testing view harbors a concept of education as a collection of individual elements of information that are to be mastered and then spewed back in a decontextualized setting. In this "bucket" view, it is expected that those who acquire a sufficient amount of such knowledge will necessarily (or at least likely) become effective members of the society.

The assessment view advanced here values the development of productive and reflective skills cultivated through long-term projects. The animating impulse seeks to bridge the gap between school activities and productive activities outside school, with the thought that the same habits of mind and discipline can be useful in both kinds of undertakings. Special attention is paid to individual strengths. Assessment should occur as unobtrusively as possible during the course of daily activities, and the information obtained should be furnished to gatekeepers in useful and economical form.

The assessment view fits comfortably with a vision of individual-centered schooling. Some observers sympathetic to a focus on assessment might still object to the individual-centered view, seeing it as an impractical or romantic conception of education. They would endorse modes of assessment in the service of a rigorous curriculum. To these individuals I would respond, perhaps surprising them, by unequivocally endorsing the importance of rigor. There is nothing in an individual-centered approach that questions rigor; indeed, in any decent apprenticeship, rigor is assumed. If anything, it is the sophomoric multiple-choice-cum-isolated-fact mentality that sacrifices genuine rigor for superficial conformity. I fully embrace rigorous curricula in an individual-based school: I simply call for a broader menu of curricular options.

Karl Marx hoped that one day the state would simply wither away, no longer needed and hardly missed. In my personal millennial vision, I imagine the apparatus of intelligence testing as eventually becoming unnecessary, its waning unmourned. An hour-long standardized test may at certain points in history have served as a reasonable way of indicating who should be performing better at school or who is capable of military service or of performing at officer rank. But as we come to understand the variety of roles and the variety of ways in which scholastic or military accomplishment can come about, we need far more differentiated and far more sensitive ways of assessing what individuals are capable of accomplishing. In place of standardized tests, I hope that we can develop environments (or even societies) in which individuals' natural and acquired strengths will become manifest—environments in which their daily solutions of problems or fashioning of products will indicate clearly which vocational and avocational roles most suit them.

As we move toward constructing such environments, there will be less need for formal and context-free kinds of evaluations; the distance between what students are doing and what they will need (or want) to do in the society will be correspondingly narrowed. We do not have tests to determine who will become a good leader because leadership abilities emerge under naturally occurring circumstances, and this kind of evidence speaks for itself. Nor do we have tests for sex appeal, football playing, musical performance, or, for much the same reasons, legislative skills. We designed tests for intelligence because this alleged global property is not easy to observe in the real world, but it may well be elusive precisely because the notion of intelligence as a single, measurable capacity was never well conceived to begin with.

If the kinds of naturally occurring cognition that I have described are valid, then their several manifestations ought to be readily discernible through judicious observations in the individual's ordinary environment. Far from rendering psychologists or psychometricians unemployable, however, a shift to this kind of subtle measurement would require committed efforts from a much larger, more broadly trained, and more imaginative cadre of workers. When one thinks about the enormous human potential currently wasted in a society that values only a small subset of human talents, such an investment seems worthwhile.

In contrast to a testing society, I believe, the assessment approach and the individual-centered school constitute a more noble educational vision. Both are more in keeping with American democratic and pluralistic values. I also believe that this vision is more consistent with what has been established in recent decades by scientific study of human growth and learning. Schools in the future ought to be crafted so that they are consistent with this vision. In the end, whatever the forms and the incidence of official assessments, the actual daily learning in schools, as well as the learning pursued long after formal school has been completed, should be its own reward.

REFERENCES

Perkins, D. (1981). *The mind's best work*. Harvard University Press.
Schaler, J. (2006) *Howard Gardner under fire*. Open Court.

HIGHER EDUCATION

As noted in the introduction to this collection, when I was a child, I assumed that one day I would be a teacher, and I would, accordingly, teach at all different levels.

And as it turns out, as a researcher, I have worked at all levels of education. In preschool, I collaborated for several years in the development of Project Spectrum—as far as I know, the most ambitious attempt to assess multiple intelligences in context. And, of course, I have visited the schools in Reggio Emilia for 4 decades (see Essay 3).

In K–12 education, for over a decade, I worked very closely with the Key School, an innovative educational experiment in the Indianapolis Public Schools. I also worked with the New City School in St. Louis. For some time, the Key School was much celebrated—indeed, in 1991, it was selected by *Newsweek* magazine as one of the best schools in the world (see Essay 14).

Our work with Arts PROPEL focused on secondary school, but the ideas and techniques developed there have turned out to be applicable across a far wider age range (see Essay 15).

Finally, for a decade, co-led by Wendy Fischman and involving many other colleagues, I've carried out an ambitious study of nonvocational higher education in the United States. Specifically, our team interviewed over 2,000 students, faculty, administrators, trustees, parents, alums, and job recruiters at 10 quite different colleges. The results of this study have been reported in many places, including our book *The Real World of College*. In this forward-looking essay, we present a summary of some of our principal findings and recommendations. And in a brief follow-up essay, I make one heartfelt curricular recommendation.

If We Were Designing a New College...

Wendy Fischman and Howard Gardner

For some years, we have been reading about the decline of American colleges. Dozens, maybe hundreds, have closed down; dozens more have merged with institutions that are financially more secure; and, of course, it's become more difficult for international students, even those who can afford full tuition, to matriculate.

But these trends have not prevented the launching of new colleges. A few, like Olin College of Engineering, have already been pronounced a success and are being emulated; Minerva, with learning based on insights from cognitive sciences and with a "campus" distributed across the globe, has attracted much attention. The recently inaugurated University of Austin has already stimulated major write-ups, both supportive and critical. And, of course, there are hundreds of individuals wealthy enough to launch new schools—sometimes for-profit institutions.

But the emergence of new colleges or universities—no matter how much ballyhoo attends them—does not necessarily yield ones that are better or more appropriate. They might even magnify the mistakes of existing ones. What if we were to design a 21st-century college based on questions posed, data collected, and answers scrutinized in our study over the last decade?

In 2012, we launched a major study of American nonvocational higher education. We conducted in-depth interviews with over 2,000 individuals, spread over 10 campuses—some campuses with names known to nearly all readers, others that we ourselves had not known. And we did not just speak to one group of stakeholders: instead, we interviewed members of eight *different groups*—first-year college students, graduating students, faculty, senior administrators, trustees, recent alumni/ae, parents, and job recruiters.

Research alone can never tell you what to do, but it can certainly reveal what's possible and plausible, and what's doomed to fail. What did we learn?

Here are lessons for those who might want to launch a new college, somewhere/anywhere in the world.

1. WHY COLLEGE?

Finding: Relatively few informants have a well-thought-through response to this question.

Some stakeholders are simply *inertial*: College is what you have to do after high school. A reasonable number are *exploratory*—learn new things, make new associations. A somewhat smaller number are *transformative or transformational* open to becoming a different kind of person. But almost half are *transactional*—go to college to get a job. That's it.

Moreover, there is a huge divide among respondents. Of the eight groups that we interviewed, only college administrators and faculty regularly embraced exploratory or transformative responses. The other six constituencies were largely transactional—we want a college degree so that we can get a job. And when we followed up with "And what happens if the job disappears after a few years?," almost no respondent had even thought seriously about this issue.

Recommendation: From the moment of admission, make it clear to students and their families that the principal goal—the raison d'être—of higher education is to train—to strengthen and cultivate—the mind. We term such messaging "onboarding." This clear and vivid message should be reinforced throughout the college experience—in academic courses as well as extracurricular activities—and perhaps even after graduation, in materials that go out to alums. We call this process "intertwining."

Recommendation: Make it clear to students (and their families) what is meant by training the mind. We describe it as the enhancement of "Higher Education Capital" (HEDCAP for short). HEDCAP entails the abilities to attend, analyze, reflect, connect, and communicate. These capacities are valued across the professional landscape and serve one well for a lifetime of productive work as well as well-spent leisure. Taking advantage of the experiences and testimony of older students and graduates, demonstrate the advantages of HEDCAP. And feel free to draw on the rough-and-ready measures of HEDCAP that we have developed.

Recommendation: Make clear that college can change you—you might become a different kind of person, one who thinks and acts differently than you did upon arrival. Make clear the rewards that attend such exploration and possible transformation. We won't tell you what kind of a person to become, nor will we insist that you change. But we will present the options so that you can make informed choices.

2. LESS IS MORE

Finding: In an effort to please all students and stakeholders, schools launch dozens of programs—we've labeled this condition "projectitis." Sometimes, each program requires its own new building—or a new building (typically donated by wealthy alums) provides a rationale for a new program. As a result, students are often confused by why they are there, what's truly important, and which options they should (or should not) pursue.

At most, college should support one other mission besides academics. And both missions should be made clear from the outset; be understood by all faculty and staff; and be reinforced by regular conversation and by personal embodiment.

Recommendation: If a school embraces one additional mission (e.g., citizenship, service, globalization, ethics, preparation for the workplace), that mission needs to be carefully intertwined with the academic coursework. For example, suppose a school embraces (as a second mission) the ability to deal with ethical dilemmas that may arise in work and/or in citizenship. Appropriate dilemmas should be incorporated across the range of courses and other activities. A stand-alone course on ethics does not suffice!

3. MORE ALIKE THAN DIFFERENT

Finding: To our considerable surprise, we found that whether they go to a highly selective school or one that admits almost everyone, students have very much the same attitudes and concerns. Two major concerns emerged everywhere: student mental health (many are very stressed, and the schools' treatment facilities are accordingly overwhelmed); and expressions of "alienation" and lack of "belonging." Clearly, these challenges need to be addressed as skillfully as possible.

Recommendation: Schools can do much to enhance belonging: for example, having all students take the same courses initially, avoiding high-stakes grading, and banning exclusive fraternities and other clubs, while encouraging interest or affinity groups that remain throughout college. If students feel that they truly belong and are valued for who *they* are and who *they* are becoming, mental health problems may well be alleviated.

Since we are not experts in mental health and treatments, we are reluctant to make specific recommendations. But we note that many of the students trace mental health problems to a belief that they need to get high grades and be perfect, with resulting anxiety and even depression. A focus on improvement, rather than on perfection, would seem to be indicated.

FINAL THOUGHTS

One might wonder what's left to those who create and operate the hypothetical new college. The surprising answer: a great deal.

We have said nothing specific about curriculum; how students might explore and be changed; the kind of work life or civic life that graduates should pursue after college; or the kinds of interventions that can enhance belonging. And indeed, colleges cannot and should not assume all of the obligations of a community. (Remember the risk of projectitis!) Instead, colleges should focus with laser sharpness on what they are—and have long been—uniquely capable of accomplishing with their students.

Indeed, both among the colleges that we studied in depth and the many other campuses that we visited, we find promising efforts with respect to at least one of these goals. For example, faculty at some colleges share the ups and downs of their own lives, thus enhancing the students' sense that they are not alone. Leaders at other schools highlight—by teaching as well as preaching—the centrality of the learning experience. As one teacher-dean quipped, "Here, the weekend begins on Saturday evening." Perhaps most important, schools with a well-known mission—faith-based or military—have less need to explain their raison d'être. But nearly every school that we know of could do more to enhance the college experience for their students.

We believe that a funder or an entity that launches a college according to these specifications would be a success—for the students and their families. As important—though it would not be easy to prove—we believe that a college that focuses on cultivation of the mind and the person in the fullest sense will lead to a less divisive, more constructive, and healthier society. Certainly, we'd consider sending our children (or our grandchildren) to its campus.

REFERENCE

Fischman, W., & Gardner, H. (2022). *The real world of college*. MIT Press.

Why We Should Require All Students to Take Two Philosophy Courses

While focused on the overall status and health of the American higher education system, I occasionally made specific recommendations, as in this essay where I recommended that every student in a nonvocational college take two courses in philosophy.

If I were the czar of higher education that is not explicitly vocational, I would require every undergraduate to study philosophy. And if I were both czar and czarina, I would require all students to take two philosophy courses—one in their first year and another just before graduation.

At first blush, that requirement may seem bizarre, especially coming from me. I am a psychologist and, more broadly, a social scientist, not a philosopher or a humanist. Indeed, in the previous essay, I warned against dictating curricula. Even more deplorably, I have never taken a philosophy course myself.

But I've been thinking about philosophy in recent months because of two developments. Some years ago, Mills College eliminated its philosophy major and merged the department into an interdisciplinary unit—just one example of a growing number of institutions that have eliminated majors in certain humanities fields. On a more positive note, Johns Hopkins University won a $75 million donation to bolster its philosophy department. It occurred to me that a good use of that money would be to design new required courses in philosophy for the benefit of both philosophy departments and undergraduates in general.

The goal: to equip graduates with a philosophical armamentarium they could draw from—and contribute to—for the rest of their lives.

The kinds of courses I would require probably wouldn't necessarily have "philosophy" in the name, although they would all be taught by academics trained in that field. Indeed, except in certain explicitly liberal arts contexts, I might well avoid the word entirely, since it would frighten some students (and, even more, their parents) and confuse others ("Is this about my personal philosophy?").

Instead, I would call the requirement something like "Big Questions of Life." Every student in their first year of college would choose one course from a list with titles like:

"Questions of Identity" (Who am I? Who are we?)
"Questions of Purpose" (Why are we here? What's it all for?)
"Questions of Virtues and Vices" (What is truth? What is beauty? What is morality?)
"Questions of Existence" (What does it mean to be alive, to die, indeed, to be? Or not to be?)

Moreover, I would start with the students' own individual and collective answers to the Big Questions of Life. But—and here is the crucial move—I would not end there.

Instead, I would help students understand that reflective human beings have been asking and answering such questions for millennia, across many cultures and many epochs. Some of the answers those people came up with to the perennial riddles of life have been profound, as indeed have some of the subsequent critiques of their answers.

I want students to appreciate that this conversation over time and across cultures is important and—crucially—that they can and should join in. But they should do so with some humility and respect, building on what has been thought and said before.

There are two powerful reasons for requiring students to start (and end) their education with philosophical questions and thinking. First, scholarly disciplines, however they may have evolved in recent times, began because of human beings' interest in understanding diverse aspects of their world, ranging from the movement of the stars to the strivings of the soul. A compelling way to understand the spectrum of knowledge is to encounter some of the intriguing ways in which our predecessors (who were also our early relatives!) thought about those same issues. Second, for most of us, it's only in the later years of adolescence that we become able to reflect on bodies of knowledge and their relation to one another.

Philosophical ways of reading, thinking, and arguing would constitute good training for 4 years of college—whether or not the "ph" word is ever uttered.

In Years 2 and 3 of a student's education, faculty members across the disciplines and at several degrees of sophistication could build on the initial exposure to philosophical thought, contouring it in ways appropriate to their particular courses. Whether you are teaching poetry, psychology, or physics, you should be able to talk about the ideas that originally motivated the practices in your discipline, the ways in which those ideas have remained constant or changed, and how they relate to ideas in other fields, both neighboring and more remote.

To do that, faculty members need not be masters of philosophy, just as a philosopher need not be a master of the other fields. But all professors should be able to—indeed, should *want* to—provide a context for their field of study. Imagine how inspiring and motivating those conversations could be from course to course, and from discipline to discipline.

During an undergraduate's senior year, philosophical topics and concerns would return as a required course, once again taught by philosophers or philosophically trained scholars. But this time, students would approach the discipline more directly through the use of philosophical texts that deal with timeless as well as contemporary issues—for example, seminal texts on just and unjust wars, human and artificial intelligence, bioethics, or the nature of consciousness.

Underscoring goal: to equip graduates with a philosophical armamentarium they could draw from—and contribute to—for the rest of their lives.

At Mills College, now merged with Northeastern University, the loss of the philosophy department and major will decrease the likelihood that students will master the critical ways of thinking that have been the hallmark of philosophical thinking since classical times. It will be far more difficult for students there to understand the origin and development of different lines of scholarship and how they relate to one another. At Johns Hopkins, a generous donation should mean that more graduating students will be armed with powerful cognitive tools that should serve them well in whatever work and leisure pursuits they elect.

It would be disappointing, even tragic, if less wealthy institutions elected to banish philosophical thinking from their campuses. Leaders of such campuses should, instead, be ingenious in drawing on philosophically trained instructors to inform foundational first-year courses and provide culminating courses of synthesis.

Indeed, in the 19th century, it was customary for the president of a college to provide an overview course at the end of the students' education. Think of the powerful message that a president would send by advocating required philosophy courses for all incoming and graduating students. Why, that kind of initiative might even attract a multimillion-dollar donation.

CONTEMPORARY CHALLENGES AND OPPORTUNITIES

Perhaps every generation believes that it has been subjected to more changes, more quickly, than previous generations. Indeed, one can probably find documentary evidence for this claim—Plautus, the Roman playwright, allegedly quipped "Manners are always declining."

That conceded, one can probably make a convincing case that the changes in my lifetime have been notable, to say the least. With Katie Davis and others, I have sought to document the ways in which the "app generation" comes to know the world—and, in particular, the educational implications of living in a world that is garlanded with apps for almost every conceivable human activity. An "app world" changes experience—but whether those changes are mobilized in a positive or stultifying way constitutes an educational challenge.

A pivotal part of the digital world is the emergence of AI approaches to teaching, studying, and learning. For someone of my generation and my experience, the personal touch in education remains essential. But AI and other computational approaches can execute routine aspects of teaching; match each student with the best pedagogy and the most appropriate curricula; and thereby liberate teachers to become modelers, coaches, and enablers. In a happy scenario, that is what should happen—and perhaps what will happen!

There may also be forms (if not frames!) of mind that are particularly privileged in the 21st century. As one candidate, I nominate the ability to synthesize well—to survey vast amounts of information and assemble them in ways that are useful to oneself and to others. In Essays 23, 24, and 26, I define and present the basic educational steps of synthesizing.

And what of my original conception of education—the idealization of truth, beauty, and goodness that has animated me for a lifetime? In the final chapter in this part, I rethink the relationship between these virtues—and in so doing, invoking the memory of the German philosopher Georg Wilhelm Friedrich Hegel, I intertwine my educational vision with the animating idea of synthesis.

ESSAY 22

Education in the Era of the Apps

With Katie Davis

We consider here an important and timely issue: how digital media are affecting and may continue to affect education. It is appropriate to begin with a vital implication that has yet to be fully acknowledged: education is no longer restricted to K–12 or even K-through-graduate-school. Indeed, it is lifelong! Education (and, it must be added, mis-education) begins as early as the time when toddlers can play with phones, tablets, or remote-control devices, and it continues as long as individuals are able and desire to be involved actively in the world.

Digital devices make possible a degree of individuation and pluralization that would have been virtually (excuse the pun!) inconceivable in earlier epochs. We live in an era when individuals can study, or attempt to acquire a skill, when they want to, at a pace of their own selection, alone or with others, with or without badges or other forms of certification—no two persons have to be educated or to educate themselves in a single mandated way. One-size-fits-all curricula or pedagogy deserve to be anachronistic, if not indictable, offenses. As emphasized in Essays 8 and 12, the time of individualized education is here!

The possibility of entering and mastering important topics and skills in multiple ways is also enabled by digital media. There are now many ways—involving many media and varying in degrees of proactivity—in which to learn to play chess or the piano, to speak French or read Chinese characters, or to gain knowledge of economics, statistics, history, or philosophy.

Furthermore, in our era, digital devices also enable a degree of collaboration with those far away, as well as those nearby, that would not have been possible or even conceivable in earlier eras. This is all to the good!

But less palatable aspects of learning also mark a digital era.

One is the threat to residential learning. To be sure, residential learning is expensive, and its dividends are not always demonstrable, particularly in the short run. Why pay thousands of dollars and move to another city if one can sit at home and master a well-designed MOOC (massive online open course)?

But there are many reasons for cohorts of learners—whether in liberal arts colleges or in professional schools dedicated to law, medicine, nursing, or engineering—to spend time together, in the company of well-trained and informed teachers and mentors. So much of what is important in work is not easily, or not usually, put into spoken words or texts; it is best picked up by being around those who carry out key practices in well-worked-out ways every day. Many years ago, philosopher Michael Polanyi pointed out that one could read about science for one's whole life in a far corner of the world, but this literary immersion would not compare with spending a few weeks in a well-run scientific laboratory in the developed world. We might well ponder whether we would want to have surgery performed or our bridges built or our case presented to a jury by an individual who may have received a high score on a certification exam but has never stood shoulder-to-shoulder with peers and mentors in an actual work setting.

Should an "app mentality" be imposed on lifelong education, an even greater danger lurks. All over the world, prodded by a consensus among policymakers (though not necessarily teachers), there is a belief that there is one body of knowledge that deserves to be mastered (typically, the STEM tetrad of science, technology, engineering, and mathematics—itself an "app quartet"); a best way to present it; and a best way to measure it (typically by a multiple-choice, machine-administered, and machine-scored examination issued by the Educational Testing Service). And there is also the dream (or is it a nightmare?) that one can rank all students, all teachers, indeed all nations, in terms of their performances on these allegedly fair and comprehensive instruments.

Almost none of the highly creative individuals of the past whom we have studied—among them painter Pablo Picasso, poet T. S. Eliot, dancer and choreographer Martha Graham, and leader Mahatma Gandhi—would likely have stood out on such measures. And among contemporary artists, it can be said that Princeton University would have been poorer without painter Frank Stella or writer F. Scott Fitzgerald, just as Harvard University would have been the loser had cellist Yo-Yo Ma or poet John Ashbery or actor John Lithgow or poet Amanda Gorman not elected to study there. (We hope that they also appreciated their broad liberal arts education—see Essay 20.)

We have no doubt that on the part of some, the motivation to carry out "objective education with objective measurements" is laudable. And we have no doubt that some individuals have misused a system in which more subjective or idiosyncratic or hyperpluralistic approaches were sanctioned. But we are equally convinced that education is too important, and too subtle, to be outsourced to the Educational Testing Service, or to what Finnish educator Pasi Sahlberg (2014) wryly terms the GERM approach of Anglo-American education: Global Educational Reform Movement.

Using approaches to health care as a model, Howard has commented, "When it comes to health care, there's a lot to be said for the 'check-list approach' favored by surgeon Atul Gawande. But when it comes to education, this sector remains in many ways an art, and one does well to follow the advice of surgeon Jerome Groopman—'listen, listen hard, and then listen even harder.'"

Contemplating the current Anglo-American intoxication with objective measurement of certain performances and a concomitant insensitivity to differences in human gifts and human aspirations, we have been concerned about an approach to education that is overly reliant on apps.

In fact, we've faced this conundrum of assessment with our own work. In studying Good Work, we have tried to define the features of such work with clarity. A group of teacher colleagues in India converted our prose definitions into carefully calibrated 10-point scales of ethical behavior. At first glance, this feat was an achievement that sharpened our thinking. And yet, it seemed to imply a precision in assessing ethics that could not realistically be achieved. Asked what he thought of the scoring system, Howard praised the devisers for their thoughtfulness and their diligence. But he added that perhaps the system promised more than it could deliver. Instead, Howard suggested, "Why not simply indicate where the school is headed in the ethical sphere—an arrow pointing 'up' means that progress has been made, while one pointed downward suggests the need for more work?"

Leading a series of conversations in which college freshmen reflected on their lives, Howard asked the dozen or so students to indicate their personal goals for the series. He was surprised by one of the responses: "I don't want to work on issues where there are no answers." Howard made a mental note of this response, but at the time said nothing to the student.

Later, after the sessions were over, Howard spent some time with the student and learned that he intended to major in biology (he wanted to become a surgeon) but also in philosophy. Since philosophy has traditionally focused on questions for which there are no answers, or at least no glib or definitive ones, Howard asked the student why he had said that he did not want to spend time on questions with no answers. The student said, "I don't like sessions where people just talk around in circles." But he then admitted what seemed evident to Howard, that an interest in philosophy is hard to square with a belief that all questions must have neat answers.

We suspect that this 18-year-old, growing up in an app world, was impatient with conversation that did not seem goal-directed. And this sentiment, which seems to be increasingly widespread, spells trouble for the study of the traditional liberal arts: interests in literature, philosophy, and history are difficult to sustain if you believe that all knowledge is—or should be—susceptible to an algorithmic process culminating in a consensually accepted correct answer or "product." In fact, the two strands in the student's psyche epitomize well this enigmatic statement (see Essay 20): "Civilization advances by extending the number of important operations which we can perform, without thinking about them."

On one reading of philosopher Alfred North Whitehead's words, the avid student is well advised to be able to automate as many features of living as possible, whether it entails mastering human anatomy so that surgery can be performed expertly or avoiding conversations that lead nowhere and seem to be time wasters. And yet, how can one know in advance which circumstances in surgery might require an instant decision involving an obscure bit of anatomical knowledge or which stray comment in an evening bull session might cause one to rethink an important life decision just in time?

There's a curious disjunction today in the world of those who speak publicly about educational means and goals. On the one hand, particularly among leaders in business, there is much talk about 21st-century skills—the "four Cs" of critical thinking, creative thinking, collaboration, and community. On the other hand, almost all policymakers in education occupying positions of authority in the United States call for the kind of constrained curriculum and traditional standard tests that at their best capture skills of a bygone era.

Given this disjunction, the status of digital learning in general, and apps in particular, is invoked by both sides in the debate. Those favoring the more open-ended skills focus on the enabling qualities of the digital world, whereas those defending the traditional skills seek to mobilize digital media to increase the efficiency and effectiveness of existing delivery and assessment processes.

Let's dive directly into the world of educational apps. Our survey suggests that the majority—one might even say, the vast majority—of educational apps encourage pursuit of the goals and means of traditional education by digital means. They constitute convenient, neat, sometimes even seductive pathways to accomplish what were already goals in an earlier era: mastering concepts, learning arithmetical operations, identifying geographical locations or historical figures or key biological or chemical or physical processes. We could dub them "digital textbooks" or "lectures" or "preprogrammed educational conversations."

Decades ago, renowned behavioral psychologist B. F. Skinner called for teaching machines that would automate the traditional classroom, allow students to proceed at their own rate, provide positive feedback on correct answers, and either repeat a missed item or present that item via another pathway. Those sympathetic to Skinner's brand of psychology—and to its associated educational regimen—would easily recognize many apps today and would likely nod in approval at their slick, seductive interfaces.

Just as generals are prone to fight the last war, it is probably not surprising that the first generation of educational apps resemble pre-app education. (In fact, no less an authority than Marshall McLuhan noted that new media predictably begin by presenting the contents of the previous media.) Yet in our view, this tried-and-true pathway represents a missed opportunity. (And given how slowly change happens in our public education system, it risks becoming codified in the curriculum for many years to come.)

Let's turn the educational challenge on its head. What features are newly enabled by the new media, and how can one create and deploy apps that take maximum advantage of these affordances?

As we see it, the new media offer two dramatically fresh opportunities. One is the chance to initiate and fashion one's own products. As we transition from Web 1.0 to Web 2.0 and beyond, there is no reason anymore simply to respond to stimuli fashioned by others, no matter how scintillating and inviting they may be. Rather, any person in possession of a smart device can begin to sketch, publish, take notes, network, and create works of reflection, art, science—in short, each person can be his or her own creator of knowledge.

The second opportunity entails the capacity to make use of diverse forms of understanding, knowing, expressing, and critiquing—in terms that Howard has made familiar, our multiple forms of intelligence. Until recently, education was largely constrained to highlight two forms of human intelligence: linguistic and logical-mathematical. (Indeed, until the end of the 19th century, linguistic intelligence was prioritized; in the 20th century, logical-mathematical intelligence gained equal if not greater importance.)

The digital media enable a far greater spectrum of intellectual tools. Not only does this opening-up of options allow many more forms of expression and understanding; it also exposes young people to different forms and formulations of knowledge. It gives additional forms of expression to all, and most especially to those whose strengths may not lay in the traditional arenas of language and logic—for example, to future architects, musicians, designers, craftspeople, and maybe even creators of innovative new software.

An example: We turn here to Scratch, a wonderful application created over the past few decades by Mitch Resnick, a valued colleague at MIT, and his colleagues. Building on Seymour Papert's pioneering work with LOGO—a prototypical example of constructivist education—Scratch is a simple programming language accessible even to youngsters who have just reached school age. By piecing together forms that resemble pieces of a jigsaw puzzle, users of Scratch can create their own messages, be they stories, works of art, games, musical compositions, dances, or animated cartoons—indeed, just about any form in any kind of format. Moreover, users of Scratch can and do post their creations. Others around the world can visit these creations, react to them, build on them, and perhaps even re-create them in their own favored symbolic system.

The genius of Scratch is twofold. First of all, it opens up a plethora of modes of expression, so that nearly every child can find an approach that is congenial with his or her own goals, strengths, and imaginations. Second, educational ends and priorities are not dictated from on high; rather, they can and do emerge from the child's own explorations of the Scratch universe. In that sense, Scratch brings pleasure and comfort to those who believe in the constructivist view of knowledge. Not only are users building their own forms of meaning and constructing knowledge that they personally value; but they epitomize the claim of cognitively oriented psychologists that one learns by taking the initiative, making one's own often instructive mistakes along the way, and then, on the basis of feedback from self and others, altering course and moving ahead.

Still, just as a hammer in the hands of a vandal can be used simply to strike every item in sight, it would be possible to misuse Scratch, to miss its genius, and to convert it into yet another behavioral tool. This less happy outcome occurs when adults—no doubt, well meaning in most cases—hijack Scratch in the exclusive service of traditional educational goals and means. For example, in an educational setting wedded to a behaviorist approach, it would be possible to use Scratch to model one specific way of drawing objects in the world or for providing the definitive model of how to represent fractions or write a sentence, a paragraph, or indeed an essay.

We see, then, that the app itself is never a foolproof avenue to one or another educational use or philosophy. Depending on the context in which it is used, and the priorities of the educators (which includes those present in the classroom, looking over homework at home, or at their drawing boards or computer screens at an educational publisher), one can skew the same application toward app-dependent or app-enabling ends.

Nonetheless, we have no intention of letting the app creators off the hook. Those who design apps can skew them toward *dependence*; this is what happens when powerful instructions and constraints are built into the app. Consider Songwriter's Pad, an app for writing songs and poems on the iPad. Choose a mood from the list of available moods, and the app returns a corresponding list of words and phrases associated with that mood that you can then insert into your song or poem. We don't doubt that some people will use this app in creative, unexpected ways. However, the constraints built into Songwriter's Pad—in the form of packaged poetic words and phrases—strike us as leaning toward app dependence.

Alternatively, app designers can skew an app's constraints toward *enabling*; this is what happens when, à la Scratch, the apps are wide-open, when they offer multiple forms of expression, and when the responses from adults and other users are not constrained.

Nor do we intend to leave adults—be they parents or teachers—off the hook. Depending on the milieu at home or at school, adults can signal that apps are simply the latest and most efficient means to a given educational goal—typically, the traditional "mastery of prior knowledge" that has been the staple of education for many years. Or they can signal that apps represent a new avenue for individuals to explore different pathways, to record their own forms of understanding, and to solicit reactions from others, ranging from those with much knowledge to those who may themselves be edified by the product or project in question.

Take, for example, an app created by Sesame Workshop, famous for the innovative television series *Sesame Street*. As described by its creators, the Big Bird's Words app lays the groundwork for learning new words. Using text recognition technology, the app prompts children to identify various words—grouped in categories—in their surrounding environment. The online demo shows a young boy of 3 or 4 working in the food category. He chooses the word *milk* from a list of food words (each item in the list has a picture next to the word), then holds up his smartphone to a milk carton. Big Bird says, "Milk," and congratulates the child for finding the correct word.

Used in an enabling spirit, this app can encourage children to explore the words around them and connect these words to their daily activities. This might lead to exploration of other words in the children's environment but perhaps not in the app's lexical database. These explorations might even involve discussions with parents and siblings. Used in a dependent spirit, however, the app might engender an overreliance on it for word recognition and perhaps send the message to some children that the only words worth knowing are those that are included in the app's database.

Considered in this light, the app-dependent use limits how children explore and learn from their world. And so we look toward mindful adults—whether new young parents or wise elderly folks—to furnish the settings within which apps will be encountered and used. It's in our hands to provide nudges in the direction of flexible use of apps; to offer initial scaffolds in the form or use of apps but then to remove these as soon as feasible; and to sanction the implementation of spaces and of times in which one puts aside the devices and the apps and fends for oneself.

Seth Kugel, author of the "Frugal Traveler" column for *The New York Times*, describes the freedom encountered when he renounces his dependence on travel apps: "I believe everyone should use the vast online database of the travel world with moderation. Save a day or two for spontaneity: seek advice from a stranger on the Seoul subway; take a day to explore an Italian town just because you stopped there for gas; trust your instinct to find a Parisian bistro to call your own. Maybe you'll find out later that its croque-madame has been praised 717 times on TripAdvisor. Who cares? You discovered it yourself."

When we began to write this book, neither of us had in mind the educational writings of Alfred North Whitehead (1911, 1929). Yet, as it happens, we find extremely useful Whitehead's own approach to education, as expressed in his little volume *The Aims of Education* (1929).

In surveying the steps involved in becoming an educated human being, Whitehead identified the recurring sequence of *romance, precision,* and *generalization.* As Whitehead saw it, genuine learning begins when one is excited, moved, inspired, or stimulated by an early encounter with a question, phenomenon, or mystery—this is the time of *romance.*

But one remains stuck at this point, or becomes bored or alienated or anxious, unless one can begin to acquire tools that allow one to gain a firmer understanding of the initially seductive phenomenon. (Of course, the acquisition of *precision* can be done in many ways, ranging from the strict behaviorist regimen to the flexible, exploring constructivist tack.)

Ultimately, the acquired knowledge and skills need to be put into a broader context; related to other forms of knowledge and understanding; and serve as a prod to further learning, with its initial romantic encounters. That's generalization, or, to use Howard's preferred term, synthesis (see Essay 23).

Please note that by no means are we dismissing the importance of learning what prior generations have already established. We certainly do not believe that individuals can or should construct all of their knowledge on their own. That would be absurd! Indeed, new knowledge must be built on what has already been consolidated by earlier thoughtful individuals and groups—in educator Matthew Arnold's well-turned phrase, "to make the best that has been thought and known in the world current everywhere" (1869).

Our point is different. Put directly, we are not unduly worried about avenues to precision; many exist. What we are here urging is that apps can and should facilitate the initial romance; present multiple ways of attaining precision; and, in the end, provide ample opportunities to make novel as well as expected use of what has been learned. This stance should occur both with respect to constrained educational goals—say, the understanding of multiplication—and with respect to the broadest educational goals—say, the appreciation of how scientific knowledge is created and used and misused. Indeed—and here is where we draw the line sharply between behaviorists and constructivists—precision should always be the means toward making knowledge one's own and ultimately using it to raise new questions and build additional knowledge.

You may well be saying, "You authors are certainly giving apps a hard time." And we might even plead "nolo contendere"—that is, we wouldn't dispute your characterization in court.

It is time to say, loudly and clearly, that there are many wonderful apps, designed to do well, better than most of us could do on our own, what needs to be done. To paraphrase Whitehead, they free us to focus on what we want to do or what remains to be done. Moreover, many apps have been created by ordinary citizens who have discerned a problem and have found a way to address it, to fix it. Two cheers for apps!

APPS FOR A BETTER WORLD

An impressive example of what apps can accomplish comes from the work of an organization called Code for America. As explained by founder Jennifer Pahlka, Code for America fellows are chosen to undertake a year's assignment. During that period they work closely with public officials in city governments to create apps that solve problems identified by administrators or citizens. These needs range from finding the optimal flow of traffic to placing children in appropriate schools and helping people who use food stamps to locate high-quality, affordable foods. To give an example, an app developed in Boston to identify potholes is open source and can be used by any other municipality.

What's striking about Code for America is that its fellows can often solve problems at a fraction of the estimated cost, and a fraction of the estimated time span, than anyone at City Hall could have anticipated. A belief in the power of apps—coupled with a sense of important problems and how they might be addressed efficiently and effectively—yields a win all around. And, of course, the existence of Code for America does not preclude the addressing of problems that are more vexed and do not lend themselves to a neat application. Indeed, in the ideal, it can free officials to devote more time to larger, less tractable challenges.

For those of us in the social sciences, there is an apt analogy. In the middle of the 20th century, at the same time that Howard was restricted to a few media outlets, he also had to perform most statistical tests with pen and pencil or the aid of a handheld calculator. These were time-consuming tasks. But in carrying out these computations, Howard got to know his data very well.

Nowadays, powerful computers (along with more sophisticated statistical techniques) allow one to arrive at findings at warp speed. If the time saved gets translated into closer scrutiny of the data and a deeper, more cogent analysis of what they mean, the apps have been invaluable. If, however, they create the illusion that the data (let alone the "big data") speak for themselves, or simply make the researcher impatient to collect and analyze the next trove of data, then the app has not been so helpful.

As an example from a very different realm, consider the creation by composer Tod Machover of a work called *A Toronto Symphony*. Dubbed "America's most wired composer," Machover has pioneered the use of electronic and digital instrumentation in many compositions; he has also created new approaches to scoring and devised toylike instruments that can be played by individuals with no formal training in music.

A Toronto Symphony breaks new ground. This massively collaborative composition (which goes beyond crowdsourcing) involves ordinary citizens—chiefly from Toronto, though anyone can play—in the co-creation of a major symphonic work. For one section of the work, inhabitants are invited to record and submit sounds that they find expressive of the city. (This can be seen as a contemporary version of the street sounds in the opening section of George Gershwin's *An American in Paris*.) For other sections of the symphony, Machover and his team have created apps that, like paintbrushes, can be applied in different colors and with differing intensity. These apps allow users to shape a melody sketched by Machover, both in terms of its broad contour and its finer details, or to create their own collages and mash-ups of musical material from the piece. Sampling and studying these various contributions garnered over several months, Machover becomes the final creator of the work. But as he has put it, "If it feels in the end like basically my piece no matter what, or like a mash-up of other people's stuff that I facilitated, I think that would be less satisfying . . . but if it's something that couldn't have been made without each other, it will feel really good" (Eichler, 2013).

Machover's symphonic composition differs in its goals and methods from Pahlka's Code for America. Whereas Pahlka is trying to solve vexing urban problems, Machover is creating a tribute to an admired urban environment: engineering versus art. But note that creating a musical work in the digital landscape is also a feat of engineering, while creating an effective municipal app is also an artistic feat. Probing further, we see the contributions of ordinary nonexperts ("what used to be called 'the audience,'" as one pundit has put it); in the case of Code for America, suggesting problems that need to be tackled and using the solutions created by the fellows. In parallel fashion, ordinary non-experts evince their best efforts to orchestrate sections of a work, and once the work has been completed and performed, the audience members can assess the success of the piece. In the finest sense, we see at work joint efforts between citizens and experts, and a fine balance between algorithms (apps) and taste (app transcendence).

REFERENCES

Arnold, M. (1869). *Culture and anarchy*. Smith, Elder, & Co.

Eichler, J. (2013, January 26). Sounds of a city: A new template for collaboration in Toronto. *The Boston Globe*. https://www.bostonglobe.com/arts/music/2013/01/26/sounds-city-machover-toronto-symphony-test-drives-new-template-for-collaboration/OBIcFVtC3Qs29Rp2XkoYXP/story.html?p1=BGSearch_Overlay_Results

Kugel, S. (2013, January 1). Using TripAdvisor? Some advice. *The New York Times*. https://archive.nytimes.com/frugaltraveler.blogs.nytimes.com/2013/01/01/using-tripadvisor-some-advice/?searchResultPosition=1

Machover, T. (2020, May 19). *A Toronto symphony*. [Video]. YouTube. https://www.youtube.com/watch?v=D8S7GnBO2go

Sahlberg, P. (2014). *Finnish lessons*. Teachers College Press.

Whitehead, A. N. (1911). *An introduction to mathematics*. Williams & Northgate.

Whitehead, A. N. (1929). *The aims of education and other essays*. Free Press.

ESSAY 23

The Five Minds for the Future

CULTIVATING NEW WAYS OF THINKING TO ACHIEVE IMPORTANT SOCIETAL GOALS

In the opening years of the millennium, we have become well attuned to considerations of the future. I refer to trends whose existence is widely acknowledged: the increasing power of science and technology; the interconnectedness of the world in economic, cultural, and social terms; and the circulation and intermingling of human beings of diverse backgrounds and aspirations.

As one who has witnessed discussions of the future in many venues, I can attest that belief in the power of education—for good or for ill—is omnipresent. We have little difficulty in seeing education as an enterprise—indeed *the* enterprise—for shaping the mind of the future.

What kind of minds should we be cultivating for the future? Five types stand out as particularly urgent. Let me bring them onto center stage.

THE DISCIPLINED MIND

In English, the word "discipline" has two distinct connotations. First, we speak of the mind as having mastered one or more disciplines—arts, crafts, professions, or scholarly pursuits. By rough estimates, it takes approximately a decade for an individual to learn a discipline well enough so that he or she can be considered an expert or master.

Perhaps at one time, an individual could rest on his or her laurels once such disciplinary mastery had been initially achieved. No longer! Disciplines themselves change, contexts change, as do the demands on individuals who have achieved initial mastery. One must continue to educate oneself and others over succeeding decades.

Such honing of expertise can only be done if an individual possesses discipline in the second sense of the word. That is, one needs to continually practice in a regular and mindful way if one is to remain at the top of one's game.

Though relatively few of us go on to become academic disciplinarians, we initially acquire a disciplined mind in school. And, indeed, that has been the traditional task of schools beyond the elementary years—helping students to grasp what it means to think mathematically, scientifically, historically, or artistically.

Note that thinking in a disciplined way is *not* knowing facts and figures. Such memorized information is discipline-neutral. Rather, it is understanding that a historical explanation of an event (e.g., a nuclear attack on a city) differs from a scientific explanation, and that the truths of mathematics are not the same as historical truths or as artistic truths—if, indeed, it is even proper to speak of truth with reference to a poem, play, or painting.

Nowadays, the mastery of more than one discipline is at a premium. We value those who are multidisciplinary (using one discipline, then another) or interdisciplinary (combining disciplines to yield new findings). But these claims must be cashed in. We would not consider someone a bilingual person unless he or she could speak more than one language. By the same token, the claim of pluri-disciplinarity (if you'll excuse this verbal monstrosity) only makes sense if a person has genuinely mastered more than one discipline and can integrate them. For most of us, the attainment of multiple perspectives is a more reasonable goal.

THE SYNTHESIZING MIND

Nobel Laureate in Physics Murray Gell-Mann, an avowed multi-disciplinarian made an intriguing claim in conversation with me: He asserted that in the 21st century the most valued mind will be the synthesizing mind—the mind that can survey a wide range of sources, decide what is important and worth paying attention to, and then arrange this information in ways that make sense to oneself and, ultimately, to others.

Gell-Mann was onto something important. Information has never been in short supply. But with the advent of new technologies and media—most notably the Internet and large language instruments—vast, seemingly indigestible amounts of information now deluge us around the clock. Shrewd triage becomes an imperative. Those who can synthesize well for themselves will rise to the top of their pack; those whose syntheses make sense to others will be invaluable teachers, communicators, and leaders.

An example from a history class: Say, as a 9th-grader, you are assigned to examine the role of immigration in your home community—in the 19th century and in recent times. The place to begin is with any already existing synthesis: fetch it, devour it, evaluate it. If none exists, you turn to the most knowledgeable individuals and ask them to provide the basic information requisite to synthesis. Given this initial input, you then decide what information seems adequate and where important additional data are required.

At the same time, you need to decide on the form and format of the ultimate synthesis—a written narrative, an oral presentation, a list of scenarios, a set of charts and graphs, perhaps a discussion of pros and cons of various waves of immigration, leading to a final judgment.

Now, the actual work of synthesis begins in earnest. New information must be acquired, probed, evaluated, followed up, or sidelined. The new information needs to fit, if possible, into the initial synthesis, and where fit is lacking, mutual adjustments must be made. Constant reflection is the order of the day.

At some point before the final synthesis is due, a protosynthesis is appropriate. This interim version needs to be tested with the most knowledgeable audience—probably a history teacher or a local historian. However, if the synthesis is to be effective as communication, it also should be shown to an individual who is sympathetic but not knowledgeable. Will he or she understand your chief findings, ask relevant questions, and make constructive suggestions?

In one sense, good teachers always have modeled synthesizing and have critiqued the adequacy of the syntheses produced by their students. But this skill has rarely been taught explicitly. Nor have clear-cut standards emerged for what counts as an excellent, an adequate, or a flawed synthesis. As educators, we must determine how to nurture synthesizing capacities more widely, since they are likely to remain at a premium in the coming era. (See also Essays 23 and 26.)

THE CREATING MIND

In our lifetimes, nearly every practice that is well understood will be automated. Mastery of existing disciplines will be necessary, but not sufficient. The creating mind forges new ground.

In our society we have come to value those individuals who keep casting about for new ideas and practices, monitoring their successes, learning quickly from their failures and near misses. And we give special honor to those rare individuals whose innovations actually change the practices of their peers in notable ways. In my trade, we call these individuals "Big C creators."

As a student of creativity, I long assumed that creating was primarily a cognitive feat—having the requisite knowledge and the apposite cognitive processes. But I have come to believe that personality and temperament are equally—and perhaps even more—important for the would-be creator. More than simply willing, the creator must be eager to take chances, to venture into the unknown, to fall flat on his or her face, and then, smiling, pick oneself up and once more jump into the fray. Even when successful, the creator does not rest on laurels. He or she is motivated again to venture into the unknown and to risk failure, buoyed by the hope that another breakthrough may just be in the offing.

In the United States, there has been discussion over the years about creativity on the streets and in the media. Creativity is an easier sell here than in many other nations. The job of schools, accordingly, is not so much the inculcation of creativity, but rather its protection. Educators protect creativity by encouraging multiple approaches to an assignment, asking students to explain their apparently flawed responses, and rewarding those who make mistakes but then learn from them.

It is important to ascertain the relation among the three kinds of minds introduced thus far. Clearly, synthesizing is not possible without some mastery of constituent disciplines—and perhaps there is, or will be, a discipline of synthesizing, quite apart from such established disciplines as mathematics or music. I would suggest that creation is unlikely to emerge in the absence of some disciplinary mastery and perhaps some capacity to synthesize as well. You can't think outside the box unless you have a box!

THE RESPECTFUL MIND

Almost from the start, infants are alert to other human beings. The attachment link between parent and child is predisposed to develop throughout the early months of life, and the nature and strength of that bond in turn determine much about the capacity of individuals to form relationships with others throughout life.

Of equal potency is the young human's capacity to distinguish among individuals, and among groups of individuals. We are wired to make such distinctions readily. Indeed, our survival depends on our ability to distinguish among those who would help and nourish us vis-à-vis those who might do us harm. But the messages in our particular environment determine how we will label individuals or groups. Our own experiences and the attitudes displayed by the peers and elders to whom we are closest determine whether we like, admire, or respect certain individuals and groups or whether, on the contrary, we come to shun, fear, or even hate them.

We live in an era when nearly every individual is likely to encounter many scores of individuals personally and when untold millions persons have the option of traveling abroad or of encountering individuals from remote cultures through digital media. A person possessed of a respectful mind welcomes this exposure to diverse persons and groups. A praiseworthy cosmopolitan individual gives others the benefit of doubt; displays initial trust; tries to form links; and avoids prejudicial judgments.

Of course, the first steps toward respect or disrespect begin in the home. But for nearly all young people, the atmosphere within a school makes an enormous contribution to the development (or lack of development) of a respectful stance. Education leaders set the tone by how they deal on a daily basis with everyone—from school boards to principals, from parents to teachers, from Jack to Jill. Just consider the different messages sent by South African leader Nelson Mandela, on the one hand, and Slobodan Milošević, the Serbian leader, on the other.

THE ETHICAL MIND

An ethical stance is in no way antithetical to a respectful one, but it involves a different and arguably more sophisticated stance toward individuals and groups. A person possessed of an ethical mind is able to think of her- or himself abstractly, able to ask, "What kind of a person do I want to be? What kind of a worker do I want to be? What kind of a citizen do I want to be?"

Going beyond the posing of such questions, the person is able to think about him or herself in a universalistic manner: "What would the world be like if all persons behaved the way that I do, if all workers in my profession took the stance that I have, if all citizens in my region or my world carried out their roles in the way that I do?" Such conceptualization involves a recognition of rights and responsibilities attendant to each role. And crucially, the ethical individual behaves in accordance with the answers he or she has forged, even when such behaviors may clash with self-interest.

The seeds that eventually lead to the sprouting of an ethical mind may begin in early life, but ethical thought typically emerges only in the adolescent years. That is because the ethical mind requires abstraction—the capacity to think of oneself not as Judy or John, but as a journalist or engineer and as a citizen of Cincinnati, China, or the entire globe.

Within schools, students do not literally have an occupation or voting rights in their community. But for most young people, schools are the first substantial institution in which they are involved. And so, it's a permissible extension to think of the vocational role of the young person as student and the citizenship role of the young person as a member of the school community. The habits of mind developed as student worker and student citizen may well help determine the ethical (or nonethical) stance of the future adult.

Deciding what is ethical (and what's not!) can prove especially challenging during times like our own—when conditions are changing very quickly and when market forces are powerful and often unmitigated. Even when one has determined the proper course, it is not always easy to behave in an ethical manner. That is particularly so when one is ambitious, when others appear to be cutting corners, when different interest groups demand contradictory things from workers, when the ethical course is less clear than one might like, and when such a course runs against one's immediate self-interest.

It is so much easier, so much more natural, to develop an ethical mind when one inhabits an ethical environment. But such an environment is neither necessary nor sufficient. That is why the ethical stances of a school and a school system are so important. Education in ethics may not begin as early as education for respect, but neither curriculum ever ends.

TENSION EXISTS

Of the five minds, the ones most likely to be confused with one another are the respectful mind and the ethical mind. In part, this is because of ordinary language. We consider respect and ethics to be virtues, and we assume that one cannot have one without the other. Moreover, often they are correlated; persons who are ethical are also respectful, and vice versa.

However, as indicated, I see these as developmentally discrete accomplishments. One can be respectful from early childhood, even without having a deep understanding of the reasons for respect. In contrast, ethical conceptions and behaviors presuppose an abstract, self-conscious attitude, a capacity to step away from the details of daily life and to conceive of oneself as a worker or as a citizen.

Whistleblowers are a good example. Many individuals observe wrongdoing at high levels in their organization and remain silent. They may want to keep their jobs; they also want to treat their leaders with respect. It takes both courage and a mental leap to think of oneself not as an acquaintance of one's supervisor, but rather as a member of an institution or profession with certain obligations attendant thereto. The whistleblower assumes an ethical stance at the cost of a respectful relation to his or her supervisor.

Sometimes respect may trump ethics. When I first learned about it, I defended the right of Danish newspapers to publish cartoons that poked fun at Islamic fundamentalism. I was taking the United States Constitution Bill of Rights at face value—guaranteed freedom of expression, no state religion. But I eventually came to the conclusion that this ethical stance needed to be weighed against the costs of disrespecting the sincere and strongly held religious beliefs of others. The costs of honoring the Islamic preferences seem less than those of honoring an abstract principle. Of course, I make no claim that I did the right thing—only that the tension between respect and ethics needs to be acknowledged and may be resolved in contrasting ways.

WAKE-UP CALLS

How can one nurture these minds in the young? Awareness of the minds—realizing the importance of synthesis, recognizing the differences between discipline and creativity—is a first step. Positive examples of each mind, either from life or from history, are valuable. So, too, one learns from contemporary or historical figures who were undisciplined or disrespectful or unethical.

A sense of the developmental trajectory is important. The serious work of disciplining the mind begins early, but it presupposes the basic literacies. Wake-up calls may be helpful. These can be positive instances—an example of a teacher whose students' creations are often notable—and they can be reactions to negative events—how the school handles a case of student cheating or a case where a teacher leaks the test to raise the scores of students.

No education leader—indeed, no person—will possess all five minds in full-blown form, but all can work to enhance each of these minds. Leaders who are not themselves expert synthesizers should make sure that others on their staff have this particular gift. Of course, experts in the specific disciplines will be needed not only in the classroom, but in key administrative roles as well. But the respectful and ethical minds cannot be outsourced. Unless leaders are paragons of respect and ethics, they cannot expect to encounter these virtues throughout the system under their jurisdiction.

No strict hierarchy exists among the minds such that one should be cultivated before the others. Yet a rhythm does exist. One needs discipline, in both senses of the term, before one can undertake a reasonable synthesis; and if the synthesis involves more than one discipline, then each of the constituent disciplines needs to be cultivated.

By the same token, any genuinely creative activity presupposes a certain mastery of discipline. While prowess at synthesizing may be unnecessary, nearly all creative breakthroughs—whether in the arts, politics, scholarship, or corporate life—are dependent to some extent on provisional syntheses. Still, too much discipline clashes with creativity, and those who excel at syntheses may be less likely to effect the most radical creative breakthroughs.

ROLE-MODELING

In the end, it is desirable for each person to have achieved aspects of all five minds for the future. Such a personal integration is most likely to occur if individuals are raised in environments where all five kinds of minds are exhibited and valued. So much the better if there *are* role models—parents, teachers, masters, supervisors at work, political leaders—who display aspects of discipline, synthesis, creation, respect, and ethics on a regular basis. In addition to embodying these kinds of minds, the best educators at school or work can provide support, advice, and coaching to inculcate discipline, encourage synthesis, prod creativity, foster respect, and encourage an ethical stance.

No one can compel the cultivation and integration of the five minds. The individual human being must come to believe that the minds are important; merit the investment of significant amounts of time and resources; and are worthy of continuing nurturance, even when external supports have faded. The individual must be aware that sometimes these minds will find themselves in tension with one another and that any resolution will be purchased at some cost.

In the future the form of mind that is likely to be at greatest premium is the synthesizing mind (see Essays 24 and 26). And so it is fitting that the melding of the minds within an individual's skin is the ultimate challenge of personal synthesis.

ESSAY 24

Synthesis 1.0
A Few Essential Tips

In Molière's play *Le Bourgeois Gentilhomme*, the protagonist (one M. Jourdain) announces—to his astonishment—that he has been speaking prose all his life. He just had not realized it!

Many of us could say the same thing about synthesis. It's a formidable word, not uttered that often, not that easy to define—but like prose, it's a vital part of living. According to the first entry in the dictionary, synthesis denotes putting things—particularly ideas or elements—into some kind of a coherent system. Simple examples include the original Greek meaning of the word—piecing parts of a garment together, or an infant's coming to understand that objects can be hidden from sight and yet will reliably reappear in most cases.

Whatever our life stage, our residence, our daily routines, or our line of work, we need to carry out syntheses, whether or not we are aware of them or think of them as such. Consider how one plans for a trip or a holiday, prepares a celebratory meal, or, less happily, arranges a memorial service, or chooses an outfit for a job interview or for one's wardrobe for the opening days of college. Each of these enterprises involves arranging and rearranging elements so that they make a coherent, or at least a tenable, whole. Of course, syntheses differ in how well composed they are, how effective they are, and how useful they prove for future challenges or opportunities.

So far, I've described quite simple forms of synthesis. Of course, there are more complex examples as well—for example, drawing on concepts from biology and statistics to explain a phenomenon in medicine, or bringing historical and psychological information to bear on the writing of a novel. We might call these Big Syntheses. In a series of blog posts (https://www.howardgardner.com/synthesizing), I've been describing striking examples of Big Syntheses. But in what follows, I focus on the elements of ordinary or "little" synthesizing.

Given the importance, as well as the ubiquity, of synthesizing, it's striking how little systematic knowledge we have of the processes involved in synthesizing and how little formal instruction exists on how to synthesize well.

Let me suggest two different—indeed contrasting—reasons for this puzzling state of affairs. On the one hand, little syntheses are so common, so ubiquitous, that (shades of M. Jourdain's belated appreciation of prose) we take them for granted—just as most of us unreflectively digest food, or jog along a path, or choose clothing for a day alone at home. On the other hand, Big Syntheses coalesce over a significant period of time, and, accordingly, it's not easy to replicate them in a laboratory experiment. Not surprisingly, we psychologists prefer to study processes that can be more easily captured—like memorizing a random list of words, or assembling blocks so that they match a target pattern.

But people do synthesize, many of us get better at synthesis, and a few of us manage to accomplish Big Syntheses. If synthesizing is not explicitly modeled or taught, how do we go about doing it? And how do we improve our performances?

I assume that some of us proceed by trial and error; some of us look for published or posted materials (how to memorize words more effectively, or how to ace an IQ test); and some of us (probably a majority) go about synthesizing much in the manner of influential role models. Half a century after the death of my grandparents, and years after the death of my parents, I organize my life very much as my close relatives did; and more than half a century after leaving graduate school, I go about studying and writing on different topics (including books and essays about synthesizing) in a manner reminiscent of certain teachers and mentors.

But take note: I don't believe that any of these role models ever used a term like "synthesis," and I don't remember any of them pointing out how they went about synthesizing. They just did it—well or not so well. I regularly observed what they did, and in my own fashion emulated them.

To wit:

My grandfather worked out ideas on a daily walk, and so do I.

My grandmother wrote poems to mark family events, and so do I.

My father kept daily "to-do" lists, and so do I—with a vengeance!

My mother (the archetypical "connector") assembled people of varying skills and dispositions to carry out diverse missions, and so do I.

My mentor, Jerome Bruner, conducted research meetings in certain ways, and so do I.

My adviser, Roger Brown, wrote textbook chapters in a certain style that I have sought to emulate.

And now that I have grown children and growing grandchildren, I can sometimes observe that they synthesize in the way that I've done—while, at other times, deliberately (and perhaps appropriately) rejecting me as a role model.

But does synthesizing need to proceed in such a catch-as-catch-can fashion? Could we teach it or model it more explicitly? And if we could, would life proceed more smoothly, more satisfyingly, and even more effectively?

I believe that the answer is a resounding yes!

Here are the ingredients for my (so far virtual) synthesizing kit:

Conceptualize the problem, the project, or the enterprise (large or small).

Identify a starting point(s).

Envision the shape of the likely end product(s)—more than one possibility is helpful.

Search for good (and not so good) models of the final product.

Reflect on the means and media at one's disposal—these include drawing on your own favored intelligences and your customary style of work (and play).

Activate these means and these media as you proceed from starting point to final synthesis.

Identify, collect, and evaluate relevant information, data, and ideas while discarding those that seem inappropriate (this should occur deliberately, but often desired information will appear without your conscious efforts).

Create drafts, sketches, or portfolios using symbol systems with which you are comfortable (numerous configurations are available—charts, grids, tables, metaphors, narratives, formulas, diagrams equations, etc.).

Arrange elements in different configurations, searching for fits and lack thereof.

Prepare and issue a protosynthesis—a first draft, so to speak.

Secure informal feedback from possible consumers of the end product—those already informed and those who want to be informed.

Lay out a penultimate draft, a "fair sample" of the final product.

Craft the final synthesis on the basis of feedback from others, especially experts (critical friends).

Of course, this kit is more than one would need if one were planning a weekend holiday, but if one were planning a year's trip around the world, it might well be appropriate. It's important to distinguish between little synthesis, middle synthesis, and Big Synthesis.

I wish you good synthesizing!

ESSAY 25

Changing Minds

If one could simply state one's goal, lay out the requisite steps, and then follow them, achieving one's goals might well be straightforward—and easy to realize.

But often there are significant obstacles toward achieving one's goals, and perhaps especially when one has customarily thought about the relevant issues in a quite different manner.

As just one example, consider what it takes to achieve disciplined thinking. As pointed out in Essays 17 and 18, children entering school are by no means blank slates. Indeed, many of them will have developed intuitive theories of mind, matter, and motion that are inimical to more sophisticated and more accurate mental models. Similarly, those who are studying history and physics in secondary school may well find that these approaches clash with their intuitive understandings of what happened in 1789 in France or Fort Sumter in 1861—or what happens when one flips a coin or parachutes off an airplane.

Questions like these stimulated me to write *Changing Minds* (2006). Here's a synopsis of one of the major arguments in that book.

80/20 AND SEVEN R'S

Mental Representations: The 80/20 Principle

Much of education entails mastering materials already part of an agreed-upon curriculum. But sometimes, one's pedagogical efforts should be directed at changing ideas, attitudes, and stereotypes that have already been well entrenched.

Consider a change of mind that many individuals have experienced over the years. From early childhood, most of us have operated under the following assumption: When confronted with a task, we should work as hard as we are able and devote approximately equal time to each part of that task. According to this 50/50 principle, if we have to learn a piece of music, or master a new game, or fill some role at home or at work, we should spread our effort equally across the various components.

Now consider another perspective on this issue. Early in the last century, the Italian economist and sociologist Vilfredo Pareto proposed what has come to be known as the "80/20 principle" or rule. As explained by Richard Koch in a charming book, *The 80/20 Principle* (1999), one can in general accomplish most of what one wants—perhaps up to 80 percent of the target—with only a relatively modest amount of effort, perhaps only 20 percent of expected effort. It is important to be judicious about where one places one's efforts, and to be alert to "tipping points" that abruptly bring a goal within (or beyond) reach. Conversely, one should avoid the natural temptation to inject equal amounts of energy into every part of a task, problem, project, or hobby; or to lavish equal amounts of attention on every employee, every friend, or every worry.

Why should anyone change his or her mind from operating under the 50/50 principle to believing Pareto's apparently counterintuitive proposition? Let's consider some concrete instances.

Studies show that in most businesses, about 80 percent of the profits come from 20 percent of the products. Clearly, it makes sense to devote attention to and retain the profitable products while dropping the losers. In most businesses, the top workers produce far more than their share of profits; thus one should reward the top workers while trying to ease out the unproductive (and unprofitable) ones. Complementing this notion (and with a nod to pessimists), 80 percent of the trouble in a workforce characteristically comes from a small number of troublemakers—who, unless they are relatives of the boss, should promptly be excised from the company. (In corporate America this policy was once practicee by companies like General Electric that singled out the top 20 percent for reward and the bottom 10 percent for oblivion.)

The same ratio applies to customers: The best customers or clients account for most of our successes, while the vast majority of clientele contribute little to our bottom line. With respect to almost any product or project, one can accomplish the basic specification and goals with only about one-fifth of the customary effort; nearly all remaining efforts are expended simply to reach personal satisfaction or to satisfy our own obsessive streak. In each case, one must ask: Do we truly desire such perfection? What are the opportunity costs of devoting significant energy to just one of a raft of possible endeavors?

The 80/20 principle even crops up in current events. According to news reports that I once read, 20 percent of baggage screeners at airports account for 80 percent of the mistakes (Moss, 2001). Responding to this need, an aviation expert designed a simple perceptual task that "screens out" the least able screeners.

By now, even if you have never heard of this principle, you have probably gotten the gist of it (maybe even 80 percent thereof!). You'll have a sense of whether this is familiar territory for you ("Pareto was just talking about cutting our losses"), or whether it represents a genuinely new way of thinking about things ("I'm going right down to the director of human resources and see how we can get rid of the most moribund 20 percent of our team"). You'll probably have some questions—for example, is it always 80/20? How do you know which 20 percent to focus on? Do we really want our pilots, our surgeons, our scientists, or our artists to practice 80/20 triage? And if you are a bit irreverent, you may ask: "How could someone named Richard Koch manage to write and publish a 300-page book on the 80/20 principle?"

Quick answer: It's a good read.

In other words, by this point, chances are that you're beginning to question previous beliefs and accept the plausibility of Pareto's proposition—in theory, at least. Indeed, from one perspective, the 80/20 principle seems easy enough to state, understand, absorb. Human beings could have been designed as the kinds of creatures who can readily learn to think about choices in such a new way.

In reality, however, nothing could be further from the truth. One of the most entrenched habits in human thought is the belief that one should operate according to a rival 50/50 principle. We should treat everyone and everything fairly and equally—and expect the same from others (particularly our parents!). We should spend the same amount of time on each person, each customer, each employee, each project, each student, each part of each project. Evolutionary psychologists go so far as to claim that this equity principle is part of the mental architecture of our species.

But there is no need to invoke a biological explanation. There is ample cultural support from earliest childhood for the notion that one should devote attention equivalently: "Now children, let's share the candy so that each of you gets exactly the same amount." And so even individuals who ardently wish to operate on a basis other than 50/50—be it 80/20, 60/40, or 99/1—find it challenging to do so. It's easy enough to state or tout the 80/20 principle; changing one's mind and henceforth operating in accordance with it proves much harder.

The 80/20 principle is perhaps best described as a concept. Human beings think in concepts, and our minds are stocked with concepts of all sorts—some tangible (the concept of furniture, the concept of a meal), others far more abstract (the concept of democracy, or gravity, or the gross national product). As concepts become more familiar, they often seem more concrete, and one becomes able to think of them in almost the same way that one thinks of something one can touch or taste. Thus, on a first encounter, the 80/20 principle may seem abstract and elusive, but after one has used it for a while, and played with it in various contexts, this principle can become as familiar and cuddly as an old stuffed teddy bear.

Moreover, the more familiar a concept, the easier it is to think of in various ways. Which brings me to an important point: Presenting multiple versions of the same concept can be an extremely powerful way to change someone's mind. So far, we have described the 80/20 principle in words and numbers—two common external marks (readily perceptible symbols that denote concepts). But the principle need not be confined to linguistic or numerical symbolization—and it is the possibility of expression in a variety of symbolic forms that often facilitates mind-changing. For example, we could create static figures, or dynamic ones, or even a computer program that allows us to put as many bottles—of any sort—in any configuration, and see to what extent these different formats capture Pareto's principle—or other concepts that denote human drinking habits.

These various ways of thinking about Pareto's principle brings us to an important point about mental representations: They have both a content and a form, or format. The content is the basic idea that is contained in the representation—what linguists would call the semantics of the message. The form or format is the particular language or system of symbols or notation in which the content is presented.

Each of the ways of viewing the 80/20 idea essentially conveys the same content or semantic: A relatively small percentage of people in any group drink most of the beer. However, the graphic means employed—the form, format, or (more technically) the syntax—is distinctive, and different people may well find one form of reportage easier to decode than the others. Note that from a formal point of view, each of these graphic systems could denote anything from the number of sunny days in Seattle during September to the rate of brain cell loss during each decade of life. Only when labels have been affixed to these visual aids is it possible to appreciate the specific meaning that the graphic artist is trying to convey.

Essentially the same semantic meaning or content, then, can be conveyed by different forms: words, numbers, dramatic renditions, bulleted lists, Cartesian coordinates, or a bar graph. At first encounter, one may find it possible to think of the 80/20 principle only with reference to a numerical ratio (4:1). Over time, however, one can think of it in terms of spatial images, verbal metaphors, bodily states, or even musical passages. Indeed, one effective way of conveying the 80/20 principle is through the use of a static cartoon or a dynamic comic strip. The same linguistic or graphic system of marking can be used to convey an indefinite number of meanings, as long as the syntactic rules that govern the particular marking system are followed and the labeling is appropriate.

Again, I argue here that multiple versions of the same point constitute an extremely powerful way in which to change minds. But what other factors might cause an individual to shift his or her perspective and begin to act on the basis of that principle—for instance, abandoning a 50/50 point of view and espousing instead an 80/20 perspective on various sectors of life?

I have identified seven factors—I'll call them *levers*—that could be at work in these and all cases of a change of mind. As it happens, each factor conveniently begins with the letters "re."

Reason

Especially among those who deem themselves to be educated, the use of reason figures heavily in matters of belief. A rational approach involves identification of relevant factors, weighing each in turn, and making an overall assessment. Reason can involve sheer logic, the use of analogies, or the creation of taxonomies.

Encountering the 80/20 principle for the first time, an individual guided by rationality would attempt to identify all of the relevant considerations and weigh them proportionately; such a procedure would help him or her to determine whether to subscribe to the 80/20 principle in general, and whether to apply it in a particular instance. Faced with a decision about how to furnish his apartment, a renter might come up with a list of pros and cons before reaching a final judgment.

Research

Complementing the use of argument is the collection of relevant data. Those with scientific training can proceed in a systematic manner, perhaps even using statistical tests to verify—or cast doubt on—promising trends. But research need not be formal; it need only entail the identification of relevant cases and a judgment about whether they warrant a change of mind. A manager who has been exposed to the 80/20 principle might study whether its claims—for example, those about sales figures or employee difficulty—are borne out on her watch. Naturally, to the extent that the research confirms the 80/20 principle, it is more likely to guide behavior and thought.

Resonance

Reason and research appeal to the cognitive aspects of the human mind, but resonance denotes the affective component. A view, idea, or perspective resonates to the extent that it *feels right* to an individual, seems to fit the current situation, and convinces the person that further considerations are superfluous. It is possible, of course, that resonance follows on the use of reason and/or research; but it is equally possible that the fit occurs at an unconscious level, and that the resonant intuition is in conflict with the more sober considerations of Rational Man or Woman. Resonance often comes about because one feels a "relation" to a mind-changer, finds that person "reliable," or "respects" that person—three additional "re" terms. To the extent that 80/20 comes to feel like a better approach than 60/40 or 50/50, it is likely to be adopted by a decision-maker in an organization.

I note that *rhetoric* is a principal vehicle for changing minds. Rhetoric may rely on many components. In most cases, rhetoric works best when it encompasses tight logic, draws on relevant research, and resonates with an audience (perhaps in light of some of the other "re" factors just mentioned). Too bad rhetoric has that "h" as a second letter!

Representational Redescriptions (Redescriptions for Short)

The fourth factor sounds technical, but the point is simple enough: A change of mind becomes convincing to the extent that it lends itself to presentation in a number of different forms, with these forms reinforcing another. I noted previously that it is possible to present the 80/20 principle in a number of different linguistic, numerical, and graphic ways; by the same token, as I've shown, a group of individuals can readily come up with different mental versions of, for example, how to repair a piece of furniture. Particularly when it comes to matters of instruction—be it in an elementary school classroom or a managerial workshop—the potential for expressing the desired lesson in many compatible formats is crucial.

Resources and Rewards

In the cases discussed so far, the possibilities for mind-changing lie within the reach of any individual whose mind is open.

Sometimes, however, mind-changing is more likely to occur when considerable resources can be drawn on. Suppose that a philanthropist decides to bankroll a nonprofit agency that is willing to adopt the 80/20 principle in all of its activities—the balance might tip. Or suppose that an enterprising interior decorator decides to give a furniture repair person all of the materials that he needs at cost, or even for free. Again, the opportunity to redecorate at little cost may tip the balance. Looked at from the psychological perspective, the provision of resources is an instance of positive reinforcement—as it turns out, another "re" term. Individuals are being rewarded for one course of behavior and thought rather than the other. Ultimately, however, unless the new course of thought is concordant with other criteria—reason, resonance, research, for example—it is unlikely to last beyond the provision of resources.

Two others factors also influence mind-changing, but in ways somewhat different from the five outlined so far.

Real-World Events

Sometimes an event occurs in the broader society that affects many individuals, not just those who are contemplating a mind change. Examples are wars, hurricanes, terrorist attacks, economic depressions—or, on a more positive side, eras of peace and prosperity, the availability of medical treatments that prevent illness or lengthen life, or the ascendancy of a benign leader or group or political party. Legislation could implement policies like the 80/20 rule.

It is conceivable that a law could be passed (say, in Singapore) that would permit or mandate special bonuses for workers who are unusually productive, while deducting wages from those who are unproductive. Such legislation would push businesses toward adopting an 80/20 principle, even in eras or areas where they had been following a more conventional 50/50 course. Turning to another example, an economic depression could nullify an individual's plans for refurnishing his apartment, whereas a long era of prosperity could make it easier.

Resistances

The six factors identified so far can all aid in an effort to change minds. However, the existence of only facilitating factors is unrealistic.

While it is relatively easy and perhaps natural to change one's mind during the first years of life, it becomes difficult to alter one's mind as the years pass. The reason, in brief, is that we develop strong views and perspectives that are resistant to change. Any effort to understand the changing of minds must take into account the power of various resistances. Such resistances make it easy, second nature, for most of us to revert to the 50/50 principle, even after the advantages of the 80/20 principle have been set forth convincingly. An owner, for example, might elect to retain his current pattern of apartment furnishing, even when reason, resonances, rewards, and the like issue their Circean song. The hassle of moving and the possibility that others might become disenchanted with the extra backhoes and forklifts might overpower several pushes toward the new furnishings.

* * *

I've now introduced the seven factors that play crucial roles in mind-changing. As we look at individual cases of successful or unsuccessful changes of mind, we can see these various factors at work in distinctive ways. For now, I will only say that a mind change is most likely to come about when the first six factors operate in consort and the resistances are relatively weak. Conversely, mind-changing is unlikely to come about when the resistances are strong and the other factors do not point strongly in one direction.

Changes of mind, of course, occur at a number of different levels of analysis, with the aforementioned seven factors being brought to bear on entities ranging from a single individual to a whole nation. Educators might keep six distinct realms in mind:

1. Large-scale changes involving heterogeneous or diverse groups, such as the population of an entire nation.
2. Large-scale changes involving a more homogeneous or uniform group, such as a corporation or a religious group.

3. Changes brought about through works of art, science, or scholarship, such as the writings of Karl Marx or Sigmund Freud, the theories of Charles Darwin or Albert Einstein, or the artistic creations of Martha Graham or Pablo Picasso.
4. Changes within formal instructional settings, such as schools or training seminars.
5. Intimate forms of mind-changing involving two people or a small number, such as family members.
6. Changes within one's own mind, such as those that might take place in musings about furniture.

I hope that this essay has caused you to reflect, and perhaps consider how you might change the mind of someone with whom you are close—or even your own mind!

REFERENCES

Gardner, H. (2006). *Changing minds.* Harvard Business Review Press.
Koch, R. (1999). *The 80/20 principle.* Crown Currency.
Moss, M. (2001, November 23). A nation challenged: Airport security: US airport task force begins with hiring. *The New York Times.* https://www.nytimes.com/2001/11/23/us/a-nation-challenged-airport-security-us-airport-task-begins-with-hiring.html?searchResultPosition=1

ESSAY 26

On Educating for the Three Virtues
A Hegelian Approach

Though it was likely not apparent to those around me, in one sense, I have always seen myself as embedded in education. As a youth, growing up 70 years ago in Pennsylvania, I daydreamed that over the course of my lifetime, I would teach all grades—from kindergarten through high school (I did not know about college or university at that time). I tried to explain things to my peers—probably in a way that was rather bossy. And to make extra money, I occasionally taught piano over a 10-year period.

Despite this inclination to teach, once I attended college, I took a turn toward pure research in psychology. I did not begin to teach regularly until I was well into my forties. As it turned out, principally because of the institutional affiliation of our research group Project Zero, my professorial appointment was in a school of education. Over the last 30 years, I have taught a variety of students across a range of subjects, and as a researcher, I have spanned the educational landscape, from preschool through the college years.

Over this period of time—effectively 70 years—education has undergone massive changes. In comparison to past centuries, all over the world education now begins earlier, lasts longer, and, happily, involves an ever-larger proportion of young people. The conditions of education have also altered. In the time of my grandparents—born toward the end of the 19th century—the range of topics, disciplines, media, and institutional settings that we take for granted today would have been unmanageable, indeed unthinkable. Some of the challenges we now take for granted—rapid and deleterious climate change, the possibility of nuclear devastation, technologies that silently gather and synthesize knowledge about each of us as individuals—would have been (and indeed sometimes were!) the stuff of science fiction. And, not to accentuate the negative, the breakthroughs in science and technology make life much easier and more pleasant (and longer!) for those of us fortunate enough to have been born in the right place at the right time with the right resources. Alas, progress in science and technology has not been matched by advances in human cooperation, empathy, and service to the wider community.

When a sector of the world—indeed, when the world as a whole—changes so rapidly, it is on occasion appropriate to step back and to consider *what might be the educational constants*, the elements, that are worth retaining over time, across space, with respect to the human family and the human condition. And even as one seeks to identify and sustain the constants, it is equally important to consider *how these educational desiderata should be conceptualized, configured, and conveyed in an ever-fast-changing environment.*

When formal education began around the world, many centuries ago, it had three primary objectives: (1) to equip young people to handle the important literacies of the era (sometimes whimsically termed the "three R's" of readin', (w)ritin', and 'rithmetic; (2) to give young people the concepts, attitudes, and moral compasses that helped them to become reasonable, constructive members of their community; and (3) to prepare youth for the livelihoods that were available, needed, and valued in the ambient culture.

The importance and the accents placed on these three educational objectives change across time (for instance, now a non-"r" discipline, coding, is increasingly deemed an essential literacy), and also across cultures (explicitly moral lessons are salient in societies influenced by Confucian ideas but very much in the background in the secular societies of Northern Europe); but I know of no culture that altogether dismisses literacies, ignores an introduction to communal and civic life, or omits preparation for the workplace.

Given this analysis, one might well claim, "These goals are more than enough." Or even "We are hardly meeting these goals adequately; what possible need is there for any additional educational goals, means, and considerations?" While bearing these strictures in mind, I take this occasion to put forth a vision of education "over the long haul" or even "for the ages."

Before turning to that vision, it's important to point out that education can be construed so broadly that it covers *everything*—every topic from astronomy to zoology, and every moment from conception to cradle to grave.

I am not going to be quite so grand. Instead, I shall focus on the three virtues that I value the most and reflect on how, in the period going forward, best to conceptualize and nurture them.

Introducing the three virtues: Wyoming Seminary, my secondary school located in northeastern Pennsylvania, proclaimed its educational goals to be *Verum, Pulchrum, Bonum*—Truth, Beauty, and Goodness. Though I had long forgotten this school motto, it clearly made a deep impression on me.

The evidence: Like almost every educator—indeed, like almost every reflective adult—I believe that education must include literacies, on the one hand, and preparation for the world of work, of labor, on the other. But in a reasonably effective educational system, the basic literacies should be covered in the first years of schooling and explicit preparation for the world of work should take place sometime during adolescence. Accordingly, we should have a considerable period—anywhere from 5 to 10 years—to pursue other educational goals. And this is where I favor a valorization and inculcation of the three virtues.

But how to think about the virtues? Enter the German philosopher Georg Wilhelm Friedrich Hegel. In a famous conceptual formulation, Hegel sought to describe progress in thinking, which he conceived in dialectical terms. Initially, he claimed, one has a thesis—a strong claim of one sort or another. Then, he argued, there is need for an antithesis—a contrasting point of view. And finally, triumphantly (one can hear the trumpets blaring in the background), one progresses to a final synthesis. (Of course, the process can be repeated—synthesis A becoming the thesis for a new cycle; and while Karl Marx may have believed that he had arrived at a final Hegelian synthesis, among political philosophers, the conversation, the dialectic launched in the 19th century by Marx, continues indefinitely, yielding various kinds of new antitheses and syntheses.)

So let me now apply Hegel to thinking about the virtues:

Thesis: When I initially thought about the virtues, during my early adolescence, I felt that they were akin to one another, or even the same thing—yoked together like the proverbial Three Musketeers. And then, several decades later, when I informally surveyed their formulation in various languages and cultures, I discovered that, in general, *these virtues were considered inseparable*. Perhaps the clearest example is in Confucian societies, where it is assumed that what is true is also beautiful and also good, and vice versa. You can't have one virtue without the others; and if any virtue is lacking, coherence falls apart.

As evidence from the other side of the planet, one can also cite the memorable couplet by poet John Keats:

"Beauty is truth, truth beauty,"—that is all
Ye know on earth, and all ye need to know.

Antithesis: When I, in the early 21st century, as a Western-educated scholar, began to reflect on these virtues, it became clear to me—perhaps too clear!—that the virtues could not be identical and also were not interchangeable.

- It's clear, it's true, that millions of deaths occurred as a result of the Spanish flu of 1918–1919; but certainly, that is not good, nor is it beautiful.
- Many of us consider the paintings of Picasso (like *Les desmoiselles d'Avignon*) or the music of Benjamin Britten (like his *War Requiem*) or the poems of Emily Dickinson to be beautiful—but it does not make sense to think of them as being "true" or "good"—at least not in any literal sense.
- And while the socialist/communist dream of Karl Marx may be good in the eyes of many, it's not yet true, and many do not find it beautiful at all.

Having arrived at this framing, I proceeded to put forth my own definitions of the three virtues. In my book *Truth, Beauty, and Goodness Reframed* (with the tantalizing subtitle *Educating for the Virtues in the Age of Truthiness and*

Twitter), I laid out the following argument: (See Essay 28 in this volume and essays in *The Essential Howard Gardner on Mind* for more details.)

Truth is the property of propositions, assertions, indeed, sentences. A proposition can be *true or false* and demonstrably so ($2+2$ is 4 and not 5 or 5,000); *not determinable* at present, but perhaps determinable in the future; or *indeterminate* and likely to remain so indefinitely.

Beauty is the property of experiences. An experience is likely to be deemed beautiful if it fulfills three conditions: it initially attracts attention; it is memorable in form as well as content; and one seeks repeatedly to revisit the experience or one that is quite similar. (Conversely, experiences are NOT beautiful if they are *not* noticeable, do *not* attract attention; if they are forgettable or readily converted into another format; and/or if one is inclined—or even determined—to avoid them in the future.) We think of our contacts with works of art as beautiful or not, but indeed, any of our experiences—from a talk to a walk, from a dialogue to a dream—can be beautiful (or ugly, or erased from memory).

Good is a description of our aspirationally benevolent relationship to other individuals—both ones close to us and those who are remote and with whom, accordingly, we have only a transactional relationship. More specifically, our relation to those whom we contact regularly entail what I have termed "neighborly morality"—and the tenets are quite well captured in the 10 Commandments or in the Golden Rule and its variations.

In contrast, and particularly characteristic of our modern and increasingly postindustrial age, *good* can also refer to relationships that are primarily transactional and transitory rather than common and long-lasting. I refer to these relations as involving "the ethics of roles." And in particular, I have in mind two roles: the role of a worker, and particularly that of a *professional*; and the role of a member of a community, and particularly that of a *citizen*.

A few more thoughts about the "good": Relationships to others (near or far) can be classified as good to the extent that one considers the impact on others of one's words, thoughts, and actions, and tries to perform in ways that are moral and ethical. And one is more likely to achieve an ethical or moral aspiration if one knows the substance of what one is doing (excellence) and if one cares about one's behavior (engagement). Hence my colleagues and I speak of the "three Es" of the good—as in good work and in good citizenship: excellence, engagement and ethics. (See thegoodproject.org and Essay 28.)

Clearly, this is a mouthful, indeed a mindful. And there's much more to say—indeed, as noted, an entire book's worth! For my present purposes, I hope that this brief introduction to my perspective on the virtues should suffice.

Full stop: In the aforementioned book, I took the position that the three virtues are independent of one another—they need to be conceptualized and realized independently. A statement like "truth is beauty"—however beautiful one may find it—is neither true nor virtuous. That was my antithesis to the earlier beliefs in the insolubility of the three virtues.

TOWARD A SYNTHESIS

As I thought about this trio of virtues, I first reached the conclusion that *the pursuit of truth* should be the primary focus of education—to repeat, in the period (often approaching a decade) between literacy and labor. And indeed, in earlier work, I maintained that the best way—indeed perhaps the *only* way—in which to ascertain what's true is to *learn and master the methods used by the different disciplines*. (I also described certain professions and trades where knowledge may not currently be encoded in verbal form but has the *potential* to be so captured and conveyed.) On this account, if we learn about the methods employed by the physicist or the historian, or the moves made by the electrician or the chef, we can figure out what is true in these realms.

I still believe that the heartland of formal education should be focused on the pursuit and the determination of truth. But I have since become convinced of two other things.

THE BEAUTY OF TRUTH-SEEKING

Even if one knows how to ascertain truth, that does not suffice. It's necessary, but it's not sufficient.

As any scientist, scholar, researcher, or journalist can tell you, there is a pleasure, a joy—even awe—in pursuing truth, in separating it from myth, mischief, or miscues. Recall the vivid testimony of Sir Isaac Newton: "I do not know what I may appear to the world, but to myself I seem to have been only like a boy playing on the seashore, and diverting myself in now and then finding a smoother pebble or a prettier shell than ordinary, whilst the great ocean of truth lay all undiscovered before me."

Not only "undiscovered." I would add: There can never be a complete, definitive truth. All one can hope for, or aspire to, is to come ever closer to the truth—whether it is about the creation of the cosmos or the causes of World War I or how the human mind works—or fails to work.

Accordingly, in formal and informal education, we need to share the joys of pursuing truth—as well as the costs of hiding or missing truth and/or spreading false information. Alas, in the era of social media, it is often superficially more pleasurable to spread alluring nonsense; only if one has a prior and firm commitment to the pursuit of truth do we have *any* hope of ignoring the superficial and arriving at the substantive, the claims that have merit and that will withstand scrutiny.

THE CONCEPTION OF THE GOOD

After *homo sapiens* had emerged, and had begun to constitute communities (as small as a family or clan, or ultimately as large as a country or, indeed, the planet), members of our species began to develop norms of behavior that are acceptable as against behavior that is not. Of course, these are not necessarily consistent with one another, nor are they necessarily permanent, though having been around for many centuries, *neighborly morality* has been much more firmly established than has the *ethics of roles*.

How does this consideration relate to the pursuit and conveyance of truth? In two ways:

First, one needs to believe that the pursuit and the promulgation of truth is important, indeed crucial. Of course, many individuals, including ones with great power and influence, do not value the truth at all. They may either be pathological liars—Hitler famously endorsed "the big lie"—or they may be transactionalists without nuance—"I pursue whatever works for me."

Indeed, that stance, that skepticism, constitutes the great risk inherent in the conception of truth held by some members of the *pragmatist school of philosophy* (truth is what works, à la William James, on some readings); and of *postmodern relativism* (there is no such thing as truthfulness (à la Jacques Derrida, on some readings). Under such skeptical formulations, the most that we can hope for is to reach tentative agreement within a community (à la Richard Rorty).

Second, one must wed the belief in truth to a personal commitment to pursue it, even when it seems easier to go with the crowd, or to sweep doubts under the rug, or even to tell a lie—often protesting it's only a white lie. And here is where goodness and truth begin to converge. We need a conception of the good that recognizes and valorizes truth, while disdaining perspectives that deny, undermine, or minimize the value of truth.

The Synthesis in Brief. So now I have done it. Having for an appreciable period of time argued for the *independence of the three virtues*, I now have come to recognize—to concede, if you will—that they are in fact *bound together* and perhaps quite tightly, perhaps even inextricably.

To state the proposed new synthesis:

1. The pursuit of truth is possible and worthwhile.
2. It's best carried out through a careful understanding and application of the methods used to arrive at propositions of various sorts, in various disciplines and in various sectors of society.
3. Individuals (and groups and societies) are most likely to pursue truth if:
    » The experience proves pleasurable, and worth pursuing and repursuing over the long haul; and

> » If that course of action fits in with one's overall conception of a good society—one that espouses and pursues neighborly morality and the ethics of roles.

Note that in reaching this conclusion, I am echoing the wisdom of Pope Francis. In an address to Italian schoolteachers in 2014, he said, "I speak of three languages: the mind, the heart and the hands. When we speak of roots and values, we can speak of truth, goodness, and creativity. Yet, we cannot educate without leading the heart to beauty" (Pope Francis, 2023, p. xvi).

FROM SYNTHESIS TO ACTION

Having sketched out my key concepts, I propose to return to the challenges of education—with a special focus on the period between *literacy* and *livelihood*. Here are the principal considerations:

1. One has to believe that these three virtues are crucial, that they are worth placing centrally as THE overarching mission of education in the period between literacy and livelihood.
2. Lessons, assessment, feedback, and trophies need to be built around the pursuit of truth, the cultivation of beautiful experiences, and the conceptions of a good society, in which these virtues are highlighted.
3. The three virtues need to be conveyed—better, they should be embodied—by teachers, administrators, staff, and older students. For their part, the learners need to have both the motivation to learn and the capacity to draw on their skills and knowledge—one might even say, their "intelligences"—to master new areas of study and practice.
4. Equally important, these virtues need to be built into the DNA, the structure, of educational institutions; whether schools, libraries, museums, educational media (either in-person or online), or even places of worship or of work, the institutions need to model and promote the pursuit of truth, the pleasure of finding it out, its importance, indeed its indispensability, for the thriving of the broader society.

    In this context, it may be helpful for this observer from the United States to mention two of the most powerful educational experiences from the early days of television: the series of *Young People's Concerts*, led and choreographed by conductor Leonard Bernstein; and the segments of *Sesame Street*, as conveyed by a few live characters and featuring the amazing Muppets. Both of these broadcast series foregrounded powerful, indeed (for me) unforgettable, intertwining of the three virtues.

And going beyond formal schooling, this modeling of the virtues should ideally characterize workplaces with which students come in contact—jobs at fast-food restaurants or grocery stores, for younger students, internships in workplaces or professional offices for older students. I've come to believe in the power of the atmosphere, the *habitus*, that pervades the first real job that students have—again, using an example from the United States, it truly matters whether one's first paying job in journalism occurs at National Public Radio or at Fox News (see Essay 3 in *The Essential Howard Gardner on Mind*).

5. And while the pursuit of truths should overall be a positive experience, we need to be able to pursue truth wherever it leads. That includes understanding the sometimes harsh realities about lethal viruses, climate change, nuclear weapons, forced separation of families, and the many ways in which social media can become vehicles of propaganda.
6. Accordingly, hand-in-hand with the acknowledgment of difficult truths, we need to be aware of the threats to truth (propaganda, lies, facile media); threats to beauty (food that seems pleasurable but is harmful, media messages that are seductive but misleading); and threats to goodness (false gods, xenophobia, misogyny, lies that are big as well as lies that present themselves as innocuous).

LINGERING QUESTIONS

1. *Arts and Humanities.* Above I have dealt at some length with questions of the truths as captured in scholarly disciplines, along with their concomitant methods of investigation. But so far this discussion has largely bypassed an important part of any curriculum—courses and experiences in the arts (music, painting, dance, drama, and the like) and the humanities (history, philosophy, the study of languages, the more qualitative strands of the social sciences, and the like).

As one devoted to the experience of beauty and the search for the good, I fully endorse—indeed, I insist on—a curriculum that features artistic and humanistic as well as scientific courses of study. To recall a quip uttered by my teacher Nelson Goodman, "We don't want an education that is halfbrained." Indeed, in view of the synthesis that I have proposed, these lines of study and experience are crucial.

Why? Unless students are provided with significant experiences in the arts, they will have a restricted (and probably rigid, even unchangeable) sense of beauty, if any at all; and unless they explore the visions of society that have been captured in the arts and humanities, they will have an impoverished sense of what is good and, alas, what does not qualify for that descriptor.

2. *Artificial Intelligence, Deep Learning, and Automatically Invoked Algorithms.* I have already alluded to the challenges to the virtues posed by social media. Without question, many of us either choose or are seduced into choosing conceptions of the virtues that are presented, implicitly or explicitly, across the spectrum of social media. These clearly challenge a belief, a faith—be it a powerful desire or a lingering hope—that we human beings ourselves *choose* and *can choose deliberately* to follow one course, rather than another.

The computercentric period in which we are living is sometimes seen—and appropriately so—as a crucial test for our species. We need to determine in which individuals, corporate bodies, governmental departments, and/or technologies we will invest a sense of agency, or whether, indeed, we will allow or encourage a competition among these respective agencies. One can envision a 1984-style rivalry emerging among three different approaches: the United States, with a great deal of latitude to corporations, their products, and their modes of operation; China, with a great deal of centralized control of computational devices and approaches; and Western Europe, with an inclination to mediate, to find a middle ground, between these polar options . . . praiseworthy but perhaps futile.

3. *Forms of Government and Governance.* For a time, after the fall of the Berlin Wall in 1989, it was assumed that Western-style democratic governance had triumphed—indeed, in Francis Fukuyama's memorable phrase, that we had come to "the end of history" (2006).

Some decades later, these predictions seem incredibly naïve. If anything, the governance pendulum has swung quite far to the right wing of the political spectrum, with authoritarian and even totalitarian regimes and systems on the rise, and many nations being democratic only in name—or in slogan. Should this trend continue, or even accelerate, thoughts or aspirations with respect to the virtues will seem naïve. Governments will control education—indeed, they will BE education. Once again, recall the three chilling oxymoronic slogans from George Orwell's prophetic allegory *1984*:

War is peace.
Freedom is slavery.
Ignorance is strength.

4. *Proximity and Remoteness in a Global Century.* In our work on issues of the good, we have long made a convenient distinction between neighborly morality—how we relate to those who live alongside us—and the ethics of roles—how we relate to those with whom we have a relationship, but not a close, or regular, or well-established connection.

We now live at a time and in a place where we can connect readily to individuals who are thousands of miles away. Moreover, we learn of their needs and their desires just as they learn about ours; and we discover and affirm our joint membership in the human species, in what has come to be called the Anthropocene era.

We must now take on one of the great challenges of our species: Are we able to think of those whom we may never meet in person in ways akin to how we think of those to whom we are related by our street address or by our genetic heritage? And in raising this question today, we need to think deeply about our relationship to the many millions who are now stranded in refugee camps and may never come to know their biological relatives.

5. *The Role of Resources.* I have set forth a very ambitious set of educational goals—one giving as much of a place to the pursuit of the classical liberal arts as to the bread-and-butter issues of literacy and labor. And I have presupposed an educational community that supports these goals, and a financial and governance infrastructure that permits—perhaps even encourages—these aspirations.

Without question, it is easier to pursue these goals if one has the resources on which to draw. But at the same time, it is crucial to point out political entities with considerable resources that fail to embrace these virtues, and to note as well that over time, schools, school systems, and even entire regions that have limited resources are nonetheless able to achieve a well-rounded and virtue-filled education. Given a forced choice between money and mission, I'd always put my money on mission!

6. *The Role of Religion and Religions.* When he was generous enough to attend the lectures on which my 2011 book *Truth, Beauty, and Goodness Reframed* was based, my colleague Marcelo Suárez-Orozco pointed out, acutely, "You have left out the 800-pound gorilla—religion." And of course, he was right! Wearing the garb of a secular academic, it is not a sphere that I ponder regularly—though as one ages, religious, spiritual, or at least existential concerns tend to loom larger.

To trace out the relationship between the great religions, on the one hand, and the three virtues, on the other, would require a lengthy treatise. Focusing primarily on the Western hemisphere, just think of the three virtues at the times of the Biblical Moses, or the life of Christ, or the height of the Roman Empire in the early centuries of the Common Era, or during the rise of the papacy in medieval times, or at the time of the challenge from Protestantism, or, more recently, the ascendancy of evangelical religion, with its belief in direct knowledge and explicit guidance from The Book. Or think of Karl Marx, who considered religion as the opiate of people, or of critics of Marx, who apply the same dismissive characterization to socialism or communism.

Suffice it to say, most individuals require a belief in something larger than themselves—perhaps even larger than their neighborhood, their clan, their nation, or, for that matter, the planet or the universe. For many, at present, it is a belief in science, in science tempered by humanism, or in what I have termed "the three sacreds."

Personally, I do not care whether individuals, groups, or societies have a religion or a worldview, or consider themselves existential in the sense made popular in the works of Jean-Paul Sartre. Personally, I favor the perspective called humanism as dissected by Sarah Bakewell (2023).

What's important is that these eschatologies, at a minimum, do not disrupt the aspiration for truth, beauty, and goodness; and that as a maximum, they work actively toward the achievement of that lofty aspiration. Ideally, if there are more than one of these worldviews, they should not cripple one another, at worst, or, more happily, they should work in consort toward the realization of the virtues.

CONCLUDING NOTE

It is not possible to predict the lay of the land in the decades and centuries ahead; we can be sure that if we survive as a species at all, our successors will encounter surprises of many sorts. While I am politically liberal, I am educationally conservative—we need to preserve and to build upon the best ideas and the best methods for educating the next generation and the generations thereafter. Indeed, during the 5-to-10-year period in childhood between the achievement of the literacies, on the one hand, and preparation for the labor market, on the other, we need to strive for educational approaches and aspirations that honor, preserve, and extend the three critical virtues. Three cheers for the liberal arts and sciences! (See Essay 20.)

In a perilous time of pandemics and unchecked climate change, I would add that we need a vision of society that is built upon the fundamental importance of truth, beauty, and goodness, one that sees their aspiration and their achievement as the adventure of a lifetime. Indeed, the goal of lifelong learning should be the pursuit and strengthening of a virtue-filled, flourishing life, one of which Socrates—and his student Plato, and Plato's student Aristotle—would have approved.

A final nod to Hegel: In the preceding pages, devoted to the portrait of an education worthy of our species and of our planet, I presented a thesis, an antithesis, and what I believe to be a new and appropriate synthesis. But as Hegel would presumably have been the first to agree, all syntheses are *pro tem*; and if these words themselves activate a new antithesis, and a better and more comprehensive synthesis, I will be pleased.

REFERENCES

Bakewell, S. (2023). *Humanly possible*. Penguin.
Fukuyama, F. (2006.) *The end of history and the last man*. Free Press.

Gardner, H. (2011). *Truth, beauty, and goodness reframed*. Basic Books.
Gardner, H. (2019). "Neuromyths": A critical consideration. *Mind, Brain, and Education*, *14*(8), 2–4. https://doi.org/10.1111/mbe.12229
Pope Francis. (2023). Address of the Holy Father (2014) on the global compact of education. In M. Suarez-Orozco & C. Suarez-Orozco (Eds.), *Education: A Global Compact for a Time of Crisis*. Columbia University Press.

ESSAY 27

The Myths in "Neuromyths"

While I worked steadily in neuropsychology for 20 years, with my move into education, that area of research waned. But I found myself back in the neurological realm when I helped to found a new area of study called Mind, Brain, and Education and to consider how neurological findings were being applied to education.

On the one hand, I was very pleased that efforts were made to join mind, brain, and education. And yet, when I saw some of the claims that were being made, I was not pleased; and when I found that my own work on multiple intelligences was being cited as a neuromyth, I realized that I had to enter that arena. I wrote a technical article on the topic (see Gardner, 2019), but the basic ideas are conveyed clearly and succinctly in this chapter.

It's good to expose myths about neuroscience.

We live in an age of debunking. It's energizing to shoot down someone or something, and sometimes, that's a good thing.

But when debunking gets out of hand, it needs to be called to account. And when you yourself are the target of a debunking, not surprisingly, you feel called upon to become the sheriff—the debunker of the debunkers, so to speak.

You may have heard the word "neuromyth" or the phrase "neural myth." It's used by researchers and, less frequently, by laypersons to describe a widely held belief that is not true. And indeed, there clearly are statements about the nervous system that deserve to be debunked.

Two examples:

- The brain has two hemispheres—left and right—and some people are left-brained, while others are right-brained.
- We only use 10 percent of our brain.

Each of these examples starts from a fact—we do have two cerebral hemispheres, and they are not identical. But even as a metaphor, the leap to two kinds of persons is not warranted.

No doubt most of us could make better use of our brains. But how to determine what percentage is used, how to account for awake, sleep, dreaming, and daydreaming, is left completely unsolved—perhaps not even considered.

Meanwhile, a whole industry has grown in which various myths are delineated, exposed, and presumably laid to rest. Yet, when one looks carefully at the assertions about the myths, many of the statements that are supposedly debunking something *do not themselves withstand scrutiny*.

Enter my own work. Over 40 years ago, I introduced the theory of multiple intelligences, a critique of the notion of a single intelligence adequately probed by a single short-answer test. In its place, I proposed that human beings have a number of relatively independent intellectual capacities. And in supporting this assertion, I drew on evidence from several scholarly disciplines, including the brain science of the day.

Never did I come close to asserting that these intelligences are inborn or genetic; or that they are completely independent of one another; or that people can be described as having one intelligence or another to the exclusion of the remaining ones. Nor did I make specific suggestions about education. I simply stated that individuals have different profiles of intelligences and that this claim should be taken into account when one is teaching, studying, assessing.

Yet, in Sarrasin et al. (2019), I found multiple intelligences (MI) theory classified as a neural myth. And this article spurred me to look more carefully at how such myths are identified and dissected.

What I found was disturbing. The article distinguished between five statements that are presumably true, and five that are asserted to be neuromyths.

First of all, of the 10 statements, only six of them even mentioned the brain or the nervous system. And so 40 percent of them are not neural at all!

Second, those that were considered myths were expressed in hyperbolic form. "All," "none," and "predominant"; anyone with any experience in taking (or making) tests would know that such global statements are likely to be false.

Third, and complementing the previous point, those that were considered true were expressed in much less totalistic form, using hedges such as "likely" and "may."

Fourth, and most telling, none of the statements actually requires mention of the brain. They are statements about learning, studying, or remembering, each of which could have been—and perhaps was!—stated 100 or 1,000 years ago. The descriptor "neuro" is entirely gratuitous.

My conclusion: The mission of neuromythology has gone too far. Obviously, all of us—researchers, teachers, or members of the general public—should scrutinize statements carefully.

A few lessons: We should be wary of absolutist statements. Just as it is useful for educators to learn about psychology and sociology, we should attempt to learn what has been established about the brain and the nervous system. But we should never change our behaviors or teachings just because of new assertions about the brain. All education is concerned with values—and so we should always ask whether a recommended tactic is consistent with what we believe should be taught and learned and why we think so. Finally, perhaps it's time to bracket the debunking phrase "neuromyths." Instead, when we encounter an assertion—be it based on psychology, pedagogy, or neuroscience—we should attempt to find out in which ways it is meritorious, or suspect, or not worth taking seriously. And if the latter, we should attempt to discover better ways to achieve the educational goals that we cherish.

REFERENCES

Gardner, H. (2019). "Neuromyths": A critical consideration. *Mind, Brain, and Education, 14*(1), 2–4. https://onlinelibrary.wiley.com/doi/10.1111/mbe.12229

Sarrasin, J, Riopel, M., & Masson, D. (2019). Neuromyths and their origins among teachers in Quebec. *Mind, Brain, and Education, 13*(2), 102–109.

ESSAY 28

Becoming a Good Person, a Good Worker, a Good Citizen in a Democratic Society

THE CHALLENGE

Within the contemporary United States, in a public school attended by 1,000 students, there will likely be one or two who may one day make a substantial positive difference for the wider community. And in a city of 250,000, there will likely be one or two students who will make a substantial positive difference for the nation or even the wider world.

Whether these "guesstimates" differ elsewhere on the planet, I don't know. But I suspect that the number would be higher in Scandinavia, and lower in a failed state.

Were there doubts that we know how to rear a significant number of good persons, these doubts have been reinforced in recent years. Throughout much of the world, there has been a shift toward more autocratic forms of government, often occurring more with the explicit or tacit support than with the opposition of the broader population. Refusal to recognize the seriousness of COVID-19—thereby endangering the lives of others, even of members of one's own family—has again underscored the selfishness, the self-centeredness on the part of much of the world's population.

In an era in which much has been expected of social science (beware the honorific "science"), we tradespersons have little to show for our efforts. To be sure, we know how to measure scholastic intelligence, but far less about other capacities and potentials. And while we have designed and carried out ingenious laboratory experiments on the human inclination to cheat or deceive, we have little solid knowledge about how to educate young people *over the long haul* about what is moral and ethical—and then to help them conduct themselves throughout their lives in ethical or moral ways.

In what follows, drawing on studies in the literature, as well as on concepts and findings from our own research on "good work" over the last 30 years, I present a way of thinking about these fundamental issues, along with proposals about how to nurture more responsible human beings (see thegoodproject.org). While some of these ideas could presumably be implemented in many places around the globe, I particularly have in mind societies that aspire to be democratic in more than name.

FRAMEWORK

My colleagues and I speak about the three characteristics of good work and of the good worker. Good workers exhibit three properties, which we have dubbed the three E's (see Figure 28.1).

Though our empirical research has focused largely on the workplace, the same fundamental description applies to citizenship (especially in a democratic society). A good citizen knows the rules, regulations, and norms (*Excellent*); cares about the issues, speaks up, votes, and is prepared to protest (*Engaged*); and strives to do the right thing, not principally for one's own self-interest but rather for the broader community (*Ethical*).

Those are the goals, the ideals.

Initially, almost all persons work within smaller circles (family, friends, neighborhood). Over time, the circle image may expand concentrically to ever-wider regions. These "rings of responsibility" (see Figure 28.2) may eventually extend to school, the first workplace, one's profession, and in some cases, the niche of the profession within the broader society.

- Their work is of *Excellent* quality.
- They are *Engaged* in their work—they enjoy it, find it meaningful, and desire to continue in that vocation.
- They behave in an *Ethical* way—they ponder what's right to do, try to do that, and, after taking action, ponder the outcome and the lessons that can be learned.

Figure 28.1. *The Three Intertwined E's of Good Work and Good Citizenship*

Excellence Ethics **Engagement**

Figure 28.2. *Rings of Responsibility That May Broaden Across the Life Span*

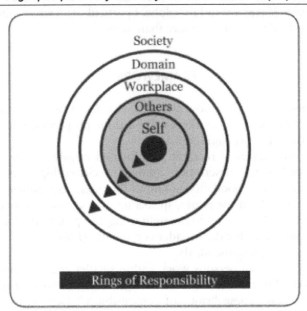

Within the smaller circles, one's behavior is carried out primarily in relation to individuals known personally—family, friends, schoolmates. We call this *neighborly morality*. The 10 Commandments and the Golden Rule provide guidelines.

As one moves geographically and vocationally, one encounters the rights and obligations attendant to one's work and one's citizenship. We term this realm *the ethics of roles*. To be sure, the rules of neighborly morality extend to these wider niches; but new issues and unexpected forces arise, technical knowledge becomes relevant, and one cannot depend reliably on norms that arose to regulate small communities thousands of years ago. We see this quite dramatically when refugees settle in a new land; typically they discover that assumptions about human relations in this new milieu are quite alien to their own familial or ethnic traditions. Here, professional codes and the laws and rules of citizenship—rights and responsibilities—come to the fore.

THE LENSES OF PSYCHOLOGY

So much for our framework for conceptualizing "the good." Assuming the stance of the psychologist, which abilities and skills prove most relevant for achieving positive societal goals?

Turning first to intellect and cognition, for many years, particularly in the United States, one's score on a test of intelligence has been the card of admission to a program of "education for the gifted." And if one is interested primarily in who can pursue advanced work in the scholarly disciplines in contemporary society, IQ is a rough-and-ready predictor. (Note: Last year's grades or class rank are better predictors.)

Once one adopts a broader lens, however, a singular notion of intellect falls short. Here the notion of *multiple intelligences*—and other pluralistic views of intellect—comes to the fore. Any intelligence can be mobilized for good or for bad work. Both Nelson Mandela and Slobodan Milošević had an abundance of interpersonal intelligence; they knew how to mobilize individuals in their respective societies—but did so in very different ways toward very different ends.

In becoming good workers and/or good citizens, three of the multiple intelligences seem key:

Interpersonal intelligences refers to the capacity to understand the personalities and motivations of other persons and the ability to make use of this knowledge productively. We think of salespersons, politicians, and actors as being strong in this intelligence

Intrapersonal intelligence denotes the capacity to understand your own personality, strengths, weaknesses, aspirations, and anxieties and to make use of that knowledge in leading your own life. We quip that only your psychiatrist can evaluate your intrapersonal intelligence—but many believe that meditation can enhance it.

Existential intelligence (about which I have speculated, though I have not formally assembled evidence sufficient to justify its addition to the ranks) is the capacity and the inclination to reflect on the large issues of life and death in the manner of a philosopher or religious leader. We sometimes joke that all children ask questions, but it's the children with an existential strain who listen to the answers and ask follow-up questions contemplating deep issues of life and death.

It's important to underscore—that is, to admit—that intelligences are not necessarily put to prosocial ends. A sadist can make use of interpersonal intelligence to torture others. Acute self-knowledge can produce depression as well as elation. And leaders of cults often draw on their own existential intelligence even as they arouse—or annihilate—the existential intelligences of others.

That said, any effort to ferret out young people with promise in the "good area" would do well to attend to these traits, while acknowledging that these gifts may not be readily assessed in a 20-minute machine-administered and machine-scored test.

Equally important is motivation. If one is to direct energies toward a particular problem or task, it's vital that one has the will and energy to devote oneself to that assignment. Invoking two concepts currently in the educational limelight, the future good worker needs both "grit" and "a sense of purpose."

Motivation, will, and an appropriate ensemble of intelligences are necessary, but they do *not* suffice. Across the centuries, autocrats have demonstrated considerable capacities to activate their followers, as well as strong motivation to succeed in their efforts, and to thwart—or even destroy—their rivals.

As indicated, psychologists have progressed in conceptualizing cognition and motivation. A more formidable challenge: deciding what is the right thing, the good thing, the proper thing, to do and then working steadily, even tirelessly, toward that goal. Yet that's precisely what's required for transformational giftedness.

You can't look it up! On any complicated issue in a contemporary democratic society, one cannot simply research the right answer—not in the Declaration of Independence, the Constitution (including amendments), the laws of the nation, the state, or the particular municipality, institution, or school.

To be sure, knowledge of history and politics is helpful, as are case studies of previous quandaries, along with proposed or pursued solutions. Indeed, these are among the reasons that we study historical events and documents, as well as important works of literature, drama, films, and the like.

But in many cases, one cannot simply say, "Look at how this dilemma was solved at the Constitutional Convention" or "That's how characters like Mark Twain's Huck Finn (or Toni Morison's Sethe or Thomas Mann's Aschenbach or the Biblical Moses) dealt with their dilemma. You do the same thing!"

Accordingly, in the perspective that our research team has developed, it's crucial to have a method for identifying dilemmas and determining how to deal with them. We speak of the five Ds of dilemmas:

Defining the dilemma.

Discussing and *Debating* the various facets.

Deciding on an action (or, equally, deciding not to act).

Debriefing (reflecting afterward on what happened, what went right or wrong, and what might be done better or differently next time).

That's it—our conceptual toolkit.

Here's an example that we've developed: Sarah is a well-known leader of a nonprofit agency devoted to worker welfare. She has been invited to a prestigious conference. When she arrives there, she discovers to her surprise that the conference is being picketed by a local union.

On the one hand, Sarah works in labor, and her grandfather was a labor organizer—she does not want to dishonor his memory or the family tradition. On the other hand, an invitation to this conference is coveted; she will be able to reach a large audience, ventilate the current issues, and perhaps garner significant financial resources for future undertaking. What should she do?

By definition, a dilemma does not have a simple, straightforward answer. One first has to recognize it as such; then determine the issues and weigh them; then make a decision; and then live with that decision. We believe that by developing this habit over many instances, people will be on the road to becoming better workers and better citizens—our admittedly ambitious goal for this undertaking.

A RECOMMENDED COURSE OF ACTION

Shifting to developmental and educational perspectives, how should one proceed?

Let's begin with the givens. We can assume that in the absence of any significant physical or mental disabilities, all human beings will have the potential to develop a range of intelligences. At the same time, because of messages in one's culture—along with the preferences of one's family and one's culture—certain intelligences will necessarily be valued more than others. As an example, in American higher education, linguistic intelligence was valorized in the 19th century, mathematical and computation skills in the 20th and early 21st century. That in itself is unobjectionable.

But if one wants to nurture good work, it is important that the personal intelligences be nurtured—specifically, we should develop understanding of others and of oneself, encompassing the emotional and affective realm, as well as matters that are essentially cognitive (and draw, accordingly, on the skills that are valorized in contemporary educational institutions).

In addition to the messages ambient in one's culture, models provided by key persons will be crucial. Of course, those models will include family members, neighbors, and friends. But just as important are the persons (and characters) presented in print, broadcast, and/or social media—with their behaviors, preferences, and idiosyncrasies. We live in a celebratory culture; the models that young people encounter regularly (night and day)—celebrities in popular music, in movies, in athletics, even in politics—exert powerful effects, for good, or for nought.

Except for sleeping and surfing sites on the media, young people spend the most time in educational settings—customarily in person, sometimes (as in the time of a pandemic) online. Over the years, what teachers say and how they say it, what they do and how they do it, will powerfully impact every child.

To be specific: Suppose that adult models are interested, indeed "immersed" in public affairs—in politics, in social challenges and solutions—and that these elders regularly and thoughtfully discuss these and model certain behaviors and attitudes. This perspective will likely be picked up by the young person (for example, around the dining room table in the home of the family of future President John F. Kennedy). And, conversely, if events in the world are not high on the radar screen, or if available role models convey disdain or uninterest in the wider world, this "distanced stance" will be absorbed and re-created as well. Importantly, if what is praised in one venue is undermined or ridiculed in others, that inconsistency will be noted, and it can have a paralyzing effect.

In the middle of the 20th century, some individuals spoke of being a "red diaper baby," or growing up in a household that subscribed to *The Daily Worker*. Such persons signaled that their parents were involved in politics (left-wing), and that immersion had made a deep impact. In more recent times, in the United States, one could make a comparable remark about being a Tea Party child or a "Fox News offspring" or a MAGA enthusiast. And there can be a more complex state of affairs: What one hears at home or reads online may be contradicted by other sources of information, whether human or digital. Such an inconsistency will be noted, and depending on the circumstances, it may prove motivating or paralyzing (see Essay 22).

The picture presented to this point is convincing—at least to me!—but it's close to self-evident. My parents and grandparents—none of whom had higher education or were conversant in the social sciences—might well have offered a similar account. But one can and should go beyond "common sense." My own observations of socially engaged individuals generate some hypotheses that could be tested.

Specifically, such individuals might be characterized by:

1. *An unusual family configuration.* Often, at an early age, future societal transformers have lost a parent—more often the father—and have had to take more of a proactive role in confronting difficult situations. Indeed, in her study of youthful social transformers my colleague Mimi Michaelson (Nakamura & Michaelson, 2001) noted that being raised by a mother—particularly one immersed in political and social events—can be crucial. A familiar example is Barack Obama, essentially raised by an activist mother, who never knew his father but who tellingly entitled his memoir *Dreams From My Father*.
2. *An early personal transformative experience.* All families experience challenges and tragedies, but the size and significance of these events differ—and some young people react to them far more passionately than others. A family illness, a physical or mental disorder, can deeply affect certain children; thereupon they commit themselves to studying it and healing it.
3. *A national or international tragedy.* A bombing, a pandemic, a flood, or a hurricane can wreak havoc on a society; it may in turn catalyze activism on the part of a sensitive youth. Joseph Walters and I have termed this a "crystallizing event" (see Essay 11).
4. *A powerful and charismatic role model.* Such a figure may be within the family but can be a neighbor, a town leader, a teacher, a scout master, or a religious leader. This role model can have a direct

personal relation to the child—we call this a mentor—or, from afar, the model can be studied and learned about—a paragon.
5. *A destructive role model.* There may also be less benign role models—we have labeled them *tormentors.* The child may vow and commit herself *never* to become like that negative example and will strive to right the misdeeds of the tormentor.

Of course, such triggers are ubiquitous. Most of us can readily think of one or more of these in our own lives and in those of family members and close friends. The question: *When* do these factors become more than one-offs; when do they become "ways of being"?

Here the ethos of larger entities and enterprises comes into play. Throughout history—and probably prehistory as well—religions have provided a framework for interpreting events and persons. Religions have also played a powerful role in seizing upon a chance event or experience and interweaving it into a larger life tapestry. Regular attendance at religious events and religious schools, confirmation, and other kinds of growth milestones, pilgrimages, or years abroad as missionaries—all can consolidate into a mission for good work. Or at least of work that *thinks of itself* as good—though when it goes wrong, such theology can also lead to carnage (from the crusades of the Middle Ages to the Cultural Revolution in China) or bombings or mass murder.

Other institutions and entities—secular—can play analogous roles. In the middle of the last century, the scouting movement played that role for many American youths (including me). Later in the 20th century, community service and civic collaboratives played analogous roles. And the ethos of certain educational institutions (e.g., those internationally oriented schools spawned or inspired by the noted pedagogue Kurt Hahn) loom large as well. However deserving of criticism, elite secondary schools and colleges in the first decades of the 20th century often led to lives of service—in the military, in the CIA or the NSA, in philanthropic organizations, or in public-interest law firms. At a time when "return on investment" of financial support looms so large in the minds of most college students and their families, it is important to recognize that within human memory, other, nonpecuniary powerful messages have been regnant.

And, of course, the lessons conveyed by teachers and by the encompassing school or school system are likely to be significant and perhaps enduring. Whether moral and ethical issues are foregrounded, and if so, how; or whether they are deliberately skirted and swept under the rug, are crucial factors in the development of one's attitude toward others—at home, at school, at work, and across the larger society. In our own research group, we have made efforts to develop curricula addressing aspects of good work (see https://www.thegoodproject.org/lesson-plans).

But the effects of these curricula—whether lessons are learned, and whether there are concomitant behavioral changes immediately or in the long run—are yet to be determined. And, of course, many research centers and educational systems around the world have also undertaken to create curricula and environments that foster an ethical orientation—see, for example, offerings described at https://www.jubileecentre.ac.uk/ or our own curricula, based on the concepts and practices described in this essay.

Finally, and importantly, we need to attend to whether these educational efforts are independent, cumulative in a positive sense, or—less happily—at odds with one another. Here it is useful to employ the tools of synthesizing or systemic thinking (see Essay 24).

While addressing educational and developmental issues, I've so far bypassed what may be the knottiest question: *How do we (indeed, how does anyone) decide what work is good?* To take just one example: Some individuals in the middle of the 20th century joined organizations that at the time would have been widely deemed benign, but some idealistic youth were actually sent abroad to undermine political regimes considered antagonistic by the United States government! We could all easily add to this list of dilemmas.

Here our own work may provide a clue. We do not simply recommend the identification of dilemmas and the invoking of the 5 D's. We provide toolkits and curricula that seek to inculcate these habits of mind in the groups that use them. We do not tell them the right answer—as if we knew it!—but rather how to define, discuss, debate, decide, and debrief. There's no guarantee that one will arrive at the right answer—if indeed there is a single optimal solution. But there's the likelihood that one's thinking and one's behavior will be more enlightened, more defensible, more constructive.

Nazi leader Heinrich Himmler famously said of the Holocaust, "This is the greatest feat of the world, which humankind can never know about." (In Wikipedia: "This page of glory in our history has never been written and will never be written.") Our response: "Sunlight is the best disinfectant."

And that is why I've cast the foregoing discussion within the parameters of a democratic society. In such a society, individuals agree to certain ground rules, but remain open to the possibility that these rules can be changed—by discussion, debate, and, crucially, by a peaceful transition of governments, most often through popular election. In the absence of these safeguards, those in power define what is good—and others lack a means for challenging that directive.

REFERENCE

Nakamura, J, & Michaelson, M., Eds. (2001). Supportive frameworks for youth engagement. *New Directions for Child and Adolescent Development, 93.*

ESSAY 29

To an Aspiring Researcher
Twelve Pieces of Advice

The essays in this volume describe my own background, the work that I have undertaken—almost always in collaboration with talented colleagues—and my thoughts about steps that might be taken to extend this work in the future,
  In the spirit of this last remark, it seems appropriate to include an essay delivered when I received a lifetime award for my research presented by the American Educational Research Association.

Thanks for this wonderful honor—it means a great deal to me. In cases like this, the honoree typically reflects on the work that he or she has carried out over many years. And that's fine.

But in these days of websites, search engines, and YouTube, information on my research is available on demand. (Or, I can now add, in the two books issued by Teachers College Press.) And so I thought—and I hope it's okay with you—that I'd use this occasion to proceed in a different direction.

I've been involved in research for a *long time*. If you start with my NSF-sponsored research on the pig heart in high school, for over 60 years; if you include my college research in sociology, 60 years; and if you focus on my sponsored work as a recently minted doctorate, for over 50 years. During that period I believe I've learned some lessons.

A THOUGHT EXPERIMENT

Let's say a motivated college junior came to see me and asked, "Dr. Gardner, what's it like to be a researcher? Can you give me some advice? Should I become a researcher?" What words of experience, and perhaps of wisdom, could I give to that student?

Here, as answers to the student's questions, are a dozen pieces of advice.

1. **What is research?**
    Scholarly research is a process that human beings can undertake—alone or with other persons—to find out the answers to questions or, at a minimum, to arrive at better ways of

conceiving questions, problems, or issues in which they have an interest.

So, ask yourself, are you curious about issues or problems, and do you have the motivation to pursue them rigorously and vigorously in the hope of getting an answer? If there is no area of knowledge that you *really* want to explore, perhaps research is not really what you want. (And rest assured, there are many other worthwhile career paths!)

2. **What are the kinds of scholarly research?**

Some require going into archives, but do not cost appreciable money—that's what historians do. Some require intensive reading or looking at works of art or listening to works of music—that's what other humanists do. These are not expensive in dollars, but they take considerable amounts of time.

Some research involves simple, or not-so-simple, equipment, and a few research assistants or postdoctoral fellows—that's what psychologists do (and what I typically have done). And, of course, "big-time research" in the sciences or medicine often involves large amounts of money (in the millions) and sizable teams of researchers (sometimes dozens or scores).

So ask yourself: Do you have a sense of what kind of research you would like to do—do you see yourself poring through paper or digital archives; pondering the poetry of John Milton or Emily Dickinson; asking subjects to solve a puzzle; or joining a large team working in a hospital on cures for a disease, or at an accelerator to understand subatomic particles?

3. **What is *your* motivation for carrying out research?**

That's a tough one. Nowadays, it is customary—in some circles, obligatory—to speak about a service motivation—you want to heal people, or save lives, or contribute to climate control. Or, if you are in education, you want to help underserved populations; or figure out the best way to spend taxpayer money on schools; or reach students with learning disabilities; or compare online with classroom or blended learning.

But I don't feel it's necessary to carry out research to solve some kind of real-life problem. Having something that you are curious about, indeed *obsessed* about—and having a method for possibly sating that curiosity—is sufficient motivation.

And there's a good reason for this seemingly nonpragmatic stance. We never know what we will find and what its implications might be. Some mission-oriented research yields nothing, and some curiosity-driven research can bring about fundamental practical changes. When young Albert Einstein arrived at the theory of relativity, he had no idea that one day the atom could be split—as it turns out, for constructive as well as destructive purposes.

Or to use a personal (less lofty!) example: When I developed the theory of multiple intelligences, I did not have a practical result in mind. I saw my work as a contribution to understanding how the mind is organized and how it operates under diverse conditions. Curiosity and altruism are both laudable goals, but they are not the same—and many saints would not be effective researchers!

4. **If the research that I want to conduct requires resources or funds to carry out, how can I get such support?**

I could easily write a book about this, and, in fact, such books should be written. Obviously, it helps to have a good project, and it helps to be persuasive—your grandparents could have told you that.

But here are some things that you—and they—might not have thought about.

Roughly speaking, in the United States (and perhaps elsewhere), there are three sources of funding:

a) The federal or national government.

b) Organized philanthropy (foundations—almost everyone has heard of the Ford Foundation, and those of us in education know and venerate the Spencer Foundation, but there are tens of thousands of other foundations in the United States alone).

c) Private philanthropists (I exclude companies and corporations here, because with notable exceptions, they rarely support disinterested research—they *know* what they want you to find).

You need to monitor all of these sources of funding constantly. And the funding landscape is constantly changing.

A personal example: Until 1980, nearly all of my research funding came from the government—NIH, NIE, and NSF. After 1980, virtually none of it did. Why?

Because when Ronald Reagan became president in 1981, he declared that "social science is socialism." And I immediately realized that given the kind of qualitative research I do, my chances of securing additional funding from "the feds" was low.

Thereafter, my sources of funding have come from well-known foundations, private individuals, and, to a lesser but still significant extent, book royalties and speaking fees. Note that if such payments go directly into a research fund, they will not be taxed—accordingly, you get more mileage from such donations.

5. **Okay, those are the sources, but please be more specific about how to get support.**

    Good point. Funders are institutions and individuals with whom you need to establish and maintain a relationship. It's no different from making a new friend or, to switch metaphors, from having a reliable client. Over the decades I've cultivated relationships with scores of funders and worked energetically to keep up these relations. And, indeed, sometimes these relationships have evolved into valued friendships.

    Even when I get a no, I maintain the relationship, and more often than one might predict, that perhaps unanticipated gesture of gratitude pays off—in recommendations of other possible funders, or even a change of heart. Occasionally I have been able to educate potential funders to see things that they had not seen before, or to construe issues in a new way. And, of course, the foundations do have to spend their money, and sometimes you can help them do so wisely!

    By my calculation, I've sent out well over 300 letters of solicitation in 50 years. In addition to welcome acceptances and frank rejections, we—thanks to Ellen Winner, my wife—have a separate file or folder dubbed "rays of hope" (a rejection that nonetheless leaves the door slightly ajar). The latter file can make a difference in the long run.

    Say "thank you," maintain contact, offer to be helpful, say thank you again, and be sure to cite gratefully on every occasion. All those etiquette lessons that your parents and grandparents sought to give you—apply them.

    This may sound overwhelming . . . and it can be. But most institutions have development offices that can help you to identify promising funders, and, of course, senior researchers can share that lore as well.

6. **What are the risks in fundraising?**

    When you accept funds from the U.S. government, or from large well-established foundations like Ford, Hewlett, Spencer, or Russell Sage, there are few risks.

    But it's different when you accept funding from a private individual or from a little-known foundation. There are risks with respect to how the funds were secured, how they are distributed, and how your findings will be used. I've made some mistakes in this area and have actually written about those poor judgments (please see https://www.thegoodproject.org/good-blog/2020/12/15/on-bad-work-in-the-academy-recognizing-it-thwarting-it). Due diligence, checking with knowledgeable others, and atoning for mistakes—all these are important parts of securing support for research.

7. **Dr. Gardner ("please call me Howard"), you are sounding very mercenary, stuck in the funding details. What about research per se?**

    Thank you so much for asking that question—it's really the most important, the fundamental question, and I got so mired in the mercenary weeds that I lost sight of the abundant, leafy garden.

    If you are curious about something and want to gain knowledge about it, there's no better way than carrying out systematic research. Of course, reflective individuals have thought systematically about puzzles for millennia, but only in the last few centuries have specific methods of research been identified, developed, and systematized. It's a good test! Sometimes what appears to be an exciting path of research turns out to be tedious or dull. And sometimes, what may seem to others to be boring or misguided catches your fancy and proves fruitful.

    To put it simply, you need to have questions or issues in which you are interested—even obsessed—and you need to find a method, or methods, by which you will approach an answer or, at a minimum, a better formulation of the problem. In my case, I lean toward qualitative methods—posing questions, reflecting on phenomena—but many others prefer experimental methods, large-scale surveys, or analyses or meta-analyses of demographic data.

    Indeed, a brief and not misleading definition of a researcher is "a person obsessed with a puzzle and equipped with at least one method for solving it."

    When I discovered the pleasures of research, it changed my life forever. And even when one research proposal after another got turned down—and it's happened—never have I regretted the path that I chose over 5 decades ago.

8. **What's helped you to be a successful researcher?**

    For me, that's an easy question to answer. By far, it's my colleagues in research—the fellow researchers, the heads of labs, and the research assistants—who make the difference between an exciting and a vexing experience in research.

    I've been extremely fortunate for the last 50-plus years. In 1967, I was a founding member of Harvard Project Zero, a research group started by philosopher Nelson Goodman at the Harvard Graduate School of Education. (Why that curious name? Goodman was making a statement about what was known about education in the arts through systematic research—*at the time*, little was known and therefore, we started at . . . Zero.) We do believe that after half a century, we have moved the number line in a positive direction. (See Essay 2 and https://pz.harvard.edu.)

For 28 years, eminent cognitive scholar David Perkins and I co-directed Project Zero. And what started out as a small endeavor in arts education is now a large set of research projects covering the disciplinary and methodological spectrum—taking place in many parts of the world. My colleagues at Project Zero are invaluable—I could not have done my work in psychology and education without them. The moment that I learned of this cherished recognition, I said, "It really should go to my colleagues."

But I had two other equally important collaborations. For 2 decades (1971–1990), I did research in neurology and neuropsychology, working at the Aphasia Research Center in the Boston Veterans Administration Medical Center. There, a group of a dozen senior researchers and I carried out work that we consider to be critical in understanding the breakdown of cognitive capacities under conditions of brain damage.

As it turned out, the work with brain-damaged patients was fundamental in the creation of the theory of multiple intelligences, the work for which I am best known (see https://www.multipleintelligencesoasis.org).

And then, starting in the mid-1990s, as a third fortunate collaboration, I had the privilege of working with two outstanding psychologists, William (Bill) Damon and Mihaly (Mike) Csikszentmihalyi. Together we explored the nature of work—and particularly what is considered to be "good work" across several professions. Each of us continued this work in our respective ways—and in my case, the collaboration led to a whole set of studies of good work, good play, good collaboration, and the like (see Essay 26 and https://www.thegoodproject.org).

9. **Interesting, Dr. Gardner (sorry, Howard). While we are at a conference education, and a society devoted to research in education has given you an honor, you have not said much directly about education.**

Yes, that's true. In my own case, ever since early childhood I assumed that I would be a teacher. And in fact, for a decade I taught piano on the side to make extra pocket money. But my own motivation in research has not been primarily educational. It's been interest in the human mind—how it works, how it develops, how it works at the top of its game, how it breaks down, and, in the last quarter-century, how it can be directed in positive ways—the goal of The Good Project.

Each of these issues—like most work in the social sciences—has clear educational implications. And in most cases I and others have followed up on these implications and possible applications—lots of work at Project Zero is applied in the field. But in truth, educational programs have *not* been the prime motivator. The motivator has been curiosity about human beings, combined more recently with a "value consideration" of how we humans can use our skills and abilities benignly.

Please be assured, I am *not* speaking for other researchers. Many are motivated initially and primarily by the desire to improve the human condition. But the individuals whom I most admire, some of whom have received lifetime-achievement accolades from AERA, are those whose primary motivation is curiosity, and the desire to add to human knowledge.

10. **You have spoken a lot about learning things and contributing to knowledge. But how does that contribution come to be known and, as appropriate, applied?**

    Another important question: You can't just have findings; you need ways to inform individuals about what you have discovered, what you have learned, and, as appropriate, how to use that knowledge.

    Here's where writing comes in. No one is born a good writer—it's definitely an acquired skill! But if you don't like to write, and you are not motivated to learn to write clearly, then I don't recommend a career in research.

    With one notable exception: If you happen to find a partner—a research partner, a life partner—who likes to write, just make a pact to collaborate with that person indefinitely. The Biblical Moses was not a good speaker, but he was fortunate to have his brother Aaron, who was very articulate. Sullivan had Gilbert, Rodgers had Hammerstein. Indeed, a few researchers—who will remain nameless—would not have achieved renown without a literarily gifted coauthor, sometimes named, sometimes anonymous.

11. **Howard, you are a well-known researcher in psychology and education. How does that feel?**

    If you work hard at research and have interesting findings, of course you'd like them to be known and recognized. But it's a big mistake to seek fame and fortune through research and writing—you can't count on getting such recognition. And let's say that you *do* become famous or rich for a particular finding or research track. You then face a choice: you either have to remain wedded to that line of work (keep singing the same tune); or be prepared to carry out work that will not necessarily become well-known (switch to a different medley of melodies). Motivation to learn, and then to share what you have learned, is more important than having a lot of money in the bank, or even (shhhhhhh. . . .) having a lot of citations in some index.

12. Howard, I want to be respectful—I am a young student, you are a venerable researcher almost 60 years older than I am. Are you carrying out research anymore? Do you have further research goals?

    An understandable and appropriate question. Of course, I cannot know how much time I have left, nor whether my mind, body, and spirit will be able to continue doing research. But at present, I have a wonderful research team with whom I work every day (including, sometimes, weekends and evenings); and I continue to write papers, post blogs, and author or coauthor books. And I'd like that to last as long as possible.

    But I am also fortunate because I'm confident that some members of the research team will continue to explore some of the questions that I am interested in. And equally importantly, I have students, and they have students (I call them grandstudents), and some of those much younger persons will raise new questions and find answers that I could not even have dreamt of. That's the greatest reward of all.

    And maybe one day, young friend, you'll be one of those individuals who discovers new things and, in the process, helps to make the world a better place.

ACKNOWLEDGMENTS

For their comments on earlier versions of this chapter and for their exemplary collegiality, I'd like to thank Lynn Barendsen, Courtney Bither, Shelby Clark, Wendy Fischman, Shinri Furuzawa, Mara Krechevsky, Kirsten McHugh, Danny Mucinskas, and Ellen Winner.

Original Publication List

I am extremely grateful to the various publications—and to my several coauthors—who have kindly granted permission to reprint articles and chapters that were written over the last half-century—or, indeed, longer! Scholarship is a collaborative project, as is publishing, and I have been very fortunate with my colleagues, many of whom have become lifelong friends. If anyone was mistakenly left unacknowledged, I offer my sincere apologies for the inadvertent oversight, which will be corrected in subsequent printings.

Except for corrections of errors or necessary updates (e.g., of dates!) and elimination of text that appears elsewhere in the volume (e.g., the list of multiple intelligences), the wording of articles and chapters remains unchanged.

It is important that all users of this book be able to access the original publications as they appeared. Accordingly, the list below includes *all available links* to *all the materials in the book*, including any articles, books, and links that are cited therein. Any source that is discussed substantively is also cited in this list.

REFERENCE LIST

From "Influences"

Gardner, H. (1989). The key in the slot: Creativity in a Chinese key. *Journal of Aesthetic Education, 23*(1), 141–158. https://doi.org/10.2307/3332893

Gardner, H. (2001). Jerome S. Bruner as educator. In J. A. Palmer & D. E. Cooper (Eds.), *Fifty modern thinkers on education*. Routledge.

Gardner, H. (2012). Foreword. In C. Edwards, L. Gandini, & G. Forman (Eds.), *The hundred languages of children: The Reggio Emilia experience in transformation* (pp. xiii-xvi). ABC-CLIO.

From "Educational Philosophy"

Gardner, H. (1991). The tensions between education and development. *Journal of Moral Education, 20*(2), 113–125. https://doi.org/10.1080/0305724910200201

Gardner, H. (2012). *Truth, beauty, and goodness reframed: Educating for the virtues in the age of truthiness and Twitter*. Basic Books.

Gardner, H., Torff, B., & Hatch, T. (1998). The age of innocence reconsidered: Preserving the best of the progressive traditions in psychology and education. In D. R. Olson & N. Torrance (Eds.), *The handbook of education and human development: New models of learning, teaching and schooling* (Chapter 3). Wiley. https://doi.org/10.1111/b.9780631211860.1998.00004.x

From "Multiple Intelligences"

Gardner, H. (1987). Beyond the IQ: Education and human development: Developing the spectrum of human intelligences. *Harvard Educational Review*, 57(2), 187–196. https://doi-org.ezp-prod1.hul.harvard.edu/10.17763/haer.57.2.l2101188 34750615

Gardner, H. (1995). Reflections on multiple intelligences: Myths and messages. *The Phi Delta Kappan*, 77(3), 200–209. http://www.jstor.org/stable/20405529

Gardner, H. (2013, October 16). Howard Gardner: "Multiple intelligences" are not "learning styles," introduced by Valerie Strauss. *The Washington Post*. https://www.washingtonpost.com/news/answer-sheet/wp/2013/10/16/howard-gardner-multiple-intelligences-are-not-learning-styles/

Walters, J., & Gardner, H. (1986). The crystallizing experience: Discovering an intellectual gift. In R. Sternberg & J. Davidson (Eds.), *Conceptions of giftedness*. Cambridge University Press.

From Educational Experiments in the Spirit of Multiple Intelligences

Chen, J-Q., Krechevsky, M., Viens, J., & E. Isberg. (1998). *Building on children's strengths: The experience of Project Spectrum.* Project Zero Frameworks for Early Childhood Education, 1. H. Gardner, D. H. Feldman, & M. Krechevsky (Gen. Eds.), Teachers College Press.

Chen, J., Moran, S., & Gardner, H. (2009). *Multiple intelligences around the world* (pp. 8–16). Jossey-Bass.

Gardner, H. (2006). *Multiple intelligences: New horizons* (pp. 113–121 and pp. 147–166). Basic Books.

From Curriculum, Pedagogy, and Assessment

Gardner, H. (1991). Assessment in context: The alternative to standardized testing. In B. R. Gifford & M.C. O'Connor (Eds.), *Changing assessments: Alternative views of aptitude, achievement, and instruction* (pp. 77–120). Kluwer.

Gardner, H. (1993). The unschooled mind: Why even the best students in the best schools do not understand. *International Schools Journal, 26*, 29–33. Originally presented as the Alec Peterson Lecture to the International Baccalaureate Conference, Geneva, Switzerland, December 1992. http://search.proquest.com.ezp-prod1.hul.harvard.edu/scholarly-journals/unschooled-mind-why-even-best-students-schools-do/docview/1293029023/se-2?accountid=11311

Gardner, H. (1999). *The disciplined mind* (pp. 138–154). Simon & Schuster.

Gardner, H., & Boix-Mansilla, V. (1994). Teaching for understanding in the disciplines— and beyond. *Teachers College Record, 96*(2), 198–218. Paper prepared for the

Conference on Teachers Conceptions of Knowledge, Tel Aviv, June 1993. https://eric.ed.gov/?id=EJ498398

From Higher Education

Fischman, W. & Gardner, H. (2022). *The real world of college: What higher education is and what it can be.* MIT Press.

Gardner, H. (2018, July 9). Why we should require all students to take 2 philosophy courses. *The Chronicle of Higher Education.* https://www.chronicle.com/article/why-we-should-require-all-students-to-take-2-philosophy-courses/

From Contemporary Challenges and Opportunities

Davis, K., & Gardner, H. (2013). *The app generation: How today's youth navigate identity, intimacy, and imagination in a digital world* (pp. 173–191). Yale University Press.

Gardner, H. To an aspiring researcher: Twelve pieces of advice. https://www.howardgardner.com/howards-blog/to-an-aspiring-researcher-twelve-pieces-of-advice

Gardner, H. (2004) *Changing minds: The art and science of changing our own and other people's minds* (pp. 7–18). Harvard Business School Press.

Gardner, H. (2006). *Changing minds: The art and science of changing our own and other people's minds* (pp. 7–18). Harvard Business Review Press.

Gardner, H. (2009). The five minds for the future: Cultivating and integrating new ways of thinking to empower the education enterprise. *The School Administrator Magazine,* 16–20. https://eric.ed.gov/?id=EJ832326

Gardner, H. (2013). It's good to expose myths about neuroscience—but debunking is getting out of hand, a world famous psychologist says, introduced by Valerie Strauss. *The Washington Post.* https://www.washingtonpost.com/news/answer-sheet/wp/2013/10/16/howard-gardner-multiple-intelligences-are-not-learning-styles/

Gardner, H. (2022). Educating for the virtues: A Hegelian synthesis. In M. Suárez-Orozco & C. Suárez-Orozco (Eds.), *Education: A global compact for a time of crisis.* Columbia University Press. https://doi.org/10.73 12/suar20434

Index

The Aims of Education (Whitehead), 253
An American in Paris (Gershwin), 255
Anthropocene era, 284
Aphasia Research Center, 304
Apprenticeship model, 58, 78, 182, 185, 217–218
Apps and digital devices, 247–256, 283
Aristotle, 285
Armstrong, Martha Gray, 16
Armstrong, Thomas, 126
Arnheim, Rudolf, 49
Arnold, Matthew, 254
Arthurs, Alberta, 132
Artificial intelligence (AI), 14, 245, 293
Arts
  artistic intelligence, 132–133
  artists, role of, 201–203, 207
  and education, 29
  See also Harvard Project Zero
The Arts and Cognition (Perkins & Leondar), 16
Arts PROPEL, 90, 132–133, 157–171
  arts education history of, 158–159
  "biography of a work," 164–165, 166
  disciplined inquiry, 159
  domain projects, 163–167
  "processfolio" assessment system, 165–166, 168–171
  Project Zero approach, 159–162
Ashbery, John, 248
Assessment
  alternative assessments, 217–234
  assessment specialists, 89–90
  in context, 224
  distributed knowledge, 225–226
  multiple measures, 228
  new approaches to, 226–230
  ongoing assessment, 187
  performance-based exams, 189–190
  "processfolio" assessment system, 165–166, 168–171
  project-based assessment, 151–154
  society-wide focus on assessment, 230–234
  Spectrum approach, 135–148
  standardized testing, 217
  and understanding, 179–180
  validity, 227
  within/across disciplines, 215
Atlantic Philanthropies, 19–20, 21
ATLAS project, 56, 174
Author's experiences
  childhood and education, 1–2, 275
  music and art, 45
  travel, 2, 29
  Wyoming Seminary, 45, 62, 276

Bakewell, Sarah, 285
Beaumarchais, Pierre, 193–194, 202
Beauty, study of, 45, 63–64, 278, 279.
  See also Virtue in education
Behaviorism, 11, 39
Bernstein, Leonard, 281
The Best and the Brightest (Halberstam), 92
Big Bird's Words (app), 252–253
Binet, Alfred, 85, 177, 218–219, 220
Bloom, B., 110
Bodily-kinesthetic intelligence, 88
Boix-Mansilla, Veronica, 174, 210
Bok, Sissela, 45
Bolanos, Patricia, 128, 149
Boulez, Pierre, 112

Brain imaging, 15
Britten, Benjamin, 277
Brooks, Ernie, 15
Brown, Marc, 18
Brown, Roger, 265
Bruner, Blanche, 8
Bruner, Jerome S., 5–10, 173, 265

Camara, Ladji, 16
Campbell, Bruce, 126
Campbell, Linda, 126
Cassirer, Ernst, 15, 52
Center of Cognitive Studies, 5
Changing Minds (Gardner), 267
Chen, Jie-Qi, 131, 136
Cheung, Happy, 126
Child development
  and education, 69–79
  stages of, 39, 47–48
  symbol systems approach, 52–55, 60–61
Children's museums, 182, 185–186
China, 128
  art as performance, 35–37
  calligraphy, 39
  childrearing practices, 31–33, 38–40
  cultural assumptions, 32–33
  curriculum, unified, 38
  educational models, 2–3, 29, 40–43
  hierarchy, 37–38
  key-slot anecdote, 31–32, 39
  life as performance, 33–35
  schools, role of, 39–40
Chomsky, Noam, 8, 12
Christopherian encounters, 186–187
Citizenship. *See* Democratic societies
Coalition of Essential Schools (Brown University), 56
Code for America, 254–255, 256
Cognitive perspectives/styles, 5–6, 9, 96
Comer, James, 56
Common sense, 199, 212–213, 214, 296
Corinth, Lovis, 15
Covert, Angela, 20
COVID-19 pandemic, 290
Creativity, 223–224, 248
  "creating mind," 259–260
Cremin, Lawrence, 19

Critique of Pure Reason (Kant), 72
Crystallizing experiences and intellectual gifts, 296
  analysis, 116–118
  mathematics, 112–114
  music, 110–112
  overview, 106–110, 121–122
  research methodology and interviews, 116
  talent as issue, 118–121
  visual arts, 114–115
Csikszentmihalyi, Mihaly, 95, 225, 304
Cultural frameworks, 6, 9, 69–71
The Culture of Education (Bruner), 9

Damon, William, 304
Da Ponte, Lorenzo, 193–194, 202
Darwin, Charles, 192–193, 196, 200, 206–207, 274
Darwin, Erasmus, 193
Davidson, Lyle, 132
Dawkins, Richard, 125
Debussy, Claude, 107
Democratic societies
  democratic practices, 129, 173–174
  role of education, 290–298
Derrida, Jacques, 280
Developmental psychology, 177–179
  approaches to testing, 221
Dewey, John, 2, 9–10, 40, 47–48, 60, 71, 130, 173–174
Dickinson, Emily, 277
Digital devices and apps, 247–256, 283
Dine people, 128
Discipline based arts education (DBAE), 11
Disciplined learners, 182
The Disciplined Mind (Gardner), 66
Disciplined minds, 257
Disciplines
  assessments, 215
  contrasted with intelligence, 95–96
  differing perspectives of, 205–209
  disciplinary knowledge, 213–214
  disciplinary to personal knowledge, 215–216
  powers and limitations, 214–215
  protodisciplinary knowledge, 213

understanding within and across, 210–216
DISCOVER method, 128
Domains contrasted with intelligence, 95–96
Dreams From My Father (Obama), 296
Duraisingh, Liz, 22

early childhood education, 135–148
Educational Testing Service, 132, 248
Eichler, J., 255
80/20 principle, 267–270
The 80/20 Principle (Koch), 268–269
Einstein, Albert, 274
Eliot, T. S., 248
Eliot-Pearson Children's School, 131, 139
Emotional intelligence, 84, 88
Emotional Intelligence (Goleman), 126
Engel, Martin, 17
Epistemic subject (Piaget), 9
Erikson, Erik, 47, 48
The Essential Howard Gardner on Mind (Gardner), 2, 53, 88, 93, 96, 98, 224, 278, 282
Ethical mind, 261
Ethnography, 8
Evolutionary biology, 192–193, 196, 200, 206–207
Existential intelligence, 93, 293
Eysenck, Hans, 85

Feeney, Charles, 20
Feldman, David, 50, 71, 95, 108, 131, 136
Finnish Lessons (Sahlberg), 91
First-order symbolic competence, 181
Fischer, Bobby, 178
Fischer, Kurt, 68
Fitzgerald, F. Scott, 248
5 Ds of dilemmas, 294–295, 298
Frames of Mind (Gardner), 83, 93, 94, 98, 129, 149
Francis (pope), 281
Freud, Sigmund, 69, 180, 274
Froebel, Friedrich, xiv

Galois, Évariste, 106
Gandhi, Mahatma, 248
Gawande, Atul, 248
Gell-Mann, Murray, 258
Gershwin, George, 255
Geschwind, Norman, 15, 16
Gilligan, Carol, 68
Gitomer, Drew, 132
Global Educational Reform Movement, 248
Goldhagen, Daniel J., 198
Goleman, Daniel, 84, 88, 126
Goodman, Katherine Sturgis, 13
Goodman, Nelson, 12–15, 16, 17, 22, 52, 282, 303
Goodness, 64–65, 278, 280–281. *See also* Virtue in education
Gorman, Amanda, 248
Graham, Martha, 202, 248, 274
Groopman, Jerome, 249
Grundtvig, Nikolaj, xiv
Guilford, J. P., 86
Guzzetti, Alfred, 16

Hahn, Ina, 16
Hahn, Kurt, 297
Halberstam, David, 92
Hamlin, George, 16
Handlan, Ray, 19–20
Hardy, G. H., 113–114, 201
Harvard Graduate School of Education (HGSE), 14, 17
Harvard Project Zero, 59, 304
 and Arts PROPEL, 149–162
 and educational reform, 18–19
 expansion of, 20–22
 funding of, 15, 19–20
 inception of, 11–16
 leadership, 16–18
 21st century, 22–23
 See also Spectrum assessments
Harvard University, 248
Harvey, Faith, 22
Hatch, Tom, 46
Haydn, Franz Joseph, 112
Hegel, Georg Wilhelm Friedrich, 246, 285
 Hegelian approach to education for virtue, 275–285

Higher education, 235, 237–240
 philosophy curricula, 241–243
Higher Education Capital (HEDCAP), 238
Himmler, Heinrich, 298
Historian, role of, 203–205, 207
Hitler, Adolf, 195, 204
Hobbes, Thomas, 70
Hockett, Charles, 8
Hoerr, Tom, 126
Holocaust, 204, 298
Howard, Vernon, 16
Howard Gardner Under Fire (Shaler), 94

Instruction Research Group (IRG), 7
Intelligence
 cultural influences, 178
 "g" factor, 96–97
 heritability of, 97
 intelligence profiles, 89–90
 IQ tests, 83, 85, 219
 Scholastic Aptitude Test (SAT), 86, 219, 228
Interpersonal intelligence, 88, 99, 293
Intrapersonal intelligence, 88, 99, 293
Intuitive conceptions, 181
Iseberg, Elise, 136

James, Carrie, 22
James, Tom, 20
James, William, 173, 280
Japan, 128
Jensen, Arthur, 85
Johns Hopkins University, 241, 243

Kant, Immanuel, 49, 72
Keats, John, 277
Kennedy, John F., 295
Key Learning Community/Key School, 126, 128, 131–132, 150
 project scaffolding, 154–156
Kinship structures, 8, 9
Kirchner, Leon, 16
Knowledge
 distributed, 225–226
 ways of knowing, 74–78
 ways of representing, 72–74

Koch, Richard, 268
Kohlberg, Lawrence, 49, 68–69, 71, 77–79
Kolers, Paul, 12
Kornhaber, Mindy, 126, 127
Krechevsky, Mara, 131
Krieger, Judy, 7
Kugel, Seth, 253
Kuhn, Thomas, 76

Langer, Susanne, 15, 52
Language acquisition, 8
Languages of Art (Goodman), 13, 14
Lazear, David, 126
Learning styles, 96, 103–105, 140
Lecoq, Jacques, 16
Leondar, Barbara, 16
Lesser, Gerald, 68
LeVine, Robert, 68
Lévi-Strauss, Claude, 62
Linguistic intelligence, 87–88
Lithgow, John, 248
Locke, John, 48, 56, 70
Logical-mathematical intelligence, 88, 112–114

Ma, Yo-Yo, 248
MacArthur, Robert, 206
Machover, Tod, 255–256
Maker, June, 128
Malaguzzi, Loris, 24–27
"Man: A Course of Study" (Bruner), 7–9, 12, 173
Mandela, Nelson, 261, 293
Markan, Manual, 11
The Marriage of Figaro, 193–194, 196, 202
Marx, Karl, 233, 274, 277, 284
Mathematics, 199–201
 crystallizing experiences, 112–114
Mayer, R., 71
McLuhan, Marshall, 250
Mein Kampf (Hitler), 204
Mental Measurements Yearbook, 219
Menuhin, Yehudi, 111
Meringoff, Laurie, 18
Messiaen, Olivier, 112
Michaelson, Mimi, 296

Miller, George, 11
Mills College, 241, 243
Milosevic, Slobodan, 261, 293
Minerva University, 237
Minute papers, 190
Montessori, Maria, xiv, 25
Moore, Michael, 129
Moral development, 76–77
Morris, Clifford, 126
Moss, M., 268
Mozart, Wolfgang Amadeus, 193–194, 196, 202
Multiple intelligence theory
  assessment instruments, 126
  assessment specialists, 89–90
  classroom applications, 98–102
  contrasted with learning styles, 96, 103–105
  development of, 85–92
  elementary school level projects, 149–156
  empirical evidence, 96
  framework, 54–55
  future applications, 257–263
  groundwork for implementation, 127–129
  as meme in popular culture, 125–127
  myths concerning, 93–102
  overview, 83–84
  policy level, 129
  and standardized testing, 222–223
  "student-curriculum brokers," 90–91
  synthesis, 264–266, 279
  understanding through disciplines, 192–209
  See also Crystallizing experiences and intellectual gifts
Musical intelligence, 88
  crystallizing experiences, 110–112

Nakamura, J., 296
A Nation at Risk, 18, 174
Naturalist intelligence, 93, 98
Natural learners, 182
Nazi Third Reich, 194–195, 196, 204, 298
Neuroscience and neuromyths, 287–289
New City School (St. Louis), 126

Newsome, Barbara Y., 17
1984 (Orwell), 283
Northeastern University, 243

Obama, Barack, 296
Odbert, Henry, 17
Olin College of Engineering, 237
Olson, D. R., 50
On Lying (Bok), 45
Oppenheimer, Frank, 185
Orwell, George, 283

Pahlka, Jennifer, 254, 256
Papert, Seymour, 251
Pareto, Vilfredo, 268
Pareto Principle, 267–270
Performances of Understanding, 59
Perkins, David, 14, 15, 16, 17, 18, 20, 223, 304
  formula for innovation, 25
Persinger, Louis, 111
Pestalozzi, Johann, xiv
Peyser, J., 112
Philosophy curricula, 241–243
Piaget, Jean, 9, 47–51, 60, 69, 71–72, 88, 177–178, 221
Picasso, Pablo, 248, 274, 277
Pittsburgh Public Schools, 162. *See also* Arts PROPEL
Plato, 285
Plato's Academy, 56
Polanyi, Michael, 248
Princeton University, 248
The Process of Education (Bruner), 5, 6–7
Programme for International Student Assessment (PISA), 129
Progressivism, 45–46, 47–61
  child-centered education, 48–49
  contextual and mediated experiences, 51
  developmental stages, 47–48
  domains beyond universals, 49–50
  educational practice and application, 56–60
  individual differences, 50
  misconceptions, 50–51
  specific knowledge, 50

Progressivism (*continued*)
  standards, application of, 51–52
  symbol systems approach, 52–55, 60–61
Project-based assessment, 151–154
Project on Human Potential, 83
Project scaffolding, 154–156
Project Spectrum, 131
Project Zero. *See* Harvard Project Zero

Ramanujan, Srinivasa, 113–114
Ramos-Ford, Valerie, 136
Ravel, Maurice, 15
Reagan, Ronald, 19, 301
The Real World of College (Gardner & Fischman), 235
Redescriptions, 272
Reeve, Christopher, 16
Reggio Emilia schools, 2, 9, 24–27
Religion, role of, 284–285
Renoir, Pierre-Auguste, 107
Research, guiding principles, 299–306
Resnick, Mitch, 251
Resonance, 271–272
resources, role of, 284
Respectful mind, 260–261
Richards, I. A., 16, 184–185
Role models, 263, 296–297
Rorty, Richard, 280
Rousseau, Jean-Jacques, xv, 56, 70
Rubinstein, Arthur, 111

Sahlberg, Pasi, 91, 248
Sarrasin, J., 288
Sartre, Jean-Paul, 285
Scaffolding, project, 154–156
Schaler, Jeffrey, 94
Schoenberg, Arnold, 202
Scholastic Aptitude/Assessment Test (SAT), 86, 219, 228
Scholastic learners, 182
School Development Program (Yale University), 56
Schools
  individual-centered schools, 89
  purpose of, 57
Scientific thinking/paradigms, 76, 199–201

Scratch (app), 251–252
Scripts/stereotypes, 184
Seidel, Steve, 22, 132, 152
Simmons, Seymour, 132
Simon, Théodore, 177
Sims-Gunzenhauser, Alice, 132
Sizer, Theodore, 12, 15, 17, 56
Skinner, B. F., 5, 39, 48, 250
Snow, Catherine, 68
Social organization of cultures, 8
Songwriter's Pad (app), 252
Spatial intelligence, 88
Spectrum assessments, 135–148
  compared to Stanford-Binet Intelligence Scale, 143–148
  parent and teacher reactions, 142–143
  Spectrum Reports, 138–139
  working styles, 140–142
Spencer Foundation, 19, 20
Sputnik (1957) and educational reform, 6, 11, 18
Standardized testing, 217. *See also* Assessment
Stanford-Binet Intelligence Scale, 135
  compared to Spectrum assessments, 143–148
Stella, Frank, 248
Stork, Janet, 131, 136
Stravinsky, Igor, 111
"Student-curriculum brokers," 90–91
Stupid White Men (Moore), 129
Suárez-Orozco, Marcelo, 284
Symbol-system approaches, 52–55, 60–61, 221–222
Synthesizing mind, 258–259

Talent and crystallizing experiences, 118–121
Teaching for Understanding (TFU), 19, 174, 211
Theory of life, 181
Theory of matter, 181
Theory of mind, 181
Thorndike, E. L., 5
Thurstone, L. L., 86
Tishman, Shari, 22
Torff, Bruce, 46
A Toronto Symphony, 255–256

Truth, 63, 278, 279. *See also* Virtue in education
Truth, Beauty, and Goodness Reframed (Gardner), 62–63, 277–278, 284

Underserved students, 129
Understanding through the disciplines, 192–209
University of Austin, 237
"Unschooled mind," 100, 177–191, 210

Viens, Julie, 131, 136
Virtue in education, 45–46, 62–67, 275–285
Visionary models, 25
von Ranke, Leopold, 205
Vygotsky, Lev, 51, 70, 71

Wagner, Richard, 111
Walters, Joseph, 106, 296

Washburn, Sherwood, 8
Wechsler Intelligence Scale, 228
Werner, Heinz, 69
White, Sheldon, 68
Whitehead, Alfred North, 58, 249–250, 253
Whitla, Janet, 56
Wilson, Daniel, 22
Wilson, E. O., 206
Winner, Ellen, 18, 23, 62, 132, 167, 170, 302
  China trip, 31
Wolf, Dennie, 18, 132
Woods Hole, Massachusetts 1959, 6, 11
Woolf, Virginia, 202
Working styles, 96, 140–142
Wyoming Seminary, 45, 62, 276

Ylvisaker, Paul, 17
Young People's Concerts, 281

Permissions

Essay 1: From: *100 Great Thinkers on Education*, A. Palmer, & D. E. Cooper Editor(s), Copyright 2001. Routledge. Reproduced by permission of Taylor & Francis Group. Reproduced with permission of the Licensor through PLSclear.

Essay 3: From the foreword of Edwards, C., Gandini, L., & Forman, G. (Eds.), *The hundred languages of children: The Reggio Emilia experience in transformation*. Praeger.

Essay 4: Originally published as Gardner H. (2006). The key in the key slot: Creativity in a Chinese key. *The Journal of Aesthetic Education* 23(1), 141–158.

Essay 6: From *Truth, Beauty, and Goodness Reframed* by Howard Gardner, copyright © 2012. Reprinted by permission of Basic Books, an imprint of Hachette Book Group, Inc.

Essay 7: With permission from the *Journal of Moral Education*.

Essay 14: From *Multiple Intelligences* by Howard Gardner, copyright © 2006. Reprinted by permission of Basic Books, an imprint of Hachette BookGroup, Inc.

Essay 16: First Published in the *International Schools Journal*—isjournal.edu.

Essay 17: From *The Disciplined Mind: What All Students Should Understand* by Howard Gardner. Copyright © 1999 by Howard Gardner. Reprinted with the permission of Simon & Schuster. All rights reserved.

Essay 18: From the January 1994 edition of *Educational Leadership, 51(5)*. © 1994 by ASCD. Reproduced with permission. All rights reserved.

Essay 21: Courtesy of *The Chronicle of Higher Education*.

Essay 22: From Gardner, H., & Davis, K. (2013). *The app generation: How today's youth navigate identity, intimacy, and imagination in a digital world*. Yale University Press.

Essay 23: Reprinted with permission from the February 2009 issue of *School Administrator* magazine, published by AASA, The School Superintendents Association.

About the Author

Howard Gardner is the Hobbs Research Professor of Cognition and Education at the Harvard Graduate School of Education. He is a leading thinker on education, human development, and cognition. In 30 books, translated into over 30 languages, Gardner has written extensively about intelligence, creativity, leadership, and professional ethics. He has received honorary degrees from 31 colleges and universities, including institutions in Bulgaria, Canada, Chile, Greece, Hong Kong, Ireland, Israel, Italy, South Korea, and Spain. A MacArthur Prize Fellow in 1981, he is the winner of the 1990 Grawemeyer Award in Education, the 2011 Prince of Asturias Prize in Social Science, the 2015 Brock International Prize in Education, and the 2021 AERA Distinguished Contributions to Research in Education Award.

In recent years Gardner has completed a national study of higher education. *The Real World of College,* co-authored by Wendy Fischman, appeared in 2022. Gardner also directed an international study of the United World Colleges, a network of secondary schools, and, with Wendy Fischman and William Kirby, has co-edited a collection on innovations in higher education around the world. Other recent books include *Good Work; Changing Minds; The Development and Education of the Mind; Multiple Intelligences: New Horizons; Truth, Beauty, and Goodness Reframed;* and *The App Generation,* co-authored with Katie Davis. His intellectual memoir, *A Synthesizing Mind,* was published in 2020. A Festschrift marking Gardner's 70th birthday is available online at howardgardner.com. A regular, committed blogger, Gardner's current thinking about good work, multiple intelligences, and synthesizing can be followed on his website.